Judges Against Justice

Hans Petter Graver

Judges Against Justice

On Judges When the Rule of Law is Under Attack

Springer

Hans Petter Graver
Faculty of Law
University of Oslo
Oslo, Norway

The author of this book has received financial support from the Norwegian Non-fiction Literature Fund and the E.ON Stipendienfond.

ISBN 978-3-662-44292-0 ISBN 978-3-662-44293-7 (eBook)
DOI 10.1007/978-3-662-44293-7
Springer Heidelberg New York Dordrecht London

Library of Congress Control Number: 2014950244

Printed on acid-free paper

Springer is part of Springer Science+Business Media (www.springer.com)

Acknowledgements

This book was conceived and researched during a sabbatical I spent in 2012–2013 at the Institut für deutsches und europäisches Gesellschafts- und Wirtschaftsrecht at the Faculty of Law at the University of Heidelberg. I thank my long-time friend and colleague professor Peter-Christian Müller-Graff for inviting me and taking me under his wings. I also thank my other colleagues at the law faculty in Heidelberg for a wonderful time.

My year in Heidelberg was financially supported by the E.ON Stipendienfonds and Norwegian Non-fiction Literature Fund.

I would like to thank Jørn Jacobsen, Kristen Rundle, and Erling Kielland, who all read versions of my manuscript and contributed valuable comments. Also thanks to colleagues in Bergen, Heidelberg, Helsinki, Mannheim, Oslo, and Vienna for comments and discussions to my presentations of themes from the book.

The book draws on sources in several different languages. Unless otherwise indicted the translations into English are by the author.

Oslo, Norway
June 2014

Contents

Chapter 1
The Judicial Role and the Rule of Law

Introduction

The judge is under pressure when the legislator attacks the law. Should the judge enforce laws that intentionally and incessantly violate basic rights of individuals, deprive them of due process and the protection of the law, and submit them to draconic and disproportionate punishments? Should he contribute to turning the law into a systematic instrument of persecution on racial, political, or other grounds?

Many will perhaps be inclined to answer the above questions with a clear "no". This is also my answer. One might say that the answer is obvious and in no need of deeper thought. According to the ideals of our western legal tradition, judges and courts should be the protectors of rights and liberty. At the same time, they should uphold the law; sometimes these two expectations are in conflict. In such situations, the judge has to choose whether to side with the legislator or to side with the ideals of the rule of law. Many judges, when the questions have arisen in practical real-life situations, have answered yes, they should uphold the law. This shows that the answer is not as clear-cut as we would like to have it.

Not only do many judges uphold oppressive law and enforce tyranny. In many cases, they at the same time believe that they are defending the rule of law as they carry out evil policies. Trying to show why this is the wrong answer while at the same time taking the situation of the judges seriously is what this book is about. The book revolves around three basic questions: what happens in situations when states turn oppressive and the judiciary contributes to the oppression? How can we, from a legal point of view, judge the judges who contribute to oppression? And how can we understand their participation from a moral point of view and support their inclination to oppose?

In oppressive regimes, there are always people who wholeheartedly support the oppression for ideological or personal reasons. Renowned jurist, Nazi ideologist, and president of the Peoples' Court Roland Freisler of Hitler's Germany is an example of this. Another example is Oswald Rothaug, of whom the US Military

H.P. Graver, *Judges Against Justice*, DOI 10.1007/978-3-662-44293-7_1

Tribunal said: "He was and is a sadistic and evil man".[1] This book is not for them and their likes.

The book is addressed to judges who experience oppressive legislation as a challenge to their conscience: should they follow the law and participate in the undermining of the rule of law, or should they follow their conscience and bend or depart from the law? I believe these to be the majority of the judges participating in the oppression of authoritarian regimes. They are performing a task that is distasteful and disagreeable to them but that they feel obligated to carry out.[2] My aim is to show that there are other answers to the question of contributing to turning the law into a systematic instrument of persecution than the answer most often given by judges who are faced with this dilemma. I try to describe the situation of judges in some recent historical examples, test the limits of judicial cooperation to oppression under international and national criminal laws, and argue the extent to which judicial cooperation and resistance are justifiable from the point of view of legal and moral theory.

Judicial contribution to oppression and tyranny is a classic topic of critical legal theory and of sociolegal studies. This tradition seeks the explanations of judicial participation in social and political contextual factors. Judges do not always participate in oppression by authoritarian regimes and are sometimes together with others trained in law, such as the legal profession and civil servants engaged in activities to obtain, maintain, and defend the basic legal freedoms of liberal society. In many parts of the world today, judges and the legal complex are engaged in the struggle for liberal rule. In such struggles, the legal complex often plays a progressive role in line with the ideals of the rule of law and protection of basic legal rights. In fact, there is evidence to say that the "legal complex", which is the body of legally trained occupations, in general mobilises in protection of basic legal freedoms. There are exceptions to this, particularly in situations of widespread public fears about internal disorder or threats to domestic security, when an otherwise liberal legal complex tends to support oppression by the executive.[3]

I wish to explore the endurance of the rule of law when it exists but is under attack. The main emphasis of the book is where there is a transition from the rule of law to a state where the legislator and the rule of law are in conflict. The examples I study all have in common a transition from a society with respect for the rule of law to authoritarian and oppressive rule. The book is a case study of examples from our recent western legal history where judges have supported the regimes in departure from the rule of law, notably Nazi Germany, South Africa of apartheid, and military dictatorships in Argentina, Brazil, and Chile. In addition, I study western European countries under Nazi dominance during World War II. All these cases are examples where public security has figured high on the list of social priorities. I am particularly interested in the development of legal thought and reasons as expressed in the

[1] The Justice Case (1951), p. 1156.

[2] Milgram (1974), p. 167.

[3] See Halliday et al. (2007), pp. 32–33.

rulings of the courts in such situations. In the study of Germany and South Africa, I go to original legal sources; in the other cases, my studies are based on secondary literature.[4]

One can ask whether there is anything of a general nature to be said about judges disembedded from their differing social and political contexts. In some of the situations described in the book, the society has been in a state of war. In others, the authoritarian regime has emerged from deep social conflicts and unrest. Some have been under foreign occupation. In some cases, the legislator has had at least some sort of basis in the existing constitution such as in Germany after 1933 and in South Africa. In others, the rulers have come to power through an unconstitutional coup. In most cases, the courts have been taken over by the new regime with the corps of judges more or less intact. Some authoritarian regimes make changes at least in the higher levels of the judiciary by packing the Supreme Court like in South Africa or by substituting its judges as in Argentina. In many cases, the regime established special courts or military courts to enforce oppressive legislation.

The issue of whether one can draw general conclusions from such a diverse set of circumstances is obviously a valid concern regarding a survey as the one I undertake here in the book. The reason I believe it is a worthwhile undertaking is that despite differences in role, function, legal tradition, and social conditions, judges of our western legal tradition do have some things in common. According to American legal historian Harold J Berman, western legal tradition has common roots and a history where law at different points in time has been invoked to protect the dissident and the heretic against the prevailing political and moral forces of society.[5] I believe Berman is right about this. The ideology of law as something autonomous dedicated to protecting more general values such as justice, equality, and the rule of law binds judges together across time and space. The purpose of the book is to examine to what extent this is true. This binding may be subtle and fragile at times, but it is nevertheless there in the way we speak about law in out societies. The ideology that the law is autonomous is the very reason why also authoritarian rules seek the legitimacy that can be bestowed upon them by the law. The book is a survey of how judges struggle to accommodate this ideology, how they defend it, and how they depart from it when it is under attack from the legislator or the executive. In order to test the extent to which there is such a common line binding judges together, it is necessary to cut across a lot of different settings where the rule of law has been systematically imperilled.

Judges in the situations I study have in common the fact that the basic values of the western legal tradition are under attack from the state and the judges are called upon to join this attack against the tradition. I will argue in the book that there are some standards by which to measure the response of the judges to the attacks on the rule of law. Based on criminal cases against judges for participation in atrocities of

---

[4] For a brilliant analysis of the reasoning of South African judges under apartheid with the aim of testing positions in legal theory on authoritarianism and law, see Dyzenhaus (2010).

[5] See Berman (1983), p. 43.

authoritarian regimes, it is possible to perform an evaluation regardless of the specific social and political situations. These standards entail a minimum core of justice applicable to any legal regime. They are not based on natural law but on decisions of international tribunals and national courts and codified in international conventions. I will also argue that there are common dilemmas facing a judge in the situation where positive law contradicts standards of justice, equality, and the rule of law. The answers to these dilemmas will vary with place and time, but the type of reasons the judge must consider in order to take a sound and defensible course of action is the same in all situations.

Drawing upon the tradition of David Dyzenhaus, I focus my study around "wicked legal systems", societies where the law is used to enforce a repugnant moral ideology, be it an ideology of racism, such as Nazi Germany or South Africa, or an ideology of severe oppression of any opposition, such as the military dictatorships of many Latin American countries of the second half of the last century. Laws that are systematically employed in the persecution of people on racial, ethnical, or political grounds may easily be characterised as evil. The same characterisation may be given to laws that mete out grossly disproportionate punishments and that treat persons accused of a wrong according to who they are and not what they have done. Evil also are laws that depart fundamentally from standards of equality before the law and from the demand that the subjects of the law should be able to predict the outcome of legal proceedings on the basis of laws that are enacted in advance. Such laws are immoral and in clear contradiction to any notion of justice and the rule of law. The so-called positivism debate on whether such laws can be rightly characterised as "law" or not lies outside the scope of this analysis. The question of whether positivism is to blame and can offer an explanation for wicked judging is, on the other hand, part of my analysis.

One may ask whether conclusions relevant to our time can be drawn from studying pathological cases of authoritarian law. The Nazi experience, in particular, was extreme in the way it dissolved normal legal principles and safeguards. The law was reshaped to serve the ideology and the aims of the Nazi Party and any traits of a liberal concept of law actively and systematically exorcised. It is true that the material content of Nazi law was abominable. It is also true that there was less regard for formal legal sources. Instead, informal and flexible sources, such as Nazi ideology of race, the party programme of the Nazi Party, and the will of the Führer, were the main sources, breaking down legal predictability and the rule of law. Many would, for these reasons, deny the categorisation of "law" to the Nazi legal order. But the legal order was administered by the traditional legal institutions of courts, prosecutors, and the bar with a continuation of the personnel. This continuation persisted into the Federal Republic of Germany. These lawyers and judges applied familiar legal techniques in their legal reasoning, such as the letter or the spirit of the law; textual, purposive, and contextual approaches to statutes; extensive or restrictive interpretation; reasoning by analogy and systemic integrity; and finding and filling of gaps in the law.

We might not be able to draw general conclusions about law from the study of Nazi law, but we can certainly draw conclusions of a general nature from the study of Nazi lawyers and judges. The same is the case for studies of judges in other authoritarian settings. By examining these examples, I try to explain and understand the nature of amoral and even immoral lawyering. As Eric L. Muller, I believe that studies of amoral lawyering can be an educational tool for the ethical instruction of judges and lawyers.[6] The knowledge that judges have positive duties towards the rule of law, especially if it means that they can be punished for upholding the laws of the regime by employing normal legal methods, tells us something about the nature of law as such in our society.

The book surveys judges in many different contexts in many different social settings. They all have two things in common, however: firstly, in all the situations studied, the judges were given their legal training and had professional background in legal orders that cherished the rule of law and the protection of individual rights. This excludes judges from, for instance, the former communist countries or countries with legal systems from outside of our western tradition from the ambit of my study. Secondly, in all the situations, the judges were faced with a legislator and an executive who consciously and systematically departed from these ideals. Although the examples examined have different social and ideological trajectories—anti-Semitism in Nazi Germany, racism in South Africa, and deep social differences in Latin America—they have in common the fact that a judicial practice committed to the rule of law evaporated almost overnight. This happened when the Nazis took power in Germany in 1939, when the apartheid regime enacted its security legislation in South Africa in 1960 after the Sharpeville shootings, and it happened when the military seized power in Argentina, Brazil, and Chile in the 1960s and 1970s.

Can we really say something of a general nature that is not trivial and that covers situations of so great difference? I think we can. At least we can tell the stories of the judges. This will show the variety of situations judges are faced with and also reveal their common elements. In all cases, the judge who is faced with a law that so dramatically departs from an ideology of the rule of law that is at the core of the legal tradition of both civil law and common law has to come to terms with himself on the issue of whether he should apply the law in the way demanded by those in power or whether he should follow his conscience and abstain from contributing to oppression and evil. Precisely because this fundamental question appears in so many different varieties that also determine how it should be answered, I will argue that it is necessary to examine it across differences in role, function, legal tradition, and social conditions of the judge.

The theoretical starting point of my analysis is that judges have both the freedom to make such choices and a scope to act upon them. Legal oppression does not follow from the law but is the result of judges applying and enforcing the law and thus determining what becomes law. Judges, not laws, put men in prison. The book studies legal institutions and judges, not the law as such. The theoretical basis for the study is that the law cannot in a meaningful way be studied in separation from legal institutions and legal practices. In this respect, it builds on the insights of legal

[6] Muller (2012).

realism and of the institutional theory of law. In these traditions, law is perceived as a social institution in line with other social institutions, albeit with a certain measure of autonomy. For ideological reasons, judges resist pressure and undue influence from the outside of what is recognised as sources of law. How is it that this resistance is broken down under certain circumstances? The historical studies seek to show how this happens through internalisation of oppressive policies by adaptation of the legal method applied by the judiciary in the interpretation and application of the law.

Given the close connection between law and legal institutions, judges cannot be studied in separation from the law. Since the main task for judges is to apply the law, and since legal reasoning is their main instrument, the book is about legal method. Studies of judges under authoritarian settings show when the question of legal reasoning becomes a political question and the choice of argument and method a moral choice. A main thesis of the book is that the question of legal reasoning becomes a fundamentally political issue when the legislator attacks the rule of law. The law ceases to be a neutral instance elevated above the political struggles of the society. Some would argue that this is inherent in law at all times. I make the more modest claim that this, at least, is the case when the rule of law is under attack. In such situations, the basis to argue for the autonomy and neutrality of the law simply erodes. Based on this thesis, the main topic of the study is the moral responsibility each judge has for his choice of legal method.

We know a great deal about the dynamics of the relationship between the legal complex and basic legal values enshrined in the rule of law and political liberalism. While this relationship is important in understanding the role of law and legal institutions, such analyses do not address the dynamics and the dilemma of the judge when there is a perceived serious threat to society. In such situations, it is often claimed that basic rights must be suspended, and those in control of the legislature and the executive often demand by ostensible legal means that the judiciary sanction and enforce oppressive legal rules.

Presently authoritarian rule seems far away in Europe and the Unites States. On the other hand, reactions of the legislator, administration, and even the courts in the Unites States and Europe after 9/11 show that we cannot take our liberal values and traditions for granted. In the first years of the "war on terror", lower courts of the US unquestioningly accepted the administration's claim that they lacked jurisdiction over Guantanamo. The deep disagreement among the American judges over the necessity and legality of limiting the liberty of individuals gave the executive the opportunity to act without judicial control for many years. "Faced with a determined executive and a complicit or complacent legislature in the world's only superpower, the rest of the legal complex—lawyers, legal academics, professional associations, judges and the NGOs—could do little to protect political liberalism", Richard Abel writes.[7] "Extraordinary renditions", torture, detention without trial,

[7] Abel (2007), pp. 392–398.

and the use of drones are all defended as legal and are not always successfully challenged in the courts.

History shows that public opinion may be easily swayed given the right (or wrong) circumstances, and principles that are valued highly today may become objects of attack by the public and by our leaders. Law is not as resistant to change as many believe. In Nazi Germany, the liberal ideology of the rule of law tumbled like a house of cards within months of the Nazi ascension to power. Right now, there are countries in Europe where the public authorities and even the courts discriminate against Roma and deny it the protection of law that is supposed to apply universally to all.[8]

The examples reviewed in the book, although extreme, tell us something about the moral dilemmas that judges are faced with also in less extreme situations. If it can be convincingly established that judges have a duty to depart from the law at some point, then the issue in all situations is not whether judges *can* depart but when they *should* depart from the law. Judges who are seen to depart from strict law are often accused of "judicial activism". From this starting point, it could be argued that judicial deviance to avoid doing bad is something that is qualitatively different from judicial activism to achieve good.

One basic starting point is common to all legal theories: the judge has a duty to apply the law. Accepting the position as judge in any legal system entails with necessity accepting the passing of judgment based on the rules and values of the legal order and not one's own personal rules and values. The problem, of course, is how to determine what the law is. "Law" in itself is not a clear concept. Does it refer to the legislation or something else? I will not engage in the important and wide-ranging question of defining law. For my purposes, it is enough to have a concept of "law" that refers to law as it should be construed according to prevailing canons of interpretation in a given society. Law construed according to Nazi theories of interpretation was therefore the law in Germany in 1933–1945 just as law construed according to contemporary German theories of interpretation is the law in Germany today.

Much has been written on the historical facts of judicial involvement in oppression, especially on Germany and, to some extent, on South Africa and Latin America. There is also an extensive literature on the relation between legal theory and judicial oppression, based on the discussion on positivism and natural law between H.L.A. Hart and Lon L. Fuller in 1958. Drawing on this literature, I attempt to understand the judges who find themselves in settings where they are expected to apply and enforce oppressive legislation and to show when they have to step outside of the law and exercise personal choices. My hope is that such understanding can provide insight that can serve as inspiration to judges who are confronted with difficult ethical issues—because they are faced with immoral laws or because the regime under which they operate is turning in an authoritarian direction.

---

[8] See Korando (2012).

Overview of the Book

The book surveys instances of judicial participation in oppression through the law in many countries in the twentieth century, seeking to outline what happened, to address the question of criminal liability for the participating judges, and to understand the moral dilemmas that judges face. The first part of the book is descriptive, the second doctrinal, and the third an excursion into legal methodology, as well as into legal theory and ethics.

The first part of the book gives an overview of how authoritarian rulers use law as a means of oppression and how judges comply with this and, in many cases, become part of the oppression of the state. There are complex relationships between oppressive rule and the law, ranging from situations where the law is bypassed completely to situations where the oppression takes place within ordinary proceedings of law. Judges contribute by closing their eyes to that which occurs outside of the legal institutions, by refusing to hear charges against the government or to provide habeas corpus, and by reinterpreting the law to accommodate the demands of the authoritarian rulers.

The relationship between oppressive rule and the law is first investigated from the perspective of the rulers in power. Of special interest is the question of why oppressive rulers seek the support of the judiciary in the first place and how they go about obtaining it. Rulers seek the legitimacy of the law that only courts and judges can give them. For this reason, judges are seldom persecuted and disciplined for opposing judgments, even in totalitarian settings such as Nazi Germany. This gives the judge a certain scope of action. Authoritarian rulers, however, employ other means than direct repression to seek compliance and loyalty from the judges and seek to limit their jurisdiction so that they do not challenge the core interests of the regime.

Next, we look at it from the perspective of the judge to see how judges exercise the choice between loyalty to the legislator and loyalty to the ideals of the rule of law. Oppressive rulers often have a basis of power that is at least questionable from a legal point of view. In many cases, however, the courts refuse to address the legality of the regime, and in some cases they outright give it their legal sanction.

Judges may, in many instances, feel compelled or coerced to support and comply with the measures taken by authoritarian rulers. This cannot be the whole picture, however, when we see the extent of the legal creativity that judges in many instances employ in support of oppression. We see such creativity in the German courts in developing the law in Nazi Germany on anti-Semitism and in the courts of South Africa developing apartheid and security legislation to oppress opposition. Such examples show that judges are not always unwilling supporters but act as convinced believers in the ideology underlying the authoritarian policies of the regime. This supports and generalises the findings of Robert M. Cover in his study of US antislavery judges in the nineteenth century. Acceptance of such underlying ideologies can also be found in liberal settings when oppressive means are used against social outcasts.

Judicial acceptance is fortunately not absolute. At the end of the first part, I relate examples of judicial opposition. The duality between loyalty to the legislator and loyalty to the ideals of the rule of law is not totally abolished, even in as oppressive settings as in Nazi Germany. It is important to keep this in mind and to learn from the examples where judges have opposed oppressive rulers and their measures.

The second part deals with the criminal liability of judges who participate in the oppression of authoritarian regimes. Experience shows that judges are seldom brought to answer for their oppressive deeds from the bench. This is in line with the trend that democratic successor regimes in general are more concerned about reconciliation and bridging social clefts than about retribution and criminal sanctions. But even in cases where perpetrators of the oppression are brought to account, the judiciary is treated more leniently.

There are, in fact, only two instances where the responsibility of judges has been a major topic: after the breakdown of the Nazi regime and after the reunification of the two German states in the 1990s. The judiciary was a topic for the Truth and Reconciliation committees of South Africa and Chile and had to suffer some criticism, but no sanctions were applied.

The main body of case law on criminal responsibility of judges in oppressive regimes thus stems from international and national cases after World War II and from German cases after the reunification. The main international case is the US Military Tribunal "Justice Case" against leading officials of the Nazi legal system. The accused were tried under international law and convicted for war crimes and crimes against the humanity. Those convicted in a judicial capacity were found guilty of discriminatory persecution and application of oppressive laws against Jews and Poles and of applying and enforcing the "Night and Fog" legislation against nationals of occupied countries. This programme was a scheme where persons accused of resistance were brought to Germany where they were convicted in secrecy in trials where they had no opportunity to defend themselves and subsequently brought to disappear in the night and fog of the concentration camps.

In Germany, several judges were accused but acquitted for lack of malicious intent. The end result of the cases after the Nazi regime was that few judges were brought to account and that international tribunals and national courts alike allowed for a set of excuses and exonerating circumstances amounting to a special judicial immunity. Judges should, however, be responsible in the same way as other representatives and officials of oppressive regimes. After the international adoption of the Rome Statute of the International Criminal Court, judges can be guilty of genocide and crimes against humanity when applying and enforcing the municipal law. This should, in the future, be the standard according to which judges should be brought to account.

The third part of the book starts with the question of why judges contribute to the evil of oppressive systems. With a starting point being the positivism debate after World War II, I examine these topics from the perspective of the judge. The decision taken by the individual judge on whether to submit to the authority of the regime or not is, in certain senses, not free. It is influenced by the socialisation he has been through in becoming a judge, his family status and dependents, his social and economic means of subsistence, and many other factors. But it is also a moral decision that can be explained, understood, and justified or criticised. In order to pass judgment, it is important to understand the situation of the judge.

Although the pressure on the judge in oppressive settings seldom includes criminal liability, there is still cause to investigate the choices open to him and how he exercises that choice. At one level, the reasons that judges often side with authoritarian rulers seem obvious. Judges, like others, have to yield to overwhelming force. Playing along and applying the new rules may also appear to be the best alternative with all things considered. From a sociological point of view, it is no mystery that judges comply with the measures of the regime.

Nevertheless, the question of why judges contribute to atrocities has been an issue of controversy within legal theory. In particular, the question has been whether legal atrocities can be attributed to a certain legal methodology or to defects in the methodology as applied by the judge. The other side of this discussion is whether the judge can avoid taking part in oppression by applying "correct" legal methodology.

These issues are the theme of Part III of the book. Here, I fist review the debate on whether legal positivism can be seen as an explanation. The arguments against this proposition are quite convincing as the theory that legal positivism is to blame confuses legal theory with adherence to authority and the general expectation that the judge avoids mixing politics and law.

Experience shows that oppression can be legitimised through a plethora of legal approaches and methods. This has led some to make the assumption that there is no connection between legal methodology and contribution to oppression through the law. I draw the conclusion that this situation shows the political side of legal reasoning. Legal reasoning is about different ways of valuing stability and change. It is also about different appraisals of legislative purpose, legal principles, and contextual conditions. All these are values inherent in the law where choices have to be made all the time as part of doing law. But in a situation where the legislator is at war with the rule of law, this choice acquires a particular political dimension that the judge cannot avoid. In this situation, the judge cannot only be a judge. He must also make a personal choice. And this choice is an inherently moral choice where the judge is accountable. The judge has a wider scope of alternatives than "just following the law". In the final chapter, I draw upon the experiences from evil regimes to give advice on how to make more sound choices of action. I employ advice worked out by the psychologist Philip Zimbardo and the political scientist Gene Sharp on how to counter factors that pull towards submission and participation in the oppression of the regime.

References

Abel RL (2007) Contesting legality in the United States after September 11. In: Halliday TC, Karpik L, Feeley MM (eds) Fighting for political freedom comparative studies of the legal complex and political liberalism. Hart, Oxford and Portland

Berman HJ (1983) Law and revolution: the formation of the western legal tradition. Harvard University Press, Cambridge, Mass

Dyzenhaus D (2010) Hard cases in wicked legal systems pathologies of legality, 2nd edn. Oxford University Press, Oxford

Halliday TC, Karpik L, Feeley MM (2007) The legal complex in struggles for political liberalism. In: Halliday TC, Karpik L, Feeley MM (eds) Fighting for political freedom comparative studies of the legal complex and political liberalism. Hart, Oxford and Portland

Korando AM (2012) Roma go home: the plight of European Roma. Law Inequality 30:125–147

Milgram S (1974) Obedience to authority, New York 1974 published by Perennial Classics with a foreword by Jerome S. Bruner New York, 2000

Muller EL (2012) Of Nazis, Americans and educating against catastrophe. Buffalo Law Rev 60:323–365

Trials of War Criminals before the Nuremberg Military Tribunals, vol III, the Justice Case, Washington, 1951

Part I
The War of Law

Chapter 2
State Repression and the Rule of Law

Rule of Law and Wicked Rulers

The Ideal of the Rule of Law

In the legal traditions both of common law and European civil law, legislators and judges work together to uphold the rule of law and to protect individual rights. The legislator, preferably on a democratic basis, enacts general legislation. This legislation is binding on the officials of the state, as well as on the citizens. The courts interpret and apply this legislation and ensure that the commitments and rights are awarded according to law. This is the prevailing self-understanding of liberal democracies. Since the birth of liberal constitutions in the United States and Europe after the Enlightenment, individuals have been given constitutional rights that limit the state's use of power over them. Central elements of the rule of law as understood in liberal democracies are the principle of legality, the division of power, and due process. The state should use its power according to laws enacted by a democratic legislator that acts according to a legitimate authorisation. These laws should be general in nature and apply equally to all. The scope of the laws should be determined by independent courts, which should also be responsible for their application and enforcement. The proceedings before the courts should be impartial and treat all parties equally, giving them the opportunity to present their case and protect their rights before any decision is made.

In some cases, the rulers in power depart from this model. They exercise powers outside of the scope of the law and even in contradiction to it. They issue discriminatory legislation and disempower the courts so that these no longer have the final word on the interpretation and application of the law. They use their power to wage war against law as it is perceived in liberal societies.

The judge in any legal order is expected to apply the law, not to create or modify it. The separation of functions between the legislator and the judges is a crucial distinction in most legal orders. It is definitely a part of the values recognised by the

H.P. Graver, *Judges Against Justice*, DOI 10.1007/978-3-662-44293-7_2

rule of law. This separation of functions requires that judges show restraint when they consider policy and that they do not substitute their own values and preferences for those of the law. In this sense, "positivism" explains the cooperation of the judge with the aims of the legislator. A wicked law places the judge in conflict with the core of the judicial role.

All legal theories accept that the legislation, both its positive wording and the aims behind it, is a main source of law. That the judge has a duty to take the legislation into account is not a matter of controversy. The difficulty arises if the duty to follow the law also entails a duty to apply non-positive norms and values even in opposition to legislation and, further, if there are limits to the duty to apply the law. Some make the case that the judge under certain circumstances has a duty to depart from the law in order to avoid an unjust result. Also, the question of what the judge should do in cases where he has no duty to apply the law is controversial. Should he abstain, resign, or even take decisions against the law?

One of the challenges to judges in such situations is how to cope with the expectations that stem from the established judicial role. This is not, first and foremost, a problem of legal theory but of professional ethics. The words of South African judges in their written submission to the Truth and Reconciliation Commission are typical of the way this is seen by judges:

> A judge, whether positioned by personal conviction on the left, center, or right of the political spectrum, who feels free to ignore the oath of office when compliance with it conflicts with his or her own credo, is no hero. Such conduct is bereft of integrity and is a self-indulgent abuse of judicial power. There are only two honest courses open to a judge in such a situation: either resign or comply with the oath of office.[1]

This might be framing the question in too simplistic terms. The judicial role can be understood in several ways and entails varying degrees of both autonomy in relation to the legislation and scope for judicial creativity. The rule of law entails more than just applying the laws enacted by the legislator. Also, the rule of law is an elusive concept and comprises many values and principles. It is furthermore difficult to speak with precision on this subject across the divide of common law and civil law jurisdictions.

The ideology of the rule of law draws its origins from the idea of the secular state established in Europe in the eleventh century. The forces that constituted the secular state were in essence the idea of a state "ruled by law", a *Rechtsstaat*. Its two main elements were that the heads of the states would enact laws and establish legal orders, rule *by* law, and that they would be bound by the laws thus enacted until they changed the law in lawful forms, rule *under* law.[2] It is a feature of the concept of the rule of law that law is derived from or rooted in a reality transcending the existing structure of political power, be it in divine and natural justice or in beliefs in human

[1] Submission to the South African Truth and Reconciliation Commission by the following members of the Supreme Court of Appeal: Mr. Justice J.W. Smalberger, Mr. Justice C.T. Howie, Mr. Justice R.M. Marais, and Mr. Justice D.G. Scott.

[2] Berman (1983), p. 292.

rights and democratic values.[3] Also, today we can speak of a core common to the western legal orders. Many would agree with Ronald Dworkin's claim "that the most abstract and fundamental point of legal practice is to guide and constrain the power of government in the following way. Law insists that force not be used or withheld, no matter how useful that would be to ends in view, no matter how beneficial and noble these ends, except as licensed or required by individual rights and responsibilities flowing from past political decisions about when collective force is justified".[4]

Recent research on judges and authoritarian regimes has employed a working concept of the rule of law in studies on legal institutions and the role of legal professionals, referring to a common minimum core of demands to a legal order. These demands comprise two different norms: firstly, that the government rule by law, that is by general rules, and is itself governed by and obey the rules and, secondly, that there must be a core of individual rights inherent in the law.[5] The concept of the rule of law thus coincides with a legal concept of political liberalism also employed in such studies. Political liberalism in this sense consists of a society that protects basic freedoms, where the state is moderate and where civil society is present.[6]

Departures from the Ideal

Liberty and rule of law are ideals, and as ideals they are realised in various degrees in any given society. There are no universal, generally accepted standards to determine what limits the rule of law imposes on legislative discretion. Positive law has limits, such as the various human rights regimes and the constitutional law of many municipal legal orders. But the lack of universal criteria shows itself when the legislator changes the constitution or enacts law in open contradiction to international law.

More often than not, social, economic, and cultural circumstances contribute to departures from the rule of law. Not all members of society are represented by the elected legislator. Access to courts depends on financial and legal resources. Power is exercised outside the ambit of formal relations. Such deviations are unavoidable and well known, and much of the political mobilisation and conflicts in society are about correcting them.

Even judges are not always able or willing to live up to the ideals of the rule of law. This is well known also in contemporary western democracies, such as when the administration is given unnecessary wide discretionary powers or when the toll

[3] Berman (1983), p. 294.
[4] Dworkin (1986), p. 93.
[5] See Shapiro (2008), p. 329.
[6] Halliday et al. (2007), pp. 10–11.

on individuals or minorities in the interest of a dominating party or a majority is excessive. This is part of normal operations of society and becomes a topic both for political controversies and for the courts. Such disputes may concern the question of the scope for the legislator to decide on what is required by the rule of law and the limits to be set by law and by the courts.

Under normal circumstances, conflicts between the legislator and the courts do not threaten the rule of law in any fundamental way. Infringements on the rule of law by the legislator and the administration are corrected by the courts according to the corresponding legal tradition, sometimes with the aid of international courts, and these adjustments by the judiciary are accepted by the administrative and political community.

Different from such normal and inevitable challenges to the relations between politics and law under ordinary circumstances are situations where those in power over legislation use legal means to systematically undermine democracy, liberty, and the rule of law. In Nazi Germany, law was used as a "nationwide government-organised system of cruelty and injustice, in violation of the laws of war and of humanity, and perpetrated in the name of law by the authority of the Ministry of Justice".[7] The old rule of law approach in judicial conduct and in legal doctrine evaporated within the first months after the Nazi takeover of power in 1933. In South Africa, "wicked" legislators launched a "war against law" to further and protect the discriminating apartheid policy.[8] The military of Brazil launched a revolution committed to the rule of law with the role of the courts to promote the advancement of a "revolutionary legality".[9] In Chile, the "repression from 1973 to 1978 was a military usurpation of judicial power, with the complicity of the legal establishment".[10]

Such situations are vastly different from our everyday arguments over legislative and judicial discretion and division of power. At the same time, they defy our concept of and faith in the rule of law. When rule of law is under attack by the legislator, who is there to protect us if not the courts? As pointed out by the Chilean National Commission on Truth and Reconciliation, legal defences are most needed when the legislator and administration systematically undermine the rule of law.[11] If the courts fail and even contribute to the breakdown of the rule of law, one may say with the US Military Tribunal in the case against leading members of the Nazi legal system: "The prostitution of a judicial system for the accomplishment of criminal ends involves an element of evil to the State which is not found in frank atrocities which do not sully judicial robes".[12]

---

[7] The Justice Case (1951), p. 985.

[8] See the terms employed by Dyzenhaus (2010), chapter 6.

[9] Osiel (1995), pp. 527–528.

[10] Pereira (2005), Kindle edition, location 2293.

[11] Report of the Chilean National Commission on Truth and Reconciliation, University of Notre Dame Press, Notre Dame, Indiana 1993, p. 143.

[12] The Justice Case (1951), p. 1086.

To be betrayed by the courts is particularly painful to our sense of justice. In convicting the defendant Rothaug, the Senior Public Prosecutor of the People's Court, formerly the Chief Justice of the Special Court in Nuremberg, the US Military Tribunal said:

> That the number the defendant could wipe out within his competency was smaller than the number involved in the mass persecutions and exterminations by the leaders whom he served, does not mitigate his contribution to the program of those leaders. His acts were more terrible in that those who might have hoped for a last refuge in the institutions of justice found these institutions turned against them and a part of the program of terror and oppression.[13]

These words are a forceful reminder of the importance of law and justice, not only in our normal liberal and democratic settings but not least in settings where other social institutions fail. The expectation of courts in orders based on the rule of law is that they can keep the other branches of government in check if they violate basic legal principles. This is not to say that judges and members of the legal profession are better or worse than those who occupy other roles in society. But when it comes to justice, the expectations are higher.

Some believe that a legal culture has "deeper" elements of basic concepts and principles that are more resistant to change than the more superficial levels of legislation and specific decisions by the courts.[14] Such a view is challenged in cases where previous democratic political systems experience radical shifts in political power and change into authoritarian or totalitarian regimes. The study of such cases and how the courts react to such changes is, therefore, of interest in how we perceive and conceptualise law in a liberal state.

In the following chapters, we will look at the relations between oppressive rulers and the courts in situations where there is a change in regime from the rule of law to authoritarianism. Two main questions underlie the presentation. The first is: to what extent and why do authoritarian rulers employ the law and legal institutions in their oppressive policies? And the second is: how do judges react to being used by authoritarian rulers as instruments of the oppression?

Transition from Rule of Law to Tyranny

Contrary to what one could presume based on the ideology of the rule of law, law and authoritarian rule are not mutually exclusive. In fact, many authoritarian rulers actively employ law and legal institutions in their oppression and go to great pains to maintain a working legal order with independent courts. Why they do so and how they go about achieving it are important questions for the topic of law and oppression.

---

[13] The Justice Case (1951), pp. 1155–1156.

[14] See, for instance, Loewenstein (1935–1936) and, more generally, Tuori (2002).

Oppressive regimes are found in many forms around the world. Of special interest to the role of law as perceived within the western legal tradition are situations where the regime establishes itself or operates in opposition to a functioning legal order based on the rule of law. Several examples of transitions from a state of rule of law to an authoritarian state can be found within the sphere of the western legal tradition. The most renowned is the transition from the liberal Weimar Republic in Germany to the totalitarian state of the Nazi Party.

The general impression that was formed after the defeat of the Nazi system was that the Nazis abolished law and transformed the regime into a system of lawless violence. This was the picture portrayed by Chief Prosecutor Telford Taylor in the Nuremberg Justice Case against the higher officials of the Nazi legal system. As a rule, the judiciary and the officials of the legal system let themselves be used by the Nazis and turned themselves into their willing servants. In the words of Taylor in his opening statement of the trial against the leaders of the Nazi legal system, the defendants:

> . . . leaders of the German judicial system, consciously and deliberately suppressed the law, engaged in an unholy masquerade of brutish tyranny disguised as justice, and converted the German judicial system to an engine of despotism, conquest, pillage, and slaughter.[15]

This picture of the Nazi regime must, however, be understood in its legal and political context with the need for the allies to establish the legitimacy of their proceedings against the German leaders and officials during the Nazi time.[16] The Nazi leaders did not abolish law or the legal institutions of the predecessor Weimar Republic. To paraphrase Ronald Dworkin, lawyers inside and outside of Germany had no difficulty in identifying collectively the institutions and practices that counted as legal practices in Germany in 1933–1945.[17] To a large extent, the Nazis ruled by measures "structured by legality"[18] and operated through the legal order and the courts.

This seeming paradox has been explained by the theory of Ernst Fraenkel of the "dual state" where the traditional legal institutions wrestled for power with the "prerogative" National Socialist party. According to this influential theory, the Nazi state could be characterised as a "dual state", where the "normative" and "prerogative" states existed as competitive parts of the German Reich.[19] The prerogative state consisted of the field of the political where law was abolished. The prerogative state did not accept any legal restraint or formal bonds and reserved the right to intervene into any field of law and to define its own boundaries. The existence of the dual state in this sense entailed that there existed a double jurisdiction in all matters regarded as political. The police, meaning the SS, could and did execute

---

[15] The Justice Case (1951), p. 31.

[16] See Wilke (2009), pp. 181–201.

[17] Dworkin (1986), p. 91. See Fraser (2005), pp. 84–107.

[18] See Rundle (2009), p. 76.

[19] Fraenkel (1941), p. 46.

administrative punishment in addition to or instead of criminal punishments executed by the courts so that people dismissed from the judicial system because of lack of evidence or after having served a sentence could be sent to the concentration camps.[20] Insofar as the political authorities did not exercise their power, private life and public life were regulated by the traditionally prevailing or the newly enacted law.[21]

To a large extent, it is correct that important institutions of oppression, such as the SS, the concentration camps, and the holocaust, operated outside of the jurisdictions of the normal bureaucracy and the courts. This does not mean, however, that the normative state operated along the lines of the rule of law as understood in the traditional sense and that the prerogative state was without legal norms. Fraenkel recognised that the dual state is characterised by "the complete abolition of the inviolability of the law".[22] In this way, the normative state was fundamentally subordinated to the prerogative state. On the other hand also the prerogative state operated under some normativity and was thus not pure arbitrariness. The SS had its own courts where "judges were torn between their ideological mission and their self-understanding as lawyers. The judges who had undertaken formal legal training were not always mere instruments of the Nazi system; they were also driven in part by their traditional conceptions of law and legality".[23]

Nazi Germany is not the only case where liberal legal institutions have been transformed and employed as a means of repression. Other examples of oppression through the law are the introduction of apartheid in South Africa after the accession to power of the National Party in 1948 and the military dictatorships in a number of Latin American countries of the 1970s and 1980s.[24] In South Africa, the Truth and Reconciliation Committee stated:

> The courts and the organised legal profession generally and subconsciously or unwittingly connived in the legislative and executive pursuit of injustice ... Perhaps the most common form of subservience can be captured in the maxim *qui tacet consentire* (silence gives consent). There were, nevertheless, many parts of the profession that actively contributed to the entrenchment and defence of apartheid through the courts.[25]

The commission further stated that judges had taken part "in the greatest injustices of all, [where] judges ... too easily made sense of the illogical and the

---

[20] Fraenkel (1941), p. 41.

[21] Fraenkel (1941), p. 57.

[22] Fraenkel (1941), p. 107.

[23] Pauer-Studer (2012), p. 378.

[24] Argentina signed the International Covenant on Civil and Political Rights on 19 February 1968 and ratified on 8 August 1986, Brazil signed and ratified on 24 January 1992, Chile signed on 16 September 1969 and ratified on 10 February 1972, South Africa signed on 3 October 1994 and ratified on 10 December 1998.

[25] Report of the Truth and Reconciliation Commission of South Africa, vol. 4, p. 101.

unjust in legislative language, and who too quickly accepted the word of the police or official witness in preference to that of the accused".[26]

The Chilean Truth and Reconciliation Committee said for its part:

> The judiciary, which in view of the Constitution, the law, and the nature of its functions, was the government institution called to protect those rights, failed by not acting more forcefully. Moreover, they failed to do so even though from the beginning churches, lawyers, the victims' relatives, and international human rights agencies were furnishing the courts with information on actions by government officials that violated human rights. The country was surprised to see the courts take such a stance, for it was accustomed to regard the judiciary as a staunch defender of the rule of law.[27]

These two observations from two very different societies are remarkably similar. Both have as their starting point a reverence of the law and the courts. In the South African case, this is more tacit, based on the respect of the legal tradition and the judges in common law. In the Chilean example, the regard for the judiciary is stated directly. In both cases, the courts let the people down. They generally failed in protecting the rights that the people were guaranteed—in the South African case, under the liberal traditions of common law; in the Chilean case, under the Constitution and under the International Covenant on Civil and Political Rights that was signed by Chile in 1969 and ratified in 1972. Already these examples show that oppression through law is not contained to a civil law or a common law legal culture and that a failure of the courts to uphold the rule of law is not specifically tied to either of these legal traditions.

Oppression in Legal Forms: Is It Really Law?

One might suppose that authoritarian regimes cannot rely on law and legal institutions and that authoritarian repression is, by its very nature, contrary to law. Or one might believe that courts in authoritarian regimes are nothing but pawns for their regimes upholding the interests of the ruling elites. Both views assume that law in any meaningful sense, as general rules applied according to acknowledged techniques by independent courts, is something reserved for democratic or at least liberal regimes. These understandings are false.[28] And if they were true, how could we have normative expectations that courts protect individual rights and rule of law in authoritarian settings and criticise judges for not doing it?

Robert Barros, in a study of judicial failure in Argentina and Chile, distinguishes between the following four different forms of state repression and their relationship with law[29]:

[26] Report of the Truth and Reconciliation Commission of South Africa, vol. 4, p. 103.

[27] Report of the Chilean National Commission on Truth and Reconciliation, p. 141.

[28] See the cases reported in Halliday et al. (2007).

[29] Barros (2008), pp. 167–168.

1. extrajudicial repression in the form of punitive acts inflicted by state agents without any prior authority or adherence to judicial or administrative formalities;
2. administrative repression, which includes detentions and other coercive measures authorised by the state without any prior review or sentence by the courts;
3. summary or quasi-judicial repression, which involves some sort of judicial proceeding but which departs from normal rule of law standards;
4. legal repression, which involves political repression but proceeds via regular judicial mechanisms that afford full protection from arbitrariness.

All these forms of repression involve judges and the courts. In extrajudicial repression without prior authority, such as the 20,000–30,000 disappearances under the military dictatorship of Argentina in the 1970s, courts may be involved by petitions of habeas corpus to force the government to provide evidence of persons abducted by government forces. In Argentina, the courts generally failed to use the formal legal power that they had to challenge the state and demand the release of prisoners where the state could not provide specific grounds for their arrest according to the laws in force.[30]

Administrative repression is based on formal legal powers that, in least in theory, can be challenged by the courts. This was the form of repression in South Africa under apartheid and in Nazi Germany under the euthanasia programme and the orders to destruct millions of Jews and members of other non-Aryan races. Failure to challenge such repression represents not only a failure to protect but even amounts to legal sanction of atrocities.

Summary or quasi-judicial repression through special courts and tribunals often involves members of the judiciary directly, as in the dictatorship of Chile and in the Peoples' Court and the special courts of Nazi Germany. To the extent that their jurisdiction is not challenged by the ordinary courts, these courts offer the blessing of the law to such tribunals. When political repression is undertaken through the regular courts, the contribution of the judges is direct. This may contribute to tempering the repression, such as in Brazil as compared to Chile, but it may also contribute to extending it, as in the measures against the Jews developed by the German courts in the 1930s.

Germany during the Nazi time pursued its policies along all four of the categories above. A large amount of the repression took place within the legal system and was sanctioned and enforced by judicial means by the courts. And although the legal sources were changed, they were applied with traditional and familiar legal techniques and modes of reasoning. Even in the countries occupied by Germany during the war, the German legal institutions were perceived as institutions of law and the judges of the German courts as judges going about their business in a manner consistent with law. A Norwegian public defender at the German *Reichkriegsgericht* (Supreme Court acting in cases related to the war) writes in a lecture published 10 years after the end of the war: "In dealing with the

[30] Osiel (1995), p. 518.

Reichkriegsgericht we had to deal with lawyers on an equal footing in a manner appropriate to a supreme court".[31]

The question of "law" or "not law" has been extensively debated in legal theory as a battle between a positivist and a naturalist concept of law. I shall return to this debate later. In this context, my point is not the philosophical or moral issue of whether it is right to characterise the Nazi persecutions as legal or not. The point I wish to make here is that the judges and courts engaged in the policies of the Nazi regime as lawyers, not by departing from their legal role. This entails that the question of "what is law" is relative to its framing. The Holocaust, the concentration camps, the "Night and Fog" policy, and the euthanasia programme were all perceived as lawful under the operating German legal order. Even if there were discussions over the legality of these measures, such as over the legal status of Hitler's ordering of the euthanasia programme, the courts would never have deemed it as illegal had it come up. According to the legislation on the Gestapo, the Gestapo was given powers to "deal with" enemies of the state and to intern them in the concentration camps outside of the jurisdiction of the courts. Once a person was put in a camp, he was deprived of his right to access to justice. The measures of the prerogative state were not only regretfully accepted by the judiciary but were perceived as according with Nazi legality. The one judge who courageously did question the legality of the euthanasia programme was dismissed by the ministry of justice with the remark that a judge who could not accept the order of the Führer as the highest law had no business as a judge in the Nazi legal order.[32]

Administrative repression, which takes place without prior review by judges and without recourse to courts, can still be characterised as legal in nature if it adheres to principles of legality, generality, and enforcement of rules. To the extent that acts were perpetrated by people who believed in the legality of the system and that they were acting under legal obligations, the extralegal atrocities of Nazi Germany were "law" too.[33]

It is true that law as such was alien to the Nazi ideology. Hitler himself refused to be bound by any law.[34] Professor Jahrreiss, a witness for the defendants at the Justice Case, put it in this way:

> If now in the European meaning one asks about legal restrictions, and first of all one asks about restrictions of the German law, one will have to say that restrictions under German law did not exist for Hitler. He was *legibus solutus* in the same meaning in which Louis XIV claimed that for himself in France. Anybody who said something different expresses a wish that does not describe the actual legal facts.[35]

[31] Rode (1983), p. 331.

[32] See further on Lothar Kreyssig on pp. 103–104 below.

[33] See Fraser (2005), pp. 330–331.

[34] See, for an overview of Hitler's and the other leading Nazis' expressions on law and lawyers, Rüthers (2012), pp. 101–111.

[35] The Justice Case (1951), p. 1011.

This view of Hitler's role was also accepted at the legal theoretical level and incorporated into the theoretical understanding of law. "Law is the will of the Führer" was elevated to the basic norm for all legal reasoning and tied to the will and the aims of the dictator.[36]

The controversy over the euthanasia programme that was enacted to kill mentally ill and disabled persons in hospitals and institutions, where over 70,000 people were killed, is a case in point. The formal basis for this programme was a secret order by the Führer empowering leaders of the Reich medical service with "the responsibility of enlarging the authority of certain physicians to be designated by name in such a manner that persons who, according to human judgment, are incurable can, upon a most careful diagnosis of their condition of sickness, be accorded a mercy death".[37]

The legality of the programme was initially contested by officials in the ministry of justice since it was not based on any formal law. Wanting to keep the programme secret, Hitler refused to issue a formal law or regulation. The argument of the defence at Nuremberg was that the Führer order was clear and constituted law. The lack of legislation was only a matter of form and not of substance, and Hitler was authorised to alter the formal requirements. After taking cognizance of the decree, all authorities acknowledged it as the legal basis.[38]

The communication between the ministry and Judge Lothar Kreyssig is illustrating. Kreyssig wrote a letter, dated 8 July 1940, protesting against the legality of the killings of mentally ill in institutions within his jurisdiction. After two meetings with the ministry where the ministry failed to provide an explanation of the legal basis for the euthanasia, Kreyssig wrote to the institutions within his jurisdiction, forbidding them to take the life of any person without his prior authorisation. On 13 November, he was called to a meeting with the Minister of Justice. The minister offered him a "golden bridge". He could keep his position if he recognised that the authorisation by a judge was not necessary for the execution of the euthanasia programme. When he refused, he was told to resign since a person who "did not recognize the will of the Führer as a source of law and legal rules could not hold the position as a judge".[39] As far as is known, no other judge protested against the carrying out of the euthanasia programme, and the courts of the Federal Republic of Germany eventually also accepted the defence of persons accused of participating in the programme that their belief in its legality was an exonerating circumstance in the criminal proceedings against them.[40] German courts after the war, however, did not accept euthanasia as legal.

---

[36] See Rüthers (2012), p. 272.

[37] Führer decree of 1 September 1939; see The Medical case (1951), vol. I, p. 795.

[38] The Medical case (1951), vol. I, pp. 815–817.

[39] Döring (2011), p. 45 and further on pp. 103–104 below.

[40] See Freudiger (2002), pp. 347–350.

Hitler also intervened in the actual administration of justice in individual cases, some of which are described in the Justice Case.[41] Upon his personal orders, persons who had been sentenced to prison terms were turned over to the Gestapo for execution. In several cases, Hitler ordered death sentences to be passed when he heard of sentences of prison terms that he found too lenient. In one case mentioned by the US Military Tribunal, a Jew, Luftgas, had been sentenced to two-and-a-half years in prison for hoarding eggs. Hitler ordered that he be sentenced to death. In this case, Luftgas was handed directly over by the Ministry of Justice to the Gestapo for execution. In other cases, the president of the court was informed of Hitler's order and directed to perform a retrial.

Such arbitrary interventions in the workings of the legal system, unbound by any norms or generality, can hardly be characterised as "law" even by the strictest positivist definitions. But such interventions in the working of the judiciary were not very frequent and did not prevent the German lawyers from relating both to legislation and Nazi ideology in a traditional legal manner, thus upholding the normal legal functions of interpretation, application, and adjudication in a manner recognisable as legal both to observers at the time and to observations made in the posterity of the Nazi regime. It is therefore too easy to deny the Nazi legal system the characterisation of "law" with reference to such examples of arbitrariness and a "complete willingness of the Nazis to disregard even their own enactments".[42] Even to lawyers today, the patterns of argument and legal methodology of the Nazi judges are recognisable and comparable to current legal activities. In the words of David Fraser: "There is no inherent epistemological, ontological juridical set of ideas, concepts or practices which distinguish Nazi law from our law".[43]

In the perspective of the judiciary, law was not reduced to mere ideology or the mechanical application of utilitarian argument. On the contrary, German judges applied the whole range of legal arguments and methods in their reshaping of the law. As an illustrating example of what I think many would recognise as legal reasoning despite its tragic subject matter, we can look at a case from the German Supreme Court from 1938 on the application of German penal provisions on acts performed outside of the territory of Germany.[44] According to a provision in the German penal code, penal provisions were applicable to all acts committed on the territory of German Reich. In the case, a German couple, the man a Jew and the woman an Aryan, had had sexual relations during their meeting in Prague. They met there to say goodbye because the man had decided to leave Germany for South America. He stopped over in Prague to earn money for his journey. The Grand Senate of the Supreme Court was asked to rule on whether the penal provisions

[41] The Justice Case (1951), pp. 1014–1017.

[42] See Fuller (1957), p. 652.

[43] Fraser (2005), p. 438.

[44] Großer Senat für Straffsachen, 23 February 1938, Entscheidungen des Reichsgerichts, Strafsachen 72 91.

could be applied in the case where the act was committed, not within the territories of the Reich but in Czechoslovakia.

The Grand Senate emphasised that the courts were bound by the law and could only punish offences covered by a law, either by its wording or by the basic aim behind it. This also applied to legislation enacted before the Nazi takeover of power: "Laws that the Führer until further notice has left untouched form part of his legislation. It is up to him, if and when such laws should be repealed".

The courts should take regard not only to the wording of the legislation but also to the aims and purposes of the legislator. The Grand Chamber warned against drawing more general rules or purposes out of specific instances. It then went on to state that the particular act according to general opinion was as worthy of punishment as similar offences committed on German territory. It also noted that the limitation in the penal code was obviously too restrictive in light of the need to protect the German people. The extent to which crimes committed abroad should be punishable in German courts must, however, be regarded as a matter for the legislator and not the courts. In light of this, it was particularly important not to draw general rules out of one specific instance.

In this specific case, the Senate did not find it necessary to rule on the general question of whether acts that were punishable also could be punished when committed outside of German territory. It stated that, despite the fact that the Nuremberg Blood Law did not entail an explicit provision for the punishment of offences committed abroad, such a provision must be regarded as implied in it. The Senate defended this result by pointing to the fact that "the Blood Law is one of the basic laws of the National Socialist state. Its purpose is to keep the German blood pure as a condition for preserving the German people for all perpetuity. This aim would be seriously compromised if it were not possible, under certain conditions, to punish offenses committed outside of the territory of Germany".[45]

Given the premise of the importance and centrality of the racial policy, this argument can be defended as a legal argument. It disregards the law in that the limits on the application of the German penal law were not respected. On the other hand, the extension of the application of the Blood Law beyond the limits of the criminal code could be defended on the basis of the basic nature of this law. The Blood Law was at the time regarded as part of the constitution of the Nazi State.[46] It could be argued that the resemblance to legal reasoning is only superficial and that the courts in such cases departed from any reasonable approach to interpretation of statutes.[47] On the other hand, it is known from all interpretation of statutes that courts sometimes deviate from the wording and from previous interpretations of these by way of restrictive interpretation or analogy. It is also common in judicial opinions that not all arguments against the opinion are dealt with explicitly. Such a

[45] Großer Senat für Straffsachen, 23 February 1938, Entscheidungen des Reichsgerichts, Strafsachen 72 91.

[46] See Pauer-Studer (2014), p. 55.

[47] In this direction, Ogorek (2008), p. 304.

result in itself cannot be characterised as "a willingness to disregard the law". In the example mentioned, the Supreme Court stresses the importance of legislation and of judicial restraint; nevertheless, some basic principles must take precedence.

A preference given to basic laws and principles can be found also in reasoning of courts today with the same type of sweeping statements with questionable empirical assertions ("the aim would be seriously compromised . . ."). Some might object to employing such arguments as a basis for applying criminal sanctions. It is, however, difficult to say that the reasoning is clearly in conflict with the principle of *nulla poene sin lege*, and the approach of the Court must be regarded as cautious in light of the principle established in the Law to Change the Penal Code promulgated on 28 June 1935, which stated that "Whoever commits an act which the law declares as punishable or which deserves punishment according to the fundamental idea of a penal law and the sound concept of the people, shall be punished. If no specific penal law can be directly applied to this act, then it shall be punished according to the law whose underlying principle can be most readily applied to the act". The Court did not resort to this piece of legislation as a basis for its application of criminal sanctions.

The objectionable aspect of this decision is therefore not that it is not legal in its approach; nor can one object in principle to the readiness to give effect to the purpose behind an essential piece of legislation. Such a teleological approach is fundamental to the interpretation of basic laws in many jurisdictions. Modern examples can be found in the approach of the two European courts, the European Court of Human Rights and the European Union Court of Justice. What is objectionable from a present point of view is the readiness of the Court to adopt the terrible racial policy of the regime and to extend the legal effects of this policy beyond the clear wording of the legislation that was adopted to implement this policy. According to the analysis of Ernst Fraenkel, the courts surrendered to the pressures of the prerogative state in Jewish affairs.[48]

However, not all accept that the atrocities that took place in Nazi Germany with the Holocaust can be seen as law. Fraenkel himself is ambiguous about this. On one hand, he analyses cases involving Jews as part of his analysis of the normative state. On the other hand, he claims that "all cases in which Jews are involved fall within the jurisdiction of the prerogative state".[49] In an article based on the discussion between Hart and Fuller, Kristen Rundle argues that there was a basic difference between the Nazi legal programme against the Jews in the 1930s and the extermination programme enacted after 1942.[50] Notwithstanding the fact that the legal campaign was flagrantly racist, persecutory, and a crime against humanity, it was still law even in the sense perceived by Lon Fuller. Rundle's argument for this is that law in the first phase recognised the Jews as agents, whereas it did not when it

[48] Fraenkel (1941), p. 96.

[49] Fraenkel (1941), p. 89.

[50] Rundle (2009).

came to the policy of extermination. The measures against the Jews were structured by legality and were not purely instrumental in character.

The extent to which the Jews in fact were recognised as legal agents even in the early stages of Nazi law may be debated, especially in light of the decision by the Supreme Court of June 1936, which described the legal personality of the Jews as "destroyed" and equalled their situation to physical death.[51] This illustrates that, substantially, Jews were already deprived of legal recognition early on in the Nazi regime.

On the other hand, the issue of where to draw the line between Jews and non-Jews both generally and in the individual case was a matter of administrative dispute right until the end. The dispute was fought with classical legal reasoning over the contents of new decrees and regulations. In individual cases, evidence was evaluated and standards of proof applied in determining whether a person was of Jewish ancestry or not. Right up to the collapse of the regime, most Jews married to Germans, and also persons of mixed ancestry, were exempt from extermination. Bernard Loesener, who served as the official "Jewish Expert" in the German Third Reich's Ministry of the Interior, the government body responsible for the Nazi's legislative assault on German Jewry, gives a vivid account of this in his memoirs.[52]

There was even a legal institution of clemency under Hitler, where by September 1942 he personally had exempted 991 persons from different effects of persecution.[53] On the other hand, the legal construction in these cases when a person gained a reclassification from Jew to Aryan was not that he had been saved from extermination but that the Aryan people had reclaimed a member who otherwise would have been lost.[54] So maybe this institution cannot be seen as evidence of the treatment of supposed Jews as persons in their own right.

Seen from the perspective of the Jews of Germany, there was a clear break in 1938 when a new measure of lawlessness and uncertainty was introduced, which may be described as their being placed outside of the law. The measures taken against them were, in this respect, no longer "law". On the other hand, the measures taken after 1938 where the responsibility of dealing with the "Jewish problem" was put firmly in the hands of the SS and the Gestapo can also be seen as an end to the unregulated street violence of the SA that culminated with the pogrom of 9 November 1938. After this, the persecution of the Jews was brought over in a regulated form under the responsibility of the SS.[55] It was only after this that the limits of the persecution were clearly drawn by the legal categorisation of a person as a "Jew" or "non-Jew". Seen from the perspective of the lawyers interpreting and applying the norms, they were still engaged in an activity of a legal nature and their actions were not illegal from the perspective of the system. Even though the laws

---

[51] RG., 1 Siv.Sen., 27. June 1936, Seufferts Archiv 91, 65; see further on p. 66–67.

[52] See Schleunes (2001).

[53] See Essner (2002), pp. 201–214.

[54] Essner (2002), p. 204.

[55] See Herbert (2011), p. 224.

changed, the procedures and methods employed to determine their content and application did not change.

The legal approach was even applied to the programme of the Nazi Party as such, which otherwise has been described as sketchy, incoherent, and opaque.[56] In an article from 1939, state attorney Friedrich Wilhelm Adami sought to show, through examples from case law, the extent to which a realisation of the programme of the National Socialist Party was "conceivable and compulsory".[57]

According to Adami, the principles of National Socialism gave legal certainty a new foundation. Adami explains how under the previous regime it was necessary in the interest of legal certainty to give the wording of the statutes overriding authority because the legislation due to the political process could not be informed by one unified worldview. This had now changed, and law under Nazi rule was tied to one specific worldview, making it possible to state that "Law is what serves the German people, illegality what harms it" and "Law of life before formal law".

Adami concluded that the correctness of a judicial decision according to the worldview is always a matter of political judgment that requires a clear political attitude, political tactfulness, and political flair. Therefore, the implementation of National Socialism into the legal order was first and foremost a question of the personality, character, and national socialist learning of the judge. This also accords with the statement of the Secretary of State in the Ministry of Justice, the later infamous president of the People's Court, Roland Freisler: "Not a reform of the law, a reform of the lawyers is what is needed".[58]

The Nazi experience shows how a dictatorship can take over almost all of the legal norms of a preceding regime and transform them by legal reinterpretation to a system of oppression.[59] The continuity of the legal order was ensured by maintaining legal language and concepts such as legislation, constitution, legal certainty, contract, property, public security, and the like, and by giving them a totally new content. This conceived the nature of the new regime and led judges and others to fail to notice its revolutionary character.[60] Even the emergency legislation that was used by the regime to legally implement the totalitarian state was modelled on the measures of the Weimar Republic and, because of this, was perceived as nothing out of the ordinary.[61]

---

[56] Lippman (1992–1993), pp. 257–318.

[57] Adami (1939), pp. 486–491.

[58] Cited Schmitt (1933), p. 43.

[59] See Rüthers (2012), p. 505.

[60] See Majer (1988), pp. 46–73.

[61] Strenge (2002), pp. 170ff.

Inside and Outside of Law

Not all oppressive states operate under the pretence of legality through legal measures. Whereas, for example, the military leaders of Brazil used peacetime military courts to prosecute political dissidents and did not suspend the constitution, the courts in Argentina were largely uninvolved in the repressive system, except to deny writs of habeas corpus and serve as a cover for state terror.[62]

In many cases, oppression and violence are performed unofficially, without any claim to being legal or sanctioned by law, as the case was in Argentina. To the extent that the actual acts of oppression are not kept secret, the perpetrators, lines of command, and the ultimate responsibilities are.

Sometimes oppressive measures are enacted through the law, as in Nazi Germany and in South Africa. In many cases, oppression takes place both within and outside of the law. Also in regimes with high claims to legality of the basis of power and of the means employed, such as Nazi Germany and South Africa during apartheid, atrocities take place outside of the law. In the time right after the Nazi's ascension to power, the SA storm troopers were employed as death squads to quash and terrorise political opposition. An observer from Berlin in 1933 writes:

> An example that became public knowledge because of its scale occurred some months later in the Cöpenick area of Berlin, where a Social Democratic trade unionist defended himself, with the help of his sons, against an SA patrol that broke into his home at night to 'arrest' him. In obvious self-defence he shot two SA men. As a result, he and his sons were overcome by a larger troop of SA men and hanged in a shed in the yard that same night. Next day the SA patrols appeared in Cöpenick, in disciplined order, entered the home of every known Social Democrat an killed them on the spot. The exact number of deaths was never made public.[63]

Haffner here describes the "wild" terror of the thugs of the SA. Later, the so-called dual state was established in a more systematic way, with the SS, Gestapo, and the police operating as a force outside the scope of the law. This was the result of a conscious policy by leaders of the SS where the police was to be seen as a force unbound by any restrictions in order to fight internal enemies of the German people, whereas the public administration would continue to be based on the principle of legality.[64] People over whom the Gestapo took jurisdiction were effectively placed outside of the law. In principle, the ordinary courts had jurisdiction over inmates of the camps. If they committed criminal offences, charges were to be brought against them in the ordinary courts. In practice, this never happened.[65] Harsh discipline was enforced within the camps without any recourse to laws or the courts. This was, however, technically illegal under valid laws, and officers of the camps were in

---

[62] See Pereira (2005), Kindle edition, location 128 and 141.

[63] Haffner (2003), p. 126.

[64] See Herbert (2011), pp. 177–181.

[65] Statement by SS-Oberfuehrer Dr. Günther Reinecke, Institut für Zeitgeschichte, Reinecke, Dr. Guenther ZS-0121 http://www.ifz-muenchen.de/archiv/zs/zs-0121.pdf (accessed 11.04.14).

some instances punished in the SS Courts for the killing of inmates. In this respect, it is important to stress that the systematic killing as part of the extermination of Jews was not illegal.

This "prerogative state" also had the unregulated power to intervene into the operations of the "normative state". Ernst Fraenkel in 1940 writes on the situation: "The important result of the co-existence of authorities bound by the law and of other independent of law are these: when it is politically desirable, the decisions of the courts are corrected by the police authorities who confine persons acquitted by the judiciary in concentration camps for indefinite periods (. . .) The co-existence of legal and arbitrary actions, most impressively demonstrated by the confinement in concentration camps of persons who have been acquitted by the courts, is a crucial development of the recent German constitutional status".[66] There were no defined limits as to issues into which the prerogative state could not intervene. On the other hand, the party and the SS were restricted from interfering directly with the operations of the courts; instructions to the judges had to go through the Ministry of Justice. Also, the extent of whom were subject to deportation and extermination as part of the holocaust was limited to the legal categorisation of "Jew" despite the fact that Himmler and SS pushed to extent the scope to "half Jews" and Jews married to Aryans.

The law is often called upon to give a facade of legality, sometimes even under circumstances of predominantly extrajudicial oppression. Law and legal functionaries are important. Even such a non-legal setting as the war and killings in the Balkans after the breakdown of Yugoslavia had its ties to the law. Osiel tells of the case of a Serbian investigating judge who was appointed to inquire into a recent massacre. When she arrived at the scene and found some victims still alive, she gave instructions to the present members of the Special Forces accompanying her to kill them.[67]

In the case of Nazi Germany, it is obvious that the great numbers of killings and crimes took place outside the ambit of the judicial system. But the legal system was an integrated part and instrument of the policy of repression of the Nazis. It is, therefore, misleading to say that law and legal institutions were abolished by the Nazi regime or that it was transformed to a lawless state. The legal institutions took part in the general oppression of aliens to the German people, criminal elements, and political opponents.

Attitudes and actions of the judges can serve as an encouragement to an authoritarian regime. One can easily imagine that the failure of the judiciary to protest against the purge of their Jewish colleagues in April 1933 and their acceptance of the legality of the emergency powers to Hitler were a welcome reassurance to the Nazis in the first and unsure weeks and months of their rule.

There is an obvious interplay between the actions of a regime outside the courts and outside of the scope of the law, on one hand, and judicial action and reaction, on

[66] Fraenkel (1941), p. 39.

[67] Osiel (2009) p. 37.

the other. Failure by the courts to protect basic rights in the way that the Truth and Reconciliation committees of Chile and South Africa criticise the courts for may therefore amount to active support of the oppression of the regime, by the encouragement this represents to the regime.

Studies of various authoritarian regimes show that, in some cases, courts and law contribute to repression in ways that go beyond mere compliance with the demands of the rulers and, in this way, contribute to make the repression more extensive and efficient. In other cases, judges challenge repressive measures and provide arenas for legal struggles over the policy of the regime. In most cases, courts provide legitimacy for oppressive policies by not challenging them and thus endowing them with the cloak of legality.

References

Adami FW (1939) Das Programm der NSDAP und die Rechtsprechung. Deutsches Recht 486–491

Barros R (2008) Courts out of context: authoritarian sources of judicial failure in Chile (1973–1990) and Argentina (1976–1983). In: Ginsburg T, Moustafa T (eds) Rule by law: the politics of courts in authoritarian regimes. Cambridge University Press, Cambridge

Berman HJ (1983) Law and revolution: the formation of the western legal tradition. Harvard University Press, Cambridge, Mass

Döring H-J (ed) (2011) Lothar Kreyssig Aufsätze, Autobiographie und Dokumente. Evangelische Verlagsanstalt, Leipzig

Dworkin R (1986) Law's empire. Fontana Press, London

Dyzenhaus D (2010) Hard cases in wicked legal systems pathologies of legality, 2nd edn. Oxford University Press, Oxford

Essner C (2002) Die "Nürnberger Gesetze" oder Die Verwaltung des Rassenwahns 1933–1945. Paderborn, München

Fraenkel E (1941) The dual state a contribution to the theory of dictatorship. Oxford University Press, New York

Fraser D (2005) Law after Auschwitz: towards a jurisprudence of the Holocaust. Carolina Academic Press, Durham

Freudiger K (2002) Die juristische Aufarbeitung von NS-Verbrechen. Mohr Siebeck, Tübingen

Fuller LL (1957) Positivism and fidelity to law – a reply to Professor Hart. Harv Law Rev 71:630–672

Haffner S (2003) Defying Hitler: a memoir. Phoenix, London

Halliday TC, Karpik L, Feeley MM (2007) The legal complex in struggles for political liberalism. In: Halliday TC, Karpik L, Feeley MM (eds) Fighting for political freedom comparative studies of the legal complex and political liberalism. Hart, Oxford and Portland

Herbert U (2011) Best Biographische Studien über Radikalismus, Weltanschauung und Vernunft 1903–1989, 5th edn. Verlag J.H.W Dietz Nachf, Bonn

Lippman M (1992–1993) They shoot lawyers don't they? Law in the Third Reich and the global threat to the independence of the judiciary. Calif West Int Law J 23:257–318

Loewenstein K (1935–1936) Law in the Third Reich. Yale Law Rev 45:779–815

Majer D (1988) Richter und Rechtswesen in Otto Borst Hrsg. Das Dritte Reich in Baden und Württemberg, Theis Verlag Stuttgart, pp 46–73

Ogorek R (2008) "Rassenschande" und juristische Methode Die argumentative Grammatik des Reichsgerichts bei der Anwendung des Blutschutzgesetzes von 1935. In: Regina Ogorek,

Aufklärung über Justiz, 1. Halbbd.: Abhandlungen und Rezensionen, V. Klostermann, Frankfurt am Main
Osiel MJ (1995) Dialogue with dictators: judicial resistance in Argentina and Brazil. Law Soc Inq 20:481–560
Osiel M (2009) Making sense of mass atrocity. Cambridge University Press, Cambridge
Pauer-Studer H (2012) Law and morality under evil conditions: the SS Judge Konrad Morgen. Jurisprudence 3(2):367–390
Pauer-Studer H (2014) Einleitung: Rechtfertigung des Unrechts. Das Rechtsdenken im Nationalsozialismus. In: Pauer-Studer H, Fink J (eds) Rechtfertigungen des Unrechts Da Rechtsdenken im Nationalsozialismus in Originaltexten. Suhrkamp, Berlin
Pereira AW (2005) Political (in)justice authoritarianism and the rule of law in Brazil, Chile and Argentina. University of Pittsburgh Press, Pittsburgh (Kindle edition)
Rode LS (1983) De tyske krigsretter, in Den Norske Advokatforening, Advokaten – rettens og samfunnets tjener Den Norske Advokatforening 1908–1983, Oslo, pp 329–362
Rundle K (2009) The impossibility of an exterminatory legality: law and the Holocaust. Univ Toronto Law J 59:65–125
Rüthers B (2012) Die unbegrenzte Auslegung: Zum Wandel der Privatrechtsordnung im Nationalsozialismus 7. Ausg. Mohr Siebeck, Tübingen
Schleunes K (ed) (2001) Legislating the Holocaust: the Bernhard Loesener memoirs and supporting documents. Westview, Boulder (Kindle edition)
Schmitt C (1933) Staat, Bewegung, Volk, Die Dreigliederung der politischen Einheit. Hamburg
Shapiro M (2008) Courts in authoritarian regimes. In: Ginsburg T, Moustafa T (eds) Rule by law: the politics of courts in authoritarian regimes. Cambridge University Press, Cambridge
Strenge I (2002) Machtübernahme 1933: Alles auf dem legalen Weg? Ducker und Humblot, Berlin
Trials of War Criminals before the Nuremberg Military Tribunals, vol I, the Medical case, Washington, 1951
Trials of War Criminals before the Nuremberg Military Tribunals, vol III, the Justice Case, Washington, 1951
Tuori K (2002) Critical legal positivism. Ashgate, Dartmouth
Wilke C (2009) Reconsecrating the temple of justice: invocations of civilization and humanity in the Nuremberg Justice Case. Can J Law Soc 24:181–201

Chapter 3
Repression of the Judiciary

The Need for Legitimacy

In his book on political justice, Otto Kirchheimer claims that judicial proceedings serve to authenticate and thus to limit political action. By this, those in power stand to gain as much as their subjects. Authentication removes the fear of protests and reprisals from victims and encourages a friendly and understanding attitude towards the security needs of the power holders.[1]

The legal system is not the main arena for battles between the regime and its opponents. The courts may therefore often serve to provide sanction to solutions and decisions reached elsewhere. The regime may resort to the service of the courts out of necessity, choice, or convenience.[2] Courts are mostly not the most efficient means for dealing with a political or social issue. But their connection to the law and legality gives their proceedings and decisions a special quality that is sought by democratic and authoritarian rulers alike.

Courts, law, and legitimacy are important even to oppressive regimes. Courts are needed for many different purposes. They are needed to establish social control and sideline political opponents, to provide legitimacy, to strengthen and control administrative compliance, to attract foreign investment, and to implement controversial policies.[3] Legitimacy is important for the acceptance of the regime and its measures among the social elites and for the possibility to economise on the use of direct force. Legitimacy can also be important to the foreign relations of a regime. For instance, the postwar authoritarian regimes in South Korea and Taiwan kept an appearance of formal constitutional legality for the sake of their security relations

---

[1] Kirchheimer (1961), p. 6.

[2] Kirchheimer (1961), pp. 419–423.

[3] Ginsburg and Moustafa (2008), p. 4.

H.P. Graver, *Judges Against Justice*, DOI 10.1007/978-3-662-44293-7_3

with the United States, but the scope of the independent courts internally was carefully circumscribed.[4] The rule of law and independent courts are important also to maintain the legal stability needed by the economic order. Even in Nazi Germany, the economic law in the narrower sense was in the most untouched by the "national socialist revolution".[5]

All authoritarian regimes do not equally depend on courts pronouncing on their legality. Stalin's Soviet, Mao's China, and Pol Pot's Cambodia did not engage courts in any important degree in their repression and the legitimation of their repression. The atrocities in former Yugoslavia and in Rwanda did not request legality.

Many authoritarian regimes, on the other hand, do seek the support of the courts, and with good reason. The Truth and Reconciliation Commission of South Africa claimed that "part of the reason for the longevity of apartheid was the superficial adherence to 'rule by law' by the National Party (NP), whose leaders craved the aura of legitimacy that 'the law' bestowed on their harsh injustice".[6] Research suggests that the Commission was correct in its observation. A study of confidence in the legal system of South Africa shows that more than half of the population had a great deal or quite a lot of confidence in the legal system during apartheid and that the confidence of the black portion of the population was on level with the confidence of the white portion.[7] It seems that support of the courts and the law is of particular importance to countries belonging to the western legal tradition.

Even a totalitarian state like Nazi Germany showed great deference to legality and its conception by the public. The Nazi takeover of power was carefully designed and employed as a legal strategy and was perceived in its time as legal in a substantive sense.[8] The same was true seen from the outside. Although many foreign observers were critical, the legality of the legal development under the Nazis was not questioned as such by contemporary commentators.[9] Nazi rule had a preference of converting Germans to its cause and using force only against fringes that could be identified as criminal.[10] This preference gave the law and the legal institutions an important role in securing legitimacy for the regime.

Courts hold the final word of that which is to be regarded as legal and that which is regarded as illegal in a given society. The relationships between the determinations of the courts and the extent to which people in society regard the regime as legitimate are indirect and complex, as are the relationships between the perceptions of legitimacy and the ability of the regime to pursue its policies. These

---

[4] Ginsburg and Moustafa (2008), p. 6.

[5] Fraenkel (1941), p. 72.

[6] Truth and Reconciliation Commission (1998), vol. 4 Chapter 4 Institutional Hearing: The Legal Community, p. 101.

[7] Ellmann (1995), p. 426.

[8] See Strenge (2002), p. 17.

[9] See Fraser (2005), chapter 4.

[10] Stoltzfus (1996).

relationships vary between different societies and probably depend on a whole range of conditions such as tradition, culture, and economic and social complexity. This is one of the reasons why the concept of legitimacy is so difficult to social theory.

In countries of the western legal tradition, notions of the rule of law seem to play an important part in establishing legitimacy for the rulers. Therefore, in these countries, courts by their control over legality hold an important condition for the actual and normative legitimacy of the other organs of state. How they exercise this control is of crucial importance to the destiny of the rule of law when it is under attack and may also be of importance even to authoritarian rulers. There are many examples of how the Nazi regime needed the judges for the appearance of legality and how this affected the functioning of the judiciary and the courts. Goebbels originally intended for the trials against the conspirators behind the attempt on Hitler's life on 20 July 1944 to be utilised for propaganda purposes. He therefore arranged to have the proceedings filmed. However, after seeing how openly shockingly biased the first trial was conducted by the president of the People's Court, Roland Freisler, he dropped the plan of having the film shown to the public with the words "Freisler's clamour is not suited for the public. It would seem repulsive to the uninitiated".[11]

Another example of how the concern of reactions from the public influenced the conduction of justice can be found in a ruling of the Supreme Court in 1938, where it overruled a decision by a lower court to incarcerate a witness who refused to give evidence.[12] Such a decision "affects the basics of judicial procedure", and it could compromise the confidence of the people in this procedure if one employed "such means to pursue the truth as the Regional Court has employed in this case". Similar arguments were employed by the Supreme Court of Argentina in an opinion where it rejected the arguments of the military and stated that the administration could enhance its public esteem by "proving its respect for the judicial power".[13]

Deference to legality seems also to underlie the policy that the Nazi regime took in implementing the euthanasia programme of the mentally disabled and incurable sick. At Berlin, 1 September 1939, Hitler signed the secret order charging Reichsleiter Bouhler and Dr. Brandt, MD, "with the responsibility of enlarging the authority of certain physicians to be designated by name in such a manner that persons who, according to human judgment, are incurable can, upon a most careful diagnosis of their condition of sickness, be accorded a mercy death". The order was not based on any previously existing German law, and the only authority for the execution of euthanasia was the secret order issued by Hitler. Following this order, over 70,000 people were put to death. Officials in the ministry of justice protested that the Hitler letter was not a law and that official legislation was necessary to

[11] Knopp (2004), p. 285. A film prepared for the Nazi leaders documenting the court of Roland Freisler can be seen at http://www.youtube.com/watch?v=x_bwucQ7l3g (accessed 30.10.2013).

[12] RGH Urteil vom 13.07.1938 73 RGSt. S. 31–36.

[13] Osiel (1995), p. 484.

legalise euthanasia. The Reich Minister of Justice even wrote a letter to the chancellery of Hitler stating that as the Führer had refused to issue a law, it was necessary to discontinue immediately the secret extermination of insane persons.

The desire to keep the killings out of public view was probably the reason why the necessary legislation was not enacted. The killings were not discontinued at this point, however, and prevailed until the public protests reached a disquieting level. At that point, the official euthanasia programme was discontinued, although some killings, especially of children, were kept on as "wild euthanasia" in certain clinics.

The same pattern can be seen in the lengthy discussions within Nazi Germany over the definition of "Jew" according to the Nuremberg laws and whether to include persons of mixed ancestry and Jews married to Germans in the deportations and extermination. As adopted in 1935, the Jew laws included persons with at least three Jewish grandparents. Circles within the Party and the SS pressured expanding the scope so as to include "every drop of Jewish blood" in the purging of Jews from the German community. The SS also wanted to deport persons not formally recognised as Jews and also deport the Jews married to Germans. These efforts were for the most part unsuccessful, and persons of mixed ancestry and Jews married to Germans were, to a large extent, saved from the Holocaust. According to officials within the Ministry of the Interior and the Ministry of Justice, this was largely due to their moderating influence and the resistance of bureaucrats in opposition to the measures against the Jews.[14] A more probable explanation is that the leading Nazis were concerned about public reaction to laws and measures breaking up the institution of marriage and breaking into large numbers of German families.

> Goebbels realized he could not murder all the people he wanted to murder – the Jewish relatives, spouses, sympathizers. At some point the Germans would have begun to identify with one another rather than with a government that kept demanding ever more human victims.[15]

National Socialist jurisprudence was at great pains not to be blamed for discarding the concept of the "Rechtsstaat" and did so partly by applying a new construction to the old term.[16] This policy of striving for legitimacy by reference to legality, albeit grounded in new concepts such as "the need of the German people" and "the will of the Führer", required certain self-restraints in order to maintain the belief in legality and the support of the German people. The fact that this restraint was shown by the Nazi leaders when public protests became evident shows the importance the regime attached to the appearance of legality.

---

[14] See Schleunes (2001) and pp. 254–256 below.

[15] See Stoltzfus (1996), p. 245.

[16] Loewenstein (1935–1936), pp. 779–813.

Judicial Independence

When authoritarian groups take control over the state and destroy its legislative and executive organs, the courts are often allowed to continue their functions. Where parliaments are disempowered and dissolved and civilian governments replaced by the military, courts are often allowed to continue their functions with a continuance both of the institutions and the personnel. This was the case even in the German occupation of the Western European nations during World War II, and it has also been the case in most coups d'état in postcolonial states.[17] The situation of the judges is, in this respect, similar to the situation of the civil servants, who also most often continue their functions after a regime change. There is, however, one major difference between judges and civil servants. Whereas civil servants are so many and specialised that they are required in order to maintain the state functions of governance, judges could more easily be replaced or dispensed with all together. The fact that judges are allowed to continue therefore indicates something about the need of the regime to uphold pretence of judicial independence.

Judicial independence involves a spectre of issues, including institutional, ideological, and personal aspects, and requires that "the judiciary shall decide matters before them impartially, on the basis of facts and in accordance with the law, without any restrictions, improper influences, inducements, pressures, threats or interferences, direct or indirect, from any quarter or for any reason".[18] In this sense, many authoritarian regimes violate the independence of the judiciary in that they try to coerce or pressure the judiciary to accommodate the needs of the regime. On the other hand, the pressure often seems to stop short of ordering the judge how to decide the individual case or applying sanctions against a judge who decides contrary to the interests of the regime. In cases where sanctions are applied, they are often limited to reposting or removal of the judge. Criminal sanctions and reprisals seem rare. The rulers may try to exert influence over the judiciary through different means: by appointment of judges loyal to the regime, by dismissal of judges who do not perform in accordance with the preferences of the regime, and by interference in judicial proceedings.[19]

The Nazis stressed the importance that the independence of the judiciary be formally upheld. There was a lot of ideological pressure on the judiciary through the mass media, scholarly journals, and letters to the judges from the Ministry of Justice. Many judgments had to be confirmed by the executive in order to become final. If the executive disagreed with the judgment, a retrial was ordered. On the other hand, the regime showed restraint in exerting influence through appointment

---

[17] See Mahmud (1994), pp. 49–140, p. 103.

[18] See UN Basic Principles on the Independence of the Judiciary Adopted by the Seventh United Nations Congress on the Prevention of Crime and the Treatment of Offenders held at Milan from 26 August to 6 September 1985 and endorsed by General Assembly resolutions 40/32 of 29 November 1985 and 40/146 of 13 December 1985.

[19] See Aall (2014), p. 33.

and dismissal of judges and also in the interference in the individual legal process. The independence of judges was seen as one of the central features distinguishing Nazi Germany from "Bolshevism". Hans Frank, the head of the Nazi Lawyers' Association, was of the opinion that the very existence of their "bourgeois culture" depended upon the independence of the judges.[20] Even as late as 1944, the German High Command issued a regulation stating that "The military judges are not under any orders when it comes to deciding the facts of the matter and their exercise of judicial functions. They are to decide according to their conviction based on all that has been presented during the case, according to soldierly values and an interpretation of the law based on the national socialist view of the world (Weltanschauung)".[21]

The control over the courts that Hitler and his cabinet exercised did not go through party lines. After some initial struggles of power between the party and the civil servants in the first years of the Nazi takeover, Hitler's control over the judiciary was mainly exercised by the delegation of his power to the Reich Minister of Justice. This ensured a measure of judicial independence from political pressure and influence, as the Ministry, until a policy change in 1942 towards the judiciary, only intervened in a few politically sensitive cases.[22] The party was given some influence on the recruitment of judges, but the main grounds for recruitment were on professional merit. Up until the 1940s, there was no pronounced control over the rulings of the judiciary, and the majority of the judges do not seem to have been under the impression that they could risk political scrutiny of their decisions at any time.[23]

The regime had clear interests in maintaining formal judicial independence. Herman Jahrreiss, professor in public law and public international law and defender at trial at Nuremberg against the major war criminals, expressed it this way during this trial:

> ... The only thing that was not quite clear was Hitler's relationship to the judiciary. For, even in Hitler Germany, it was not possible to exterminate the idea that it was essential to allow justice to be exercised by independent courts, at least in matters which concern the bulk of the people in their everyday life. Up to the top group of Party officials this was shown by some of the speeches by the Reich Leader of jurists, the Defendant Dr. Frank, as quoted here – there showed resistance, which, it is true, was not very effective, when justice in civil and ordinary criminal cases was equally to be subjected to the *sic volo sic jubeo* of one man. But apart from the judiciary, which in the end also was beginning to succumb, absolute monocracy was complete.[24]

The pressures on the judiciary increased during the war. On 26 April 1942, Hitler addressed the Reichstag in part as follows:

---

[20] See Linder (1987), p. 15.

[21] Garbe (2000), p. 100.

[22] Angermund (1990), pp. 87–92.

[23] Angermund (1990), p. 93.

[24] Trial of the Major War Criminals before the International Military Tribunal, Nuremberg 14 November 1945–1 October 1946, vol. 17, p. 487.

> I do expect one thing: That the nation gives me the right to intervene immediately and to take action myself wherever a person has failed to render unqualified obedience...
>
> I therefore ask the German Reichstag to confirm expressly that I have the legal right to keep everybody to his duty and to cashier or remove from office or position without regard for his person, or his established rights, whoever, in my view and according to my considered opinion, has failed to do his duty...
>
> From now on, I shall intervene in these cases and remove from office those judges who evidently do not understand the demand of the hour.[25]

In the opinion of the US Military Tribunal, this speech changed the position of the German judiciary and formed the basis for the situation described by the Tribunal where one could no longer speak of an independent judiciary in any meaningful sense. The US Military Tribunal stated that at this time "the function of the Nazi courts was judicial only in a limited sense. They more closely resembled administrative tribunals acting under directives from above in a quasi-judicial manner".[26] The ministry at the time saw it differently and considered that they failed to control the judges even in so sensitive areas as the laws governing the military necessity of war.[27]

In fact, it may be an open question as to how much of a real change Hitler's speech represented. Hitler took measures to ensure that there was no direct influence on judges by party officials but that conflicts were sorted out at the ministerial level.[28] One of these measures was the change of personnel at the top of the Ministry of Justice and the introduction of the "judge letters" where individual decisions were commented on for the benefit of educating the judges in National Socialist legal flair.

Even after the change in 1942, and Hitler's speech in the Reichstag, the situation was not totally under the control of the regime. The judges themselves read Hitler's criticism with disbelief and blamed his—what they saw as ill-founded—allegations on his advisors. They did not believe that Hitler would allow direct interventions in the affairs of the courts, and they were confident that he would protect the independence of the judiciary.[29] The judges were assured, and they believed, that Hitler would not allow interference with individual judges and that he would protect judicial independence.[30] All in all, judicial practice shows that the judges functioned to a certain extent independently, even after 1942 when the scope of their freedom had been decreased.

Judicial independence is evidenced also by the fact that the Nazis, to a very limited extent, disciplined or sanctioned judges for non-conforming rulings. A contemporary observer, Karl Loewenstein, wrote in his report on the reconstruction of German law after Nazism:

---

[25] The Justice Case (1951), pp. 1011–1012.

[26] The Justice Case (1951), pp. 1024–1025.

[27] Angermund (1990), pp. 244–245.

[28] Angermund (1990), pp. 253–265.

[29] Angermund (1990), p. 248.

[30] Angermund (1990), p. 248.

> But not a single case is reported in which a judge who resigned was sent to a concentration camp, or even lost his pension. If he wished, he could leave the service and "sit the regime out" on his pension. Though such cases occurred not too frequently, they were known and widely commented on by the judiciary. Moreover – and this too was fully known – there were some judges, particularly among the older generation, who, neither resigning nor yielding, resisted pressure to the end. Nor is it correct to assume that non-party members among the judiciary were invariably denied promotion. No doubt one reason for this is that very few judges mounted any opposition against the regime. But some did quite openly without meeting with more serious sanctions than transfer to a different jurisdiction, lack of promotion or removal from office with a pension.[31]

Judges who opposed the Nazi policies were given mild reprimands and in the more substantive cases where pensioned off.[32] This happened to Lothar Kreyssig, for his protests against the euthanasia programme, and to Hubert Schorn. Judges who refused to enter the Nazi Party experienced that they were passed over for promotion and that it took longer for them to advance in their careers.[33] Nevertheless, it cannot be denied that many judges may have maintained their loyalty to the regime and contributed by meeting out draconic punishments out fear of the consequences of seeming disobedience.[34]

Judicial independence was respected to a degree also in countries under German influence during the war. In Vichy France, lawyers could, without significant risk, protest against oppressive Vichy laws.[35] Even in the occupied countries, the Germans were, in general, moderate in their dealings with opposition from the national judiciary. In Norway, the judges of the Supreme Court did not encounter any sanctions for their protest when they resigned over a controversy with the German Reichskommissar.[36] Also, the lawyers appearing before the German war tribunals and SS courts were surprised over the extent to which they were allowed to speak and criticise freely the occupation authorities in court without being reprimanded.[37] In the Netherlands, two judges were dismissed when they sentenced a criminal with a lenient sentence in order to save him from having to serve a sentence in a German detention camp, which had been exposed for its ill-treatment of prisoners.[38]

In Belgium, the confrontations were more severe and the German measures harder. The Belgian judges were told when they discontinued their work in protest against a demand to apply the legal measures of the German occupier that such an act would be regarded as an illegal strike subject to criminal proceedings against them, and they were subject to arrest and hostage taking during the occupation.

---

[31] Loewenstein (1948), p. 444. See also Oppler (1947).

[32] Rasehorn (2000), p. 130.

[33] Schorn (1959), pp. 39–40.

[34] See Angermund (1990), p. 245.

[35] Weisberg (1996), p. 10.

[36] See further pp. 95–96 below.

[37] See Rode (1983), p. 353.

[38] See Michielsen (2004), pp. 161–162.

The judges of Belgium were in constant opposition to the German occupiers throughout the occupation. As the occupation progressed, the German occupiers resorted to intimidation to persuade the judges not to rule unfavourably. In several cases, judges were arrested and punished for "anti-German behaviour".[39] Judges who ruled contrary to the expressed interests of the occupier were placed on lists for hostage taking. The Court of Cassation protested against measures against judges who had acted within their official capacity and in compliance with Belgian law and who considered such measures an attack on the independence and dignity of the courts. In cases where judges were removed from their office for ex officio acts, the Court of Cassation intervened successfully, but it had less success when judges were removed for vicarious reasons.[40]

One dramatic example involved a dispute over an administrative regulation in a reorganisation of the Belgian administrative structure. When the legality of this was contested, the military administration ordered a stay in the proceedings before the Brussels Court of Appeal and the Court of Cassation. The Court of Cassation complied, but the Brussels Court considered the letter an attack on its judicial independence and rendered judgment where the administrative regulation was declared ultra vires. The military administration reacted by arresting the three judges who had participated in the decision and taking several other judges hostage. The administration, however, denied that the hostage taking had anything to do with the judgment of the Brussels Court.

The Court of Cassation decided to stay its work until further notice and was followed by the Brussels Court of Appeal and one other court. The military administration declared that if the work was not resumed, severe measures would be taken. According to a regulation for the protection of labour peace, strikes bore the maximum of the death penalty. The Brussels Court decided to resume its "activities in confidence" that the civilian authorities would find a solution for the release of the arrested judges. The Court of Cassation also resumed its activities based on an assurance from the Secretary General of Justice that a release was imminent. The judges were subsequently released, but only after 2 weeks.[41] The legal community in Belgium also protested when their Jewish colleagues were purged from their positions, and unlike their colleagues in Germany and France, Belgian judges did not introduce a legal category of "Jew" into the private and commercial laws, resisting attempts to introduce German anti-Jewish norms into Belgian law.[42]

In South Africa, the regime "carefully refrained from direct action against any judge", even though several of them were liberal in their outlook and tried to curtail the oppressive measures that were enacted by the regime.[43] The generals of

---

[39] Michielsen (2004), pp. 45–46.

[40] Michielsen (2004), pp. 47–50 and 81–92.

[41] Michielsen (2004), pp. 70–77.

[42] Fraser (2009), pp. 47–51 and p. 211.

[43] Dugard (1987), p. 494.

Argentina, Brazil, and Chile depended on the courts to keep up necessary support among the bureaucratic and economic elites.[44] Despite the constant resistance of the Brazilian Supreme Court to the regime, the Court for a long time was allowed to continue its protests. The officers instead responded by redrafting the laws and decrees, by taking repressive measures underground, and by reallocating jurisdiction in politically significant offences to the military courts.[45] The generals of Chile took great pains to give their policies a patina of legal formality. They claimed to have seized power to uphold the rule of law, which they blamed the socialist government of Allende for undermining. They cultivated an image of respect and commitment to law and to an independent judiciary, and the judges were in fact not subject to threats or other types of interference from the military government.[46] The military of Argentina, though, were not committed to preserving the appearance of the rule of law and even included "ingenious legalists" among the class of subversives to be oppressed. But even they could not afford to shed all legalist pretentions to secure support among domestic elites.[47] Studies on courts in authoritarian regimes suggest as a general finding that direct attacks on judges are rare.[48]

The refraining of authoritarian regimes to interfere directly in judicial decisions and to sanction judges for their rulings says something about the core of the judicial role. A judge who is under direct orders is no longer acting in a judicial capacity. In the words of Nazi Judge Oeschey:

> Now it is an absurdity to tell the judge in an individual case which is subject to his decision how he has to decide. Such a system would make the judge superfluous. I was never a supporter of the stubborn doctrine of the independence of the judge which granted the judge within the frame of the law the position of a public servant, only subordinated to his conscience but otherwise 'neutral', that is, politically completely independent... Naturally it (instructing the judge) was not done in an open manner; but even the most camouflaged form could not hide the fact that a directive was to be given. Thereby the office of judge is naturally abolished and the proceedings in a trial become a farce.[49]

In light of this, it is perhaps not surprising that judicial independence in this limited sense is respected even by authoritarian regimes. To the extent that the regime wishes to or is dependent upon maintaining judicial institutions, this independence is a necessity. Without it, the regime loses the benefits that it can gain by maintaining law and legal institutions as vehicles for its policies.

Such dependency on the courts gives judges even in authoritarian settings a certain amount of power. But it also makes their position a precarious one; it is in the nature of authoritarianism not to accept challenges to the exercise of power. The courts are dependent upon the regime for the enforcement of their decisions, and the

---

[44] Osiel (1995), p. 510.

[45] Osiel (1995), p. 537.

[46] See Hilbink (2008), pp. 104 and 113.

[47] Osiel (1995), pp. 510–511.

[48] See Ginsburg and Moustafa (2008), p. 14.

[49] The Justice Case (1951), p. 1020.

regime has in its power to remove judges and appoint new ones, and even to abolish courts all together. The dilemma for such regimes is that by subverting the judiciary excessively, they also undermine their own efficiency. By this fact, judges often have more scope for action than might be believed, and as we see, this can be the case even under totalitarian regimes.

Purge of the Judiciary and Court Packing

Oppressive regimes have a wide set of means other than suppressing individual judges to secure the support of the judiciary. Rulers often seek to appoint cooperative judges to ensure judicial support for their policies and to ensure a more compliant administration of the politically sensitive criminal law. It is quite common for regimes with a political agenda to obtain support by relieving "politically unsound" judges and appointing sympathetic judges to the bench.

One of the first measures of the Nazi regime was the passing of the April 7, 1933, "law for the reestablishment of the civil service".[50] The law established the famous "Aryan clause" and provided for the retirement or dismissal of such civil servants who, in view of their political activities prior to the advent of the regime to power, did not offer sufficient guarantees that they would defend the regime without reservations. Under this Act, Jews and members of the Social Democrat Party were purged from the legal profession. This did not, however, affect many judges: the composition of the bench was left basically unchanged by this move.[51]

To a certain extent, the purge nevertheless opened up opportunities for young lawyers to engage in a judicial career. These opportunities increased, particularly with the war and administration of occupied territories, which created a demand for judges and prosecutors. By 1942, the number of judges and prosecutors had increased from around 10,000 in 1933 to almost 17,000.[52] It is difficult to establish whether this expansion, with the considerable recruitment of new judges, as such strengthened the loyalty of the judiciary to the Nazi regime. Few of the newly appointed judges were old party members. But loyal party members were recruited to the more strategic positions, such as to vacancies in the Supreme Court and to the People's Court and the special courts that were established as criminal courts for treason, political offences, and other cases of special importance to the regime. But even for these courts, juridical qualifications were the main criteria for recruitment.[53]

Purge of judges and court packing are also common in less totalitarian regimes. In South Africa, as a result of the controversy between the government and the

---

[50] Gesetz zur Wiederherstellung des Berufsbeamtentums of April 7, 1933, RGBI. I, 175.

[51] See Angermund (1990), p. 54.

[52] Angermund (1990), p. 102.

[53] See Angermund (1990), p. 138.

Appellate Division of the Supreme Court over judicial review of legislation, the government in 1955 packed the Appellate Division by enlarging it from 6 to 11 judges and by providing that all the judges had to sit in cases where the validity of legislation was to be determined.[54] In this way, the government finally secured support for its measures to disenfranchise coloured voters.[55] In Argentina, the generals immediately after the coup purged the bench and appointed new judges supportive of the coup. This was in line with the established tradition of radical changes in government, which Argentina experienced regularly from the 1930s to 1980, where it was customary for each new regime to replace the members of the Supreme Court. In Brazil, the judges were left in office, but the number of judges in the Supreme Court was increased after the Court began to rule against the regime and decreased to its original number again after two judges resigned in protest against military actions.[56]

The Junta in Chile left the courts untouched and refrained from dictating or otherwise manipulating judicial decisions.[57] Here, the judiciary was controlled by the Supreme Court, which had a strong conservative faction that was supportive of the coup. As overseer of the judiciary, the Supreme Court in 1974 used its power to dismiss 12 % of the judicial employees, among those approximately 40 judges.[58]

Similar experiences can be found in other cases. In Norway, during the occupation, the German occupiers and the Quisling regime tried to ensure a cooperative judiciary by lowering the compulsory pension age, combined with a selective renewal of the tenure of compliant judges. When the Supreme Court refused to recognise the legality of such a scheme, Quisling and Riisnæs, the Minister of Justice, deliberated on appointing new, additional judges to the Supreme Court to ensure a majority for their view. Before any measures were taken, the Supreme Court judges collectively resigned their positions over the dispute and over a controversy on the right to judicial review by national courts of decrees issued by the German occupation authority.[59] Quisling subsequently appointed new judges supportive of the regime, after ensuring they would vote against a right to judicial review.

As we see, it is not uncommon for oppressive regimes to exercise control over who holds judicial positions, especially within the higher courts. With the general tendency of judges to look to the higher courts for directions on the law, these courts naturally hold a strategically important position. The higher courts are an important source of law even in civil law regimes, and in any case they can overrule on appeal decisions by lower courts that are unfavourable to the regime.

---

[54] See Dyzenhaus (1998), p. 154.

[55] See further below p. 93–95.

[56] Osiel (1995), p. 513 and P. 531.

[57] Hilbink (2008), p. 102.

[58] Hilbink (2008), p. 123.

[59] See p. 95–96 below.

Limits to Jurisdiction and Special Courts

Another common procedure of oppressive regimes is to limit the access to the court by limiting the scope of the competence of the courts to review acts and decisions by organs and agencies of the state. During the German Weimar Republic, the Supreme Court and the government had taken different positions on judicial review, with the Supreme Court stating that the courts had to correct the failings of the legislator.[60] After the Nazi takeover of power, review of statutes by the courts was ultra vires because the statutes were the commands of the Führer, who was the supreme source of law and the ultimate judge at the same time. The German Supreme Court ruled in 1934 that acts of government of a political nature undertaken for the sake of political expediency were beyond judicial control.[61]

The Supreme Court of Chile ruled only 2 months after the military coup that military tribunals in the time of war fell outside of its jurisdiction.[62] It generally refused to hear appeals for habeas corpus. In his speech opening the judicial year on March 1, 1975, the Supreme Court president said:

> As a result of appeals presented, the Appeals Court in Santiago and this Supreme Court have been overwhelmed with a large number of habeas corpus actions that have been introduced, alleging arrests made by the executive branch. The administration of justice has thereby been impeded, since the higher courts, particularly in Santiago, have been prevented from attending to urgent matters entrusted to them.[63]

The courts of Argentina periodically sought to limit the oppressive measures of the regime, for instance, by granting habeas corpus in favour of persons who were illegally detained. In most cases, however, the Court confined itself to ordering the executive to conduct a thorough enquiry.[64] Snyder argues that the effect of these measures was only to provide the government with a comparatively uncomplicated formula to follow to establish the legality of its actions.[65] The courts of Brazil covered up the systematic torture of prisoners and did not investigate allegations of torture. In rare instances, they acquitted defendants because of claims of torture, but this did not occur until towards the end of the 1970s.[66] In neither Argentina, Brazil, or Chile was there any efficient oversight by the courts over the use of administrative powers or state violence, nor did the courts question the denials by the authorities of any knowledge of disappeared persons. A remarkable feature of the Brazilian courts was, however, the relatively high rate of acquittal of persons charged with political offences.[67]

---

[60] Angermund (1990), pp. 39–40.

[61] Loewenstein (1935–1936), p. 810.

[62] Barros (2008), p. 174.

[63] Report of the Chilean National Commission on Truth and Reconciliation (1993), p. 141.

[64] Osiel (1995), p. 518.

[65] Snyder (1983–1984), p. 516.

[66] Pereira (2005), Kindle edition, loc. 1072.

[67] Pereira (2005), Kindle edition, loc. 1096.

Another way of limiting the power of the judiciary is by the setting up of special courts and tribunals, staffed with "reliables", to deal with the politically more sensitive cases. Moustafa talks about the engineering of "fragmented judicial systems" with exceptional courts where the regime retains tight controls alongside the regular court system.[68] According to Osiel, the most common strategy of authoritarian rulers is to limit the jurisdiction of the courts to hear cases that are likely to raise their suspicions about the executive's commitment to the rule of law.[69] But special courts may also be used more actively to ensure efficient implementation of policy.

To ensure vigorous enforcement of treason laws and political cases, the Nazi regime established special courts within the district of every court of appeal with a decree dated 21 March 1933. Their jurisdiction included the trial of cases of insidious attacks against the government of the national revolution. During the war, they were given jurisdiction in cases against looting.[70] Judges were appointed to these courts not only based on their party affiliation but also based on their legal qualifications. The judges in the special courts also continued to serve in their positions on the bench of the regular courts.[71]

As a result of the ruling of the Supreme Court in the case of the Reichstagsfire, a People's Court was established by an Act of 24 April 1934. The People' Court had jurisdiction in cases of treason, economic sabotage and failure to report intended crimes, and undermining of the war effort. Its jurisdiction was constantly increased, especially during the war years.

In South Africa, the major part of judicial oppression was undertaken by the magistrates, lower courts staffed from the ranks of the public service rather than the private legal profession. The magistrates for this reason had a lower status than judges within the legal profession. The bulk of political trials were actually heard not by the judges but by magistrates. Magistrates also performed crucial functions in relation to political detainees, including overseeing complaints and safeguarding prisoners' rights. Magistrates received directives from the Department of Justice, could be transferred without their consent, were dependent on merit assessments for promotion and salary increases, and could face an inquiry by the executive into charges of inefficiency or misconduct.[72]

The Argentinean leaders set up military courts and gave them jurisdiction in matters of infringements of rules by military personnel, security forces, and the police. In this way, in such issues, the ordinary courts were deprived of jurisdiction over the oppressive measures of the regime.[73] In Brazil, the leaders limited the jurisdiction of the regular courts in habeas corpus petitions and let established

[68] Moustafa (2007), Kindle edition, location 546.

[69] Osiel (1995), p. 500, footnote 64.

[70] The special courts are described by the Tribunal in the Justice Case on pp. 999–1002.

[71] Angermund (1990), pp. 138–139.

[72] See Gready and Kgalema (2003), pp. 145–146.

[73] Snyder (1983–1984), pp. 503–520.

military courts deal with matters of national security.[74] The military government of Chile appointed military courts to deal with political offences. Due to a wide jurisdiction over civilians, these courts tried four civilians to every one military person. They were staffed by mid-level officials, without legal training, and who were hierarchically subordinate to the commanders in chief. They dispensed 200 death sentences between 1973 and 1976, and thousands of others were sentenced to harsh disproportionate prison sentences.[75]

During the occupation, the Norwegian collaborator regime also appointed a People's Court and special courts to deal with political crimes and crimes of opposition against the regime and the occupying forces.

Special courts are ways of bypassing the established courts and ensuring courts that are loyal to the general aims and policies of the regime. In some cases, they are staffed by judges who do not have legal training or experience as judges from the ordinary bench. In other cases, such as in occupied Norway, political criteria are used for recruiting judges. Further examples include ordinary judges participating in the special courts, recruited according to ordinary criteria of merit.

Special courts are not illegitimate as such. Some countries use specialised courts as an ordinary way of dispensing justice under the rule of law, while in other countries specialised courts are frowned upon. In any case, there are no general standards by which special courts can be deemed as illegitimate once the internal conditions for their establishment and empowerment are met. Even the notorious special courts and the People's Court of Nazi Germany were recognised as legitimate courts by the US Military Tribunal after the war, by courts of allied countries dealing with war crimes, and by the courts of the Federal Republic of Germany.[76]

In contrast to a judge in a court that is established before an authoritarian regime comes to power, judges of the special courts of the regime owe allegiance only to this regime. If the regime operates in contradiction to the constitutional order or rights of the old regime, judges in courts that continue through the regime change have to decide to be loyal either to the regime and constitution that appointed them or to the regime in power. They may use the fact that they have their basis in a constitution based on the rule of law as an argument to check the measures of the new regime. This opportunity is not available to judges appointed to courts established by the new regime. They too, however, owe allegiance to the law. To the extent that the law still contains elements of the rule of law, they therefore also have a source of arguments to hold the regime in check, as the experience with the military courts of Brazil shows. The military courts of Brazil acquitted nearly 70 % of the people who were charged before them and contributed to lessen the repression that was sought by the military rulers.[77]

---

[74] Osiel (1995), p. 531.

[75] Hilbink (2008), p. 107.

[76] See Chap. 10 below.

[77] Osiel (1995), p. 538.

Persuasion and Conditioning of Legal Minds

In addition to seeking out sympathetic judges and limiting the scope of their control and supervision of oppressive means, authoritarian regimes rely on a wide range of mechanisms to convince, persuade, and coerce judges to apply their legal minds to the benefit of the regime. In Nazi Germany, the judiciary was subject to public criticism and rulings that were disliked by the SS or the Party were condemned in the press.

The legal system and the judiciary were under attack by the Nazis long before their takeover of power in 1933. German law under the Weimar Republic was deemed as "Roman" as contrasted to "Germanic", "liberalistic", and "Jewish".[78] After the takeover, judicial independence was not formally abolished: the judges received assurances from Hitler himself that judicial independence would be respected.

On the other hand, the Law for the Restoration of the Professional Civil Service of 7 April 1933 required political reliability as a condition for public office, including judicial offices. Under this Act, non-Aryan judges, as well as judges belonging to the Social Democrat Party, were removed from office. The judges' unions were disbanded, and the judges were encouraged to join the *Bund Nationalsozialistichen Deutschen Juristen*. The membership of this union increased from 1,600 in June 1933 to 30,000 by the end of 1933 and 80,000, including 15,000 judges, in 1935.[79] This meant that virtually all judges and prosecutors were members of the Nazi lawyer's association.

Judges were instructed by the Ministry of Justice to disregard the wording of old statutes and to apply the "values and principles of National Socialism". Individual judges and rulings were criticised publically in the press and in legal journals. Hitler proclaimed himself as supreme judge, unbound by the law in the purge of the SA and Ernst Röhm in 1934. Despite all this, according to later historians, there was no total control over the judiciary by the Nazi Party; the majority of judges were not under the impression of being under the risk of disciplinary action for their judgments.[80]

To "educate" the judges and guide them in National Socialist principles of law, the Ministry of Justice in 1942 started issuing letters to the judges, commenting on and criticising judicial decisions for the benefit of the whole judiciary. These were letters by the ministry addressed to the judges, discussing particular decisions that were chosen for their exemplary or blameworthy nature and giving political guidance on the legal effects of the Nazi ideology. The letters were classified and guarded from outsiders.[81]

---

[78] Loewenstein (1935–1936), p. 782.

[79] Angermund (1990), p. 61.

[80] Angermund (1990), p. 93.

[81] The judge letters are discussed in the Justice Trial, pp. 1017–1019.

References

Aall J (2014) Requirements concerning the independence of the judiciary according to Norwegian and international law. In: Engstad NA, Frøseth AL, Tønder B (eds) The independence of judges. Eleven Publishing, The Hague

Angermund R (1990) Deutsche Richtershaft 1919–1945. Fischer, Frankfurt am Main

Barros R (2008) Courts out of context: authoritarian sources of judicial failure in Chile (1973–1990) and Argentina (1976–1983). In: Ginsburg T, Moustafa T (eds) Rule by law: the politics of courts in authoritarian regimes. Cambridge University Press, Cambridge

Dugard J (1987) The judiciary in a state of national crisis – with special reference to the South African experience. Wash Lee Law Rev 44:477–501

Dyzenhaus D (1998) Judging the judges, judging ourselves truth, reconciliation and the apartheid legal order. Hart, Oxford

Ellmann S (1995) Law and legitimacy in South Africa. Law Soc Inq 20:407–479

Fraenkel E (1941) The dual state a contribution to the theory of dictatorship. Oxford University Press, New York

Fraser D (2005) Law after Auschwitz: towards a jurisprudence of the Holocaust. Carolina Academic Press, Durham

Fraser D (2009) The fragility of law constitutional patriotism and the Jews of Belgium, 1940–1945. Routledge-Cavendish, Oxon

Garbe D (2000) Im Namen des Volkes?! Die Rechtlichen Grundlagen der Militärjustiz im NS-Staat und ihre "Bewältigung" nach 1945. In: Nolz B, Popp W (eds) Erinnerungsarbeit Grundlage einer Kultur des Friedens. Lit Verlag, Münster

Ginsburg T, Moustafa T (2008) Introduction: the functions of courts in authoritarian politics. In: Ginsburg T, Moustafa T (eds) Rule by law: the politics of courts in authoritarian regimes. Cambridge University Press, Cambridge

Gready P, Kgalema L (2003) Magistrates under Apartheid: a case study of the politicisation of justice and complicity in human rights abuse. S Afr J Hum Rights 19:141–188

Hilbink L (2008) Agents of anti-politics: courts in Pinochet's Chile. In: Ginsburg T, Moustafa T (eds) Rule by law: the politics of courts in authoritarian regimes. Cambridge University Press, Cambridge

Kirchheimer O (1961) Political justice: the use of legal procedure for political ends. Princeton University Press, New Jersey

Knopp G (2004) Sie wollten Hitler Töten. C. Bertelsmann, München

Linder M (1987) The Supreme Labor Court in Nazi Germany: a jurisprudential analysis. Vittorio Klostermann, Frankfurt am Main

Loewenstein K (1935–1936) Law in the Third Reich. Yale Law Rev 45:779–815

Loewenstein K (1948) Reconstruction of the administration of justice in the American occupied Germany. Harv Law Rev 61:419–467

Mahmud T (1994) Jurisprudence of successful treason: Coup d'Etat and common law. Cornell Int Law J 27:49–140

Michielsen JNME (2004) The "Nazification" and "Denazification" of the Courts in Belgium, Luxembourg and the Netherlands. University of Maastricht, Maastricht

Moustafa T (2007) The struggle for constitutional power law, politics, and economic development in Egypt. Cambridge University Press, Cambridge (Kindle edition)

Oppler K (1947) Justiz und Politik. Deutsche Rechts-Zeitschrift 2:323–326

Osiel MJ (1995) Dialogue with dictators: judicial resistance in Argentina and Brazil. Law Soc Inq 20:481–560

Pereira AW (2005) Political (in)justice authoritarianism and the rule of law in Brazil, Chile and Argentina. University of Pittsburgh Press, Pittsburgh (Kindle edition)

Rasehorn Z (2000) "Renazifizierung" der Nachkriegsjustiz. ZRP 127–131

Report of the Chilean National Commission on Truth and Reconciliation, University of Notre Dame Press, Notre Dame, 1993

Report of the Truth and Reconciliation Commission of South Africa Vol. 4 Chapter 4 Institutional Hearing: The Legal Community, 1998

Rode LS (1983) De tyske krigsretter, in Den Norske Advokatforening, Advokaten – rettens og samfunnets tjener Den Norske Advokatforening 1908–1983, Oslo, pp 329–362

Schleunes K (ed) (2001) Legislating the Holocaust: the Bernhard Loesener memoirs and supporting documents. Westview, Boulder (Kindle edition)

Schorn H (1959) Der Richter im Dritten Reich Geschichte und Dokumente. Vittorio Klostermann, Frankfurt am Main

Snyder F (1983–1984) State of Siege and rule of law in Argentina: the politics and rhetoric of vindication. Lawyer Americas 15:503–520

Stoltzfus N (1996) Resistance of the heart intermarriage and the Rosenstrasse protest in Nazi Germany. W.W. Norton & Company, New York

Strenge I (2002) Machtübernahme 1933: Alles auf dem legalen Weg? Ducker und Humblot, Berlin

Trials of War Criminals before the Nuremberg Military Tribunals, vol III, the Justice Case, Washington, 1951

Weisberg RH (1996) Vichy law and the Holocaust in France. Harwood Academic Publisher, Amsterdam

Chapter 4
Judicial Acceptance of Oppression

Acceptance of the Legality of Authoritarian Regimes

What do judges do, what can they do, and what should they do when authoritarian rulers call upon them to employ and enforce means of oppression and to lend legitimacy to the oppression? According to the ideals of the rule of law, they should hold stand, defend their independence, and protect the basic rights of individuals. Experience from history teaches that this is, unfortunately, the exception rather than the rule.

Courts often accept the legality of new authoritarian regimes. It is a basic realist fact that a regime established by force can only be effectively challenged by a stronger force; no judicial dictum can prevail against it.[1] Tayyab Mahmud concludes in his study of all postcolonial common law cases dealing with the aftermath of coups d'état up to 1994 that "most courts have opted for the worst choice, namely, validation and legitimation of extra-constitutional usurpation".[2] As Mahmud points out, the options facing the courts when confronted with rulers who depart from the established procedural and substantive requirements of legality are not many. They may choose to validate the new rule, they may stick to the established constitutional arrangement and invalidate it after performing judicial review, they may resign their office, or they may declare that ruling on the legality of the new regime is outside of the scope of judicial powers.

It appears that rulers may, in general, depend upon judges not challenging the core interests of the regime. This in itself is important and means that authoritarian rulers receive legitimation from the courts. As pointed out by the Truth and Reconciliation commissions of Chile and South Africa, this support is all the more valuable when it comes from courts that have a standing from previous liberal times as independent guardians of the law. One must not underrate the value to an

---

[1] Carmen (1972), pp. 1059–1060.

[2] Mahmud (1994), pp. 138–139.

H.P. Graver, *Judges Against Justice*, DOI 10.1007/978-3-662-44293-7_4

authoritarian regime of even passive support in the form of omission of effective judicial review. In a situation where the regime actively attacks the rule of law and established legal principles, omission of defence by the courts, who are the very guardians of these values, amounts to positive support of the policies of the regime.

In his survey, Mahmud is dealing with coups d'état, that is, radical regime changes that take place outside of the rules established for power successions. In such cases, the new regime cannot derive its formal legitimacy from the established positive rules of the constitution. It must seek to legitimise itself through emergency rules, through the necessity of the situation, or through the established fact of effective control over the state apparatus. As the experience from the transition in Germany into Nazi rule shows, there is a gradual line from instances when an established regime resorts to authoritarian measures by invoking emergency measures to instances of total revolution.

In the last years of the Weimar Republic, the German Parliament was, to a large extent, bypassed and the country was ruled by emergency legislation enacted by the Reichspresident von Hindenburg. Many of the civil and political rights of the constitution were suspended under this legislation. When Hitler came to power, it was by similar measures passed by Hindenburg. The basic powers of the Nazi government in the enabling law of 22 March 1933, which passed legislative powers directly to Adolf Hitler, including the power to change the constitution, were formally based in the Weimar Constitution. On the other hand, Nazi lawyers immediately started to treat the Nazi takeover as a revolution with its own legal basis as a successor to, and therefore not based on, the Weimar Constitution.[3]

The blurred lines between continuance and break with the established legal regime can also be seen in the Latin American experiences. Despite the similarities between the social and political facts in Argentina, Brazil, and Chile, the authoritarian regimes portrayed their relationships to the existing constitution differently.[4] In Argentina, the generals derived their authority from the constitution and its provisions for a state of emergency. They did not proclaim their rule as revolutionary, declaring that all previous legislation remained in force to the extent that it had not been specifically repealed by the new regime. The Brazilian armed forces proclaimed their role as revolutionary and the role of the courts as the advancement of revolutionary legality. They portrayed the revolution as self-justifying and owing no duties to the previously valid constitution. In Chile, the Junta seized power in the name of the rule of law, claiming to re-establish this after the violations of the rule of law that they ascribed to the previous regime.[5]

Whether there is a change in regime or not, and whether such a change openly portrays itself as a coup, the courts are faced with the question of whether to accept or reject authoritarian measures that break with civil or political rights of established constitutional principles. Under liberal constitutions, there are strict

---

[3] See Pauer-Studer (2014), pp. 36–38.

[4] See Osiel (1995), pp. 511–512 on Argentina and pp. 527–528 on Brazil.

[5] Hilbink (2008), p. 104.

limits for such departures from recognised rights. Normally, individual rights can only be limited under requirements of necessity and proportionality, and under the supervision of judicial review. In many cases, there are absolute limits in the form of rights from which there is no derogation, such as the prohibition against torture.

In all cases where the regime claims to be unbound by the ordinary limits of the constitution, it must support its claim on reasons external to the constitution—whether these are reasons of fact, such as necessity, or reasons of principles that are seen as overriding the positive constitutional norms. Only a few courts have taken the high road of strict constitutionalism and actively challenged the legality of successful coups. In "dozens of authoritarian states", we can observe what Ginsburg and Moustafa name "core compliance" with regime interests by the judiciary.[6] This was the fact in Germany, Argentina, and Chile. The courts in Argentina never directly addressed the core questions of the legality of the military regime.[7] In habeas corpus cases that were brought to the Supreme Court, the Court required that the regime provide specific evidence of the arrest so that it could review the grounds. But in most cases when the regime refused to do this, the Court did not respond with ordering the release of the prisoner.[8] In Germany, the courts never questioned the legality of the Nazi takeover of power, of the emergency laws or of the powers exercised under these powers.[9] On the contrary, the right to judicial review, recognised under the Weimar Republic, was explicitly dismantled through arguments in the legal doctrine and by decisions of the courts. Studies of the contemporary legal literature show a distinct positive approach to the concept of dictatorship during the preceding period of the Weimar Republic and an untroubled attitude towards it.[10] To many judges, the Nazi takeover was nothing more dramatic than the transition from dictatorial rule to slightly more dictatorial rule.

The Supreme Court of Brazil did review the legality of measures by the Junta and sometimes repudiated them. The same was the case with the Appellate Division of the South African Supreme Court, which initially refused to accept as constitutional legislative measures to disenfranchise coloured voters of the Cape of Good Hope.[11] The legality of this Act was only accepted by the Court after two litigations, a change of the constitutional law and a packing of the Court with additional judges who were sympathetic to the government. Also in the cases reviewed by Mustafa on coups d'état in postcolonial common law countries, there are some examples of courts refusing to accept the legality of the coups. One of them is the

[6] Ginsburg and Moustafa (2008), p. 15, mentioning specifically Egypt, the Philippines, Pakistan, Ghana, Zimbabwe, Uganda, Nigeria, Cyprus, Seychelles, and Grenada. Osiel (1995) has references in footnote 58 to rulings of the supreme courts of Pakistan, Uganda, and Rhodesia all accepting the coups d'état on the basis that the new rulers were successful in replacing the former regimes and in establishing public order on a new basis. See p. 497.

[7] Snyder (1983–1984), p. 517.

[8] Osiel (1995), p. 521.

[9] See Strenge (2002) for a study of the transition to Nazi rule from a legal point of view.

[10] Strenge (2002), p. 191.

[11] See more closely below pp. 93–95.

decision by the Privy Council of Great Britain on the proclamation of the Smith government of Rhodesia.[12] In this case, however, we are dealing with a court based firmly on the constitution that was rebelled against and that could review the legality of the revolution from a safe distance being based in London. The others are instances where the courts have ruled after the coups have been defeated and the old order re-established. This leaves then only Brazil and South Africa as cases of some measure of judicial resistance to authoritarian rule.

Even courts in states occupied by foreign forces often bend to the force of the situation and lend legitimacy to the oppressive means of the occupier. The options outlined by Mahmud for coup situations are the same even for courts when the country is under occupation of a foreign power. Experiences from the German occupation of European states during World War II display courts that comply, protest, resign, or define the occupation regime outside the scope of their jurisdiction. The courts of Denmark and the Netherlands basically complied with the core interests of the German occupier and applied oppressive laws passed in the interest of the occupier. The Norwegian Supreme Court reserved the right to review the legality of the measures of the German occupation authority and resigned when they were denied this possibility. The Belgian courts regarded the occupation measures as outside of their competence and refused to apply them as law.

The Supreme Court of the Netherlands never questioned the legality of the measures taken by the German occupying authority or the measures by the Netherlands' authorities under powers delegated by the Germans, and it was mostly followed by judges in the other courts. This even led to the Nazis being able to use the Netherland courts to implement their measures against Jews.[13] The judges appointed during the occupation accepted taking an oath of allegiance to "the laws in force on the occupied Netherlands territory", which clearly included the measures of the occupying force.[14] The Supreme Court defended its position by reference to the rights of an occupier under public international law and that "it was customary that judicial officials would fulfil their duties in the interest of their country, as long as sufficient independence was left to them and they were not forced to dispense justice in the name of another sovereign".[15]

In Denmark, the courts cooperated with the efforts of the government to keep the administration of internal affairs in Danish hands. There was no change in the Danish government with the German occupation, and, unlike in many of the other occupied countries, the established government or the head of state did not go into exile. One of the overriding considerations of the government in the field of administration of justice was to maintain jurisdiction over Danish citizens for the Danish police and courts. In order to achieve this, the government enacted oppressive reforms of the criminal law and the criminal procedure in order to

[12] Madzimbamuto v. Lardner-Burke [1969] 1 AC 645.

[13] Michielsen (2004), pp. 125–131.

[14] Michielsen (2004), p. 122.

[15] Michielsen (2004), p. 153.

accommodate German demands. The Danish courts followed a strict line in the application of these laws imposing strict punishment.[16]

One notable example is the case against a Danish officer who had been arrested in Berlin in 1940 for attempting to persuade Danish pilots to enter the war on the side of the British. The Danish authorities negotiated with the Germans to have him extradited to Denmark. The German authorities set as a condition for extradition that he could be sentenced to a punishment no less than life imprisonment. This was not possible under Danish law, but Parliament passed a law in January 1941 that criminalised aid to enemy forces with a maximum punishment of life imprisonment. The officer was returned to Denmark the same day and shortly afterwards was convicted and sentenced to imprisonment for life by the Copenhagen City Court.[17]

Political rights of freedom of speech and freedom of assembly were also severely restricted and violations of the restrictions criminalised. One of the most controversial measures was the internment of all known members of the Communist Party after the German attack on the Soviet Union on 22 June 1941. The Supreme Court upheld the detention of the communists based on a law passed retroactively in August 1941 as constitutional without entering into argument or giving any reasons.[18] Tamm explains the decision of the Court as that it could not be expected that the Supreme Court should reject the policy of negotiations with the Germans that the government and Parliament had committed to. To this it could be countered that the role of the courts is precisely to draw the limits to policy and not to enter into such policy.

As long as judges are independent in a narrow sense, that is they are not specifically ordered as to how to decide an individual case, the regime depends on the reasoning and choices of the individual judge. Although causes and motives for judicial choice may vary, judicial decisions are most often framed as legal. Judges portray their decisions as compulsive according to the law, whether they support or challenge the regime, and the legal reasoning that they employ is often beyond reproach seen from a methodological point of view. Judges in authoritarian settings use the same forms of legal reasoning as judges in liberal and democratic settings.

When faced with measures that attack fundamental legal rules and values, the judge has basically two choices: he can follow the law and overrule the measure, or he can depart from the law and accept it. Often, following the law also implies making choices since the law is not always settled. These choices may be choices of evaluation in determining the best possible interpretation of the law or the fact or choices of policy in deciding which rule to establish.[19] The judge often has a certain scope of action in the establishment and interpretation of the law. Based on studies of the South African courts under apartheid, Dyzenhaus draws a distinction

---

[16] See Tamm (1984), pp. 35–62.

[17] Tamm (1984), pp. 44–45.

[18] Tamm (1984), p. 60.

[19] Dodson et al. (1997), p. 61.

between a "plain fact approach" and a "common law approach" to legal interpretation.[20] In the plain fact approach, law is applied as it exists and not according to what morality requires. The judge "looks to a pattern that exists as a matter of historical fact in the legal acts and decisions of the past, mainly those of the legislator". In the "common law approach", the interpretative context and not the intent of the historical content is the "master over legal meaning". In the plain fact approach, principles embedded in common law, such as equality and rule of law, have to yield to the clear discriminatory intent of the apartheid legislator. This was the approach used by the majority of the South African judges. The approach enabled them to uphold and even extend the authoritarian measures of the regime and disregard the protection of individual rights and liberty traditionally entailed in the common law. Judges who employed the common law approach could and would question oppressive measures and interpret them narrowly. This approach was therefore a way of balancing the dual loyalties of the judge to both the underlying fundamental legal values and to the positive legal demands of the regime.

A similar balancing was performed by the Supreme Court of Argentina. The Supreme Court of Brazil, on the other hand, went further and, in some cases, even refused to give effect to positive legal measures by invalidating them based on uncodified legal principles of natural law. Osiel explains the differences in the approaches of the two courts in their social setting and the differences in the relationships between the judiciary and the ruling establishment in the two countries.

The Supreme Court in Argentina operated in a common jurisprudential framework with the Junta, that of legal realism. It directed its legal reasoning to the Junta, and in cases where measures of the regime were reviewed, the review was performed by adherence to standards shared by the regime. The Argentine Supreme Court thus was in a judicial dialogue with the dictators. The Supreme Court of Brazil, on the other hand, employed standards other than the ones employed by the regime. Where the regime enacted positive law, the Court drew on naturalist arguments. The decisions of the Supreme Court of Brazil do therefore not evidence the same sense of shared membership of a common legal culture with the Junta as the decisions of the Argentine court do. In this respect, Brazilian judges were like the common law judges of South Africa. In their willingness to invalidate positive law, the Brazilian judges, however, went even further than their South African colleagues. The Brazilian judges did not engage much in dialogue with the regime. Their arguments, according to Osiel, were directed more to the public and civilian professional figures and to the wider legal community.[21]

The reasons for these differences in choice of audiences may be differences in political sympathy. The judges of Argentina were more sympathetic of the military regime, whereas the judges of Brazil were more unsympathetic. On the other hand,

[20] Dyzenhaus (2010), pp. 48–54.

[21] Osiel (1995), pp. 548–549.

this may only have been at the superficial level. According to Pereira, organisational relations between the military and the judiciary were much closer in Brazil than in Argentina and Chile, and in Brazil there were several leading members of the legal profession who provided links between the legal profession and the military.[22] It could therefore also be that in Brazil there was more room for a broader legal debate on the workings of the regime, whereas the role of the judges was more marginal and precarious in Argentine, thus forcing them into operating on the premises established by the regime.

This hypothesis also accords with the study by Pereira of the military courts in Argentina and Brazil. The Brazilian government utilised established military courts with long-standing and good relations between the judges and the military. In Argentina, new courts were established. In Brazil, the government used the military courts as an active instrument in their oppression and the courts operated in a relatively independent fashion with a relatively high rate of acquittal and with relatively lenient punishments. In Argentina, most of the repression was undertaken outside of the scope of the law by military and extra-military death squads.

Judges are bound by an obligation to apply the law. After all, legal reasoning differs from general moral or political reasoning in that it relies on authoritative legal sources provided by the state. No matter what approach to legal theory one takes, one cannot totally disregard such sources and still practice law. This means that when the authority in power is established and oppressive measures are enacted as legislation, oppressive measures will be included among the sources that at least *prima facie* count as authoritative to the judge. So both the judicial role and basic power relations contribute to the fact that courts seldom challenge the core interests of the regime such as its basic legality and main instruments of power.

Acceptance of Oppressive Aims and Policies

That the courts have to give way to overwhelming force is hardly surprising. It is more critical to the function of the judges that they, in many cases, seem to give active support to the new regimes and their authoritarian measures. Judges are members of the social elites in a society, and in many cases authoritarian rulers draw upon these elites for support for their policies. The judiciaries of Argentina, Brazil, and Chile, for instance, were quite receptive to the arguments by the military coup makers for the need for authoritarian rule to protect society from "subversive" elements. The German judges in 1933 were, as many of their colleagues among the academic lawyers, critical of the Weimar Republic and saw the Nazi regime as a way to re-establish the old order. In Vichy France, the prewar anti-Semitic propaganda paved the way for the anti-Semitic laws. The South African judges accepted the arguments of the government and its strict measures on security legislation.

[22] Pereira (2005), loc. 942–950.

That judges defer to authoritarian power may therefore be not only a question of might influencing right.

Otto Kirchheimer claims that courts and juries generally tend to follow the line of the government as the presumed expert in the field of subversion and that they often even outbid the government as a custodian of state protection.[23] In his study on judges and evil, Douglas Linder states:

> 'The strange interdependence of thoughtlessness and evil' that Arendt observed in Jerusalem underlies many of the injustices that have dishonored the American legal system in recent years. Overidentification with popular causes of the day and immersion in professional legal culture has blinded many of the key players in our justice system to the human consequences of their decisions. Bureaucratic thinking has enabled people who should know better to conclude that they are mere functionaries who, if they did not do what they did, would watch as others carried out the same injustices. Arendt concluded, from the Eichman trial, that 'remoteness from reality and thoughtlessness can wreak more havoc than all the evil instincts taken together.' So, also, we might conclude today.[24]

In some cases, the judiciary actually takes the lead in developing oppressive law. Illustrative examples are the role of the Nazi judiciary in developing the legal category of "Jew" and giving this effect in different fields of law, such as family law, labour law, and the law of contracts, and the role of the South African judiciary in developing racial segregation and security law. In such cases, we are no longer faced with a judiciary forced to comply but with judges taking a primary role in undermining the rule of law through an over-identification, with the aims of the regime and a perception of their role as mere technical, legal.

Nazi Anti-semitism

In authoritarian and totalitarian settings where the legislature and the administration show no self-restraint, we can see tragic consequences when the oppressive ideology of the regime is shared by the judiciary. It can be claimed that the laws of "Nazi Germany did not fall fortuitously on unwilling or unwitting populations and judiciaries. The judiciaries applied laws which on the whole had met with judicial approval, just as the population followed laws which on the whole had met with popular approval".[25]

The German judges of the first half of the twentieth century held the same resentments against homosexuals, persons alien to the German community, antisocials, and members of inferior races as the rest of the population.[26] In Germany, there were elements of anti-Semitic sentiments in the courts even before the Nazi

[23] Kirchheimer (1961), p. 197.

[24] Linder (1993), p. 1113.

[25] Curran (1998–1999), p. 31.

[26] See Angermund (1990), p. 191.

accession to power,[27] and the courts had no difficulty in rapidly accepting and implementing this part of Nazi ideology. The effect of this was that the courts, in many ways, were forerunners to the legislator and the Nazi administration when it came to depriving Jews of rights and legal status in Germany. In this, the courts went beyond the mere acceptance of the legal basis of the Nazi regime and entered into the active advancement of the Nazi legal ideology.

The reform of German law in the first years after 1933 in the direction of a "Germanic renewal" was not first and foremost carried out by the legislator. Rüthers shows how this task was undertaken by the legal doctrine and the judiciary in close cooperation, where the tools and techniques for a legal reform were developed for a loyal transformation of the liberal legal order into an order of repression.[28]

Family law and the relationship between German and Jewish spouses are a field where the active role of the judiciary in developing anti-Semitic measures is very clear. The first of these cases was decided by the Supreme Court on 12 July 1934.[29] The case concerned a married couple where the husband sought annulment of the marriage. The parties had married in August 1930 after having met during the summer of 1928. The husband was an Aryan, former priest, and now a student of medicine. The wife was a Jewess. The husband had applied for divorce already in the spring of 1931, but the application was rejected.

The husband's application of 1931 was based on allegations that the wife was hysterical and that she had not fulfilled her promise of being able to support herself. The application that he now made was based on the rule of German marriage law in BGB § 1333, which stated that "A marriage can be challenged by the spouse who has been in error about the identity of the other spouse, or about such personal characteristics of the other spouse, which by reasonable consideration would have withheld him from the marriage, had they been known to him at the time of entering into the marriage".[30] The applicant was familiar with the fact that the parent of his spouse were Jews, but he claimed that he was in error of "such personal characteristics of the other spouse, which by reasonable consideration would have withheld him from the marriage", since he had not realised the implications of the differences of race between the parties. He claimed that this realisation first came to him with the National Socialist revolution, which made the differences between the German and the Jewish races common knowledge.

The Supreme Court stated that a person's race, in particular when it concerned a Jew, according to "a natural conception of life", must be considered a "personal

---

[27] Critch (2012), p. 362.

[28] Rüthers (2012), p. 479.

[29] Case IV 94/34 12. July 1934, Juristische Wochenschrift 1934, pp. 2613–2615.

[30] Eine Ehe kann von dem Ehegatten angefochten werden, der sich bei der Eheschließung in der Person des anderen Ehegatten oder über solche persönliche Eigenschaften des anderen Ehegatten geirrt hat, die ihn bei Kenntnis der Sachlage und bei verständiger Würdigung des Wesens der Ehe von der Eingehung der Ehe abgehalten haben würden, BGB § 1333.

characteristic" in the meaning of the law. Since the racial traits also are inherited by the offspring of a married couple, this personal characteristic, according to the Court, must be of the kind that by reasonable consideration would have withheld the erring spouse from the marriage had it been known to him or her at the time.

The Court of Appeals had granted the husband an annulment of the marriage. The Court based the annulment on the fact that it "was just recently acknowledged that the Jewish race differs from the Aryan race totally in regards to blood, character and way of life" and that intermarriage is "not only undesirable, but also pernicious and unnatural". The Supreme Court did not follow this line of reasoning, however, and denied annulment. In contemporary literature, this decision was therefore cited as an example where the courts resisted the political pressure to give legal effect to Nazi ideology.[31] This is, in my opinion, misleading since the Supreme Court did accept the racial ideology of differences between Aryan and Jews as a matter of fact.

The Court did not distance itself from the characterisation of the undesirability of intermarriages. Rather, it reasoned that the importance of racial differences had been well known since the middle of the previous century and that at least since the publication of the party programme of the Nazi Party in February 1920, it would be difficult to claim unawareness of this fact. The condition that the personal characteristics of the spouse were *unknown* to the husband at the time of the marriage was therefore not met. Neither could the annulment be based on the fact that the husband at the time of the marriage could not know that he and his children would be subject to the Aryan legislation of the Nazi regime. This legislation was a later fact and could therefore not be said to be characteristics present in the spouse at the time of the marriage.

The Supreme Court recognised that the courts had to take into account the racial legislation of the present regime and stated this legislation as grounds for interpreting the BGB § 1333 to include race as a "personal characteristic". But it continued, "The courts are not authorised to take the insights of National Socialism further than the limits that have been drawn by the legislation of the National Socialist state itself". It pointed out that interracial marriages were not prohibited by law and that new marriages could not be annulled under BGB § 1333 by spouses who knowingly married a Jew. It also rejected the possibility of treating § 1333 as a general clause where the courts could develop the law in accordance with National Socialist thought. According to the law, § 1333 was one of a set of specified grounds for annulment and "the judges are presently as previously bound by the law".

The Court in this case balanced loyalty to the ideas of the new regime, on one side, and the limits to judicial discretion set by the law, on the other. The racial ideology was accepted by the Court and even regarded as so evident that the Court rejected the husband's claim that he could not have realised the importance of the differences in race prior to the Nazis' accession to power. The grounds that the Court bases this statement on are rather shaky. It refers only to the public policy of

[31] Loewenstein (1935–1936), p. 796.

the Nazi Party and makes no problem out of basing statements of fact on the programme of a political party. What the Court in fact demands is that the population in Germany prior to 1933 should have taken the programme of the Nazi Party as evidence of the biological facts of the existence of races and racial differences.

The reality, of course, is that racial differences were differences not in biological facts but in ideology, and as such the Nazi programme was sufficient basis for asserting this difference. But in this view, 1933 is a relevant turning point because the fact of these ideological differences was not established as compelling for the German population prior to the Nazi takeover of power. These differences between facts and ideology must have been evident also to the German Supreme Court in 1934. Why did it then engage in such obviously weak arguments?

One reason may be that the Court in this case perceived the husband's claim as unreasonable. One may suspect that the Court judged the husband's claims to be made on opportunistic grounds and that his real motives were to have a new go at divorcing his wife for the same reasons he had tried the last time. To avoid the annulment of the marriage, the Court either had to reject the notion that being a Jew was a personal characteristic in the meaning of the law or that this characteristic was unknown to the spouse at the time of marriage. The Court chose the latter. In not rejecting the former, the Court accepted the whole stock of racial ideology of the regime and welcomed it into the body of family law. The whole argumentation of the Supreme Court is based on the ideology of racial differences and of the social undesirability of intermarriages. It was precisely because of this being so obvious to all that the husband could not be heard with the claim that it had been unknown to him. Had it not been for the seriousness of the matter and the formal attitude of judges, one could be tempted to read the reasoning of the Court as ironic.

It is of course difficult to say whether the Court here is paying lip service to the regime or whether it is arguing out of sincere belief. The effect is in any case the same—that the courts have to take due account of the racial ideology of the regime when applying any part of the law. On the other hand, the Supreme Court also states and demonstrates that this duty to take the ideology into account is limited by law and by the established role of the courts. This underlines the fact that even if the courts are transforming the law into Nazi law, it is still law in the sense that it is applied independently by the courts according to familiar modes of legal reasoning.

Why did the Court not choose to reject the racial ideology and base its result on denying that race was a personal characteristic in the meaning of § 1333? Answering this question will inevitably be pure speculation. One factor may be the general perception of Jews at the time; the courts had a record of racial prejudice prior to 1933.[32] Nevertheless, this was a creative interpretation of the law, with few practical consequences, since race as a ground for annulment would be unavailable to most due to the strict requirements that the Court placed on the ignorance of the other party. The interpretation was therefore not in any way necessary in order to

[32] See Angermund (1990), p. 33.

establish a legal remedy for anyone. Another reason could be that denial of the racial ideology could have been seen more as a provocation of the regime, which perhaps the Court wished to avoid. In that case, the Court could be accused of sacrificing humanity and a basic requirement of the rule of law for the sake of its own standing in the new political order. In any case, the Court in its decision did not in any way protect the fundamental concept that "all men are created equal".

By its decision, the Supreme Court accepted and endorsed the racial myth of National Socialism where purity of race is the foremost objective of legislation and of the new Germanic law, as opposed to the past Romanistic liberalism.[33]

A second case was decided by a different senate of the Supreme Court on the same day. In this case, the Court accepted that the complainant was not aware of the implications of marrying a Jew at the time of the marriage. Gradually, the fundamental differences of the spouses dawned on him and after some years, in 1926, he left his wife because he felt they had nothing in common was the argument of the husband. At this point, according to the Court, the consequences of their racial differences were obviously known to him. The legal issue then was whether the time limit of 6 months stipulated by the law to make a claim for annulment had expired. His realisation of the relevant facts happened in 1926, so the question was, what was the relevant starting point for calculation of the deadline? If the starting point was when he left his wife, it was obviously too late to claim annulment in 1933.

The Court referred to a provision in the BGB that stated that a deadline is suspended as long as "access to justice is hindered by circumstances outside of control of the party". Commenting on this, the Court said that such a circumstance was present as long as there was no prospect of receiving an annulment by the courts. It declared that getting an annulment on the ground that the spouse was Jewish would have been unthinkable before the National Socialist revolution. This had changed with the Law for the Restoration of the Professional Civil Service of 7 April 1933, which represented a formal recognition by the state of the implications of race. From this date on, the deadline was no longer suspended and the complainant had 6 months to lodge his complaint.

In regarding the legal recognition of a right as a relevant removal of a hindrance to access to justice, the Court referred to a previous ruling of 1923 where a new precedent was given the same legal effect. One might question to what extent one can draw parallels between new legislation and court rulings. Where court rulings in their nature are retrospective, changes in legislation usually regulate future legal issues. The Court, however, does not comment on this difference. One may also question the way the Court accepted the claim of the husband that the personal estrangement of the parties was a consequence of their racial differences. This issue was decided by the Court of Appeals, and therefore not an issue before the Supreme Court, but it does show that the Court was ready not only to accept and apply Nazi racial ideology but also to treat is as self-evident. Or maybe the treating of it as self-

[33] See further Loewenstein (1935–1936), pp. 785–787.

evident and beyond question was a way of distancing itself from it and shoving the responsibility for it on the rulers of the state a sort of symbolic "washing of hands"?

In the next case, from 1935, we encounter a more aggressive Supreme Court. The applicant applied for divorce from his Jewish wife after joining the Nazi Party. The application was filed in December 1933. During the proceedings, in October 1934, he claimed that the marriage should be dissolved in accordance with BGB § 1333.

The Supreme Court referred to its rulings from 1934. It reaffirmed that intermarriages were undesirable and stated that "under a reasonable understanding of the nature of marriage as it appears to the worldview of National Socialism, mixed marriages are not allowed". It is interesting to note that this opinion on the legality of intermarriages was stated 1 year before the consequence was drawn by the legislator in the infamous Nuremberg law on the protection of the German blood and honour.

The Court stated that the view taken by the Court previously, that the consequences of Jewishness must be held to be known by most after the party programme of the Nazis was published in 1920, had been challenged by lower courts and in doctrine and could not be upheld. Even though the racial question had been recognised in society prior to the National Socialist revolution, Jewishness was by most perceived as a religious issue and not as a racial problem. The Court also asserted that in the political debates and campaigns against the Nazis, their racial programme in particular had met the strongest opposition and had been under attack from all other political factions. Under such conditions, it could not be expected of people in general that they realised the importance of the racial issue before the takeover. The relevant cut-off date was set to the date of the Law for the Restoration of the Professional Civil Service when the racial question was given official recognition by the state.

This in itself did not solve the case in favour of the applicant since he had not claimed annulment before October 1934, well after the expiration of the 6-month deadline. Creative reasoning of the Court came to his aid. Foremost, the Court stated that when proceedings for a divorce have been brought, new legal grounds for a divorce may be introduced into the case. This must also be applied when new legal grounds to dissolve the marriage are introduced. Since the claimant had brought divorce proceedings in December 1933, this date, and not October 1934 when he made the claim for annulment, should be regarded as the date when the claim was brought to the Court.

But this was also too late to meet the deadline. The Court reaffirmed the approach taken in the second of the 1934 cases that the deadline was suspended as long as there was an obstacle to the claiming of the right. It then pointed to the fact that the applicant had launched an application for legal aid in August 1933 and that he had filed for the divorce immediately after having been granted legal aid. Since he did not have the means to file for a divorce before he had been granted legal aid, the deadline in his case did not expire until his application was granted. The reason he did not file within the October 1933 deadline was that the authorities had not yet responded to his application for legal aid, and he should not be blamed for this.

The cases we have just been through illustrate how national socialist ideology of race was regarded as a source for legal reasoning with authority to support a reinterpretation and development of the law, thus reaching results conforming to the Nazi ideology without formally disregarding the law. In all these cases, the Supreme Court demonstrated that it did not consider itself bound by the original meaning or the intent of the legislator of the existing provisions of family law. All cases concerned the "old" legislator. Then what about its loyalty to the legislator when it came to "new" law?

The cases from the Supreme Court on the Nuremberg laws of 1935 to protect the German blood and honour are telling. In its case law, the Court went far beyond both the wording of the Act and the legislative intent in order to criminalise relations between Jews and Aryans. The Supreme Court turned what, from the legislator, was enacted as a measure of racial hygiene into an instrument of general racial policy.[34] A case from 1938 exemplifies the relationship between legislative intent and Nazi ideology. In this case, a spouse filed for annulment with the argument that one of the grandparents of the other spouse was Jewish. The application was rejected by the appeals court because marriage between two people where one of them had a Jewish grandparent was not forbidden by the 1935 law for protection of the German blood and honour. The Supreme Court, however, rejected this argument:

> It does not follow from the fact that the blood protection act does not forbid marriages that such marriages are straightforward from a racial point of view, and it does not follow that a German-blooded person might not want to abstain from entering into such a marriage... Even though the law itself does not regard the disadvantages of such marriages as great enough to outright prohibit them, a person conscious of the National Socialist understanding of the racial differences might be deterred from it out of consideration to the mother and the child should the marriage result in pregnancy.[35]

A different approach could has been to refer to the line drawn in the legislation and regard this as a limit to when parentage could be regarded as a "personal characteristic" in the meaning of BGB § 1333. Here, however, the Court appealed to the arguments behind the law to interpret the law in an expansive way to give better effect to these arguments. As such, the case is an example of a teleological approach to legislation, based on the objectives or purposes that the legislator aimed to pursue with the legislation.

In a case of June 27, 1937, the defendant had received all copyrights to a manuscript—"in particular the film rights"—from the applicant according to a contract agreed on February 24.[36] In addition, she received the services of director *Ch.* For this, she agreed to pay 130,000 Reichsmarks, payable in instalments. The

[34] Ogorek (2008), pp. 292–293.

[35] RG., IV. SivSen., 2. May 1938, Juristische Wochenschrift 1938, p. 2475.

[36] RG., 1 Siv.Sen., 27. June 1936, Seufferts Archiv 91, 65.

first instalment was paid on March 1. On April 5, she withdrew from the contract and claimed refund of her payment on the ground that Ch. was Jewish and therefore no longer allowed under German law to contribute to films aimed at the German public.

The legal issue of the case concerned the interpretation of clause 6 of the agreement, which gave the complainant right to withdraw from the contract "should it become impossible to fulfil the contract because Ch. due to death, illness or similar circumstances is unable to direct the movie".

The trial court solved the case in favour of the complainant. It argued that the clause "due to death, illness or similar circumstances" must be interpreted as to include all circumstances connected with the person of the director, not only physical or mental incapacity. Further, it held that "unable" included not only physical inability to direct the film but also inability to fulfil the assignment according to the intentions of the contract, i.e. produce a film showable to the German public.

The trial court here reasons in a traditional way. The issue is which party should bear the risk for the altered circumstances based on an interpretation of the parties' contract. One could, of course, question whether the new evaluation of the implications of race should be regarded as a condition of the person or as a changed social condition and that the issue should have been framed as an issue of which of the parties should bear the risk of new public regulations. We can see already how the court accepted the racial ideology in regarding "Jewishness" as a personal disability from the fact that this was not raised in the case.

The Supreme Court went even further in its reasoning. Concurring with the result and reasoning of the trial court, it added that the result could be supported by the fact that "since the National Socialist takeover the scope of power and privileges of the person is linked with race". Referring to historical times, the court stated that "the deprivation of all rights was likened to physical death, because the legal personality was completely destroyed". Based on this, the Court stated that it was straightforward to state that the director was unable to perform due to circumstances similar to death or illness.

The additional reasoning of the Supreme Court was not strictly necessary to decide the case in favour of the complainant. As we have seen, the legal issue in the case was a familiar one, that is, one of the allocation of risks between the parties due to changing circumstances. The weak point, however, of the reasoning of the trial court was why the new situation regarding Jews should be seen as circumstances related to the person and not as changed social or regulatory circumstances. It is obviously this hole the Supreme Court aims to fill by its supplemental reason. And in filling this hole, the court likens the situation of the Jews to their physical death and describes their situation after March 1933 as deprived of all rights with destroyed legal personalities.

It is remarkable that the Supreme Court took this approach in June 1936. In handling the racial legislation, the courts could have taken two alternative approaches: they could see the new legislation as specific limits to the rights of the Jews, or they could see them as instances of a new legal situation where the Jews were deprived of their legal personality. The case is an indication that the latter approach was firmly established in the Supreme Court by 1936. This means that the Supreme Court not only implemented and applied a legislative programme to ostracise the Jews but that it itself took a leading role in developing the law into an instrument of exclusion.[37]

The same can be said about the decisions of the Grand Senate of the Supreme Court in its case law on sexual relations between a Jew and an Aryan. It extended the prohibition against extramarital relations to encompass all relations with a sexual suggestion, disregarding whether it could lead to or even had anything to do with sexual intercourse.[38] It also extended the prohibition to include acts committed outside of Germany (see the case presented above on page 26–28).[39] These cases show an active approach by the courts to the deconstruction of the Jewish population as legal subjects. The courts went beyond not only the letter of the law but also its scope as defined by the Nazi legislator. It is difficult from such cases to say that the courts were passive participants in the transformation of German law, doing no more than they were forced to by their judicial roles.

Extension Beyond Race

The influence of National Socialism in the legal order was not limited to the racial question and the treatment of the Jews. On the contrary, National Socialism and National Socialist ideology infiltrated the whole legal order and changed it in a fundamental way.[40] Ernst Fraenkel shows how the German courts in the years after 1933 systematically extended the sphere of the political and thereby the dominance of the Gestapo and the prerogative state over law and society.[41] In this way, it was the courts themselves that "pronounced the death sentence on the Rule of Law".[42]

In his article from 1939, state attorney Friedrich Wilhelm Adami shows how many legal institutions are changed in their "essence and contents" under the influence of the basic worldview of National Socialism.[43] As examples, he mentions labour law, which has become permeated by the concept of the community of the enterprise, and landlord and tenant law, which is permeated by the concept of the community of the inhabitation. Also, the concept of freedom in the marketplace

[37] See Angermund (1990), p. 124.

[38] See Ogorek (2008).

[39] Großer Senat für Straffsachen, 23. February 1938, Entscheidungen des Reichsgerichts, Strafsachen 72 91.

[40] The seminal study of this, with an emphasis on German private law, is Rüthers (2012).

[41] Fraenkel (1941), p. 43.

[42] Fraenkel (1941), p. 45.

[43] Adami (1939), pp. 486–491.

has been modified by the duty of all to act within the common framework and to the good of all.

Another example mentioned by the vice president of the Prussian Administrative Appeals Court shows the influence of Nazi ideology on the concept of women and women's role in society. A case had been brought by the police against an establishment in Berlin to prohibit the public display of female boxing. The establishment had also been taken to court on an earlier occasion for the same issue, and the Court ruled at that time that the shows were permitted provided the combatants were not inappropriately dressed. In the new case of 9 November 1933, the court stated that the concept of "public order" changes with changes in social outlooks and mores. The breakthrough of the "national revolution" had now caused a changed view of the role of women in society without precedent in the development of the German soul. Whereas the permissibility of female boxing previously was seen as an issue of decency, it must now be seen in relation to the "essential characteristics of womanhood, her position and value within the German community". Female boxing, with two women engaged in battle, mutually hitting and wounding each other to the "satisfaction of the voyeurism in public establishments", must be regarded as contrary to this.[44]

The spirit of the laws in the new era is changed, Adami says. In a parliamentary system where several political parties compete, the laws reflect compromises and changing majorities so that not one worldview permeates the law. Under National Socialism, this is different: the law is based on a single view of the world, National Socialism. Adami structures the party programme on eight basic principles: the principle of the community of the German people, the concept of race, common good before individual good, abolishment of interest slavery, combat against "vermin, notorious criminals, usurers, pushers and the like", the grounding of the law in the German people, freedom of religion, and formation of chambers for the professions. He refers to court cases in relation to all these principles and shows how they have been taken into account by the courts and how the principles of the programme offer various opportunities to be transformed into law. He shows how law under Nazi rule is tied to one specific worldview, making it possible to state that "Law is what serves the German people, illegality what harms it" and "Law of life before formal law".

The basic tenet of National Socialist law—"law is what serves the German people"—was transformed into "law is the will of the Führer". This became the basic norm upon which all legal reasoning was based and also the foundation of German legal theory.[45] The traditional loyalty of the German judges to legislation was substituted with a loyalty to the will and political goals of the dictator. The cases from the Supreme Court on Jewry show that this transformation of loyalty occurred very rapidly.

---

[44] Bach (1938), p. 203.

[45] Rüthers (2012), p. 277.

South African Courts and Apartheid

South Africa is another example where oppression and discrimination were achieved by the regime by legal means. "What makes apartheid exceptional was that it was implemented and sustained through law", writes David Dyzenhaus.[46] As in Nazi Germany, the law was based on an ideology of the differences of races and of a perceived need to protect the community.[47] In South Africa, the community to be protected was the white Christian civilisation.

Although law in South Africa was discriminatory, it did not deprive people of their status as legal subjects or confer upon them an inferior status as legal subjects. Two legal scholars, Haysom and Plasket, wrote towards the end of the apartheid regime:

> One of the peculiar features of South African society is that the courts allow an impoverished black employee to call his or her white employer to account, and a voteless black resident to summon a white cabinet minister before court. Law has been used as an attenuated form of accountability in a country where the majority of citizens are denied the right to exercise the more conventional form of accountability, the franchise.[48]

Apartheid law had two main branches: (1) racial segregation and discrimination and (2) security laws enacted to curb, control, and stamp out extra-parliamentary opposition to apartheid.[49] The "constitution" of apartheid was a set of statutes enacted over two decades that provided for the physical separation of the races, created a system of tribal government of Africans in the rural areas, and regulated Africans in the urban areas.[50] Central to these statutes were the Population Registration Act and the Group Areas Act, both enacted in 1950. The Population Registration Act comprised definitions of the races and required the director of the census to classify and register every resident. The Group Areas Act established separate areas in every region in which each race should dwell and do business.

All of the country outside of the reserves was established as white man's land where Africans could live and work only through the tolerance of the white. In rural areas, Africans could register and work as labour tenants on white farms. In urban areas, entry of Africans was restricted. According to a provision in the Urban Areas Act, any African could be arrested without a warrant on the belief that he was an idle or undesirable person and brought before a magistrate. If found to be idle or undesirable, the person could be removed and sent to his home, a work colony or similar institution, or any other indicated place. The courts, in their application of this law, gave some substance to the concepts of "idle" and "undesirable" and

---

[46] Dyzenhaus (1998), p. 149.

[47] See Landis (1961), pp. 2–3. For a brief historical background to the apartheid legislation, see Dyzenhaus (2010), pp. 34–38.

[48] Haysom and Plasket (1988), p. 307.

[49] Dyzenhaus (2010), p. 74.

[50] Landis (1961), p. 16.

insisted on scrupulous respect for judicial standards in the hearing but respected the findings of the authorities when the facts were clear.[51]

Following a police attack on a peaceful demonstration at Sharpville in 1960, which killed 69 and wounded 180, a state of emergency was declared, and South Africa entered into a new stage as regards the rule of law, with powers for the police to detain and hold persons for long periods without access to judicial review and with restriction on civil and political rights.[52]

The South African judges extended the apartheid laws much in the same way as the Nazi judges extended the discrimination of the Jews. In a case from 1934, the court had to decide whether an instruction by the Postmaster General to divide the post office in Transvaal into one section for Europeans only and one for non-Europeans was legal.[53] The relevant legislation did not authorise such discrimination, so it was not an issue of giving effect to an Act by the legislator. The crucial issue of the case was whether the fundamental principle of equality before the law required that racial discrimination could only be implemented by express provision of Parliament or whether discrimination between races was a sensible and rational measure that in itself could not be seen as unreasonable.

The Postmaster General was empowered to establish, maintain, and abolish post offices and to supervise and control their services, as well as to "issue such instructions as he may deem necessary for the conduct and guidance of officers in carrying out the provisions of the Act". Prior to this order, there was a separate room for natives. The order resulted in people of Indian origin being barred from the European counter and obliged to go to the non-European room. The lower courts found the instructions to be invalid as effecting discrimination based on race or colour.

Justice Stratford of the Appellate Division took as a legal starting point that "an enabling Act must not be construed to confer the power to do unreasonable things unless such latter power is specifically given". When it came to dividing the community into white and coloured, he could not see that in itself as unreasonable "for such conclusion runs counter to accepted principle and good sense". Justice De Villiers distinguished between discrimination on gratuitous grounds and discrimination for which "reasons may be conceived upon which such discriminations might justify and reasonably be made" and placed discrimination based upon race and colour in the latter category. In his opinion, discrimination between Europeans and non-Europeans was not per se unreasonable as long as it did not entail differences in rights, duties, privileges, or treatment.

Justice Gardiner dissented. He said that there is a fundamental principle that in the eyes of the law all men are equal and that separating on account of colour or race is humiliating treatment. Based on this view, he maintained that it could not be held that the general terms of the Act authorising the Postmaster General to issue rules

[51] Landis (1961), p. 52.

[52] See Dyzenhaus (2010), pp. 39–40.

[53] Minister of Post and Telegraphs v. Rasool, 1934 AD 167.

could include power to what was contrary to the fundamental principle of the law. Race distinctions could, in his opinion, only be drawn by express provision of Parliament.

Although the decision by the majority of the court was based on the premise that the services provided to the two groups were equal, the effect of the decision was to authorise discriminatory measures by the administration. The case would become a valuable precedent after the introduction of apartheid as the official national policy.[54]

In 1960, the Appellate Division decided a case where a lawyer named Pitje from the offices of Mandela and Tambo was held for contempt of court.[55] The reason he was fined was that he refused to address the Court from the table set aside by the magistrate for non-Europeans. The setting up of two separate tables had been ordered by the magistrate. Justice Steyn of the Appellate Division referred to Minister of Post and Telegraphs v. Rasool and stated that a magistrate could order matters incidental to the proceedings by his own discretion as long as they were not contrary to law or unreasonable.

Pitje would have contended that having to address the Court from a separate table would have entailed it not being in the best interests of his client to be represented by him. He was not allowed to make this submission, however, because the magistrate refused to hear any argument from him unless he addressed him from the table for non-whites, which Pitje refused. Justice Steyn commented on this as an "insulting statement he intended to make".

There was no expressed basis for a separation in the Separate Amenities Act. Nevertheless, Justice Steyn found support in this Act:

> Although I accept it that no action was taken under the 1953 Act, the fact that such action could have been taken is not entirely irrelevant. It shows that the distinction drawn by the provision of separate tables in this magistrate's court is of a nature sanctioned by the legislature, and makes it more difficult to attack the magistrate's order on the ground of unreasonableness.

The conclusion to be drawn from this ruling was that in the view of the courts, the legislation was not the sole machinery for reserving separate amenities and the courts should be willing to sanction discrimination that went further than what was provided for in the legislation.[56]

In 1961, the Appellate Division had to decide if a law that provided for discrimination also allowed discrimination that was in effect unreasonable.[57] An Indian contested the division of the city of Durban into group areas on the ground that the best areas had been given to the whites and the inferior areas to the coloureds where there was not even suitable accommodation available to everyone at the time. In its earlier case law, the Court had stated that unreasonable

---

[54] See Dyzenhaus (2010), pp. 44–48.

[55] R v. Pitje, 1960 (4) SA 709 (A).

[56] See Dyzenhaus (2010), pp. 69.

[57] Minister of the Interior v. Lockhat 1961 (2) SA 587 (A).

discrimination presupposed an express provision in the legislation. In the case in 1961, the Court departed from this condition with the argument that division of the country into group areas was a "colossal social experiment" and that "Parliament must have envisioned that compulsory shifts of persons occupying certain areas would inevitably cause disruption and, within the foreseeable future, substantial inequalities". As Dyzenhaus has argued, the Court here is giving effect to the general design and implementation of apartheid policy, which was to leave whites in a vastly superior position to blacks in every possible dimension of social and political life.[58]

The South African Appellate Division did not limit this expansive approach to the legislation of apartheid. It also applied this approach to the security legislation enacted by the regime. A well-known example is the case of Rossouw v. Sachs. The issue in this case was whether a person detained under the 90-day detention rule of Section 17 of Act 37 of 1963 could be denied access to reading matter and writing material during the duration of his detention.[59] Access to reading matter and writing material was allowed for persons in custody awaiting trial, according to general prison rules. The Commissioner of the Police had, however, issued orders on how persons detained under the 90-day rule should be treated, and in these rules access to reading matter and writing material was in general denied.

Act 37 did not contain any provision of the conditions of the internment, save the fact that access to the detainee was conditioned upon consent of the Ministry of Justice. This also included access to an attorney. Further, the Act explicitly stated that no court should have jurisdiction to order the release of a person interned. The Act did not have any provision empowering the administration or the police to issue regulations on the conditions of the internment. The orders of the Commissioner of the Police were not disclosed to the Court.

The Cape Provincial Division Court had found in favour of Mr. Sachs and ordered that he was entitled to access to reading matter and writing material. The Provincial Court expressed the view that an individual has the right to an adequate supply of reading matter and writing materials and that to deprive a detainee of that right "amounts in effect to punishment". The Court held that "It would be surprising to find that the Legislature intended punishment to be meted out to an unconvicted prisoner".

The Appellate Division did not enter into a discussion on the legal basis for the Commissioner of the Police to issue orders on the treatment of persons detained and did not ask whether such a basis included a power to order that the detainee was deprived of reading matter and writing material. Rather, the issue was framed as a question of whether a person detained had a right to reading matter and writing material. To answer this question, Justice Thompson, with whom the other justices concurred, turned to Act 37 and "the true purpose of the continued detention authorized by sec. 17".

---

[58] Dyzenhaus (2010), p. 71.

[59] Rossouw v. Sachs 1964 (2) SA 551 (A), Judgment March 24, 1964.

Justice Thompson held that the true purpose of the statute was "to induce him to speak". The issue then to be decided was whether Parliament intended that the detainee should continue to enjoy his ordinary rights and privileges or whether it intended the "continued detention should be as effective as possible". Since the Act was silent on this, the intent of Parliament had to be inferred from the circumstances.

As the object of the statute was to protect against crimes directed towards the public order and the safety of the state, there was no place for a restrictive interpretation in favour of individual liberty. Justice Thompson pointed that the Act itself set aside two basic principles of criminal law: the protection against self-incrimination and the right to access to legal counsel. This was taken as an argument that Parliament intended for the use of the means necessary to induce those detained to reveal any information they had. Justice Thompson found that "it was not the intention of Parliament that detainees should as of right be permitted to relieve the tedium of their detention with reading matter or writing materials".

In the same way that the German judges had adopted the anti-Semitic ideology prior to the Nazi takeover, the South African judiciary had adopted as appropriate an ideology of racial separation.[60] In both cases then, the readiness of the judges to accept, apply, and extend the oppressive laws of the regime cannot be explained in full by reference to their legal approach or sense of obligation. They were not enforcing legislation that diverged from their general views of what they thought was appropriate. They were, on the contrary, implementing measures that accorded with their views of appropriateness. The same can be seen in other jurisdictions. The judges of the Supreme Court of Argentina were generally political conservatives who supported the military coup and believed in the continuing legitimacy of military rule.[61]

Agreement with Oppressive Measures in Liberal Societies

Protection of Vital State Interests

Acceptance of authoritarian measures in times of emergency is not limited to situations with tyrannical regimes. The courts of liberal democracies also have a record of such acceptance. Can we draw any parallels between oppressive measures in authoritarian regimes and democracies? And are there lessons to be learned from them?

Well-known examples are the acceptance of the unfettered discretion of the Home Secretary to detain persons without trial by the UK's House of Lords in 1941,[62] the United States Supreme Court's acceptance of the internment of the

[60] Dyzenhaus (2010), pp. 53–54.

[61] Osiel (1995), p. 526.

[62] Liversidge v. Anderson and Morrison (1941) 3 All E.R. 338 (H.L.).

Japanese, and the acceptance by the same court of the anti-communist legislation in 1950.[63] Such cases show that when judges share the view of the government that drastic measures are required to combat dangers to society, individual freedoms and rights are placed in a subordinate position.

The British Regulation 18B provided that the Secretary of State could detain any person he had "reasonable cause to believe to be of hostile origin or associations or to have been recently concerned in acts prejudicial to the public safety or the defence of the realm or in the preparation or instigation of such acts". The regulation presupposed that there could be certain persons against whom no offence was proved nor any charge formulated but against whom it would be expedient to authorise the Secretary of State to make an order for detention. In total, 1,874 orders were made under this regulation, including about 750 members of the British Fascist Party.[64] Pilot officer Liversidge was arrested on 28 May 1940. He was not given any reason for the detention. He appealed to the courts for an order under which he could receive the grounds upon which the authorities had reasonable cause to believe him to be a person of hostile associations, of the grounds upon which it was necessary to exercise control over him. The legal issue in the case before the House of Lords was whether the Court could review the "belief" of the Secretary of State that there were reasonable grounds to intern pilot officer Liversidge. The alternatives were framed in the following way by Viscount Maugham speaking for the majority:

> If A.B. has reasonable cause to believe a certain circumstance or thing, it should be construed as meaning 'if there is in fact reasonable cause for believing' that thing, or if A.B. acting on what he thinks is reasonable cause (and, of course, acting in good faith) believes the thing in question.

Under the first alternative, it would be up to the courts to review whether there were reasonable grounds for believing; under the second, it would be sufficient for the authorities to state that they so believed. The second interpretation would, of course, in practice give unrestricted powers to the administration and leave any judicial review totally ineffective.

In the opinion of Viscount Maugham, the approach to interpretation of the statute that the Court should take was that "if there is a reasonable doubt as to the meaning of the words used, we should prefer a construction which will carry into effect the plain intention of those responsible for the Order in Council rather than one which will defeat that intention". Based on this approach, the majority settled for the second meaning. Against the argument that it was a settled rule that in cases where the liberty of the subject is involved, statutes must, if possible, be construed in favour of the subject and against the Crown, Viscount Maugham stated that "I hold that the suggested rule has 'no relevance in dealing with an executive measure by way of preventing a public danger' when the safety of the state is involved".

---

[63] Korematsu v. United States, 323 U.S. 214 (1944) and Dennis v. United States 341 U.S. 494 (1951).

[64] Simpson (1988), p. 124.

In a famous dissent, Lord Atkin stated:

> In this country, amid the clash of arms, the laws are not silent. They may be changed, but they speak the same language in war as in peace. It has always been one of the pillars of freedom, one of the principles of liberty for which on recent authority we are now fighting, that the judges are no respecters of persons and stand between the subject and any attempted encroachments on his liberty by the executive, alert to see that any coercive action is justified in law.

The view of Viscount Maugham and the others, however, prevailed.

Liversidge was decided when Britain was at war, and it has later been held to apply only under special circumstances. "But times of peace hold their dangers too. Spies, subverters and saboteurs may be mingling amongst us, putting on a most innocent exterior", speaks Lord Denning in a case from 1977 about the deportation of a foreign journalist.[65] By reference to Liversidge, the Court of Appeal rejected a request for an order of certiorari to quash the deportation order on the grounds that it was wrong in law, there was a failure to comply with the principles of natural justice in that he was not informed of the matters on which he was to be heard, and leave to appeal to the House of Lords was refused. Liversidge was also an important precedent and source of argument for the South African Appellate Court in upholding and expanding on the repressive security legislation of the apartheid regime.[66]

Acceptance of emergency measures is not limited to situations of open war. In 1950, the United States Supreme Court was asked to rule on whether the Smith Act violated the First or Fifth Amendments of the United States Constitution in making it a crime "for any person knowingly or willfully to advocate the overthrow or destruction of the Government of the United States by force or violence, to organise or help to organise any group which does so, or to conspire to do so".[67] General Secretary of the Communist Party of America, Eugene Dennis, argued that the prohibition of the Act violated the freedom of speech and that it was too indefinite to form the basis of a criminal conviction.

A unanimous Supreme Court upheld the Act. Justice Vinson, speaking for the majority, fully accepted the government's assessment of the communist threat and the need to move against it with criminal measures. He stated:

> The formation by petitioners of such a highly organized conspiracy, with rigidly disciplined members subject to call when the leaders, these petitioners, felt that the time had come for action, coupled with the inflammable nature of world conditions, similar uprisings in other countries, and the touch-and-go nature of our relations with countries with whom petitioners were in the very least ideologically attuned, convince us that their convictions were justified on this score.

He concluded this line of reasoning with this statement:

> If the ingredients of the reaction are present, we cannot bind the Government to wait until the catalyst is added.

---

[65] R v. Secretary of State for the Home Department, ex parte Hosenball [1977] 3 All E.R. 452.

[66] See Dyzenhaus (2010), chapter 3.

[67] Dennis v. United States 341 U.S. 494.

Justice Frankfurter cited previous cases to establish the following:

> To preserve its independence, and give security against foreign aggression and encroachment, is the highest duty of every nation, and to attain these ends nearly all other considerations are to be subordinated. It matters not in what form such aggression and encroachment come... The government, possessing the powers which are to be exercised for protection and security, is clothed with authority to determine the occasion on which the powers shall be called forth....

Characterising the political statements of the Communist Party, he declared that "on any scales of values which we have hitherto recognised, speech of this sort ranks low".

Eugenics

Judicial accord with oppressive measures is limited neither to authoritarian or totalitarian regimes nor to situations of social unrest or dangers to the state. Many liberal states from the 1920s onwards, and up to as late as the 1970s, went quite a long way based on perceptions on eugenics in repressive means against people who were perceived as mentally degenerate. For instance, in Sweden, it is estimated that as many as 21,000 people were forcibly sterilised, most of them between 1935 and 1955.[68] All those who supported measures such as enforced sterilisation were not motivated by a desire to protect the race from inferior genetic material; many of the supporters were motivated by social policy reasons, to protect against crime and antisocial behaviour, and even to prevent new individuals being born into social misery and poverty. The oppressive measures were generally accepted and enforced by the judiciary.

In 1927, the first case on enforced sterilisation was decided by the United States Supreme Court. Carrie Buck was a "feeble minded" institutionalised daughter of a "feeble minded" mother in the same institution who had given birth to an "illegitimate feeble minded child". The authorities held that Carrie Buck was "the probable potential parent of a socially inadequate offspring, likewise afflicted", and "that she may be sexually sterilised without detriment to her general health and that her welfare and that of society will be promoted by her sterilization". In his opinion for the Court, the famous justice, Oliver Wendell Holmes, wrote:

> We have seen more than once that the public welfare may call upon the best citizens for their lives. It would be strange if it could not call upon those who already sap the strength of the State for these lesser sacrifices, often not felt to be such by those concerned, in order to prevent our being swamped with incompetence. It is better for all the world, if instead of waiting to execute degenerate offspring for crime, or to let them starve for their imbecility, society can prevent those who are manifestly unfit from continuing their kind... Three generations of imbeciles are enough.[69]

---

[68] SOU 2000:20, p. 33.

[69] Buck v. Bell, Superintendent of State Colony for Epileptics and Feeble Minded, 271 U.S. 200 1927.

It is undisputable that the American legislation and practice on sterilisation were utilised by the Nazis in their propaganda and in their justification of their racial ideology on preserving the health of the Aryan race.

The Buck v. Bell case also illustrates the fact that judges often share the basic underlying ideological assumptions in society, also when these assumptions are grounds for vicious measures. It would be speculation to maintain anything on whether it was restraint on the side of the legislators or the courts that prevented worse things from happening under the belief that society had to be purified from the degenerates. It stands as a fact, however, that it was not the courts that were the restraining factor in the application of such measures.

Disproportionate Punishment

A current example in the United States of judicial support for oppressive measures is the use of criminal sanctions that are disproportionate in relation to the criminal act. Under European law, the European Court of Human Rights has accepted "that while, in principle, matters of appropriate sentencing largely fall outside the scope of the Convention (Léger, cited above, § 72), a grossly disproportionate sentence could amount to ill-treatment contrary to Article 3 (on the protection against torture and inhuman or degrading treatment or punishment) at the moment of its imposition".[70] However, the "gross disproportionality" is a strict test, and it will only be on "rare and unique occasions" that the test will be met. Even sentences for life imprisonment without possibility of parole are not regarded as contrary to Article 3 if they are imposed for offences of the utmost severity, such as murder or manslaughter, after due consideration of all relevant mitigating and aggravating factors.

In the United States, the Eighth Amendment to the United States Constitution provides that cruel and unusual punishments shall not be inflicted. It has been interpreted by the Supreme Court as prohibiting extreme sentences that are grossly disproportionate to the crime. The threshold for disproportionality, however, is considerably higher than in European countries and allows for death penalties and for life imprisonment for less serious crimes for reasons of criminal policy.

I will not address the issue of death penalty here as there is no obvious consensus that this penalty as such and as a punishment for very serious offences is against the basic minimum of civilised society, although this view is held in many countries. What I will address, though, is the more general issue of proportionality. There is consensus that the right of the state to impose punishment is not unlimited and that some restrictions follow from a principle of proportionality or a principle against punishments that are cruel and unusual.

[70] ECtHR, judgment 17 January 2012 The case of Vinter and Others v. the United Kingdom, (Applications nos. 66069/09 and 130/10 and 3896/10), paragraph 89.

Judges in the United States are faced with a moral dilemma arising from a sentencing regime with rigid sentencing guidelines and strict minimal punishments. The US Supreme Court has held that capital punishment, though not unconstitutional per se, is categorically too harsh a penalty to apply to certain types of crimes and certain classes of offenders, thus restricting it to homicide and prohibiting it for offenders under 18 at the time of the crime. Also, the use of severe prison sentences has been reviewed under the prohibition against "cruel and unusual punishment" of the Eighth Amendment of the Constitution, and the Supreme Court has established that a sentence grossly disproportionate to the offence for which it is imposed is unconstitutional. At the same time, however, in the cases it has reviewed it has instituted a very stringent test, which in practice accepts all mandatory minimum sentences enacted by state and federal legislature.[71]

In the case before the US Supreme Court of Lockyer v. Andrade, the majority upheld a sentence of two consecutive terms of 25 years to life for the theft of videotapes worth USD 150 in total on two separate occasions.[72] Andrade had been a heroin addict since 1977 and had been in and out of prison for different offences since 1982. The State of California charged Andrade with two felony counts of petty theft with a prior conviction. Under California's three strikes law, any felony can constitute the third strike, subjecting a defendant to a prison term of 25 years to life. The jury found Andrade guilty and then found that he had three prior convictions that qualified as serious or violent felonies under the three strikes regime. Justice Souter stated in a dissent that "if Andrade's sentence is not grossly disproportionate, the principle has no meaning".

Many trial and appeal court judges have struggled with this state of law. In the case of United States of America v. Marion Hungerford, this caused a judge to voice his frustration in a concurring opinion upholding an "irrational, inhumane, and absurd the sentence".[73] Marion Hungerford, 52, and severely mentally disturbed, had no criminal history and had apparently led a spotless, law-abiding existence. After meeting her codefendant Canfield, who moved in with her, she participated in a string of armed robberies. Although she conspired with and aided and abetted Canfield, her participation in the robberies themselves was quite limited, particularly when compared to Canfield's dominant role. During most of the robberies, Hungerford took no active part other than driving Canfield to or from the scene of the crime or casing the stores that Canfield later robbed. No one was physically injured in any of the robberies, and the total loss resulting from them was less than $10,000.

Hungerford was convicted of conspiracy, seven counts of robbery, and seven counts of using a firearm in relation to a crime of violence. Although she never touched a gun, she received 57 months of imprisonment for the conspiracy and robbery counts, to run concurrently, plus 60 months for the first firearm charge and

[71] See Ewing v. California, 538 U.S. 11 (2003).

[72] Lockyer v. Andrade, 538 U.S. 63 (2003).

[73] United States of America v. Marion Hungerford 465 F.3d 1113.

300 months for each of the other firearm charges, to run consecutively—a total of 1,917 months, which amounted to 159 years' imprisonment.

The severe sentence was a result of the minimum sentencing laws of the United States and the fact that Hungerford refused to accept a plea bargain offer. Canfield, who accepted the offer of the prosecutor, received a sentence of 32 years. Her appeal of the sentence was rejected by a unanimous appeals court.

One of the judges of the Appeals Court stated in his opinion, however, that "it cannot be left unsaid how irrational, inhumane, and absurd the sentence in this case is, and moreover, how this particular sentence is a predictable by-product of the cruel and unjust mandatory minimum sentencing scheme adopted by Congress". He also stated that the sentence "should shock the conscience of anyone who believes that reasonable proportionality between a crime and the sentence is a necessary condition of fair sentencing".

In another case, in the United States District Court of Utah, Weldon Angelos was sentenced to minimum of 55 years in prison for the sale of marihuana worth USD 350 in total to a police informant on several occasions.[74] As a result of the sentence, the earliest possible release date for Mr. Angelos was at 77 years of age. The trial judge stated that "the fifty-five-year sentence mandated by § 924(c) in this case appears to be unjust, cruel, and irrational" and added that "our constitutional system of government requires the court to follow the law, not its own personal views about what the law ought to be".

Angelos had no previous criminal record. His misfortune was that he was carrying a weapon on these occasions and that he was in possession of weapons, together with marihuana, at his house. This brought him within the scope of the federal code, which provides for mandatory sentences for dealers who carry firearms during their drug transactions.

The district court judge reviewed the applicable law and concluded that he had no alternative but to apply the mandatory punishment. While stating that the law "imposes unjust punishment and creates irrational classifications", he upheld the law based on the test of whether "any ground can be conceived to justify [the statutory scheme] as rationally related to a legitimate government interest". As a result, the judge perceived himself obliged to apply the law. In addition, the judge reviewed whether the result of the law in the present case would amount to a cruel and unusual punishment in violation of the Eighth Amendment. The judge answered this in the affirmative, but for the ruling of the Supreme Court in Hutto v. Davis, where "the Supreme Court held that two consecutive twenty-year sentences—totaling forty years—for possession of nine ounces of marijuana said to be worth $200 did not violate the Eighth Amendment". With reference to this ruling by the Supreme Court, the judge wrote:

> The court believes it is it obligated to follow its holding here. Indeed, in Davis the Supreme Court pointedly reminded district court judges that "unless we wish anarchy to prevail within the federal judicial system, a precedent of this Court must be followed by the lower

[74] D. Utah v. Angelos, 2004 U.S. 345 F.Supp.2d 1227.

> federal courts...." Under Davis, Mr. Angelos' sentence is not cruel and unusual punishment. Therefore, his Eighth Amendment challenge must be rejected.

Having disposed of the legal arguments in the case, the judge found it "appropriate to make some concluding, personal observations". He characterised the penalty as "unjust, disproportionate to his offense, demeaning to victims of actual criminal violence". He therefore recommended that "the President commute Mr. Angelos' sentence to a prison term of no more than 18 years, the average sentence recommended by the jury that heard this case". He also recommended that Congress revise the legislation.

The sentence of Angelos was upheld on appeal. In the words of the Appeals Court, the "district court failed to accord proper deference to Congress's decision to severely punish criminals who repeatedly possess firearms in connection with drug-trafficking crimes, and erroneously downplayed the seriousness of Angelos's crimes".[75]

We see that judges apply and enforce punishments that they believe to be unjust and irrational. In this they are upholding laws that require them to meet out the sentence of an offender, not out of the inherent moral or social reprehensibility of the triggering offence but out of considerations of criminal policy enacted by the state. In the words of Supreme Court Justice Souter, "The triggering offense is treated so seriously, rather, because of its confirmation of the defendant's danger to society and the need to counter his threat with incapacitation".[76] The sentence is, in other words, not determined from the nature of the offence and an evaluation of aggravating and mitigating circumstances in connection with it but from the nature of the offender.

The judges in these cases enforce the law and refer to their judicial duty to uphold the law. The United States courts have not, however, limited themselves to applying the legislation narrowly construed. In several cases, the Supreme Court has chosen interpretations of the law that have been more invading on individual liberty than available alternative interpretations. In the case of Deal v. the United States, the defendant was convicted, in a single proceeding, of six counts of carrying and using a firearm during and in relation to a crime of violence for six bank robberies on different dates.[77] The legal issue before the Supreme Court was whether Section 924(c)(1) of the Criminal Code, which prescribed a 5-year prison term for the first such conviction and required a 20-year sentence in the case of a second or subsequent conviction, should be applied to multiple convictions under a single proceeding. The District Court sentenced Deal to 5 years' imprisonment on the first count and to 20 years on each of the other five counts, the terms to run consecutively. The Court of Appeals affirmed the convictions and sentence.

The provision was enacted by Congress in 1968, and the 20-year minimum sentence was in the first years treated both by prosecutors and courts as a rule

[75] C.A.10 (Utah) 2006 U.S. v. Angelos 433 F.3d 738.

[76] Ewing v. California, 538 U.S. 11 (2003).

[77] Deal v. U.S. 508 US 129 (1993).

applicable to repeat offenders. At some point, some prosecutors changed their position and argued for its use also for first-time offenders. This construction was accepted by one of the Courts of Appeal, the Eleventh Circuit, in 1987. In 1993, the controversy reached the United States Supreme Court.

Justice Scalia, voting for the majority, applied a textual approach and held that "conviction" in the statute could only refer to the finding of guilt by the jury and that there could therefore be "subsequent convictions" in the meaning of the stature within one proceeding. He held that a claim that Congress intended to address those with previous convictions who committed new crimes was "nothing but personal conviction" and an "ungarnished policy view" that could not even exclude other policy views such as taking repeat offenders off the streets for especially long periods or visiting society's revenge on repeat offenders more severely. Justice Stevens pointed out in his dissent that it could hardly be argued that "a construction surfacing for the first time 19 years after enactment is the only available construction" and thus rejected Justice Scalia's textual argument.

In another case, Smith v. the United States, the defendant had offered to trade an automatic weapon to an undercover officer for cocaine.[78] In relation to the same provision of the Criminal Code as in Deal, the issue here was whether the use of a firearm as payment amounted to using a firearm "during and in relation to... [a] drug trafficking crime". Justice O'Connor, delivering the opinion of the Court, argued that Smith "used" the gun as an item of barter and thus came under the meaning of the words using the gun in relation to a drug trafficking offence. There was no indication in the wording of the statute that it was limited to the use of a gun *as a weapon*.

In this case, Justice Scalia was in the minority. Also in this case, he employed a textual approach, but this time in defence of the defendant. He argued that although use as an item of barter falls within a possible meaning of the word "use", this is not within the "ordinary" meaning of the term "use of a firearm".

In both of these cases, there were means and alternatives available to judges who wished to restrict the application of the mandatory sentencing rules. In both cases, however, the majority of the Court opted for the most expansive interpretation of the statute. One can therefore not accurately portray the situation in the United States as one where the judiciary is committed to the protection of individual rights and liberty and construes statutes encroaching upon these values narrowly in order to defend them. Even in the US, the courts have had as much a part in restricting liberty as the legislator. From the two cases, we also see that there is no simple relationship between the interpretative approach employed by a judge and the application of or resistance to oppressive legislation. In the Deal case, the textual approach led to expanding the scope of the legislation. Also in the Smith case, the statute was expanded by the employment of a textual approach, but here the same approach could also be used to restrict it as Justice Scalia's dissent demonstrated.

[78] Smith v. US 508 US 223 (1993).

There are indications that the view of the Supreme Court on what constitutes a grossly disproportionate punishment is evolving towards a less oppressive direction. In its 2010 case of Graham v. Florida, the majority of the Court held that the US Constitution prohibits the imposition of a life without parole sentence on a juvenile offender who did not commit homicide.[79] This was characterised by the dissenting judges as a break with the previous case law.

Terrance Jamar Graham was born on January 6, 1987. His parents were addicted to crack cocaine, and their drug use persisted in his early years. Graham was diagnosed with attention deficit hyperactivity disorder in elementary school. He began drinking alcohol and using tobacco at age 9 and smoked marijuana at age 13. In July 2003, when Graham was age 16, he and three other school-age youths attempted to rob a barbeque restaurant in Jacksonville, Florida. The attempt failed, and Graham was arrested. Graham pleaded guilty to charges under a plea agreement. Graham wrote a letter to the trial court. After reciting "this is my first and last time getting in trouble", he continued, "I've decided to turn my life around". Graham said, "I made a promise to God and myself that if I get a second chance, I'm going to do whatever it takes to get to the [National Football League]".

The trial court accepted the plea agreement and sentenced Graham to two concurrent 3-year terms of probation. Less than 6 months later, Graham again was arrested, this time for armed robbery. The night that Graham allegedly committed the robbery, he was 34 days short of his 18th birthday. When Graham again was brought to trial, the trial court, this time with a different judge, noted that Graham, in admitting an attempt to avoid arrest, had acknowledged violating his probation.[80] The court further found that Graham had violated his probation by committing a home invasion robbery, by possessing a firearm, and by associating with persons engaged in criminal activity.

Under Florida law, the minimum sentence Graham could receive absent a downward departure by the judge was 5 years' imprisonment. The maximum was life imprisonment. When sentencing him to the maximum sentence authorised by law on each charge, life imprisonment for the armed burglary and 15 years for the attempted armed robbery, the judge said:

> And I don't understand why you would be given such a great opportunity to do something with your life and why you would throw it away. The only thing that I can rationalize is that you decided that this is how you were going to lead your life and that there is nothing that we can do for you. And as the state pointed out, that this is an escalating pattern of criminal conduct on your part and that we can't help you any further. We can't do anything to deter you. This is the way you are going to lead your life, and I don't know why you are going to. You've made that decision. I have no idea. But, evidently, that is what you decided to do.
>
> So then it becomes a focus, if I can't do anything to help you, if I can't do anything to get you back on the right path, then I have to start focusing on the community and trying to protect the community from your actions. And, unfortunately, that is where we are today is I don't see where I can do anything to help you any further. You've evidently decided this is the direction you're going to take in life, and it's unfortunate that you made that choice.

---

[79] Graham v. Florida 560 US—08-7412 (2010).

[80] Circuit Court of Florida, Fourth Judicial Circuit. Duval County State of Florida v. Terrance Graham. No. 16-2003-CF-11912-AXXX-MA. May 25, 2006, 2006 WL 6283414 (Fla.Cir.Ct.).

> I have reviewed the statute. I don't see where any further juvenile sanctions would be appropriate. I don't see where any youthful offender sanctions would be appropriate. Given your escalating pattern of criminal conduct, it is apparent to the Court that you have decided that this is the way you are going to live your life and that the only thing I can do now is to try and protect the community from your actions.[81]

Because Florida has abolished its parole system, a life sentence gives a defendant no possibility of release unless he is granted executive clemency. At the age of 19, Graham was in effect locked up for life with the key thrown away for a crime committed before he was 18.

As part of his reasoning, Supreme Court Justice Kennedy, delivering the opinion of the Court, stated that defendants who do not kill, intend to kill, or foresee that life will be taken are categorically less deserving of the most serious forms of punishment than are murderers and that offences like robbery or rape are "serious crime [s] deserving serious punishment", which nevertheless differ from homicide crimes in a moral sense. He also pointed out that life without parole sentences share some characteristics with death sentences that are shared by no other sentences. Further, he held that minors have less moral culpability than adults and have a greater possibility of a change in their personality and behaviour. The majority of the court thus emphasised the importance of taking regard of both the seriousness of the actual crime and the moral blameworthiness of the offender in the test of the proportionality of the punishment imposed. These two factors therefore limit the extent to which the legislator may pursue its aims of criminal policy through harsh punishments. The Supreme Court, therefore, no longer lacks "clear objective standards to distinguish between sentences for different terms of years", which has been the argument holding it back in its previous cases.[82]

In his dissent, Justice Thomas expressed the view that "the Court is willing to impose such an exacting constraint on democratic sentencing choices based on such an untestable philosophical conclusion is remarkable. The question of what act is 'deserving' of what punishment is bound so tightly with questions of morality and social conditions as to make it, almost by definition, a question for legislative resolution".

Punishing the offender for who he is rather that what act he has committed has parallels to the criminal justice of Nazi Germany. In criminal trials of the German courts at that time, the main thing was not that the defendant had violated a specific law but whether he belonged to the community or not, writes Ingo Müller.[83] Compare this to the words of the trial judge in sentencing Graham:

> We can't do anything to deter you. This is the way you are going to lead your life, and I don't know why you are going to... If I can't do anything to get you back on the right path, then I have to start focusing on the community and trying to protect the community from your actions.

---

[81] Cited from. Graham v. State 982 So.2d 43 Fla.App. 1 Dist. 2008 April 10, 2008.

[82] See the overview of Justice O'Connor in Lockyer v. Andrade 538 US 63 (2003), pp. 72–73.

[83] Müller (1989), p. 87.

The important element, according to Müller, was not the actual crime but the criminal personality. This fact does not of course entail that justice as such in the US resembles justice in Nazi Germany. As claimed by Otto Kirchheimer:

> Each society has such islands where the rule of law is at best uncertain, conjectural and often nonexistent. These islands may connote identifiable geographic areas or specific group relations; in other cases they may be nothing more than predispositions of certain groups ready to enter the field if the sociopolitical configuration changes and restraining influences remain weak. The decisive difference, in separating a normal from a criminal state, involves the degree to which such islands are kept under control and whether they are encroaching in wider and wider fields of social activity.[84]

There are crucial differences between the two systems in that the American punishment rules are not part of an ideology dividing the population into the "people" and "enemies of the people" based on a racial myth with the perceived necessity of waging war to uphold the state and the national culture. But also the criminal law in the US is subject to becoming an instrument of the state in the pursuit of its policy, in departure from a central principle of the rule of law that punishment should stand in relation to the guilt of the offender. Seen from this perspective, the difference between the two systems are differences in the nature of the policies pursued and of scope. Whereas Germany under the Nazis engaged in evil policies of persecution on racial grounds and total domination of the population by the state, the crime prevention aims of the United States are not evil. On the other hand, this should not be allowed to imply that they can be pursued by any means. The US sentencing practice acutely raises the question of whether it is conceivable to require that judges refrain from upholding and enforcing authoritarian measures within a regime that is not, as such, authoritarian.

If judges are operating within islands lacking of rule of law, upholding and enforcing lawlessness, should they be judged by other standards than judges operating in a criminal state? Many of the sentences imposed and sanctioned by the Supreme Court most probably would not withstand the test of the European Court of Human Rights when sentences that amount to life imprisonment without parole have no necessary relation to the gravity of the crime and are not reserved for offences of the utmost severity, such as murder or manslaughter. Does the doctrine of the duty to obey the law hold greater force on judges in a democratic setting than on judges in a totalitarian setting?

In the view of some, the sentencing system leads the judges to having to choose between what is lawful and what is right.[85] There are voices in the US debate that claim that US judges should refuse to apply the law when it leads to results that are grossly unjust and irrational. In a comment to the Hungerford decision, the editorial writer in the Harvard Law Review stated:

> By dutifully affirming a lengthy and inappropriate prison sentence, the Hungerford judges passed up a chance to engage in a powerful, symbolic act of civil disobedience – the kind of

[84] Kirchheimer (1961), p. 322.

[85] See Oleson (2007), p. 679.

> direct public repudiation of unwise and unjust laws that has been central to social change throughout our history. The court, like hundreds of others each year, missed an opportunity to play a role in ensuring America's substantive commitment to its formal values in an area likely to be ignored by popular government and unlikely to engender a spontaneous, organic, and effective social movement.[86]

It is also reported that some judges have resigned from the bench over the frustration of having to cope with a sentencing system that they find cruel and rigid.[87] Maybe such reactions by scholars and judges are one factor behind the apparent change of course by the Supreme Court in Graham.

The Courts and Legal Repression

What conclusions of a general nature can be drawn from the acceptance of authoritarian measures in democracies? Courts in general seem quite ready to accept the need to protect the institutions of the state when they are in a situation where their existence or stability or what is perceived as core values are seriously challenged independent of the nature of the regime. The regime is allowed to define whether there is a situation that calls for emergency measures and also to employ measures that would otherwise be regarded as infringements of fundamental rights. Oppressive measures are accepted if the issue at stake seems high enough.

There is sympathy between judges faced with extreme situations across the divide of tyranny and democracy. The US judges in the Military Tribunal of Nuremberg went quite far in their empathic understanding of their German colleagues and the measures they accepted and imposed in the name of national security in a passage like the following:

> Questions of far greater difficulty are involved when we consider the cases involving punishment for undermining military efficiency. The limitations on freedom of speech which were imposed in the enforcement of these laws are revolting to our sense of justice. A court would have no hesitation in condemning them under any free constitution, including that of the Weimar Republic, if the limitations were applied in time of peace; but even under the protection of the Constitution of the United States a citizen is not wholly free to attack the Government or to interfere with its military aims in time of war. In the face of a real and present danger, freedom of speech may be somewhat restricted even in America. Can we then say that in the throes of total war and in the presence of impending disaster those officials who enforced these savage laws in a last desperate effort to stave off defeat were guilty of crimes against humanity?[88]

Even under the direst of circumstances, this is not, however, a view that is universally held. A contemporary German army judge characterised the savage

---

[86] Civil Disobedience—The Role of Judges—The Ninth Circuit Confirms Mandatory Sentence—*United States v. Hungerford*, 465 F.3d I i Q (9th Cir. 2006). 120 Harv. L. Rev. 1988 2006–2007.

[87] Oleson (2007), p. 696.

[88] The Justice Case (1951), p. 1026.

laws in "the last desperate effort to stave off defeat" with "It is obvious that this is the end of the legal order".[89] He, in other words, judged the readiness of his superiors and colleagues to adopt and enforce atrocious measures more harshly than the US judges holding judgment over the Nazi legal order did. However, the sympathy expressed by the US judges makes it difficult to bring judges of authoritarian regimes to account for their participation in oppression and violation of individual rights.

Judicial acceptance of authoritarian measures in democracies serve to legitimise them, and also in authoritarian settings. The Nazis referred explicitly to the experience with the sterilisation laws in the United States for their eugenics practices,[90] just as the judges of South Africa used Liversidge as authority for interpreting the security legislation. The similarities in the approach of the courts and the mutual understanding that they show for each other's challenges show that also judges in authoritarian regimes act in a judicial capacity and not as aberrant jurists.

The sympathy between judges across regimes contributes to a feeling of collegiality between judges. South African judges participated in international meetings of judges; German jurists were on cordial terms with colleagues in other countries. In June 1939, Hans Frank, head of the National Socialist Jurists Association and President of the Academy of German Law, later Governor General of occupied Poland and executed at Nuremberg in 1946, visited Denmark in an official capacity. On the evening of his visit, he gave a speech on "Law as a Bridge between Peoples" to the Danish Law Society, where he spoke of the "five pillars of Nazi law"—race, earth, labour, state, and honour. The speech was met with an enthusiastic reception, and during the dinner the chairman of the society spoke of the valuable cooperation between the Danish and the German law societies.[91]

Legal sanction of authoritarian measures in regimes otherwise entrenched in the rule of law serves as a reminder that to show understanding and empathy towards a regime using oppressive means to defend itself is not something that is limited to judges in authoritarian settings. Even in countries with long traditions of judicial protection of individual rights, the courts accept oppressive measures, and the measures of the government should not be reviewed by the courts. Such "islands where the rule of law is at best uncertain [may be] mechanisms of corrosion that are latent in most constitutional democracies, either lying dormant or functioning at lower levels of intensity... capable of surfacing should the necessary circumstances arise".[92] Vivian Curran makes this observation in relation to the legal transformation of France under the Vichy regime, where the Jews were excluded from constitutional protection of fundamental rights through a rapid succession of laws

[89] Müller-Hill (2012), p. 30.

[90] Fraser (2005), p. 109 with further references.

[91] Tamm (1984), p. 607.

[92] Kirchheimer (1961), p. 322.

that were accepted and applied by the judges, legal scholars, and the rest of the legal community.[93]

The consequences of such a judicial acceptance are, of course, different, depending on the nature of the regime—whether it is basically democratic or authoritarian. In a democratic regime, there are other institutions besides the courts exercising control with the government, and the government will use the powers it is granted in a restrained way. Democratic regimes will also generally respect lines drawn by the courts. In authoritarian regimes, restrictions imposed by the courts will often be regarded as impediments to be overcome, either by new and even more oppressive legislation or by measures taken outside the reach of the judiciary. But this also shows that the important differences between rule of law and authoritarian rule are not the function and attitudes of the courts and judges but the nature of the other social institutions and the attitudes of those who control them.

References

Adami FW (1939) Das Programm der NSDAP und die Rechtsprechung. Deutsches Recht 486–491

Angermund R (1990) Deutsche Richtershaft 1919–1945. Fischer, Frankfurt am Main

Bach (1938) Die Rechtsprechung des Preußischen Oberverwaltungsgerichts im Lichte der nationalsozialistischen Weltanschauung und Rechtsauffassung. Deutsche Verwaltung 15:203

Carmen RD (1972) Constitutionalism and the Supreme Court in a changing Philippine polity. Asian Surv 13:1050–1061

Critch R (2012) Positivism and relativism in post-war jurisprudence. Jurisprudence 3(2):347–365

Curran VG (1998–1999) The legalization of racism in a constitutional state: democracy's suicide in Vichy France. Hastings Law J 50:1–96

Dodson JM, Jackson DW, O'Shaughnessy LN (1997) Human rights and the Salvadoran judiciary: the competing values of independence and accountability. Int J Hum Rights 1(4):50–65

Dyzenhaus D (1998) Judging the judges, judging ourselves truth, reconciliation and the apartheid legal order. Hart, Oxford

Dyzenhaus D (2010) Hard cases in wicked legal systems pathologies of legality, 2nd edn. Oxford University Press, Oxford

Fraenkel E (1941) The dual state a contribution to the theory of dictatorship. Oxford University Press, New York

Fraser D (2005) Law after Auschwitz: towards a jurisprudence of the Holocaust. Carolina Academic Press, Durham

Ginsburg T, Moustafa T (2008) Introduction: the functions of courts in authoritarian politics. In: Ginsburg T, Moustafa T (eds) Rule by law: the politics of courts in authoritarian regimes. Cambridge University Press, Cambridge

Haysom N, Plasket C (1988) The war against law: judicial activism and the appellate division. S Afr J Hum Rights 4:303–333

Hilbink L (2008) Agents of anti-politics: courts in Pinochet's Chile. In: Ginsburg T, Moustafa T (eds) Rule by law: the politics of courts in authoritarian regimes. Cambridge University Press, Cambridge

Kirchheimer O (1961) Political justice: the use of legal procedure for political ends. Princeton University Press, New Jersey

[93] Curran (1998–1999), p. 11.

Landis ES (1961) South African Apartheid legislation I: fundamental structure. Yale Law J 71:1–52

Linder DO (1993) Journeying through the valley of Evil. N C Law Rev 71:1111–1150

Loewenstein K (1935–1936) Law in the Third Reich. Yale Law Rev 45:779–815

Mahmud T (1994) Jurisprudence of successful treason: Coup d'Etat and common law. Cornell Int Law J 27:49–140

Michielsen JNME (2004) The "Nazification" and "Denazification" of the Courts in Belgium, Luxembourg and the Netherlands. University of Maastricht, Maastricht

Müller I (1989) Furchtbare Juristen – Die unbewältigte Vergangenheit unsere Justiz. Knaur, München

Müller-Hill WO (2012) "Man hat es kommen sehen und ist doch erschüttert" Das Kriegstagebuch eines deutschen Heeresrichters 1944/45. Siedler, München

Ogorek R (2008) "Rassenschande" und juristische Methode Die argumentative Grammatik des Reichsgerichts bei der Anwendung des Blutschutzgesetzes von 1935. In Regina Ogorek, Aufklärung über Justiz, 1. Halbbd.: Abhandlungen und Rezensionen, V. Klostermann, Frankfurt am Main

Oleson JC (2007) The antigone dilemma: when the paths of law and morality diverge. Cardozo Law Rev 29:669–702

Osiel MJ (1995) Dialogue with dictators: judicial resistance in Argentina and Brazil. Law Soc Inq 20:481–560

Pauer-Studer H (2014) Einleitung: Rechtfertigung des Unrechts. Das Rechtsdenken im Nationalsozialismus. In: Pauer-Studer H, Fink J (eds) Rechtfertigungen des Unrechts Da Rechtsdenken im Nationalsozialismus in Originaltexten. Suhrkamp, Berlin

Pereira AW (2005) Political (in)justice authoritarianism and the rule of law in Brazil, Chile and Argentina. University of Pittsburgh Press, Pittsburgh (Kindle edition)

Rüthers B (2012) Die unbegrenzte Auslegung: Zum Wandel der Privatrechtsordnung im Nationalsozialismus 7. Ausg. Mohr Siebeck, Tübingen

Simpson AWB (1988) Rhetoric, reality and regulation 18B. Denning Law J 3:123–153

Snyder F (1983–1984) State of Siege and rule of law in Argentina: the politics and rhetoric of vindication. Lawyer Americas 15:503–520

SOU 2000:20 *Steriliseringsfrågan*, Stockholm 2000

Strenge I (2002) Machtübernahme 1933: Alles auf dem legalen Weg? Ducker und Humblot, Berlin

Tamm D (1984) Retsopgøret efter besættelsen. Jurist- og Økonomforbundets forlag, København

Trials of War Criminals before the Nuremberg Military Tribunals, vol III, the Justice Case, Washington, 1951

Chapter 5
The Opposition

"The Flame of Law Never Quite Extinguished"

Legal professions have often been active in the building of liberal institutions. In many instances of tyrannical and oppressive rule, judges, as well as lawyers, are brave protectors of the rights and freedoms of individuals. In the examples I have chosen for this book, however, the judiciary have failed and become accomplice to the oppression. Even though the judiciary in these cases has contributed to the atrocities of oppressive regimes, this is not the whole picture. "Despite the deep fall of our supreme servants of the law, the flame of law never quite extinguished in our judiciary through these most difficult years", wrote professor and former minister of justice in the Weimar Republic for the Social Democrat Party Gustav Radbruch after the collapse of the Nazi regime.[1] In a more self-satisfied vein, former justice of the Reichsgericht Emil Niethammer wrote:

> In spite of this, all the decisions of the Supreme Court were targeted on humanity, truth and justice as the main goals. Humanity, truth and justice are enduring supreme goals. They do not depend on the human conditions; they are given humanity by God. They endure even when the attitudes and outlooks on earthly matters change, in particular on matters of state. Because of this, the attempt of the legislator (to breach the ties to the previous case law) never fully succeeded. Since its inner bonds sustained, its outer freedom was crust and smoke. The true value of "the case law of the past" nevertheless persisted.[2]

It is difficult to believe in the sincerity of these statements from a man who was an active justice at the Court when it developed its racial jurisprudence against Jews far beyond the statutory requirements of the Nazi regime. And it is impossible to agree with the statement that "all the decisions of the Supreme Court were targeted on humanity, truth and justice". On the other hand, the French judges continued to believe that they were upholding the rights entailed in the constitution during the

---

[1] Radbruch (1948), col. 64.

[2] Niethammer (1946), p. 12.

H.P. Graver, *Judges Against Justice*, DOI 10.1007/978-3-662-44293-7_5

Vichy regime, despite the enactment and enforcement of racial legislation against the Jews.[3] In the same way, it should be granted that German judges could continue to believe that they were preserving the "flame of the law" in the storm of extinguishing evil forces and that some of them were actually doing so. Such statements as the one of Niethammer should therefore be taken as evidence of the state of mind of judges at the time and not as evidence of the state of the law. Both Radbruch's and Niethammer's statements are evidence that the ideology of law as something autonomous dedicated to protecting more general values such as justice, equality, and the rule of law was in existence also through the Nazi period, at least as an ideology to praise and, to some, also as a troubling conflict of conscience. To some, it was present as even more than this.

After the fall of apartheid, President of the Constitutional Court of South Africa Arthur Chaskalson wrote:

> For despite all the paradoxes they have somehow held to the infrastructure and have kept alive the principles of freedom and justice which permeate the common law. True, at times no more than lip service has been paid to these principles, and there have been landmark cases where opportunities to give substance to and uphold fundamental rights have been allowed to pass without even an expression of discomfort, let alone a vindication of the right. Yet the notion that freedom and fairness are inherent qualities of law lives on, and if not reflected in all of the decisions, is nonetheless acknowledged and reinforced in numerous judgments of the courts. This is an important legacy and one which deserves neither to be diminished nor squandered.[4]

The Truth and Reconciliation Committee also emphasised the existence of an opposition against the regime among the judges:

> Yet, for all that this was the overwhelming pattern of the law and lawyers' conduct under apartheid, there were always a few lawyers (including judges, teachers and students) who were prepared to break with the norm. These lawyers used every opportunity to speak out publicly and within the profession against the adoption and execution of rules of law that sanctioned arbitrary official conduct and injustice. They explored the limits of their forensic skills in defending those on trial for offences in terms of such legislation, or in arguing for the invalidity of vague or unreasonable administrative action. They worked ceaselessly to prepare the cases of those targeted by the state, often in trying conditions and for little material reward. They advised and educated those in the community most vulnerable to official excesses, such as the rural poor and workers, through advice offices and religious bodies. They challenged their students to confront the relationship between law and justice and to translate their ideals into practice. They forswore the comforts of commercial practice for the sake of the upliftment of those excluded from all forms of power. They exercised their judicial discretion in favour of justice and liberty wherever proper and possible.[5]

Marc Osiel points out that it is often possible for judges to engage in genuine dialogue with the rulers in oppressive states. Judicial arguments are listened to and

---

[3] Curran (1998–1999), pp. 8–9.

[4] President of the Constitutional Court of South Africa Arthur Chaskalson, quoted from Dyzenhaus (1998), p. 20.

[5] SA Truth and Reconciliation Commission Final report, p. 104.

given general consideration, even to the extent that involves a change in policy. Legal arguments do not prevail with great regularity, but they are not ignored. Judges are allowed to express criticism publicly from the bench and are often not sanctioned or forced to resign.[6] Osiel holds this as traits of authoritarian regimes, as opposed to totalitarian regimes, but there was a certain scope of judicial independence, critique, and dialogue even in Nazi Germany.

Apart from open judicial dissent in judgments, there are not many known examples of judicial resistance to the authoritarian rule in countries like Germany and South Africa, and countries in Latin America. It might be that the explanation for this is that such instances were few and far between. But there is also a methodological difficulty in the study of resistance under totalitarianism. It is in the nature of such activity that it is performed in secrecy without leaving trails for the political police to follow. Often therefore there are few sources for a historical account, and sources that are available may be intentionally deceptive.[7] At the same time, accounts given by those who took part in the happenings of their own resistance may be coloured and exaggerated by people wishing to exonerate themselves from blame after the fact.[8] This means that actual acts of resistance may be overlooked and that reported acts may be false or at least misleading. We shall start here with such resistance that at the time was openly stated in the official rulings of the courts.

Issues of Legality

Courts do not always enforce oppressive legislation without resistance. There are examples of situations where courts question the legality of oppressive measures or where they seek to limit them through restrictive interpretation or by applying them in light of general rule of law principles. A clear-cut example where the legality issue is tackled head on by a court is the approach of the Appellate Division of South Africa to the voters' registration law. In 1951, the South African Parliament passed the Separate Representation of Voters Act, "to make provision for the separate representation in Parliament and in the provincial council of the province of the Cape of Good Hope of Europeans and non-Europeans in that province".[9] The consequence of the Act was to remove the right of coloured voters to vote for ordinary constituency members of the House of Assembly and instead allow them

---

[6] Osiel (1995), p. 486.

[7] See Gerrens (2009), pp. 9–10.

[8] See Essner (2002), pp. 113–133.

[9] The Act is available at http://www.disa.ukzn.ac.za/index.php?option=com_displaydc&recordID=leg19510618.028.020.046 (01.03.2013). See Beinart (1958), pp. 587–608 and Weinrib (1998) for an overview and discussion of the conflict between Parliament and the Appellate Division over this Act.

to elect four members of the House at separate elections. The Act was based on the ideology that non-European voters were inferior and that their participation in the general elections was a threat to white supremacy.

The validity of the Act was challenged on the basis of the South Africa Act of 1909, whereby the British Parliament established the South African Union. The South African Act provided that changes in the right to vote had to be made by the chambers of the South African Parliament acting in joint session and by a two-thirds majority. This procedure had not been followed by the South African Parliament when enacting the Separate Representation of Voters Act. In its landmark case of Harris v. Minister of the Interior, the Appellate Division declared the Act invalid, null, and void.[10] The annulment of the Act was particularly noteworthy as the Court reversed a previous decision limiting its right to review Acts of Parliament.[11]

The reply from Parliament was to set up a "High Court of Parliament" comprising the two Houses of Parliament to be the final instance in cases of the validity of statutes. This "court" deliberated an appeal of the decision of the Appellate Body in the Harris case and reversed it. The statute setting up the High Court of Parliament was brought before the Appellate Division, which invalidated it too.[12] The government's response to this decision was to undertake a large-scale change in the composition and status of the Appellate Division, nominating five new judges to the Appellate Division under a power it had through the Criminal Procedures Act. Following this, Parliament in 1955 passed the Appellate Division Quorum Act, which stated that "on the hearing of an appeal, whether criminal or civil, in which the validity of any Act of Parliament (which includes any instrument which purports to be and has been assented to by the Governor-General as such an Act) is in question, eleven judges of the Appellate Division shall form a quorum".

The government did not have the two-thirds majority in the two Houses of Parliament combined but used its majority to recompose and expand the Senate, and by this it managed to obtain the necessary majority. The two Houses acting together then passed amendments to the South Africa Act and established the basis for separate registration of the voters. It also passed an amendment stating that "No court of law shall be competent to enquire into or to pronounce upon the validity of any law passed by Parliament other than a law which alters or repeals or purports to alter or repeal the provisions of section 137 or 152 of the South Africa Act, 1909". When this Act was challenged, it was upheld by the Appellate Division by a majority of 11-1.[13] The Appellate Division held that the re-established Senate was legal despite its "artificial majority".

---

[10] Harris v. Minister of the Interior 1952 (2) SA 428 (A). For a comprehensive discussion of the legal issues of the case under the English and South African doctrines of parliamentary sovereignty, see Cowen (1952), pp. 282–296 (Part I) and Cowen (1953), pp. 273–298 (part II).

[11] See Weinrib (1998), p. 356.

[12] Minister of the Interior v. Harris 1952 (4) SA 769 (A).

[13] Collins v. The Minister of the Interior 1957 (1) SA 552 (A).

The qualification that the courts still could review changes in the South Africa Act itself was no practical restriction on the government since it had established a right to reconstitute the Senate. In that way, it could always secure the necessary two-thirds majority as long as it had the simple majority of the House of Representatives.[14]

There is a parallel in the approaches of the German courts and the South African courts in that the power base of the new regime was regarded as legal once the formal requirements of the constitution were satisfied. The courts did not enter into an analysis of the substance or the way that the regime had come about satisfying the formal requirements. In the German case, the passing of the enabling law was not challenged on the ground that the Nazis achieved the necessary majority by suppressing political opponents, both before the elections and after they had been elected, to prevent them from attending the session of the Reichstag. In South Africa, the reconstitution of the Senate was left unchallenged because the South Africa Act did not contain any specific provision limiting the right of Parliament to legislate on it.

Courts under occupation do not show a consistent picture of subservience or opposition to the demands of the occupier. In many of the countries occupied by Germany during the Second World War, the national courts loyally administered laws passed to accommodate the interests of the occupying authorities. The Vichy regime of France is notorious for its enactment of anti-Semitic laws and decrees, and these were all loyally enforced by the judiciary.[15] In Denmark, the courts enforced the oppressive legislation passed in the interests of the German occupier.[16]

There are also exceptions to this image of subservience and collaboration. The Norwegian Supreme Court justices collectively resigned their posts in December 1940 over a controversy with the German Reichskommissar Terboven and the collaborating Quisling regime over the power of the occupiers to enact reforms in the judicial system.[17] Following the breakdown of the cooperation between the German and Norwegian authorities, the Germans in September 1940 appointed collaborating men as heads of the Norwegian ministries. At the same time, a whole set of laws and regulations was issued aimed at transforming Norwegian society into a National Socialist state. This legislative activity continued, and in November 1940 a regulation was issued that enabled the Ministry of Justice to appoint and dismiss juries and lay members of the courts in criminal and civil cases.

The Supreme Court wrote a letter to the ministry protesting this measure and argued that it was contrary to the general principles of justice of the Norwegian constitution and that it exceeded the powers of occupying forces under public international law. The judges got two reactions to this letter. The first was a

---

[14] See Beinart (1958), p. 603.

[15] See Curran (1998–1999), pp. 30–34.

[16] See Tamm (1984), pp. 35–62.

[17] One of the justices wrote a book describing the events regarding the Supreme Court in 1940, Schjeldrup (1945). The last chapter deals with the events described here.

regulation lowering the retirement age for public officials from 70 to 65, combined with a right for the responsible minister to prolong the tenure indefinitely. The second was a letter from the Reichskommissar stating that Norwegian courts did not have the power to review the legality of laws and regulations enacted by or on behalf of the occupation authorities.

With the new retirement arrangement, the conditions under which the justices should function became unacceptable to the judges of the Supreme Court. The "unreliables" would be dismissed at 65 and replaced with persons loyal to the regime. The letter from the Reichskommissar Terboven made clear that the Germans would not accept judicial review of the legality of occupation measures under public international law. Terboven claimed to be the supreme source of law in Norway. On December 9, all of the judges signed a letter where they asked the minster to revoke the retirement regulation. Three days later, they sent a new letter to the minister where they all resigned, because "we cannot adhere to the view expressed by the Reichskommissar on judicial review without acting in contradiction with our duties as members of the Norwegian Supreme Court". The minister replied by dismissing the judges who were 65 years or older and by summoning the remaining to individual conferences in the ministry. When these conferences failed to provide submission by any of the judges, the ministry was forced to accept the resignation of the judges as a *fait accompli*.

The judges of occupied Belgium also offered resistance to the German occupiers. In October 1940, the German occupying authorities issued a prohibition for people of Jewish ancestry to exercise public office. The Court of Cassation wrote a letter to General Falkenhorst protesting and declaring the measure contrary to Belgian constitutional law and legislation.[18] The Belgian courts more or less openly refused to apply regulations enacted by the military administration. They also refused to recognise the delegation of power to the Belgian secretaries general who were heads of the Belgian administration but recognised their measures when they were within the scope of Belgian law.

Following a case in the Court of Cassation where the Court asserted its right to review the measures of the Belgian Secretaries General, the military administration on 14 May 1942 enacted a regulation prohibiting judicial review. In reply to this, the Court issued a statement where it held that the result of this regulation was that Belgian courts could not try cases involving the application of sanctions based on measures enacted by a secretary general. The German authorities prohibited the publication of this statement and considered it a call for a strike. Nevertheless, the attitude of the Court of Cassation became known among the judiciary who adjourned all cases involving decrees of the secretaries general.

The occupant's response to this was the discontinuing of payment of salaries to the judges, together with threats to arrest and execute ten judges and send the rest of the protesting judges to the east. An enormous pressure built up against the Court. The secretaries general were dependent on the courts for a legal basis in Belgian

[18] Michielsen (2004), pp. 32–33 and 50–55.

law for their administration—the alternative would have been a transfer of the administration to German hands. Finally, in July 1942, the Court gave in and accepted a compromise solution.[19]

A main difference between the approaches of the Norwegian and Belgian courts was that the Norwegian Supreme Court was willing to apply the regulations of the occupation authority provided that they were within its competence under public international law. The Belgian courts refused to apply the occupying authority's regulations or the regulations by the Belgian authorities based on a delegation from the Germans. But they were willing to apply measures by the Belgian authorities provided that they had a basis in Belgian law as interpreted under the emergency conditions of the occupation.

In both cases, the national courts reserved the right to review, and in both cases this right was denied by the occupying authority. The Norwegian judges found it unacceptable to continue under these circumstances and resigned. Staying in office would have involved a transfer of their loyalty from the Norwegian constitution to the occupation regime. The Belgian judges, on the other hand, stayed in office. They were prevented under Belgian law enacted before the German occupation to abandon their post. However, they attempted to refuse to try cases where regulations by the authorities were grounds for criminal sanctions, but they were pressured into submission. When they tried to lay down their work in protest against repressive measures, they were threatened with criminal proceedings with a possible death penalty.

Restrictive Interpretation

Another form of resistance is to reduce the effect of the restrictive measures by interpreting them narrowly and in light of established rules and principles of law that protect the individual. Marc Osiel describes how the Argentine Supreme Court, in many cases, interpreted the scope of emergency measures narrowly so as to allow their reconciliation with a more liberal, preexisting law. Instead of taking the plain facts approach of the South African Appellate Court to give effect to the intentions of the regime, it applied existing laws in a positivist way. Osiel mentions as an illustration the question of extending the length of detention of prisoners without trial beyond the time stipulated in the constitution for emergency measures. The regime argued that it would be illogical to release from custody those held for disrupting the social order on the ground of their success in disrupting the order for a longer time than envisioned by the constitution. The Court rejected such argument.[20]

---

[19] Michielsen (2004), pp. 55–68.

[20] Osiel (1995), pp. 524–526.

The Supreme Court of Brazil consistently engaged in a narrow interpretation of the oppressive measures of the military regime. Initially, it interpreted repressive legislation in light of rights and liberties in the legislation predating the coup. As the regime enacted new legislation with more precise abrogation of earlier law and even changed the constitution, the Court resorted to underlying moral principles implied in the constitution for its narrow interpretations.[21]

An example of a court that approached the measures of the Nazi regime in this way was the Prussian Administrative Appeals Court. The Prussian Administrative Appeals Court in Berlin represents, according to Schorn, a "hall of fame" of German justice during the Nazi regime.[22] According to Schorn, it maintained its old traditions through a series of "brave and uncompromising" decisions.

The legal credo of the Prussian Administrative Appeals Court is presented in an article in 1936 by Senatsprezident Dr. Franz Scholz.[23] He affirms that there has been a transition to a "new legal thought" in the case law of the Court but maintains that this transition started before the Nazi takeover of power and dates back to the rulings where the courts departed from the "Mark equals Mark" approach because of the hyperinflation. In these rulings, the courts departed from a strict textual approach to contractual obligations to take account of the diminished value of money due to inflation. The rulings marked the turn away from a formalistic legal reasoning tied to the letter of the law and paved the way for an approach based on substance and justice. Scholz describes the approach of the Prussian Administrative Appeals Court as based on reliance, rule of law, equal treatment, and loyalty to the intentions and aims of the legislator as core values of the community of the German people (Volksgemeinschaft).

Scholz stresses that the Prussian Administrative Appeals Court never put in doubt the fact that older legislation must be applied insofar as it had not explicitly been repealed by the new regime or must be regarded as contrary to "the totality of the new law". Illustrative of this are several cases where the Gestapo had closed down the businesses of Jews, socialists, and other "unreliables". The issue in such cases was whether the merchants were protected by the freedom of enterprise in the old legislation. In a consistent line of cases, the Court protected the merchants. In one case, it stated:

> It is true that the freedom of enterprise contained in § 1 of the RGO in order to accommodate the interests of the people has been restricted to a large extent by the National Socialist legislator, so that it no longer is the ruling principle of the market place. On the other hand, §§ 1 and 143 have not been repealed... Precisely from the fact that the legislator in order to reach its goals has chosen not to repeal §§ 1 and 143 follows that it is the will of the legislator not to further encroach upon these provisions, and that they, in the lack of specific legislative provisions remain in force.[24]

[21] Osiel (1995), pp. 534–535.

[22] Schorn (1959), pp. 144–169.

[23] Scholz (1936), pp. 401–422.

[24] Hempfer (1974), p. 105.

The judges accordingly were obliged to apply older legislation, "even when they believe that the older legislation contradicts the National Socialist worldview". On the other hand, Scholz conceded that the general clauses of the law, such as good faith, essential concern, public order, etc. must be applied according to the National Socialist outlook.

The case law of the Court shows that the description of the practice of the Court given by Scholz was not only casing but actually represented attitudes applied by the Court in its rulings.[25] Scholz mentions cases where the Court allowed judicial review of actions taken by the Gestapo to close down opposition newspapers. In a decision of 25 October 1934, the Court drew a distinction between review of the legality of the action, which was admissible, and review of the discretion of the police, which the courts should not undertake. Under the review of the legality, courts should assess whether police action was undertaken in the "prevention of communist acts of violence", which was the requirement of the relevant legislation. That courts should review the legality of police action followed from established administrative law, which courts were not allowed to deviate from.

It was not clear from the beginning of the Nazi regime that actions of the secret police, the SS, and the concentration camps would be outside the review of the courts. Discussions over this issue prevailed over a period of 3 years between the SS, on one hand, and the ministries of Justice and Interior, on the other, resulting in three different acts, each of them narrowing the scope of judicial review. The ministries kept insisting that also the SS and its branches must be subject to judicial review when operating state functions such as police and concentration camps. The issue was finally settled by Hitler personally, and the third Gestapo Act was enacted on 10 February 1936, stating that all actions and affairs within the jurisdiction of the secret police fell outside the jurisdiction of the administrative courts.[26]

The Prussian Administrative Appeals Court took a narrow approach to the different acts. The second Gestapo act explicitly excluded acts by the Gestapo itself from legal review. This was reflected in a decision of 2 May 1935, where judicial review was denied by the Court. On the other hand, the Court interpreted this statue narrowly: a case of 23 May 1935 stated that assistance offered by the normal police to the Gestapo was subject to judicial review. When the third law was enacted, the Court had to adapt again. But also this time, the Court gave the statute a narrow interpretation. When reviewing the assistance of the normal police, the Court stated in a decision of 19 March 1936 that it was a matter for the Court to review whether the decision to assist was, in fact, based on matters of the Gestapo and that this was expressed in the decision to assist or followed evidently from the facts. The mere declaration from the police that the action was made to assist the Gestapo would not suffice to exclude judicial review. Scholz's comment on the legal development was that it lead to the unsatisfactory situation that the courts had

---

[25] Schorn (1959) gives a digest of some of the case law of the court. For a thorough analysis of case law against basic tenets of the rule of law, see Hempfer (1974).

[26] See Herbert (2011), pp. 150–163 on this conflict.

no means to protect against arbitrary police actions originating from an office of the Gestapo since this mere formal circumstance was enough to prohibit judicial review. Only for acts originating from the normal police could the courts determine whether the actions in fact were matters of a political nature or not. According to Fraenkel, the 1936 decision represented the abolishment of "the last vestige of the Rule of Law in Germany".[27] It seems that the court had to give in once the SS had defeated the resistance of the two ministries.

Scholz accentuates the importance of judicial protection of the law in administrative measures. He gives an example of a case where the licence for itinerant trade was revoked from a member of the Roma population. The Court stated in its ruling of 30 December 1935 that the licence could not be revoked solely on the ground that Roma, in general, uses such a licence as a cover for theft and fraud. A revocation would have to be based on the individual circumstances of the trader.

In reply to the criticism that the Court in this way adhered to an obsolete theory of subjective rights, Scholz argued that a theory of subjective rights had never been a part of the jurisprudence of the Court and that one must distinguish between the granting of subjective rights and upholding the law. Scholz declares that "That judicial protection at the same time protects the interests of the community and the state is obvious".[28] The Court in several decisions also underlined the importance of due process, access to documents and evidence, and impartiality and argued that this followed from the "fundamental foundations of any legal process".

At the same time as the Court followed its traditional concern for legality and judicial protection, it emphasised that its jurisprudence was based on the new law and on National Socialist legal thought. In an article from 1938, the vice president of the Court, Dr. Bach, underlined that the Court consciously and purposely aimed its case law at the worldview and legal thought of National Socialism.[29] He stressed that the important thing to look at was not the wording used in the rulings but the spirit. He then went on to show with specific examples how the slogans of "common good before individual good"; "good faith, reasonableness, good customs, living perception of law etc."; "purposive interpretation"; and "rejection of formalism" were reflected in the case law of the Court. It is notable, however, that Bach makes no mention of other more sinister basic dogmas of Nazi legal thought, such as the concept of race and combat against "vermin, notorious criminals, usurers, pushers and the like".[30]

The attitude of the Prussian Administrative Appeals Court was not left without comment. In a harsh criticism by Professor Reinhard Höhn, the approach of the Berlin court was compared to that of the court in Hamburg. The Hamburg court had, according to Höhn, taken the correct line in realising that the "essence of the state

[27] Fraenkel (1941), p. 27.

[28] Scholz (1936), p. 421.

[29] Bach (1938), pp. 199–205.

[30] See Adami (1939), pp. 486–491.

must be reflected in the legal situation of the police". The Berlin court had not yet "dared to take this step". The court

> severs law and reality in a hostile manner. In its view, the Police would have an existence as an order of force separate from the conditions of the life of the German people. If the National Socialist police had acted according to such a view after the takeover of power, it would have failed in protecting the inner security of the Reich. The Prussian Administrative Appeals Court puts itself with its jurisprudence in direct contradiction to the actual facts.[31]

To a certain extent, the Prussian Administrative Appeals Court actually managed to take the ideology of the Nazis and merge it with traditional rule of law values. Walter Hempfer concludes his comprehensive study of the case law of the Prussian Administrative Appeals Court by stating that the Court managed to avoid liberal protections being abolished by the Nazi legal approach through its insistence on upholding legislation that was not formally repealed.[32] The National Socialist ideology of law and state was reflected in the jurisprudence of the Court, but the Court refused to accept it as a source of law superior to positive legislation. The Court troubled itself to limit the consequences of the constitutional transformation. On the other hand, the Court's loyalty towards positive law showed its weaknesses in the fact that it had nothing to cling to in the face of a repressive legislator; it had to accept the power of the Nazis as legitimate and enforce their legislation, even when they departed from fundamental elements of the rule of law.

The approach of the Prussian Administrative Appeals Court is remarkable compared to that of the other higher courts in Germany, for instance the Reichsgericht (the Supreme Court). The Reichsgericht quickly became a Nazified court, and its rulings by 1938 were described by former Justice of the Court Emil Niethammer as subservient, indecisive, sickly passionate, and blinded.[33] Niethammer himself left the Court in 1937, so he is characterising the time after he left. As we have seen above in many cases involving the rights of Jews, after the Nazi seizure of power, the Court contributed early and actively through its rulings to develop and further the discriminatory and oppressive policy of the Nazis, perhaps culminating with a ruling in 1936 likening the situation of the Jews to their physical death and describing their situation after March 1933 as deprived of all rights with destroyed legal personalities.[34]

The active opposition and contributor to several plots to assassinate Hitler, Hans von Dohnanyi, was active as a judge with the Court from 1938 to 1941. Dohnanyi was a member of the resistance group around Wilhelm Canaris and was executed in April 1945 after a proceeding that later on resulted in his prosecutor and judge being charged with murder.[35] He was an excellent lawyer who made a successful career

---

[31] Höhn (1938), pp. 330–333.

[32] Hempfer (1974), pp. 175–178.

[33] Niethammer (1946), pp. 11–14.

[34] RG., 1 Siv.Sen., 27. June 1936, Seufferts Archiv 91, 65; see, for a comment, Rüthers (2007), pp. 258–259.

[35] Concerning this case, see p. 180–181.

within the Ministry of Justice. In 1938, he was removed from his office and promoted to the Supreme Court due to doubts about his political loyalty based on his criticism of the racial policy of the regime. He left the Court in 1941 because he found it difficult to serve as a judge in criminal cases and took a position in the management of the Credit Bank of Rheinland Westfalen.[36]

It is difficult to see traces of Dohnanyi's oppositional views in the rulings of the Supreme Court that he participated in.[37] This is perhaps not very surprising. When he was called to the Court, Dohnanyi was its youngest member, and he served with the Court for a short period. At the time, he was already involved in plots against Hitler, so he might have felt the need to keep a low profile. In 1935, however, he actively opposed Roland Freisler in a commission to reform the criminal law they were both members of. He wrote to his wife that he was engaged in a "fearsome debate over the protection of honour of the community" and that it was impossible to resolve the controversy since the issue was related to "regarding the law as political or apolitical". He wrote ironically from another session of the commission that "we were presented with subtleties that deeply wounded my feelings for blood and honour (Blut und Boden)".[38] These and other skirmishes with one of the leading and most notorious Nazi lawyers did not seem to have harmed him personally. When he was arrested in 1943 and later executed, this was due to Gestapo's suspicion and later uncovering of his role in active resistance against the regime and not because of his activities as a lawyer and a judge.

There were, however, instances where judges of the Supreme Court obstructed the aims of the regime, even after 1938. Hubert Schorn reports of a case involving Senatspräsident Paul Vogt from 1944.[39] An innkeeper was convicted for dealings with prisoners of war. His appeal was channelled by the prosecutor through the Ministry of Justice. The Ministry gave an order that the appeal be promptly rejected as unfounded so that the sentence could be executed. Vogt, however, informed the prosecutor that this would not be possible as the conviction was tainted both by formal and substantial faults. He proposed to his co-judges that the conviction be overruled, and he also informed them of the ministerial order and that there would probably be a reaction from the ministry. They concurred with his opinion; the conviction was overruled, and the case was referred to a different court.

Vogt was called in to Minister Thierack in Berlin, who scolded him for the political gloom of the judgment. Vogt replied that as judges they were not bound by orders from the ministry and that the minister, with his order, had offended the independence of the judiciary. Vogt was invited to retire but refused. Six months later, he received his retirement by reaching the age of 65. Even this was probably a political decision, though, since most judges were retained beyond the age of 65 due to the shortage of judges.

---

[36] See Gerrens (2009), pp. 130–131.

[37] Smid (2002), pp. 203–209.

[38] The quotes from the letters are taken from Gerrens (2009), p. 108.

[39] Schorn (1959), pp. 442–444.

There are also other reported instances of judges who opposed the regime in their judgments. Of renown as a courageous judge is the District Court judge Lothar Kreyssig.[40] Kreyssig was appointed as a judge in 1928 and was regarded by his superiors as a very competent and able jurist and judge. After the Nazi takeover, he repeatedly came into the sights of the Nazis due to his refusal to partake in political formalities. He left the room during the uncovering of a portrait of Adolf Hitler, he "only moved his lips slightly" during a triple "Heil", and he omitted attending political training sessions. Above all, being active in the evangelical church, he sided with the church in its conflict with the Nazi regime. Several complaints to the Ministry of Justice to have him removed as a judge were not supported. The ministry did not find sufficient grounds to remove a competent judge and did not want to escalate the conflict with the church by removing one of its prominent supporters. After having bought a farm, Kreyssig applied for, and was granted, transfer to an unimportant county court in a rural area in Brandenburg. From there, he continued being reported to the ministry for political activities—distributing political leaflets in support of the church.

The issue that has made him known, and which eventually led to his being pensioned off, was his activities in relation to the euthanasia programme against the mentally ill. As a judge, he was the custodian of several people who, due to mental illness, could not take care of their own affairs. He discovered that persons under his custody were transferred to an institution where they were killed. On this basis, he wrote a letter protesting to the president of the regional court. He was asked to recall this "improper" document, but he refused. The letter was then reported by the president to the Ministry of Justice.

To the ministry, Kreyssig wrote that he protested not solely on religious grounds but also on account of the consequences the euthanasia programme would have for the concept of justice of the German people.

"In the name of the terrible slogan 'law is what serves the people', not yet contradicted by any of the guardians of justice in Germany, whole sections of society have been excluded from the law like for instance in the concentration camps and now also in our institutions for health and care", Kreyssig wrote. He admitted that the judicial role as custodian did not give him a legal right to intervene. But he saw it as his judicial duty to engage himself on the side of law and justice and to ask for a resolution from the Ministry of Justice.

After several meetings with Roland Freisler in the ministry, where no legal grounds for the killings could be demonstrated, the ministry itself being kept in the dark, Kreyssig issued orders to several institutions forbidding them to end the lives of persons under the custody of the Regional Court of Brandenburg. Again, he was called to the ministry, this time to meet with minister Gürtner in person. Present also was Hans von Dohnanyi. Kreyssig was given the option to recall his orders. But even after having been shown a photocopy of the secret order by the Führer, Kreyssig was unconvinced that the euthanasia programme was legal. The minister

[40] For his career as a judge based on his file in the Nazi Ministry of Justice, see Gruchmann (2011).

then made clear to him that it was impossible for him to continue as a judge if he could not accept the will of the Führer as the ultimate source of law. A few days later, Kreyssig wrote to the ministry, stating that he could not for his conscience withdraw his order, and he asked to be relieved of his duties as a judge.

In his proposal to the Minister of the Interior to the pensioning of Kreyssig, dated 10 May 1941, Secretary Schlegelberger wrote:

> Doctor Kreyssig expresses in these statements that in event of a conflict between his official duties and his duties as a Christian, as he sees them as a devotee of the "professing church," he will give precedence to the latter. Regarding membership of the party he sees this as incompatible to his Christian belief. He refuses to recognize the state as total in its power and to recognize a right for the state to regulate the affairs of the church. From his basic attitude he expresses doubt in the security of law in the National Socialist state and even doubts whether one can speak of the rule of law [einem Rechtsstaat] at all... Based on the conclusions from the investigation procedure it stands clear that Dr. Kreyssig is unready to give his personal convictions the necessary restraint demanded of him by his duties as an official, and this attitude rests on a conviction that is in contradiction to the National Socialist concept of the state. I therefore see the pensioning of Judge Dr. Kreyssig as compulsory.[41]

At the same time, Schlegelberger recommended that the disciplinary case against Kreyssig be withdrawn since his actions were much more due to his philosophy of life than due to violation of official duties. He went into pension and was left alone by the regime to farm his organic farm and attend his religious activities. After the war, he became the leader of the synod of the evangelical church in Magdeburg, where he lived to his death in 1986 after continuing his religious opposition under a second German dictatorship.

Another well-known instance is the so-called Berlin Coffee Case, regarding a decision by a county court judge in Berlin by Judge Dr. Willi Seidel.[42] A special coffee ration was distributed to the population of Berlin in the fall of 1940. Six thousand Jews applied for the coffee ration but did not receive it, being "excluded from the distribution per se". The food authorities imposed fines of 150 Reichsmarks upon the Jews for making the unsuccessful application. Most of them paid the fine, but 500 Jews appealed to the district court. Judge Seidel wrote a lengthy opinion stating that the interpretation on the part of the food authorities was absolutely incompatible with the established facts and that the imposition of a fine could not be upheld for legal reasons. He argued that the Jews had committed no crime. The most serious allegation that could be made against them was that they had attempted to receive rations to which they were not eligible, but the law did not make attempts of such offences criminal. In any case, the statute of limitations excluded punishing the Jews.

---

[41] See Döring (2011), p. 180. See also Lothar Kreyssig's own recollection in Bericht des Amtsgerichtsrats i. R. Dr. Lothar Kreyssig vom 16.10.1969, p. 5, Institut für Zeitgeschichte München–Berlin, Kreyssig, Dr. Lothar ZS-1956 http://www.ifz-muenchen.de/archiv/zs/zs-1956.pdf (last accessed 11.04.14).

[42] Schorn (1959), pp. 649–652. It is also mentioned in The Justice Case (1951), pp. 1016–1017 as an example of instruction of the judges by the Ministry of Justice through its Judges' Letters.

The Reich Minister of Justice commented the decision in the following way:

> The ruling of the district court, in form and content matter, borders on embarrassing a German administrative authority to the advantage of Jewry. The judge should have asked himself the question: What is the reaction of the Jew to this 20-page long ruling, which certifies that he and the 500 other Jews are right and that he won over a German authority, and does not devote one word to the reaction of our own people to this insolent and arrogant conduct of the Jews? Even if the judge was convinced that the food office had arrived at a wrong judgment of the legal position, and if he could not make up his mind to wait with his decision until the question, if necessary, was clarified by the higher authorities, he should have chosen a form for his ruling which under any circumstances avoided harming the prestige of the food office and thus putting the Jew expressly in the right toward it.

Seidel was reported by the head of the food office to the president of the Court with the request that he be transferred to another position. The president of the Court rejected this request, also when it was repeated by the regional leader of the Nazi Party (*Gauleiter*). The head of the food office appealed to the Reich Ministry of Propaganda, which after consultation with the Ministry of Justice received the reply by Roland Freisler that Dr. Seidel had been reprimanded.

Dr. Seidel was charged by the Party Court, which revoked his membership to the National Socialist Party. The Party Court found that he had shown absolute lack in political attitude through a serious misconception of the Jewish issue. Even if he believed that his decision was necessitated by the law, which, the Party Court commented, was not the case under an intelligent interpretation, he should have consulted with the Ministry of Justice before passing a judgment that could undermine the authority of state bodies before the Jews.

The ministry consequently transferred Dr. Seidel to the civil department of the Court so that he would no longer deal with criminal matters. As a judge in the civil law department, he was no longer exempt from the draft, and he was subsequently called up for military service. He survived the war and was afterwards appointed president of a Berlin district court.

A judge of a more ambiguous nature is SS judge Konrad Morgen.[43] Before the war, he served as a civil judge, but he was removed from his post after refusing to consent to a verdict according to the party line where a teacher who was not a party member was accused by the Hitler Youth of illegal excessive corporal punishment. After serving with the Waffen SS, he was appointed as SS judge in 1941. After acquitting a defendant accused of racial defilation, he was removed by Himmler in 1942. In 1943, he was recalled and ordered to serve as an SS judge at the Reich's main criminal office in Berlin. From this position, he was ordered to investigate corruption in the concentration camps. In Buchenwald, he came across evidence of illegal killings, and following his investigation the former commandant and the camp physician were arrested on charges of embezzlement and illegal killings. They were prosecuted and sentenced to death. However, Himmler ordered the investigations into the concentration camps stopped.

[43] See Pauer-Studer (2012), pp. 367–390.

After the war, Morgen cultivated a self-conception of an upright judge trying to do his best and uphold decency. He discovered the programme of mass extermination when investigating Auschwitz but regarded the killings that took part according to orders from Hitler and Himmler as legal. But he pursued killings that took part outside of this scheme, and the taking advantage of the prisoners.

Pauer-Studer observes that "Something is deeply flawed in Morgen's professional activities, though he certainly took considerable personal risks and displayed personal courage on various occasions".[44] Should he be seen as a judge "pursuing justice, trying to reach just and fair verdicts within the legal framework of the SS jurisdiction", or was he a convinced Nazi, committed to the ideology and values of the SS to promote honesty and combat financial corruption and corruption of character? Pauer-Studer concludes that Morgen portrays himself both as the judge and as the Nazi, alternating between the two according to the accounts he is asked to give to his interrogators after the war. In any case, his mission for rule of law and decency is flawed because the conditions to achieve these were lacking in the circumstances that he operated.

> Within the SS jurisdiction, Morgen could not act as a judge oriented towards the rule of law, simply because the most basic requirements defining the rule of law—such as stability, predictability and publicity of legal rules—had been violated... When the highest juridical authority orders mass extermination, aiming for the rule of law within that juridical system is not only curtailed but rendered impossible.[45]

It is difficult to assess the extent of opposition among the judiciary to Nazi laws and policies. According to Hubert Schorn, many judges recognised the conflict between law and justice and decided to depart from positive law and follow their conscience in their rulings.[46] He mentions instances where the judge placed suspects in custody even if the evidence was not sufficient, to protect them from being apprehended by the Gestapo. For the same purpose, a judge could sentence a defendant to a longer prison term instead of a short one because his release from prison would have resulted in him being placed in a concentration camp. The actual examples Schorn cites are few, especially taken into account that more than 15,000 judges were active during the Nazi regime, passing many thousands of judgments.

Most commentators state that judicial opposition to the regime was negligible. This does not mean, however, that the criminal cases of German courts were a massive body of arbitrary and disproportional application of the harshest punishments. Closer studies reveal a nuanced picture of differentiation of sentences according to the crime, the person of the accused, region, and the personality of the judge.[47]

Any opposition must have been in a covert form, unnoticed both by the regime and later historians. Only very few stories are told that can serve as illustrations.

---

[44] Pauer-Studer (2012), p. 384.

[45] Pauer-Studer (2012), p. 388.

[46] Schorn (1959), pp. 32–35.

[47] See Angermund (1990), p. 213.

Werner Otto Müller-Hill, a German army judge, writes in his diary from the last year of the war on how differences in personality of the judge could influence how the oppressive laws were enforced:

> When a defendant I prosecuted was acquitted, I let it be with that and did not try by appeal to be 'proven right'. My counterpart is an old colleague from Breslau, a self-righteous, but good-natured Prussian. He represented the phenomenon that simply transformed when dressed into the uniform of an army judge. To him, acquittals when prosecuting were personal insults and insults of the maxim of the state. He would not rest until he had gotten such an acquittal repealed, and continued this miserable practice, even though he almost always was in the wrong because the people often were acquitted again in the new trial against them. He was the kind of German with a Bismarckian power-complex and other complexes that one as a South-Westener has difficulties in coming to terms with.[48]

He writes about sentencing:

> I had to judge a miserable little Pole from around Katowitze who went AWOL and flew to Switzerland. He went from there and to France, where he was apprehended. In prison he did the incredible; he drew a map over the border-crossings to Switzerland for two imprisoned mutineers. The map was discovered. We convicted the poor bastard, who hardly understood any German, to 15 years imprisonment. The prosecutor asked for the death sentence. The commander in chief, General Fromm, repealed the sentence as too lenient. The next court here sentenced him again to 15 years. Result: repeal by From. With that the judges in our unit were spent and the command at Baden-Baden was assigned the case. A professional judge presided over the court. To his honor it must be said that the sentence again was for 15 years imprisonment.[49]

Towards the end of the war, the Nazi regime introduced ever harsher penalties against "undermining the war effort", demanding the death sentence for the voicing of critical remarks. On these measures Müller-Hill comments in the following way:

> Criticism of the Führer was and is the proper gambit of the prohibition against malicious slander (Heimtucke) which punishes those with prison who publicly make hateful, heretic or malicious statements about leading figures of state. Today such criticism is 'undermining of the defense' and countless heads are rolling for it. It is obvious that this is the end of the legal order.[50]

He also comments on the establishment of roaming special courts that were established in the last phases of the war to uphold discipline among the troops. Some of these courts even passed death sentences for desertion after the capitulation of the German forces to the Allies.

> And to us came orders from above (Himmler) on the establishment of court marshals to subdue the tendencies to disintegration, as if a last act of judicial brutality could do anything to stop it. Our 'sharpest' judge, who had made a name for himself as such in the staff-court of Stuttgart—I myself am maybe in favour for my efficiency, but in line of duty I am not because I am too lenient—was appointed chief of the court martial of Tübingen and was going to let heads roll for the final victory! Not an envious task, which is uncomfortable even to him who is really too sharp and without any compassion. I have due to my mildness

---

[48] Müller-Hill (2012), pp. 43–44.

[49] Müller-Hill (2012), p. 30.

[50] Müller-Hill (2012), p. 30.

> not been appointed, a fact I am rather proud of. I have always seen it as my task to help honest soldiers who have got themselves into trouble, and protect them from severe and unbearable punishment. In this way I believe I have served the common good, and I have seldom experienced that soldiers that I in this way have helped to the best of my ability, have disappointed me.[51]

We see from such examples that resistance is possible and that it happens sometimes, even in totalitarian settings. There are examples of total defiance, such as of the judges of the Supreme Court in Norway and of Lothar Kreyssig and of judges refusing to accept the legality of measures of the regime, such as the initial approach of the South African Appellate Division of the Supreme Court and the approach of the Prussian Administrative Appeals Court. In some cases, judges engage in a dialogue with the regime or with other elites in order to persuade the regime to temper its measures. In other cases, the opposition is more covert where the judge exercises his discretion as far as possible in favour of individual victims of oppression, without going for an outright confrontation with the regime.

Opposition in the Twilight of Authoritarianism

In order to secure their own situation by distancing themselves from the government, judges who lack institutional security start facing incentives to rule against the government once the government in office starts to lose power. In Argentina, with its tradition of replacing the justices of the Supreme Court at changes of the regime, the percentage of antigovernment rulings in the Supreme Court increased remarkably once it became likely that regime changes would occur in 1983 and 1989.[52]

As has been shown above, South African judges of the 1960s not only loyally enforced apartheid laws and security law, but they also extended their application to give best possible effect to the oppressive policies of the regime, in what David Dyzenhaus has labelled as the "plain fact approach".[53] When a state of emergency was declared again in 1985 after school and trade boycotts, several of the judiciary acted differently. Whereas the courts after the 1961 killings at Sharpeville had relentlessly turned down legal challenges to the validity of security measures, many judges in 1985 interpreted the emergency regulations in a common law context and restricted their application.[54] Where the Appellate Division in 1964 argued that legislation that went far to curtail individual rights indicated that Parliament intended for the use of the means necessary to obtain the goals of the legislation,[55]

[51] Müller-Hill (2012), p. 143.

[52] Helmke (2002), p. 296.

[53] Dyzenhaus (2010), p. 48 and, further, p. 227 below.

[54] Dyzenhaus (2010), pp. 148–164.

[55] Rossouw v. Sachs 1964 (2) SA 551 (A).

courts in 1985 could take the attitude that the more serious the expressed inroads on liberty in a statute, the more ready the court should be to fulfil its role as a protector of individual rights granted under common law.[56] Contemporary commentators could observe a "more activist trend that started to emerge in 1985 [which] continues to characterize judicial decision-making".[57] Dyzenhaus calls this the "common law approach" to interpretation.[58]

Initially, the common law approach of lower court judges was overruled by the Appellate Division, which held on to its government-friendly approach to a point where it could be said that the Court "put itself and other South African courts in a position where the courts would take jurisdiction only to decline it and this gave the government the facility to operate under the cloak of the rule of law".[59] But even the Appellate Division signalled a change in its approach once the end of apartheid was in sight. Despite this, it seems correct that the opposing judicial decisions from 1985 to 1990 by lower courts were in open defiance not only to the legislator but also to the approach dictated by the supreme court of the land.

In Brazil, the political trials were brought before the military courts. Their judgments were never entirely arbitrary, and their proceedings were open to argument on behalf of the accused by the defence lawyers. These courts also had a relatively high rate of acquittals.[60] The judgments began to lean in a more liberal direction in the mid to late 1970s, when the climate of political emergency had waned. These rulings "stretched the boundaries of permissible activity and speech within national security law and served to lay the foundations for a proto-civil society, one that demanded fuller respect for human rights".[61]

The developments in Argentina, Brazil, and South Africa may be instances of what Helmke labels "strategic defection" by judges. Also, in the Netherlands, there were some instances near the end of the German occupation where some courts started to question the powers of the occupant on the Netherlands civil administration.[62] A weak point in Helmke's argument is that she asserts that judges adapt strategically to the values of a possible new regime out of fear of sanctions. As will be shown in the next part of this book, judges seldom have much to fear in this respect. The "abandoning of ship" that can be seen may also be a reminder of the importance of having judges brought up in a tradition of the rule of law and of the resilience of rule of law values even under conditions of severe oppression. The remarkable adaptation to the new political and social conditions of the German judiciary after the fall of the Nazi rule may also be an indication of this.

[56] Nkwinti v. Commissioner of Police 1986 (2) SA 421 E.

[57] Basson (1987), p. 41.

[58] Dyzenhaus (2010), p. 53.

[59] Dyzenhaus (2010), p. 161.

[60] Osiel (1995), pp. 537–538.

[61] Pereira (2005), location 2132.

[62] Michielsen (2004), p. 179.

The different measures of resistance may not be very impressive or seem very important, but compared to the approach taken in many case of active support and even extension of legal measures to give effect to the policy of domination, they are all noteworthy. Given the atmosphere of terror and fear that authoritarian regimes often create, they are probably also often instances of high personal courage. Fear of unpleasant consequences is probably often an explanation or at least the excuse for many judges not to engage in open or covert resistance to the regime. This may also explain the fact that judicial resistance often increases once the regime is on the wane. The fact that judges seldom challenge core regime interests before it appears that the regime is on its way out of power may seem unheroic. Nevertheless, it points to the fact that judges may have an important role to play in the end phases of an authoritarian regime and in the re-establishment of the rule of law.

Resistance and Legal Method

These instances of judicial opposition, though few and far between, are important because they show that judicial resistance is possible. They are possible as actions within the law, and they are possible on the personal level. Some judges manage to give rulings that do not support the regime. In some situations, such rulings are made by the leading courts and by the judicial elite. In other cases, they are made by a minority of judges. In any case, they show that acceptance of the legality of an established authoritarian regime and of its oppressive measures is not a social or legal necessity. The examples also show that opposition is often tolerated at the personal level, although the regime will seek to find legal and institutional ways to circumvent it.

Legal opposition to the regime and to the predominant legal opinion is often made possible through alternative approaches to law. Sometimes the main battlefield even is a methodological issue like the conflicts between the Norwegian and Belgian judges and the legal view held by the German occupying authority. Both the Belgian and the Norwegian supreme courts took a stand on their approach to international law and the application of rules based on international law in national courts. The Belgian stand was that such rules could not be applied and enforced in Belgian courts. In this way, it forced the Belgian administration to legitimise its measures in the Belgian constitution. The Norwegian stand was that a precondition for the application of measures from the occupying authorities was that Norwegian courts could review their legality under international law. According to the Supreme Court, the sole legal basis for this regime was by delegation from the German occupiers. An important political consequence of this was that all measures of the Quisling regime would be reviewed under this approach since the Quisling regime had no basis in the Norwegian constitution.

The effects of the differences between the plain fact judges and the common law judges in South Africa were also political. The differences in the legal reasoning were, on the other hand, first and foremost on the methodological approach taken.

The differences will be further explored below on pp. 285–290. Here, it suffices to say that experience shows that it is possible to apply different approaches to interpretation and that different approaches may lead to the difference between supporting and resisting the oppressive measures of an authoritarian regime. The experience of the Prussian Administrative Appeals Court is an example of this, showing yet a third type of approach to legal interpretation. The debates that this Court triggered in German legal doctrine in the 1930s also show the relationship between politics and legal method.

The opposition thus presented by some judges was recognised at the time as judicial action within the scope of the law. Their methods and results were criticised and sometimes corrected by higher courts, but they were not defined as politics or "non-law". The debates over method were conducted in the usual form as legal and theoretical debates, not as political debates. But if these discussions are held, and the choice of method to be employed made without regard to the political consequences, then the participants are acting with blinders. Participation in atrocities may then result as the product of the professional narrow-mindedness that Hannah Arendt found and criticised in the person of Adolf Eichmann, and which she labelled as the banality of evil. We will return to the relationship between legal theory and judicial complicity or opposition in part three. Before that, we will examine the extent to which judges can be held responsible under criminal law for complicity in atrocities by applying and enforcing evil laws.

References

Adami FW (1939) Das Programm der NSDAP und die Rechtsprechung. Deutsches Recht 486–491

Angermund R (1990) Deutsche Richtershaft 1919–1945. Fischer, Frankfurt am Main

Bach (1938) Die Rechtsprechung des Preußischen Oberverwaltungsgerichts im Lichte der nationalsozialistischen Weltanschauung und Rechtsauffassung. Deutsche Verwaltung 15:203

Basson D (1987) Judicial activism in a state of emergency: an examination of recent decisions of the South African courts. S Afr J Hum Rights 3:28–43

Beinart B (1958) The South African appeal court and judicial review. Mod Law Rev 21:587–608

Cowen DV (1952) Legislature and the judiciary. Mod Law Rev 15:282–296 (Part I)

Cowen DV (1953) Legislature and the judiciary. Mod Law Rev 16:273–298 (part II)

Curran VG (1998–1999) The legalization of racism in a constitutional state: democracy's suicide in Vichy France. Hastings Law J 50:1–96

Döring H-J (ed) (2011) Lothar Kreyssig Aufsätze, Autobiographie und Dokumente. Evangelische Verlagsanstalt, Leipzig

Dyzenhaus D (1998) Judging the judges, judging ourselves truth, reconciliation and the apartheid legal order. Hart, Oxford

Dyzenhaus D (2010) Hard cases in wicked legal systems pathologies of legality, 2nd edn. Oxford University Press, Oxford

Essner C (2002) Die "Nürnberger Gesetze" oder Die Verwaltung des Rassenwahns 1933–1945. Paderborn, München

Fraenkel E (1941) The dual state a contribution to the theory of dictatorship. Oxford University Press, New York

Gerrens U (2009) Rüdiger Schleicher Leben zwischen Staatsdienst und Verschwörung. Gütersloher Verlagshaus, Gütersloh
Gruchmann L (2011) Ein unbequemer Amtsrichter im Dritten Reich aus den Personalakten des Dr. Lothar Kreyssig. In: Döring H-J (ed) Lothar Kreyssig Aufsätze, Autobiographie und Dokumente. Evangelische Verlagsanstalt, Leipzig
Helmke G (2002) The logic of strategic defection: court-executive relations in Argentina under dictatorship and democracy. Am Polit Sci Rev 96:291–303
Hempfer W (1974) Die nationalsozialistische Staatsauffassung in der Rechtsprechung des Preußischen Oberverwaltungsgerichts. Dunker & Humblot, Berlin
Herbert U (2011) Best Biographische Studien über Radikalismus, Weltanschauung und Vernunft 1903–1989, 5th edn. Verlag J.H.W Dietz Nachf, Bonn
Höhn R (1938) Alte und neue Polizeirechtsauffassung in der Praxis. Deutsche Verwaltung 330–333
Michielsen JNME (2004) The "Nazification" and "Denazification" of the Courts in Belgium, Luxembourg and the Netherlands. University of Maastricht, Maastricht
Müller-Hill WO (2012) "Man hat es kommen sehen und ist doch erschüttert" Das Kriegstagebuch eines deutschen Heeresrichters 1944/45. Siedler, München
Niethammer E (1946) Fortdauende Wirksamkeit der Entscheidungen des Reichgerichts. DRZ 11–14
Osiel MJ (1995) Dialogue with dictators: judicial resistance in Argentina and Brazil. Law Soc Inq 20:481–560
Pauer-Studer H (2012) Law and morality under evil conditions: the SS Judge Konrad Morgen. Jurisprudence 3(2):367–390
Pereira AW (2005) Political (in)justice authoritarianism and the rule of law in Brazil, Chile and Argentina. University of Pittsburgh Press, Pittsburgh (Kindle edition)
Radbruch G (1948) Des Reichministeriums Ruhm und Ende, Zum Nürnberger Juristenurteil. Süddeutsche Juristenzeitung col. 64
Rüthers B (2007) Hatte die Rechtsperversion in den Deutschen Diktaturen ein Gesicht? Juristenzeitung 11:556–564
Schjeldrup F (1945) Fra Norges Kamp for Retten 1940 i Høyesterett. Grøndahl & Søn, Oslo
Scholz F (1936) Die neue Rechtsprechung des Preußischen Oberverwaltungsgerichts. Verwaltungsarchiv 41:401–422
Schorn H (1959) Der Richter im Dritten Reich Geschichte und Dokumente. Vittorio Klostermann, Frankfurt am Main
Smid M (2002) Hans von Dohnanyi Christine Bonhoeffer, Eine Ehe in Widerstand gegen Hitler. Gütersloher Verlagshaus, Gütersloher, pp 203–209
Tamm D (1984) Retsopgøret efter besættelsen. Jurist- og Økonomforbundets forlag, København
Trials of War Criminals before the Nuremberg Military Tribunals, vol III, the Justice Case, Washington, 1951
Weinrib LE (1998) Sustaining constitutional values: the Schreiner legacy. S Afr J Hum Rights 14:351–372

Part II
Holding Judges Responsible for Injustice

Chapter 6
The Argument for Criminal Liability

Introduction

Under international human rights law, states have an obligation to prosecute perpetrators of serious human rights violations. It has since long been shown that also judges can be responsible under international law for atrocities committed as part of the application and enforcement of municipal law. This was first established by the US Military Tribunal against leaders of the Nazi legal system and has since been confirmed by the European Court of Human Rights. Under municipal law, however, the picture is more complex. The legislation on judicial responsibility for unlawful judging varies from country to country, as do definitions of "unlawful" in relation to judicial activity.

For the most part, judges are not brought to account for their contribution to uphold and enforce authoritarian regimes and evil institutions and laws, neither under international nor under national law. To my knowledge, apart from in Germany, no proceedings have been brought against judges for their action in their judicial capacity in cases of transitional justice after the Nazi war trials of the middle of the twentieth century. In South Africa, the judges and magistrates did not meet the Commission for Truth and Reconciliation; they got away with it. In Argentina, the military courts were stripped of their jurisdiction over civilians and the judges of the Supreme Court were replaced by the democratic regime.[1] Judges were not included, however, among the officials of the military regime who were prosecuted. In Brazil, the judiciary continued to function under democracy largely as they had under military rule. The judges were not subject to any serious criticism despite their responsibility for thousands of persecutions during the dictatorship.[2] In Chile, the judiciary was blamed for complicity by the Chilean National

---

[1] See Pereira (2005), location 2263.

[2] See Pereira (2005), location 2245.

H.P. Graver, *Judges Against Justice*, DOI 10.1007/978-3-662-44293-7_6

Commission on Truth and Reconciliation and the judicial system was reformed, but there was no criminal prosecution.[3]

The postwar trials in countries occupied by Germany during the war do give instances of how this situation was dealt with by the restored regimes after liberation. In many countries, the legitimate national institutions continued their business during the occupation under the dominance and control of the German occupying power. In some countries, notably in France and Norway, national political groups seized the opportunity to grasp power and establish themselves as illegitimate national rulers: the Petain regime of Vichy France and the Quisling regime of Norway.

Despite the fact that the German military courts and the SS court in occupied Norway during World War II were responsible for the execution of 231 members of the Norwegian resistance, not one single member of these courts was charged in the war crime proceedings after the war in Norway.[4] A charge of murder was brought against three judges of a summary trail (Standgericht), but they were acquitted by the Norwegian Supreme Court. During the past decades, research on judicial conduct in authoritarian settings has increased, and we now have quite a bit of knowledge on how judges act and their reasons for doing so. But we still have a few facts and little knowledge about the extent to which they are made to answer for these acts.

Methodological Considerations

Most of the few available cases are still from the aftermath of Nazi Germany and World War II. This means that the cases are marked by their postwar setting: the military tribunals employed international law on war crimes and crimes against humanity, and national procedures took place in a settling of the accounts with wartime collaborators and traitors. This limits the consequences that can be drawn from the cases to transitory justice issues in other contexts. Also the development of international law and human rights law limits the validity of cases from the 1940s and 1950s in the present setting. There now are highly refined standards by which to judge judicial conduct, independent from the national law that judges employ. How these standards should play out in the questions of criminal and civil liabilities of individual judges under international and national laws must, however, remain a field of speculation, given the lack of cases and other legal materials.

The legal situation is therefore that the amount of positive legal sources is limited. Apart from a few national cases, the most important source is still the US Military Tribunal Justice Case. Surprisingly, given its central importance for the criminal responsibility of officials of the law, the literature on this case is scant. It

[3] See Pereira (2005), location 2317.

[4] See Nøkleby (1996), pp. 177–178.

was more or less ignored in Germany.[5] A few articles have been written in English, which has become the focus of increased attention in the recent years, but it has hardly been analysed from a doctrinal point of view.[6]

The tenet that no one should be punished for an act that is not made punishable by law at the time it is committed—*nulla poene sin lege*—is a central principle of the rule of law. To a survey like this, it means that liability in municipal law can only be established through an investigation of the legal sources in each and every body of national law. What a general survey like the present can show is models for how to establish such liability, arguments against the most common reservations that are employed to reject responsibility, and examples of how these reservations are overcome. The actual conclusion in each jurisdiction must, however, be drawn on the basis of specific national sources. This study then, on the judicial responsibility under municipal law, can be seen as a study *de lege ferenda*, how the law ought to be, and *de sententia ferenda*, how the judges who are called upon to decide on the responsibility should reason in the case that national law gives them a scope of discretion.

The Counterarguments

The basic arguments against holding judges responsible for upholding and applying oppressive law are the following: if what the judge does is legal at the time, later legislators and courts should not judge him according to their new standards. For sanctions to be applied, a legal rule needs to be broken. And even if one should hold that a judge in an objective sense has broken some rule based on the rule of law, one should not punish a judge who has only been performing his function in the best possible way. In these cases, there is not the necessary criminal intent present for punishment to be applied. A judge who applies the law such as it is enacted by the legislator in power is bound by his role as a judge to enforce this law. In a sense, he is acting under an obligation. Any society needs judges, and the rule of law requires that judges can perform their function independently from any outside pressure. This also demands that judges are not later brought to answer for their judicial decisions. Immunity for judges is therefore a necessary part of the rule of law, not least in oppressive settings.

The answer to all these objections is that judges should be held responsible for enforcing laws that flagrantly infringe human rights and thereby commit substantial and obvious infringements of individual rights. That such acts are crimes is well established in international law, both in customary law and in the Rome Statute of

---

[5] It was presented by Radbruch (1948), pp. 57/58–63/64 and by Bader (1948), pp. 40–43. Fifty years later, the judgment and its reception were presented by Perels (1997).

[6] Notable are Lippman (1997–1998), Wilke (2009), and Fraser (2012). It also was presented and commented by Sands (2008).

the International Court of Criminal Justice. In most national legal orders, even criminal statutes can be interpreted in light of long-established principles of justice and in light of international human rights without violating basic principles of the rule of law. This means that it is possible to interpret national prohibitions against murder, deprivation of liberty, and other offences against the individual so that they override legislation passed by a regime that demands such obvious infringements.

Anyone arguing that he subjectively thought that substantial and obvious infringements of individual rights would go unpunished if the power relations changed can hardly be taken seriously. One can never commit gross violations of human rights with the legitimate expectation that one will not be punished, and the law should not protect such an expectation. Not even judicial immunity should offer this protection. Judicial immunity is important, not for the benefit of the individual judge but for the benefit of the rule of law. It must therefore not be construed in such a way as to become an obstacle to the rule of law and a protection of those who break it down.

Judges as Culprits

We often picture judges under oppressive regimes as "blood judges" who in flagrant violation of all standards of justice and due process meet out draconic measures on their hapless victims. And such judges certainly exist—the most notorious example being the Nazi legal official and judge Roland Freisler. As president of the Nazi People's Court, he personally presided over scores of cases where the defendants were mocked and harassed and sentenced to death. Killed in an American Air raid over Berlin in 1944, he never had to stand trial for his misdeeds. But most judges of the Nazi judiciary were not of his kind. In its judgment over the Nazi legal system, the US Military Tribunal in the Justice Case stated:

> [The] Nazi system forced the judges into one of two categories. In the first we find the judges who still retained ideals of judicial independence and who administered justice with a measure of impartiality and moderation. Judgments which they rendered were set aside by the employment of the nullity plea and the extraordinary objection. The defendants they sentenced were frequently transferred to the Gestapo on completion of prison terms and were then shot or sent to concentration camps. The judges themselves were threatened and criticized and sometimes removed from office. In the other category were the judges who with fanatical zeal enforced the will of the Party with such severity that they experienced no difficulties and little interference from party officials.[7]

The liability of fanatics is easily settled. Misuse of the law for external purposes is never permitted on the part of a judge or a legal official, and no doctrine of legal immunity should justify immunity for malicious judicial behaviour that causes serious harm to others.[8] When a judge knowingly and willingly departs from

[7] The Justice Case (1951), p. 1025.

[8] Shaman (1990), p. 4.

legal procedure, takes a decision that is not in accordance with the facts of the case, or applies the law wrongly, few would disagree that he should be held responsible. He is committing a crime also when measured by his own legal standards. There is little to be learnt from this for others because most people do not identify with zealots and fanatics.

A far more difficult issue to decide is to what extent a judge can be held accountable for abuses by the law, which is when the law administered in a technically impeccable way leads to atrocities. This raises the much more uncomfortable issue for most of those who try to be good lawyers, keeping to the established canons of interpretation and trying their best to treat issues of fact and law in a balanced and honest way. When appreciating the role of judges in evil settings, the concern is not with the "monsters" but with the "good" judges.[9]

When a regime commits itself to oppression of its inhabitants by discrimination, deprivation of personal liberty, and even outright killings, we do not hesitate in holding those responsible accountable. We blame the persons taking the decisions and also members of police and security forces and the personnel at institutions responsible for implementing the evil measures. Once the oppressive measures are ordered and enforced by courts, they are often perceived differently.

Take for example the euthanasia programme of Nazi Germany that killed more than 70,000 people. Most would not hesitate in calling this a programme of extermination. The same characteristic is not commonly used to describe the institution of special and military courts that killed more than 35,000 people, most of them between 1941 and 1945.[10] Reportedly, only one German judge was convicted for this in the Federal Republic of Germany after the war.

Generally, representatives of oppressive regimes are not punished for violations of the basic rights of their populations by successor regimes.[11] This is even more the case with the judiciary. With few exceptions, judges are never brought to answer for their contribution to their regimes' evil or oppression. In South Africa, after apartheid, no judge consented to attend the legal hearing of the Truth Commission, and nothing was done about it. In the US Military Tribunal Justice Case at Nuremberg after the Second World War, judges were found guilty and punished—with one exception, however: all of those found guilty by the Tribunal either had been involved in policymaking and law implementation at the Ministry of Justice or had executed their judicial duties in a cruel, fanatical, and discriminatory manner. West German courts developed a standard under which it became impossible to convict judges from the Nazi regime. In East Germany, six former judges of the military courts were tried and sentenced to death in the so-called *Waldheimer-prozesse*. The nature of these proceedings was, however, such that one

---

[9] Compare Greene (1995), pp. 1122–1129.

[10] For this parallel, see Friedrich (1983), p. 13. The numbers of death sentences reported in the literature vary, and many report much higher figures. I have chosen to follow the accounting in the latest thesis on the subject of the German trials of Nazi criminals, Freudiger (2002), pp. 295–297.

[11] See Werke (2001), pp. 3001–3008.

cannot speak of ordinary trials. Due to the great number of defendants and the time allocated to the proceedings, the Tribunal did not go into the guilt of the individual defendant and the sentencing was arbitrary.[12]

The experience with the Nazi judges is not the exception to a rule. On the contrary, it is difficult to find cases where judges have been brought to account for their support and contribution to oppressive measures and tyrannical regimes. After the reunification of Germany in 1990, a few of the judges of the former GDR were tried and punished by German courts. It is these cases that mark an exception to a more general practice around the world to exonerate the judges who cease to uphold the rule of law.[13]

The collaborator trials in Norway provide some examples of judges who were convicted. The Norwegian courts convicted all those judges who had taken office in the Supreme Court and the special courts established by the Quisling regime. They were found guilty of collaboration and for contributing to the attempt to change the constitution of Norway by illegal means by accepting office and functioning as judges for the regime. The special courts were deemed illegal. Their judges who had participated in verdicts of capital punishment were therefore convicted for accessory to murder.

Apart from this, no judges, Norwegian or German, were brought to answer for their administration of oppressive laws. The same was the case in Belgium, Denmark, and the Netherlands. Judges of German courts in other occupied countries were found guilty of war crimes in cases only where they had convicted people from these countries after proceedings that did not even have the resemblance of a fair trial.

From this, it is fair to presume that judges who had not been involved in policymaking for the Nazis or in failed attempts to overturn the government were not punished for their judicial activities as long as they conducted their office in a reasonably objective way, no matter how oppressive and contrary to the basic meanings of the rule of law the positive law was. No scrutiny was made of whether the judge accepted or departed from the basic principles of accepted legal methods, whether he sought to moderate the oppressive sides of the law or whether he sought to expand them. Attempts to bring Nazi judges to justice for participating in the special Nazi courts and practising only "vestigial remnants of legal procedure which only served to mock the hapless victims", in the words of chief prosecutor for the Americans Telford Taylor, were effectively blocked by the Supreme Court of the Federal Republic of Germany. The lack of cases from around the world from other instances of transition from tyrannies to democracies suggests that the experiences of post-Nazi times are representative. Judges are not held accountable for their contribution to uphold oppression and to enforce oppressive measures.

---

[12] See Weinke (2011), p. 76.

[13] In this, I disregard the trials that were conducted in the communist countries after the war since they were conducted for other reasons than to uphold the rule of law.

Some might argue that judges are not the main perpetrators of oppression and injustice. It could be claimed that the contribution of the judicial system to the atrocities of the Nazi regime was small and that most of the crimes of the regime were committed outside of the legal scope by the SS and *Einsatzgruppen* in the extermination camps and on the Eastern Front. Even though this is true by numbers, it does not portray the role of the judges and the legal system in Nazi Germany in a correct light. During the 12 years of the Nazi regime, more than 35,000 death sentences were issued by German courts, often for mere trivialities.[14] The legal system was an integrated part and instrument of the policy of repression of the Nazis. This is illustratively expressed by the US Military Tribunal in the Justice Case: "If the judiciary could slay their thousands, why couldn't the police slay their tens of thousands?"[15] The Tribunal also states:

> That the number the defendant could wipe out within his competency was smaller than the number involved in the mass persecutions and exterminations by the leaders whom he served, does not mitigate his contribution to the program of those leaders. His acts were more terrible in that those who might have hoped for a last refuge in the institutions of justice found these institutions turned against them and a part of the program of terror and oppression.[16]

The Tribunal points to an important aspect of the social role of the judges and the courts. Courts are central to the legitimacy of any regime. No regime can survive for long "on bayonets" only. A measure of acceptance and collaboration from a majority of the population is necessary. The judicial system is crucial in the securing of this acceptance.

Who are the monsters, and who are good when the law itself is monstrous? "Good" judges also contribute to committing terrible acts; to discriminating persons on account of their race, creed, or nationality in civil and criminal laws; to sentencing accused to death for minor offences; to sending people into the claws of brutality, like under the frightful German "Night and Fog" regime, and to the legitimacy of the regime. To what extent should the fact that such acts are committed under administration of "justice under a measure of impartiality and moderation" absolve them?

If we look at the question of when a judge can be held criminally liable for his judgments, we have to take as a starting point the general conditions for responsibility under criminal law. This entails that some rule of law must be broken and the perpetrator must have had the necessary criminal state of mind when breaking the law. The act must meet both the definition of the crime (*actus reus*) and the mental elements of the crime (*mens rea*). These simple conditions for criminal liability have grappled the minds of the few courts that have been challenged with the question of bringing judges of a former regime to justice.

---

[14] See Freudiger (2002), pp. 294–297.

[15] The Justice Case (1951), p. 1086.

[16] The Justice Case (1951), pp. 1155–1156.

The role of the judiciary is so central to the concept of law that law is even defined by reference to the courts in significant parts of legal theory, namely the influential school of legal realism. Even in other strands of thought, the courts hold a central place in the determination of the law, through doctrines of precedent or through an acknowledgement of the place of judicial discretion in legal decision-making. How then can judges break the law when they are engaged in application and interpretation of that which is recognised as law at the time by the judiciary?

The position of the courts is such in some jurisdictions that it is hard to conceive of a judicial decision, at least from a court of last instance, of breaking the law. To this comes the fact that when we consider the role of the courts in supporting oppressive laws and regimes, we are often confronted with courts that judge according to the laws of the regime and not contrary to them. The basic problems in such cases are issues where courts follow the legislative measures and legal opinions of the ruler and thereby cease to protect the rule of law and contribute to its undermining. How can judges in such cases fulfil the requirement of illegality that is necessary to find them guilty of a criminal offence?

This question has different answers in different settings. From the viewpoint of international law, the legality of judicial decisions can be viewed from a polycentric perspective—what is legal from a municipal point of view may be illegal when seen from the international point of view. The question may also come up after a failed coup or takeover of power where the old regime is re-established. In such cases, the legality of the acts of the revolutionaries will be determined by the laws of the old regime and often be regarded as acts of treason. Again, a different setting is found in a transition from one regime to another, where both are regarded as legal. It is in such cases that it is particularly difficult to establish an external reference by which to judge oppressive measures independently from the ones used by the regime itself. But it is also under these circumstances that this question is at its most pressing: how do we deal with the guardians of the rule of law when they themselves fail and leave the gates open for oppression and tyranny?

References

Bader KS (1948) Das Urteil im Nürnberger Juristenprozeß. Deutsche Rechts-Zeitschrift 40–43

Fraser D (2012) Evil law, evil lawyers? From the justice case to the torture memos. Jurisprudence 3(2):391–428

Freudiger K (2002) Die juristische Aufarbeitung von NS-Verbrechen. Mohr Siebeck, Tübingen

Friedrich J (1983) Freispruch für die Nazi Justiz Die Urteile gegen NS-Richter seit 1948 Eine Dokumentation. Rowolt Taschenbuchverlag, Hamburg

Greene NL (1995) A perspective on "Nazis in the Courtroom". Brooklyn Law Rev 61:1122–1129

Lippman M (1997–1998) The prosecution of Josef Altstoetter et al.: law, lawyers and justice in the Third Reich. Dickinson J Int Law 16:343–433

Nøkleby B (1996) Skutt blir den ... Tysk bruk av dødsstraff i Norge 1940–1945. Gyldendal Norsk Forlag, Oslo

Pereira AW (2005) Political (in)justice authoritarianism and the rule of law in Brazil, Chile and Argentina. University of Pittsburgh Press, Pittsburgh (Kindle edition)

Perels J (1997) Der Nürnberger Juristenprozess im Kontext der Nachkriegsgeschichte, Vortrag gehalten am 4.12.1997 in der Johann-Wolfgang-Goethe Universität Frankfurt/Main

Radbruch G (1948) Des Reichministeriums Ruhm und Ende, Zum Nürnberger Juristenurteil. Süddeutsche Juristenzeitung col. 64

Sands P (2008) Torture team deception, cruelty and the compromise of law. Penguin, London

Shaman JM (1990) Judicial immunity from civil and criminal liability. San Diego Law Rev 27 (12):4

Trials of War Criminals before the Nuremberg Military Tribunals, vol III, the Justice Case, Washington, 1951

Weinke A (2011) Ehemalige Wehrmachtrichter in der SBZ/DDR Elitenaustausch und verhinderte Aufarbeitung. In: Perels J, og Wette W (Hg.) Mit Reinem Gewissen Wehrmachtsrichter in der Bundesrepublik und ihre Opfer. Aufbau Verlag, Berlin

Werke G (2001) Rückwirkungsverbot und Staatskriminalität. Neue Juristische Wochenschrift 3001–3008

Wilke C (2009) Reconsecrating the temple of justice: invocations of civilization and humanity in the Nuremberg Justice Case. Can J Law Soc 24:181–201

Chapter 7
The Condition of Illegality Under International Law

The Legal Basis for the Allied War Crimes Tribunals

The basic definitions of crimes from the bench under international law were established by the US Military Tribunal in the Justice Case after the Second World War. Allied war crime tribunals based themselves on international law, and the judges were accused of the same crimes as other war criminals. The legal basis for the International Tribunal was the London Agreement of 8 August 1945, establishing the Charter of the International Military Tribunal. Article 6 of the Charter gave the Tribunal jurisdiction to rule on the individual responsibility for crimes against peace, war crimes, and crimes against humanity. Articles 7 and 8 stated that the official position of defendants or the fact that the defendant acted pursuant to orders should not be seen as freeing them of responsibility. In order to establish a uniform legal basis in Germany for the prosecution of war criminals and other similar offenders, other than those dealt with by the International Military Tribunal, the Control Council, 20 December 1945, enacted the Control Council Law No. 10. The law recognised the acts of crimes against peace, war crimes, and crimes against humanity as crimes and gave jurisdiction to deal with individual defendants. This law was the direct legal basis for the US Military Tribunal in the Justice Case.

Much has been written on the discussion on the legitimacy of basing indictments and convictions on international law, and I will not go into this discussion here.[1] Today, the individual responsibility and criminal liability for breaches of international law are well established, both in customary law and in the Rome Statute of the International Criminal Court with wide recognition, and it is also well established that such cases can be tried both by international courts and tribunals and by national courts.

---

[1] For a recent contribution, see Fraser (2012).

H.P. Graver, *Judges Against Justice*, DOI 10.1007/978-3-662-44293-7_7

The US Military Tribunal Justice Case

The Justice Case comprises the most comprehensive discussion on possible charges against judges and other legal officials yet to be found in any judicial act. The Tribunal judged crimes under international law: membership of a criminal organisation, war of aggression, war crimes, and crimes against humanity. Even when assessing the criminal responsibility of German citizens for crimes against German nationals, the Tribunal made clear that its evaluation was not in any way based on national law or jurisdiction:

> In declaring that the expressed determination of the victors to punish German officials who slaughtered their own nationals is in harmony with international principles of justice, we usurp no power; we only take judicial notice of the declarations already made by the chief executives of the United States and her former Allies. The fact that C. C. Law 10 on the face of it is limited to the punishment of German criminals does not transform this tribunal into a German court. The fact that the four powers are exercising supreme legislative authority in governing Germany and for the punishment of German criminals does not mean that the jurisdiction of this Tribunal rests in the slightest degree upon any German law, prerogative, or sovereignty. We sit as a Tribunal drawing its sole power and jurisdiction from the will and command of the four occupying Powers.[2]

This is in line with the finding of the Military Tribunal in the Ministries Case against 21 defendants charged with criminal conduct arising principally out of their functions as officials of the Reich government.[3] The Tribunal dismissed the charge against the defendants in this case "of the commission of atrocities and offenses against German nationals, including murder, extermination, ill treatment, enslavement, imprisonment, plundering and looting of property, and other persecutions and inhumane acts, committed on political, racial, and religious grounds" committed in the years 1933–1939 on the ground that they had not been committed in relation to war crimes or crimes against the peace. According to the Tribunal, "crimes against humanity perpetrated by a government against its own nationals" were at the time not of themselves crimes against international law and were in "urgent need of comprehensive legislation by the family of nations, with respect to individual human rights".[4] This legal situation is important to keep in mind when judging by the standards of today since such acts are also crimes under present international law when they are committed without any relation to international conflict.

Part of the indictment against many of the defendants in the Justice Case was membership in criminal organisations. Certain groups of the Leadership Corps, the SS, the Gestapo, and the SD were declared to be criminal organisations by the judgment of the first International Military Tribunal, and this ruling was followed by the military tribunal in the Justice Case. The fact that many judges and

---

[2] The Justice Case (1951), p. 964.

[3] The Ministries Case, Trials of War Criminals Before the Nuremberg Military Tribunals, vol. XII–XV, Nuremberg 1946–1949.

[4] The Ministries Case, vol. XIII, p. 117.

prominent lawyers had membership in criminal organisations is illustrative of the role of lawyers and legal legitimation in the Nazi regime, but it does not pertain specifically to their role as judges.

The defendants were accused of participating in war crimes in their roles as leading officials in the Ministry of Justice and as prosecutors and judges in the German legal system. Naturally, some forms of war crimes were more relevant to their activities than others. In particular, the Military Tribunal emphasises "ill treatment or deportation to slave labor or for any other purpose, of civilian population from occupied territory".[5] Of specific importance in this respect was the development and execution of the "Night and Fog" programme, whereby civilians of occupied countries accused of alleged crimes in resistance activities against German occupying forces were spirited away for secret trial by special courts in Germany by order of the Ministry of Justice. The victim's whereabouts, trial, and subsequent disposition were kept completely secret, thus serving the dual purpose of terrorising the victim's relatives and associates and barring recourse to evidence, witnesses, or counsel for defence. If the accused was acquitted, or convicted, after serving his sentence, he was handed over to the Gestapo for "protective custody" for the duration of the war. These proceedings resulted in the torture, ill treatment, and murder of thousands of persons. According to the findings of the Military Tribunal:

> The trials of the accused NN [*Nacht und Nebel*, i.e. Night and Fog] persons did not approach even a semblance of fair trial or justice. The accused NN persons were arrested and secretly transported to Germany and other countries for trial. They were held incommunicado. In many instances they were denied the right to introduce evidence, to be confronted by witnesses against them, or to present witnesses in their own behalf. They were tried secretly and denied the right of counsel of their own choice, and occasionally denied the aid of any counsel. No indictment was served in many instances and the accused learned only a few moments before the trial of the nature of the alleged crime for which he was to be tried. The entire proceedings from beginning to end were secret and no public record was allowed to be made of them.[6]

Crimes against humanity consisted of acts of "murder, extermination, enslavement, deportation, and other inhumane acts committed against any civilian population, before or during the war; or persecutions on political, racial or religious grounds in execution of or in connection with any crime within the jurisdiction of the Tribunal, whether or not in violation of the domestic law of the country where perpetrated".[7] An important aspect of this charge was that it was irrelevant to the charge whether the acts were committed against the population of occupied territories or against own nationals. Acts that were war crimes when committed against people of occupied territories could be crimes against humanity when committed against their own population:

---

[5] The Justice Case (1951), p. 972.

[6] The Justice Case (1951), pp. 1046–1047.

[7] The Justice Case (1951), p. 972.

> The evidence conclusively establishes the adoption and application of systematic government-organized and approved procedures amounting to atrocities and offenses of the kind made punishable by C. C. Law 10 and committed against "populations" and amounting to persecution on racial grounds. These procedures when carried out in occupied territory constituted war crimes and crimes against humanity. When enforced in the Alt Reich against German nationals they constituted crimes against humanity.[8]

In addition to persecution and discrimination of own nationals on racial grounds, political persecution could also be regarded as a crime against humanity. In characterising the proceedings against Count Montgelas in April 1945 by a drum-head Court Martial, the Military Tribunal stated:

> It is provided in C. C. Law 10 that persecutions on political as well as racial grounds are recognized as crimes. While the mere fact alone that Montgelas was prosecuted for remarks hostile to the Nazi regime may not constitute a violation of C. C. Law 10, the circumstances under which the defendant was brought to trial and the manner in which he was tried convince us that Montgelas was not convicted for undermining the already collapsed defensive strength of the defeated nation, but on the contrary, that the law was deliberately invoked by Gauleiter Holz and enforced by Oeschey as a last vengeful act of political persecution. If the provisions of C. C. Law 10 do not cover this case, we do not know what kind of political persecution it would cover.[9]

The Count had made insulting remarks concerning Hitler, among others, to the effect that his true name was Schickelgruber. He also expressed approval of the attempt upon Hitler's life on 20 July 1944. He was sentenced to death by the Court Martial and shot.

A particular aspect of crimes against humanity is where acts were part of the extermination of a whole group of people, genocide, and where the acts were part of a systematic discrimination of a group. In particular, the treatment of Poles and Jews formed an important part of the Justice Trial.

The law against Poles and Jews was rigorously enforced by the judicial system. Poles and Jews convicted of specific crimes were subjected to different types of punishment from that imposed upon Germans who had committed the same crimes. Their rights as defendants in court were severely circumscribed. Courts were empowered to impose death sentences on Poles and Jews even where such punishment was not prescribed by law if the evidence showed "particularly objectionable motives". And, finally, the police was given carte blanche to punish all "criminal" acts committed by Jews without any employment of the judicial process. Judges were found to distort and then apply "the laws and decrees against Poles and Jews as such in disregard of every principle of judicial behavior".[10]

Several of the accused invoked in their defence that they had acted in an official capacity in accordance with national law at the time. This defence was rejected by the Military Tribunal. Legality or illegality under municipal law was seen as irrelevant to the question of whether international law was broken or not. The Tribunal based its rejection of this defence on the legal basis for the proceedings:

---

[8] The Justice Case (1951), p. 1081.

[9] The Justice Case (1951), p. 1164.

[10] The Justice Case (1951), p. 1063.

> The argument that compliance with German law is a defense to the charge rests on a misconception of the basic theory which supports our entire proceedings. The Nuremberg Tribunals are not German courts. They are not enforcing German law. The charges are not based on violation by the defendants of German law. On the contrary, the jurisdiction of this Tribunal rests on international authority. It enforces the law as declared by the IMT Charter and C. C. Law 10, and within the limitations on the power conferred, it enforces international law as superior in authority to any German statute or decree. It is true, as defendants contend, that German courts under the Third Reich were required to follow German law (i.e., the expressed will of Hitler) even when it was contrary to international law. But no such limitation can be applied to this Tribunal. Here we have the paramount substantive law, plus a Tribunal authorized and required to apply it notwithstanding the inconsistent provisions of German local law.[11]

In its evaluation of the guilt of Ernst Lautz, who had served as a prosecutor at the People's Court, the Military Tribunal rejected national law as a defence with the following words:

> Lautz was not active in Party matters. He resisted all efforts of Party officials to influence his conduct but yielded to influence and guidance from Hitler through the Reich Ministry of Justice, believing that to be required under German law. He was a stern man and a relentless prosecutor, but it may be said in his favor that if German law were a defense, which it is not, many of his acts would be excusable.[12]

On the contrary, enforcement of national laws did, as such, form the very breach of international law. The following passage from the Tribunal makes this point clear:

> We have pointed out that governmental participation is a material element of the crime against humanity. Only when official organs of sovereignty participated in atrocities and persecutions did those crimes assume international proportions. It can scarcely be said that governmental participation, the proof of which is necessary for conviction, can also be a defense to the charge.[13]

An important consequence of the legal basis applied by the Military Tribunal is that the defendants were not punished for the breakdown of the rule of law as such. This is specifically set out by the Tribunal. First, it sets out a catalogue over the type of cases where the Nazi courts imposed the death penalty in the course of their functioning:

> The prosecution has introduced captured documents in great number which establish the draconic character of the Nazi criminal laws and prove that the death penalty was imposed by courts in thousands of cases. Cases in which the extreme penalty was imposed may in large measure be classified in the following groups:
>
> 1. Cases against habitual criminals.
> 2. Cases of looting in the devastated areas of Germany; committed after air raids and under cover of black-out.
> 3. Crimes against the war economy – rationing, hoarding, and the like.

---

[11] The Justice Case (1951), p. 984.

[12] The Justice Case (1951), p. 1128.

[13] The Justice Case (1951), p. 984.

4. Crimes amounting to an undermining of the defensive strength of the nation; defeatist remarks, criticisms of Hitler, and the like.
5. Crimes of treason and high treason.
6. Crimes of various types committed by Poles, Jews, and other foreigners.
7. Crimes committed under the Nacht und Nebel program, and similar procedures.[14]

Then it proceeds to a discussion, which it summarises in the following way:

> All of the laws to which we have referred could be and were applied in a discriminatory manner and in the case of many, the Ministry of Justice and the courts enforced them by arbitrary and brutal means, shocking to the conscience of mankind and punishable here. We merely hold that under the particular facts of this case we cannot convict any defendant merely because of the fact, without more, that laws of the first four types were passed or enforced.
>
> A different situation is presented when we consider the cases which fall within types 5, 6, and 7.[15]

In this, the Tribunal established that it would not convict any defendant merely because of the fact, without more, that he participated in the passing or enforcement of laws for the punishment of habitual criminals, looters, hoarders, or those guilty of undermining the defensive strength of the nation. On the other hand, an arbitrary and brutal enforcement of these laws "shocking to the conscience of mankind" was punishable.[16]

The Acquittal of Nazi Judges

In the Justice Case, 16 persons were indicted, and of these four were acquitted. Most of the defendants were former leading officials of the Nazi Ministry of Justice. Six of them had only been active as judges and/or prosecutors: Paul Barnickel and Ernst Lautz, senior public prosecutors at the People's Court; Günther Nebelung, Chief Justice of the People's Court; Judge Herman Cuhorst; Oswald Rothaug, prosecutor and judge; and Hans Petersen, a lay judge at the People's Court. The defendants, Barnickel, Petersen, Nebelung, and Cuhorst, were found not guilty under the counts charged against them. Rothaug was sentenced to life for crimes against humanity, Lautz to 10 years' imprisonment.

Oswald Rothaug was sentenced to life in prison based on his activities as a judge. He received the severest punishment meted out in the Justice Case trial, together with three others of the accused. He was found guilty solely on the count of crimes against humanity. He was a member of the Party Leadership Corps, but he was acquitted on the count of membership of criminal organisations. He was therefore the only defendant who was sentenced for crimes committed solely in the courtroom.

---

[14] The Justice Case (1951), p. 1025.

[15] The Justice Case (1951), p. 1027.

[16] The Justice Case (1951), p. 1165.

His attitude of virulent hostility towards Poles and Jews was proven from many sources. According to a testimony, Rothaug believed in severe measures against foreigners and particularly against Poles and Jews, who he held should be treated differently from German transgressors. Rothaug felt that there was a gap in the law in this respect, and he asserted that in his own court he achieved this discrimination by interpretation of existing laws but that other courts failed to do so. Such a gap, according to Rothaug, should be closed by singling out Poles and Jews for special treatment.[17]

As an example, the Tribunal cites a case presided by Rothaug where two Polish girls—one, 17 years of age, the other somewhat older—were accused of starting a fire in an armament plant in Bayreuth. This alleged fire did not do any material damage to the plant, but they were in the vicinity when it started and were arrested and interrogated by the Gestapo. In the view of the Tribunal, based on the evidence, these two young women did not have what amounted to a trial at all but were executed because they were Polish nationals, in conformity with the Nazi plan of persecution and extermination.[18] In a case where he sentenced a Polish farmhand to death for sexually assaulting the farmer's wife, he stated:

> Thus, the defendant gives the impression of a thoroughly degenerate personality, which is marked by excitability and a definite trend to mendacity, or to lying. The whole inferiority of the defendant, I would say, lies in the sphere of character and is obviously based on his being a part of Polish subhumanity, or in his belonging to Polish subhumanity.[19]

To Rothaug's defence that he was merely administering the law as a judge, the Tribunal remarked:

> Despite protestations that his judgments were based solely upon evidence introduced in court, we are firmly convinced that in numberless cases Rothaug's opinions were formed and decisions made, and in many instances publicly or privately announced before the trial had even commenced and certainly before it was concluded. He was in constant contact with his confidential assistant Elkar, a member of the criminal SD, who sat with him in weekly conferences in the chambers of the court. He formed his opinions from dubious records submitted to him before trial. By his manner and methods he made his court an instrumentality of terror and won the fear and hatred of the population. From the evidence of his closest associates as well as his victims, we find that Oswald Rothaug represented in Germany the personification of the secret Nazi intrigue and cruelty. He was and is a sadistic and evil man. Under any civilized judicial system he could have been impeached and removed from office or convicted of malfeasance in office on account of the scheming malevolence with which he administered injustice.[20]

Ernst Lautz served as Chief Public Prosecutor at the People's Court in Berlin from 20 September 1939 until the end of the war. He joined the NSDAP in May 1933. During the period of his service, the "higher officials" under his supervision increased from 25 to about 70. Lautz was sentenced to 10 years' imprisonment. He

---

[17] The Justice Case (1951), p. 1145.

[18] The Justice Case (1951), pp. 1146–1147.

[19] The Justice Case (1951), p. 1149.

[20] The Justice Case (1951), p. 1156.

was found criminally implicated in enforcing the law against Poles and Jews, which the Tribunal deemed to be a part of the established governmental plan for the extermination of those races. He was thereby an accessory to, and took a consenting part in, the crime of genocide. The Tribunal also found him guilty of contributing to the "Night and Fog" programme. The Court remarked in measuring out the sentence:

> There is much to be said in mitigation of punishment. Lautz was not active in Party matters. He resisted all efforts of Party officials to influence his conduct but yielded to influence and guidance from Hitler through the Reich Ministry of Justice, believing that to be required under German law. He was a stern man and a relentless prosecutor, but it may be said in his favor that if German law were a defence, which it is not, many of his acts would be excusable.[21]

The other four judges and prosecutor were acquitted. One of them was the president of the Special Court of Stuttgart, Herman Cuhorst. Cuhorst was, according to one of the defenders at the Court, a "prototype of a Nazi judge", and there was ample evidence before the Tribunal on the "arbitrariness, unfairness and lack of judicial conduct" of his proceedings.[22] The examination of such crimes was outside the scope of the Military Tribunal:

> No defendant is specifically charged in the indictment with the murder or abuse of any particular person. If he were, the indictment would, no doubt, name the alleged victim. Simple murder and isolated instances of atrocities do not constitute the gravamen of the charge. Defendants are charged with crimes of such immensity that mere specific instances of criminality appear insignificant by comparison. The charge, in brief, is that of conscious participation in a nation-wide government-organized system of cruelty and injustice, in violation of the laws of war and of humanity, and perpetrated in the name of law by the authority of the Ministry of Justice, and through the instrumentality of the courts. The dagger of the assassin was concealed beneath the robe of the jurist.[23]

The Justice Trial concerned crimes under international law: membership of a criminal organisation, war of aggression, war crimes, and crimes against humanity. The Tribunal considered whether the use of death penalty as an instrument of terror against the population constituted a crime against humanity and rejected it with the following reasons:

> Do those Draconic laws or the decisions rendered under them constitute war crimes or crimes against humanity?
>
> Concerning the punishment of habitual criminals, we think the answer is clear. In many civilized states statutory provisions require the courts to impose sentences of life imprisonment upon proof of conviction of three or more felonies. We are unable to say in one breath that life imprisonment for habitual criminals is a salutary and reasonable punishment in America in peace times, but that the imposition of the death penalty was a crime against humanity in Germany when the nation was in the throes of war. The same considerations apply largely in the case of looting. Every nation recognizes the absolute necessity of more stringent enforcement of the criminal law in times of great emergency. Anyone who has

---

[21] The Justice Case (1951), p. 1128.

[22] See Schorn (1959), pp. 113–114.

[23] The Justice Case (1951), pp. 984–985.

> seen the utter devastation of the great cities of Germany must realize that the safety of the civilian population demanded that the werewolves who roamed the streets of the burning cities, robbing the dead, and plundering the ruined homes should be severely punished. The same considerations apply, though in a lesser degree, to prosecutions to hoarders and violators of war economy decrees.
>
> Questions of far greater difficulty are involved when we consider the cases involving punishment for undermining military efficiency. The limitations on freedom of speech which were imposed in the enforcement of these laws are revolting to our sense of justice. A court would have no hesitation in condemning them under any free constitution, including that of the Weimar Republic, if the limitations were applied in time of peace; but even under the protection of the Constitution of the United States a citizen is not wholly free to attack the Government or to interfere with its military aims in time of war. In the face of a real and present danger, freedom of speech may be somewhat restricted even in America. Can we then say that in the throes of total war and in the presence of impending disaster those officials who enforced these savage laws in a last desperate effort to stave off defeat were guilty of crimes against humanity?[24]

With this reasoning, the Tribunal in many ways gave support to the notion of the German reaction after the war that the Nazi judges for the most were only applying the law of the land under difficult times, and they were not to blame for the legal atrocities.

References

Fraser D (2012) Evil law, evil lawyers? From the justice case to the torture memos. Jurisprudence 3(2):391–428

Schorn H (1959) Der Richter im Dritten Reich Geschichte und Dokumente. Vittorio Klostermann, Frankfurt am Main

Trials of War Criminals before the Nuremberg Military Tribunals, vol III, the Justice Case, Washington, 1951

[24] The Justice Case (1951), p. 1026.

Chapter 8
The Condition of Illegality and Failed Usurpations

Judges and Revolution

When judges participate in a coup d'état or serve the leaders of such an attempt to establish a new regime, establishing the legal basis for holding them accountable is more straightforward. The revolutionaries can be held accountable according to the law of the regime that they tried to overthrow, which made their acts illegal at the time. To the extent that the revolutionaries establish new institutions such as special courts and tribunals, they will lack legitimacy, and their decisions need not be regarded as an exercise of judicial functions. In practice, though, they often are.

The issue of the legality of rebel courts was put before the United States Supreme Court after the civil war.[1] The question arose in the context of a suit for compensation by a person who had been arrested and charged with treason in the District Court of the Confederate States of America for the Northern District of Alabama. The US Supreme Court ruled that the arrest had been illegal since the "Confederate States" were rebels without the power to establish courts of law on the territory of the United States. Justice Swayne stated:

> The act of the Confederate Congress creating the tribunal in question was void. It was as if it were not. The court was a nullity, and could exercise no rightful jurisdiction. The forms of law with which it clothed its proceedings gave no protection to those who, assuming to be its officers, were the instruments by which it acted.

According to this view, persons who accept office in courts established by rebels are accomplices to the rebellion and cannot be accepted as officials of a system of justice. The same view was taken by the Norwegian courts regarding judges who had accepted appointment to the special courts established by the Quisling regime under the German occupation.

[1] Hickman v. Jones, 76 U.S. 9 Wall. 197 (1869).

H.P. Graver, *Judges Against Justice*, DOI 10.1007/978-3-662-44293-7_8

The situation of the collaboration of judges in the existing courts that are taken over by the revolutionaries is more complicated. These are already judges by virtue of the established constitution. Their acts can therefore not be dismissed offhand as nonjudicial, even if they are administrating laws passed by the rebelling regime. The courts will continue to exercise their normal functions to the extent that it is possible under the circumstances and may even be forced to apply and enforce laws issued by the revolutionaries. Sound arguments can be made for the holding of the courts outside of the conflict between the competing contenders of power over the state and not forcing them to choose sides. Lord Pearce put the argument in this way in his dissenting view in Madzimbamuto v. Lardner-Burke on the obligations of the judges in Rhodesia after the coup by the Smith government:

> The practical factual situation in Rhodesia is this. The judges lawfully appointed under the 1961 constitution and representing its judicial power, have been entrusted by both sides with the duty of continuing to sit. They have continued to sit as judges under the 1961 Constitution although the country is in the control of an illegal government which does not acknowledge or obey that Constitution and does not acknowledge any right of appeal to their Lordships' Board. This is an uneasy compromise which has been adopted by both sides from, no doubt, a consideration of many factors. The primary reason, one presumes, is the reasonable and humane desire of preserving law and order and avoiding chaos which would work great hardship on the citizens of all races and which would incidentally damage that part of the realm to the detriment of whoever is ultimately successful. This would accord with the common sense view expressed by Grotius [above]. For this reason it is clearly desirable to keep the courts out of the main area of dispute, so that, whatever be [sic.] the political battle, and whatever be [sic.] the sanctions or other pressures employed to end the rebellion, the courts can carry on their peaceful tasks of protecting the fabric of society and maintaining law and order.[2]

A difficult question under such circumstances is where the line goes "between merely keeping office in order to administer to the current needs of the population and action which implicitly involves recognition of the invader's title", as well as "what is the form and style of obedience which reflects acknowledgment of the power of coercion but avoids any move towards helping to transform naked power into authority?"[3]

Judges Under Foreign Occupation

Trials in occupied countries were based on the national law of each country. In the postwar trials outside of Germany, punishing collaborators was, by far, a much larger task and priority than punishing Germans, and the large number of charges concerned treason and collaboration with the enemy.[4] These offences also applied

---

[2] Madzimbamuto v. Lardner-Burke [1969] 1 AC 645.

[3] Kirchheimer (1961), pp. 315–316.

[4] See Pendas (2009).

to judges and other members of the legal profession. In Belgium, 29 judges were under investigation during the purges of Nazis in public service after the war and five were convicted for political collaboration.[5] In Denmark, three judges were punished for collaboration.[6] In Luxembourg, the Germans reorganised the courts. All but two of the judges joined the Nazi Party. The rulings of the courts were not recognised as rulings by Luxembourg courts after the war, with all the judgments rendered nonexistent by a Grand Ducal Decree. Disciplinary procedures were initiated against 19 judges, but the files have subsequently been lost, and the outcomes are unknown.[7]

In the Netherlands, the exiled government, upon its return, distrusted the courts because of their record during the occupation and appointed special courts to undertake the purge of Nazis and collaborators. All judges appointed under the German occupation were suspended. The members of the Supreme Court short of one were suspended too. After the suspension was lifted, the Minister of Justice wrote a letter to the Supreme Court criticising it for its actions during the occupation and requested the voluntary resignation of the judges. The justices refused on the ground that their resignation would be "contrary to (their) conscientiously conducted policy during the occupation and not solve the problem".[8] Negotiations between the Court and the government resulted in the establishment of a purge authority to purge the prewar members of the courts. The Supreme Court received an organisation of the purges that ensured that it would not have to go through the purge procedure and that respected the independence of the prewar appointees as much as possible.

The special tribunal that was established conducted 16 investigations. It dismissed four judges and ended the proceeding without taking any measures in 11 cases.

The president of the Supreme Court under the occupation, who had been appointed by the Germans, was indicted and convicted for his failure to support the spirit of resistance. Apart from this case, there do not seem to have been any convictions of judges for their ex officio acts under German occupation in Belgium, Denmark, Luxembourg, or the Netherlands. In all these countries, judges appointed during the occupation were suspended and only reinstated after a screening. They were not, however, sanctioned for having accepted appointment as judges.

In Norway, there were particularly two provisions of the General Criminal Act that formed the fundamental basis for the legal purges after the occupation: § 86 of the criminal code against collaboration with the enemy and § 98 against attempts to change the constitution by illegal means.

In the trial against Vidkun Quisling, the Supreme Court determined that he was guilty on both these counts. He and his party had consciously used the German

[5] Michielsen (2004), p. 232.

[6] Tamm (1984), p. 570.

[7] Michielsen (2004), pp. 235–241.

[8] Michielsen (2004), p. 249.

occupation as a means to establish themselves as rulers with the aim of transforming Norway into a National Socialist state. This was, of course, contrary to the constitution of Norway and at the same time an aid to both the military and political aims of the enemy. Membership in the National Socialist Party was considered sufficient to establish a violation on both counts.

The Quisling administration established a People's Court and special courts after the German model. Quisling also had the opportunity to appoint a new Supreme Court since the existing Supreme Court judges resigned from their positions over the controversy surrounding the composition of the courts and the right to judicial review of orders issued by the German occupying authorities. After the war, members of these courts were brought to trial for collaboration with the enemy and for seeking to assist in changing the Norwegian constitution by illegal means. Acceptance of office in the courts established by the Nazis and in the Supreme Court after the resignation of its judges was considered collaboration, and they were all convicted.

In the collaboration trials, judges who had accepted office in the special courts established by Quisling were convicted not only of collaboration but also for the effects of their judgments. The system of special courts was established outside of the regular court system, with no basis in international law or in the constitution, in order to further the treasonous goals of the illegal regime. As a general rule, members of the special courts set up by the Nazis in Norway were convicted not only of collaboration but also of murder, where death penalties were passed and executed.[9] This means that the courts found both that the formal basis for the judgments of the special courts was illegal and that members of the courts were not allowed any defence of judicial privilege.

In this way, one can say that the Norwegian judges who collaborated with the regime were treated differently and according to a more severe standard than that of their German counterparts. The legal rules that were used as grounds for the trials in the special courts, whether German or Norwegian, all had to have their formal basis in the international rules of the rights of an occupying power, and the evaluation of the independence and soundness of the judicial proceedings of the special court should be independent of the nationality of the judges participating and of the municipal law establishing the grounds for the special courts. A German could, of course, not be accused or convicted of collaboration, but it is not self-evident that this fact should have relevance to the question of whether issuing a death sentence after judicial proceedings in a special court should make the prosecutor or the judge guilty of murder or not. The Norwegian courts were here in line with the US Military Tribunal and other national courts in not regarding it as a crime for a German judge to participate in a special court set up by the Nazi legislator, even though the proceedings were summary and the measures draconian, as long as the rulings did not amount to war crimes or crimes against humanity.[10]

---

[9] See Andenæs (1979), p. 198.

[10] See further Chap. 10.

Although the conclusion of the Norwegian courts of the illegality of participating in special courts must be understood in the special light of the war and the occupation, the reasoning on treason as attempt to change the constitution by illegal means, in principle, also applies to a purely internal situation, where a group seizes power over the state by illegal means. Contributing to the protection of such a regime by accepting appointment to special courts to deal with political crimes and subversion would, by this line of cases, be illegal and a criminal offence in Norway, even when they apply rules that are in force before the coup. Rebel courts are not courts, and their decisions are therefore not judgments according to this case law. Subsequently, their use of force is indistinguishable from any other use of force not sanctioned by legitimate state authorities.

Of special interest is the dealing with those judges who accepted service as judges in the Norwegian Supreme Court during the occupation. The ordinary members of the Supreme Court, appointed before the occupation, all collectively resigned from their posts in a letter to the Minister of Justice, dated 18 December 1940.[11] The Supreme Court was restocked with jurists who were willing to accept the position in the new Supreme Court. After the war, all of these persons were charged and convicted both on the charge of collaboration and on the charge of seeking to assist in changing the Norwegian constitution by illegal means. The first case was against the president of the Supreme Court during the occupation, Jacob Andreas Mohr.[12] Mohr was a justice at the City Court of Oslo when he was approached in December 1940 by the Minister of Justice and asked to take the office as president of the Supreme Court. He accepted this appointment and was assigned immediately.

A unanimous Supreme Court found Mohr guilty both of collaboration and of treason. Supreme Court Justice Berger stated that the clear intention of the Germans and Quisling in 1940 was that the Supreme Court should cooperate with the Quisling Party and the Germans and that the appointment of new judges was a major element in the fight against the Norwegian resistance. As to the count of coup d'état, Berger stated that the Supreme Court collaborated with Quisling, and Quisling's intent to change the constitution of Norway by illegal means was clear from the beginning. By accepting appointment to this court, Mohr contributed to substituting the legal judges, who had resigned from their offices for reasons grounded on international law and the constitution, with a set of justices who were willing tools in the hands of Quisling and the Germans.

Mohr also had the necessary criminal intent to be punished. He knew that the justices of the Supreme Court had resigned over a conflict with the German Reichskommissar. He was aware that the Minister of Justice was seeking new justices who would be accommodating towards the opinion of the Germans on the issue of judicial review. He was further aware of the dangers in making the Court dependent on the administration, and he had been clearly warned against

[11] See above on pp. 95–96.

[12] NRT 1946, p. 1139.

accepting office by a college in the District Court. He was, as a judge, under a special obligation of loyalty to the constitution and the King of Norway.

Berger further pointed out that Mohr continued in his position as judge despite the fact that the abuses of the Germans and the Quislings grew worse and more overt and despite the fact that the rule of law became totally undermined and was replaced by arbitrary rule. Mohr maintained that he had been objective and conscientious in his judicial actions and also that he had protested vigorously in a case where the regime went to action against one of the judges. In light of the gravity of Mohr's guilt, Justice Berger found no need to consider these claims. The reasoning in the case against Mohr made it a crime for all to have accepted appointment to the Supreme Court and the special courts established by the Quisling regime.

Unlike the judges in the special courts, the justices of the Quisling Supreme Court were not held accountable for their individual judgments. The political cases were mainly under the jurisdiction of the People's Court and the special courts with no appeal to the Supreme Court, so the Supreme Court was for the most part involved in civil cases that were not controversial from the point of view of the Norwegian resistance. From this, there was one notable exception. The first case for the new Supreme Court was appeal on a minor criminal case where the County Court had been set according to the Ministerial Decree of 15 November 1940. The plea in the appeal was that the composition of the County Court was illegal because the decree was in violation of the occupant's powers under international law.

This was the very issue that had started the controversy that led to the resignation of the Supreme Court judges, and the Supreme Court had then stated as its opinion that it, as a Norwegian court, had the right to review the legality of the decrees of the occupying authority under international law when asked to apply the decrees in cases before it. Now the new Supreme Court was faced with the same issue. Unanimously, it decided that it was outside the scope of the powers of a national Norwegian court to review the legality of regulations issued by or on behalf of the occupiers.[13]

Participation in this ruling was part of the indictment against the judges of the Supreme Court. In the verdict against Mohr and the others, this judgment was not seen as a separate criminal offence, and the courts after the war therefore saw no need to go into the legal issue of the relationship between an occupier and the courts in an occupied country under international rules of war. This may be also seen as according the members of the illegal Supreme Court some immunity for judgments issued according to their exercising of normal judicial functions. It may also be interpreted, however, in the light of the obvious dilemma that it was the opinion of the Quisling Court and not the opinion of the Supreme Court that is best accorded with accepted opinion in international law. In this way, the Norwegian courts, after the war, circumvented this difficult issue.

[13] NRT 1941, p. 63.

References

Andenæs J (1979) Det vanskelige oppgjøret. Tanum-Norli, Oslo
Kirchheimer O (1961) Political justice: the use of legal procedure for political ends. Princeton University Press, New Jersey
Michielsen JNME (2004) The "Nazification" and "Denazification" of the Courts in Belgium, Luxembourg and the Netherlands. University of Maastricht, Maastricht
Pendas DO (2009) Nazi trials in postwar Europe. J Mod Hist 81:347–368
Tamm D (1984) Retsopgøret efter besættelsen. Jurist- og Økonomforbundets forlag, København

Chapter 9
The Condition of Illegality in Transitional Settings

The German Post-Nazism Restoration

In Germany, the situation was that the Nazi takeover of power in 1933 had been undertaken by what was considered legal means. This was the result of a conscious and cleverly designed and executed strategy by the Nazi Party.[1] The regime was perceived as legal according to the German constitution by contemporary society, both within Germany and abroad.[2] Virtually, a whole generation of German legal scholars gave support to the legality of the new regime.[3] Despite the fact that "the constitutional basis on which the reconstruction of Germany on National Socialist lines rested was created mainly by fraud and terrorization", serious reservations against the regime's legality were not raised by the critics of the regime either.[4] The regime and its legislative measures were applied as legal by the German courts right from the beginning. As a consequence of this perception of legality of the Nazi regime, the issue of legal responsibility and criminal liability for judges and other legal officials for applying the law raised difficult questions concerning the legal basis for such responsibility after the breakdown of the Nazi regime.

The issue of a legal basis for responsibility was raised shortly after the capitulation of Germany by leading scholars who had been in opposition to the regime. It was first addressed by professor and former Minister of Justice for the Social Democratic Party under the Weimar Republic Gustav Radbruch in his much-acclaimed article, *Gesetzliches Unrecht und Übergesetzliches recht*.[5] In this article, he claimed that laws that lack the fundamental requirements of justice cannot be

[1] See the detailed description and analysis by Strenge (2002).

[2] See Fraser (2005), pp. 77–119 for the Anglo-American legal academic reactions to the developments in German law under Nazism.

[3] Rüthers (2012), p. 502.

[4] Loewenstein (1936–1937), p. 541.

[5] Radbruch (1946).

H.P. Graver, *Judges Against Justice*, DOI 10.1007/978-3-662-44293-7_9

regarded as law. Such laws therefore are legally void from the moment of their enactment.

Contrary to positivism, law must be defined by its very essence, which according to Radbruch is to create an order aiming for justice. This does not mean that any unjust law lacks the character of law. But when the injustice reaches an unbearable level, it can no longer be recognised as law. Radbruch acknowledges that drawing a line between injustice and unbearable injustice is impossible. He therefore suggests that where achieving justice is not even an aim of the legislator and where the legislator consciously challenges the claim to equality, which is the core of justice, then the resulting legislation lacks the character of law. From this he concludes that racial legislation—legislation that treated some humans as subhumans—and legislation that demanded harsh punishments without regard to the circumstances of the case were examples of legislation of the Nazi period that lacked the character of law. Such legislation should be disregarded by judges, and judgments made accordingly should be deemed unlawful.

Many of the laws of the Weimar era enacted for the protection of human rights were never repealed by the Nazis. Many acts defined as war crimes or crimes against humanity under international law were committed or permitted in direct violation of the provisions of German criminal law. If one were to disregard the Nazi legal rules that permitted such acts, they would also be illegal according to German law at the time. In Radbruch's view, this meant that judges who had based their sentences on such laws and imposed penalties such as death or imprisonment objectively committed the crimes of murder or illegal detention. The grounds for punishing a judge for following unjust legislation and orders can, in other words, be found in the existing prohibitions against illegally depriving of a person of his liberty, murder, discrimination, etc., according to the circumstances of the case. Whereas a judge is undertaking such acts legally when he is doing it in the course of his administration of justice, his acts will be illegal once the legality of the rule that he is applying is taken away. Enforcing oppressive laws is thus an illegal act to the extent that the enforcement leads to violations of rights.

Radbruch thus resorted to extralegal norms in order to hold judges responsible for their contribution to the Nazi oppression. He did not, however, advocate using natural law as a basis for determining whether a judge objectively had committed an offence. The basis for this should be sought in positive law. Natural law was used to remove the unjust law that otherwise made such invasions in the life and liberty of others legal judicial acts.

German professor in Roman and civil laws Helmut Coing addressed Radbruch's argument on the responsibility of the judge in an article from 1947.[6] He held that the judge is committed to follow both positive law and justice. When the legislator consciously and manifestly departs from justice, the judge is bound to disregard the legislation or to step down from his office.

[6] Coing (1947).

This does not mean, however, that the judge can be held criminally responsible for applying the law, even if it leads to the taking of another person's life or depriving him of his freedom. The law must reconcile two conflicting aims: on one hand, the aim of supporting justice by punishing those who depart from it and, on the other hand, the principle of *nulla poena sine lege*. Criminal sanctions may only be used to uphold positive law, i.e. law as social order, and not to uphold morality, i.e. law as justice. Coing disputed the construction that removing the legality of the basis of a judge's verdict in a capital case would make him guilty of murder. This construction supposes that judges are engaged in illegal acts when they deprive persons of their liberty by sentencing them to prison, but for the fact that exercising a judicial function is seen as a justification. But the judge's verdict is not murder made legal by exception but something totally different. This leads to, according to Coing, punishing a judge for upholding laws that are invalid because of their unjustness, amounting to punishing him for breaking a rule based on natural law and not for breaking a positive legal rule. The basic principle *of nulla poene sin lege* is even more relevant to the situation of the judge who acted in obedience to positive law.

Coing, on the other hand, states that a judge who departs from justice when justice is openly disregarded by the legislator is unfit to continue as a judge. He also points out that a judge who departs from the positive law by following an illegal order may be punished. He mentions as an example a situation where a judge secretly is told by superiors how to decide a case. German courts, after the war, used this construction to convict persons engaged in euthanasia, pursuant to Hitler's secret order of September 1939.

Coing's argument, based on natural law, led him to the same conclusion drawn by H.L.A. Hart a few years later from a positivist point of view. Hart also concluded that imposing punishments for obedience to a positive law would require the use of laws enacted after the act was committed changing its status from legal to criminal.[7] But Hart construed the issue of applying punishment as a choice between two moral requirements: the demand that atrocious acts be punished and the demand that criminal laws should not be applied retroactively. As one cannot conform to both, one has to choose to break one of them.

The Radbruch formula was accepted by the courts and employed in cases against defendants accused of participation in the Holocaust, the killing of Soviet prisoners of war and participation in the euthanasia programme.[8] In these cases, the regulations and orders sanctioning the acts were brushed aside, with the argument that they were contrary to a core of justice present in the minds of all civilised people. Persons engaged in enacting orders and directives from the Führer could therefore be convicted of murder or accessory to murder under the criminal laws in force during the Nazi regime. The orders and directives were regarded as illegal by the courts of the Federal Republic since they challenged any conception possible of a

[7] Hart (1957), pp. 619–620.

[8] See Freudiger (2002), p. 405.

common core of justice in the minds of civilised people. These were not, however, cases against judges, so the courts did not have to deal with the legal issue of a ruling of legality pronounced by a competent court. The successor courts could thus base themselves on an assessment on the illegality of these acts also under the Nazi regime itself without having to set aside specific legal authorities from the time.

Formally, the approach of the German courts was different from that taken by the Allied Military Tribunal since they based their decisions on national law interpreting the law of the Nazi time and not on international law and customs. When it comes to the heart of the matter, there were, nevertheless, similarities in the legal basis. Nazi law was reinterpreted by the German courts of the Federal Republic in light of a core of justice based on the minds of "all civilized people".[9] In the same way, "fundamental rules of justice which have been adopted or accepted by nations generally" was an important basis for the war crime trials, both by the international tribunals and by municipal courts after the war.[10]

In the German trials against prosecutors and judges, this was seen differently. Although some legal scholars were rapid in taking up the question of the legal responsibility of the Nazi legal officials, German courts did not address such issues for many years after the war. A German court, Bamberg Court of Appeals, indirectly addressed the issue in 1949 in a case where a woman was on trial for denouncing her husband to the Nazi authorities.[11] The main issue in this case, however, was the liability not of the judge but of the citizen who had denounced and therefore delivered another into the hands of the Nazi legal system.

The husband of the accused wife had been fighting in the war since 1940; the wife had, in the meantime, fallen for other men. One day, in 1944, he was home on leave and expressed the view that it was a pity that the attack on Hitler on 20 July 1944 had not united him with the devil. To get rid of her husband, she betrayed him to the local party official, with the result that the man was arrested, put on trial, and sentenced to death. The death sentence was later commuted to duty at the front.

As part of its reasons, the court considered whether the judges who tried the husband were outside the scope of justice when they sentenced him according to a law that was "without doubt manifestly unreasonable... and regarded by the majority of the German people as an instrument of fear". The court rejected this and held that the judges had not broken the commands of natural law because the relevant Nazi law only required the subjects to keep their silence and not to commit any act that was against the demands of natural law. And since the law did not require actions against the demands of natural law, the judges were bound by their duty as judges to apply it.

Surely, if positive law is limited by natural law or justice, there are grounds to disapply a law that requires citizens to perform acts that according to "godly or

[9] See Werle (1992).

[10] See Law Reports of Trials of War Criminals, vol. XV Digest of Laws and Cases, United Nations War Crimes Commission, London 1949, pp. 6–7.

[11] Beschluß v. 27.7.49—WS 152/49.

human law in the opinion of all civilized nations are prohibited".[12] But is this the whole picture? Is it not a conscious and manifest departure from justice on the part of the legislator to punish by death critical remarks about the ruler expressed in the privacy of one's home? One could raise the question at another level and ask, what about the judge sitting trial on another judge for refusing to apply the Act in a case like the one presented? One could then argue that this judge would be bound to disapply the law because it required the accused judge to perform an act that according to godly or human law in the opinion of all civilised nations is prohibited, namely to commit to death a person for his voiced opinions in the privacy of his own home. If this is the case, then the first judge could not be bound to apply the law either. It could, from the standpoint of justice, be argued that the judge was bound not to apply the law and that convicting someone to death for breaking it would amount to murder, at least in the objective sense.[13]

In a later denunciator case, the German Supreme Court decided that the use of the death penalty for criticisms of the regime was illegal because it constituted a denial and violation of the basic principle of criminal law of proportionality between deed and punishment. In cases where the law allowed for discretion—in denunciator cases, from 1-day imprisonment to death penalty—the courts could not choose the death penalty for minor offences without breaking this principle.[14]

The first case where the Supreme Court was asked to rule directly on the criminal liability of a judge was a case in 1952 against judges of a military tribunal, which after the capitulation of the German forces in May 1945 had convicted three sailors to death for desertion.[15] Also in this case, the Supreme Court stated that disproportional punishments were against an "unwritten basic assumption of German criminal law". To a certain extent, the Supreme Court by this gave its confirmation of the Radbruch formula that manifestly unjust laws are not binding laws.

The position thus taken would entail that judges who had applied the death sentence to persons accused of relatively insignificant offences would be liable to punishment. This caused former judges to mobilise.[16] In later cases, the courts departed from this line of reasoning, and the position was reversed in a ruling from 1956 against Dr. Otto Thorbeck and Walter Huppenkothen.[17]

Thorbeck and Huppenkothen were charged as judge and prosecutor of an SS Tribunal that tried Canaris and several of his associates in the concentration camps of Sachsenhausen and Flossenbürg on April 6 and 8, 1945, for participation in

---

[12] Radbruch (1946), p. 208. My translation from German.

[13] A jury in Thüringen found an informer in a similar case guilty of complicity to murder. This verdict must entail that it regarded the judge convicting the person who was informed upon as guilty of murder; see Radbruch (1946), p. 106.

[14] BGH, Urteil vom 8.7.1952—1 StR 123/51.

[15] BGH, Urteil vom 29.5.1952—2 StR 45/50.

[16] See Garbe (2000), p. 110.

[17] BGH, Urteil vom 19.06.1956—1 StR 50/56 (LG Augsburg).

attempts to assassinate Adolf Hitler. According to documents found by the Gestapo, Canaris and his associates had engaged in several plots to murder Adolf Hitler.

The Supreme Court dealt with the case three times. In the final round, it acquitted the two for their participation in the trials against Canaris and his associates. The Supreme Court took as its starting point that every state has a right to defend itself and that the right to enact strong measures against attacks on the state also must be extended to the Nazi state. Based on this circumstance, it could not be held against a judge who convicts according to the rules in force without asking himself whether the defendant acted according to a justification based on non-positive norms of a right to rebel against tyranny or oppression. This was in Germany perceived as an explicit rebuttal of the Radbruch formula, which stated that according to German law, a judge had no obligation to go beyond positive law no matter how draconic it may seem from outside standards.

In the Rehse case, the German Supreme Court stated that a judge could only be punished for pronouncing a death sentence if he did so for nefarious reasons.[18] The only crime for which a judge could be held accountable under German national law in the transition from the Nazi regime was, therefore, the crime of intentionally departing from the law as it was perceived by the judge at the time of his judgment. The result was that virtually no judges were convicted by West German courts of participation in oppression and persecution.

The Judges of the GDR

German courts were called upon again to rule upon the responsibility of judges after the reunification of Germany in 1990. After the two Germanies were reunited, the German judiciary carried out a large-scale investigation and adjudication of the crimes of the GDR regime. The trials that were held can be seen as one of the steps taken to end the situation established by the courts after the breakdown of the Nazi regime, where crimes committed by the state apparatus in oppressive regimes went unpunished.[19] Similar to the Nazi period, the judicial system of the GDR was also a system employed by the regime as an apparatus in the pursuit of political aims and an instrument of political persecution and oppression.

Cases brought against prosecutors and judges of the GDR were the largest group of cases brought against representatives of the GDR regime for crimes against its population.[20] Together, 374 such cases against 618 accused were brought, making them 36.6 % of the total. Less than 5 % of the prosecutors and judges of the GDR were charged. The charges resulted in 181 convictions for "bending the law", bringing the conviction rate to 24 % of the accusations. In many more cases, the

[18] BGH, Urteil vom 30.4.1968—5 StR 670/67.

[19] See Marxen and Werle (2007), p. XIX.

[20] Marxen and Werle (2007), p. XXIX.

courts concluded that the judicial decisions had violated basic principles of the rule of law.[21]

Initially, the legal doctrine was sceptical to applying criminal sanctions against judges of the GDR regime. According to the opinions of many scholars, sanctions were ruled out because of the statute of limitation. Many also contested the rights of the Federal Republic as a successor to enforce infringements against the law in the GDR.[22]

The first case at the German Supreme Court was a case from 1993 against members of a labour court accused of upholding an unjust dismissal.[23] The Supreme Court here stated that German courts could hold judges of the former GDR accountable but that apart from cases of clear departure from the law of the GDR at the time, liability would have to be restricted to instances where the rights of individuals were substantially infringed in an obvious way to the point of being arbitrary. This restrictive approach was demanded by the prohibition against applying present law retroactively to the detriment of the GDR judges.

In determining what was to be considered as substantial and obvious infringements of individual rights, the Court referred to the International Covenant on Civil and Political Rights, which the GDR had ratified in 1976. Since this only formed part of the argument, one can say that the Supreme Court based its reasoning partly on positive law in the form of ratified international conventions and partly on the natural law argument of Gustav Radbruch.[24] The Court expressed its opinion that the judges of the GDR had had the possibility within the prevailing legal method to interpret and apply the law of the GDR in such a way as not to commit substantial and obvious infringements of individual rights understood in this way. For this reason, their judgments were also illegal at the time when they manifestly departed from a basic core of justice.

The objective conditions for applying criminal sanctions were elaborated in later cases. In the case of 16 November 1995 against a member of the Supreme Court of the GDR, the German Supreme Court recapitulated the following requirements: substantial and manifest human rights violations, intolerable disproportionate punishments, and substantial violations of the right to a fair trial.[25]

The Supreme Court in this way made a clear break with its case law from the post-Nazi trials in its cases against the GDR judiciary, and the Court explicitly gave its accord to the criticism that had been voiced against its jurisprudence of the 1950s and 1960s. The Court recognised that the standard it now applied would have led to the trial and conviction of numerous judges from the Nazi period had it been applied by the courts in the aftermath of the Nazi regime. The Court stated that it

[21] Marxen and Werle (2007), p. XXXVII.

[22] See Schröder (2000), p. 3019.

[23] BGH, Urteil vom 13.12.1993 5 StR 76/93.

[24] See Marxen and Werle (2007), p. XLIII.

[25] BGH, Urteil vom 16.11.1995, 5 StR 747/74.

was a "momentous failure" of justice of the Federal Republic that this had not been done.[26]

References

Coing H (1947) Zur Frage der strafrechtlichen Haftung der Richter für die Anwendung naturrechtswidriger Gesetze. Süddeutsche Juristen-Zeitung, col. 62

Fraser D (2005) Law after Auschwitz: towards a jurisprudence of the Holocaust. Carolina Academic Press, Durham

Freudiger K (2002) Die juristische Aufarbeitung von NS-Verbrechen. Mohr Siebeck, Tübingen

Garbe D (2000) Im Namen des Volkes?! Die Rechtlichen Grundlagen der Militärjustiz im NS-Staat und ihre "Bewältigung" nach 1945. In: Nolz B, Popp W (eds) Erinnerungsarbeit Grundlage einer Kultur des Friedens. Lit Verlag, Münster

Hart HLA (1957) Positivism and the separation of law and morals. Harv Law Rev 71:593–629

Loewenstein K (1936–1937) The German constitution 1933–1937. Univ Chic Law Rev 4:537–574

Marxen K, Werle G (eds) (2007) Strafjustiz und DDR-Unrecht Dokumentation, Band 5/1 Teilband Rechtsbeugung. De Gruyter, Berlin

Radbruch G (1946) Gesetzliches Unrecht und übergesetzliches Recht. Süddeutsche Juristen-Zeitung 105–108 [English translation Statutory Lawlessness and Supra-Statutory Law, Translated by Bonnie Litschewski Paulson and Stanley L. Paulson, 26 Oxford Journal of Legal Studies 2006, pp. 1–11]

Rüthers B (2012) Die unbegrenzte Auslegung: Zum Wandel der Privatrechtsordnung im Nationalsozialismus 7. Ausg. Mohr Siebeck, Tübingen

Schröder F-C (2000) Zehn Jahre strafrechtliche Aufarbeitung des DDR-Unrechts. NJW 3017–3022

Strenge I (2002) Machtübernahme 1933: Alles auf dem legalen Weg? Ducker und Humblot, Berlin

Werle G (1992) Der Holocaust als Gegenstand der bundesdeutschen Strafjustiz. Neues Juristische Wochenzeitung 2529–2535

[26] "Darin, daß dies nicht geschehen ist, liegt ein folgenschweres Versagen bundesdeutscher Strafjustiz" NJW 1996, 857, on page 864.

Chapter 10
Judges in Special Courts

Authoritarian Regimes and Special Courts

The establishment of special courts to deal with sensitive cases is common in authoritarian states.[1] The more autonomy the regular courts enjoy, the more likely it is that the regime will establish such courts. And the less compliance the regime receives, the greater will the scope of jurisdiction be for the special courts.[2]

The UN Basic Principles on the Independence of the Judiciary state in paragraph 5:

> Everyone shall have the right to be tried by ordinary courts or tribunals using established legal procedures. Tribunals that do not use the duly established procedures of the legal process shall not be created to displace the jurisdiction belonging to the ordinary courts or judicial tribunals.

A question to be raised is whether one should expect judges to refuse appointments to positions as judge under such circumstances. The UN Economic and Social Council declared in 1989 that "no judge shall accept an appointment or act in a fashion that is inconsistent with the Principles".[3]

Helmut Coing stated in his article on the responsibility of the judges from 1947 that a judge has a moral duty to refuse to participate in a special court. A failure to refuse would, in Coing's opinion, make the judge unsuitable to be used as a judge in a successor regime and make him a political accomplice to the political rulers of the oppressive regime.[4] Otto Kirchheimer holds that a legitimate yardstick by which to measure the acts of complicity to evil is the withdrawal from significant participation in public life. By this yardstick, it must be obvious that a judge should refuse to accept positions that are offered by the regime in order to increase the efficiency of

---

[1] See pp. 47–49 above.

[2] See a general overview in Ginsburg and Moustafa (2008), p. 17.

[3] Se Lippman (1992–1993), p. 315.

[4] Coing (1947), col. 62.

H.P. Graver, *Judges Against Justice*, DOI 10.1007/978-3-662-44293-7_10

the policies of the regime. It is, alas, as Kirchheimer states, also a fact that "many men show a fatal proclivity toward pushing themselves, or allowing themselves to be pushed, into positions where they know in advance the honors and rewards will entail corresponding entanglement and responsibility".[5] Regimes therefore unfortunately do not seem to have difficulties in recruiting judges to their special courts.

The US Military Tribunal and Special Courts

Judges of the special courts and the People's Court of Nazi Germany were singled out by the Allies after the war as "Class II offenders (activists, militarists, and profiteers)".[6] The initial view of the Allies after the Second World War was, in other words, that judges in the special courts and the People's Court were to be investigated as war criminals in line with activists, militarists, and profiteers. This does not mean, however, that these judges were treated as criminals just from the fact that they had agreed to serve on the special courts established by the regime. The classification was open to rebuttal in the individual case. In the Justice Case, the prosecution initially indicted defendants on the basis of their having served as judges in the special courts or in the People's Court. The Tribunal did not convict anyone purely on this basis.

The Justice Case involved several defendants who had served as judges or prosecutors in the special courts or the People's Court. In the indictment, serving on the special courts was regarded as a war crime by their use for the purpose of and in fact creating a reign of terror to suppress political opposition to the Nazi regime. The special courts subjected certain German civilians and nationals of occupied countries to discriminatory and special penal laws and trials and denied them all semblance of judicial process. The opening statement of the prosecution framed the accusation in this way:

> The third group is the cases where, under alleged trials, in the People's Court, special courts, and civilian courts martial, certain of these defendants, by the use of the prescribed procedures or those actually practiced, the fixing of penalties which outrage the universal moral judgment of mankind, and through convictions based only upon the subjective conclusions of the prosecutor or judge, which we describe now only as examples, give rise to the legal conclusion that the defendants thus convicted were murdered or unlawfully enslaved under the guise of exercising a judicial process.[7]

It seems a subtle point to make that, according to this, it was not the acceptance of the position as a judge in a special court or the People's Court that was an offence

[5] Kirchheimer (1961), p. 331.

[6] There were altogether five classes: major offenders (Class I), offenders (Class II), lesser offenders, followers, and persons exonerated; see Loewenstein (1948), p. 449.

[7] The Justice Case (1951), p. 71.

but the serving as a prosecutor or judge that, by necessity, entailed committing crimes because of the nature of the proceedings taking place.

In the words of Chief Prosecutor Telford Taylor:

> The defendants and their colleagues distorted, perverted, and finally accomplished the complete overthrow of justice and law in Germany. They made the system of courts an integral part of dictatorship. They established and operated special tribunals obedient only to the political dictates of the Hitler regime. They abolished all semblance of judicial independence. They brow-beat, bullied, and denied fundamental rights to those who came before the courts. The "trials" they conducted became horrible farces, with vestigial remnants of legal procedure which only served to mock the hapless victims.[8]

The Military Tribunal, however, only considered the guilt of the defendants under international law and was not concerned with violation of constitutional guaranties or withholding of due process of law. The Tribunal did not share the prosecution's view on the criminality of serving on the special courts. This can be seen by its treatment of the defendants who were charged with participation in the special court system. Four of the defendants were judges of the People's Courts, three of the defendants were judges of the special courts, and four of the defendants were prosecutors.

The most important prosecutor among these defendants was Ernst Lautz, Chief Public Prosecutor of the Reich. In this capacity, Lautz prosecuted many important cases before the People's Court. He was not convicted for his function as chief prosecutor in the People's Court as such.

Defendant Rothaug served as president of the Special Court of Nuremberg. This was not in itself a reason for his conviction. He was convicted based on his specific conduct on the bench. The Military Tribunal characterised him as "a sadistic and evil man" who could have been impeached and removed from office or convicted of malfeasance in office under any civilised judicial system. After reviewing three of the cases that Rothaug had presided, the Military Tribunal stated:

> From the evidence it is clear that these trials lacked the essential elements of legality. In these cases the defendant's court, in spite of the legal sophistries which he employed, was merely an instrument in the program of the leaders of the Nazi State of persecution and extermination. That the number the defendant could wipe out within his competency was smaller than the number involved in the mass persecutions and exterminations by the leaders whom he served, does not mitigate his contribution to the program of those leaders. His acts were more terrible in that those who might have hoped for a last refuge in the institutions of justice found these institutions turned against them and a part of the program of terror and oppression.
>
> The individual cases in which Rothaug applied the cruel and discriminatory law against Poles and Jews cannot be considered in isolation. It is of the essence of the charges against him that he participated in the national program of racial persecution. It is of the essence of the proof that he identified himself with this national program and gave himself utterly to its accomplishment. He participated in the crime of genocide.[9]

[8] The Justice Case (1951), p. 31.

[9] The Justice Case (1951), pp. 1155–1156.

The defendants—Barnickel, public prosecutor of the People's Court; Nebelung, justice of the Fourth Senate of the People's Court; and *Petersen*, lay judge of the First Senate of the People's Court and lay judge of the Special Senate of the People's Court—were all acquitted. Accepting office and serving on the special Nazi courts was therefore not in itself a crime under the London Agreement of 8 August 1945 or the Allied Control Council Law No. 10. The general dismantling of the rule of law was outside the jurisdiction of the Tribunal. From this we see that what the Tribunal considered as criminal was not the function as a special court judge as such but the particular conduct of the individual judge. Despite the general characteristics made of the Nazi administration of justice, it was possible to serve as a judge in the special courts and try foreigners without committing war crimes if one did not apply the laws in a discriminatory manner against Jews and Poles and if one was not involved in "Night and Fog" cases.

The same view was expressed by the Norwegian Supreme Court in the case against Hans Paul Helmut Latza, who presided over a special court that condemned members of the Norwegian resistance to death.[10] Latza was first found guilty of murder, but the conviction was overturned by the Supreme Court on appeal. Naturally, the Norwegian court did not consider whether it was an offence in itself for Latza to accept the position as a judge in a German special court. But the practice of the special courts was not regarded as a war crime as such, despite the fact that they submitted nationals of the occupied countries to a denial of what is normally regarded as fundamental to a fair trial. This was a general trend in the postwar trials against German judges and prosecutors in the occupied countries, although some special court judges and prosecutors were convicted in several of them.[11]

Under national law, this is different. Central to the national dimension is not international law on war crimes against foreigners but contribution to and participation in the breaking down of the rule of law by rulers who have this as their declared policy. Accepting appointment to courts and offices that are established with this specific purpose in mind must be judged by different standards.

The View on Special Courts in Post-Nazi Germany

The German discussion after the war on the responsibility of the judges who had contributed to the atrocities of the regime focused on the application of unjust laws and not on the participation in specific courts.[12] Karl Loewenstein commented in 1948:

---

[10] The Latza Case, reported in LAW REPORTS OF TRIALS OF WAR CRIMINALS, selected and prepared by THE UNITED NATIONS WAR CRIMES COMMISSION, vol. 14, London 1949, Norwegian law reports (NRT) 1948, p. 328.

[11] See Law Reports of Trials of War Criminals (1949), vol. 14, pp. 84–85.

[12] See Radbruch (1946), Coing (1947), and Figge (1947).

> Nobody familiar with German mentality expected to see the corrupt judges of the Volksgericht and the Sondergericht, who had signed the death warrants of many "enemies of the regime" indicted by their fellow judges for multiple homicides under these statutes.[13]

Among the German judges and lawyers, there was no strong demand that members of the special courts or People's Court be punished. In fact, had participation in these courts been deemed an offence as such, this would have labelled hundreds of the postwar German judges as murderers, going even into the ranks of the Supreme Court and the German Constitutional Court.[14]

The Judges of the special courts or the People's Court were not singled out in the German debate as especially liable to criminal responsibility. The academic discussion took as its starting point the duty of the judge to follow and apply the law, and the judge's belief in the legality of Nazi law as positive law, without discriminating between judges in the ordinary courts and judges in the special courts.

An obligation to take office as a judge in a special court or in the People's Court is, however, of a very different character from the obligation of a judge to apply the law in the course of justice. The obligation to take office as a judge is no different from any other obligation resting upon citizens. It is not an obligation for the judge to administer in a judicial function but an obligation to follow or not follow the dictates of superiors.

It also appears that many German judges chose not to follow an obligation to take office as a special court judge, or were asked to be excused from office, and that the system offered many opportunities to the considerable number who made these choices.[15] These facts were mentioned by Schorn in order to demonstrate that there were many upright judges in the judiciary in Nazi Germany within the special courts too and that they should not all be condemned by the deeds committed by those who broke their basic obligations to justice. This led Kirchheimer to comment: "There is a conclusion that Schorn refrains from drawing: a silent strike of the profession, with its great majority refusing to serve on such courts, would have embarrassed the regime, lowering its prestige with the population at large".[16]

In the early denunciator cases, the German Supreme Court characterised the People's Court as an instrument of terror for illegal killings in judicial form.[17] This characterisation was not offered where the liability of the serving judges was at stake. The legality of serving as a judge in the People's Court was only finally decided by the West German Supreme Court as late as 1968, in the Rehse case.

[13] Loewenstein (1948), p. 437 (Loewenstein's comment on Figge's article in footnote 91 is difficult to understand. As I read Figge, he states the opposite of what Loewenstein attributes to him.)

[14] See Müller (1989), pp. 284–285.

[15] See Schorn (1959), pp. 114–115.

[16] Kirchheimer (1961), p. 331.

[17] BGH St 9, S. 302.

The Court here stated that the judges of the People's Court were independent, equal, and only bound by the law. Their sole duty was to follow their own legal conviction.[18] The judges serving here could only be held responsible for sentences they pronounced out of malicious reasons outside the scope of their legal beliefs. It follows that accepting office and serving in this court was not something to be criticised by the judiciary of the Federal Republic.

Should Taking Office in a Special Court Be Criminal?

Accepting office in a special court of an illegitimate regime should be regarded as a contribution to the attempts of this regime to seize and hold power. The approach of the Norwegian courts after the occupation has a more general outreach and should be applicable not only when it is a foreign invader taking power.

It is not evident that the same would be the case in a situation where such special courts were established by a legally appointed government on its way down a slope towards authoritarianism. Confronted with courts unwilling or unable to accommodate such a regime's measures to uphold internal security, the government might resort to packing the courts with more cooperative judges or establishing "more efficient" special courts with "more specialized" judges. It is difficult to characterise it as a crime to accept appointment by a legitimate regime to courts established by this regime, even if they are special courts with the task of contributing to maintain internal security. Judged from a legal perspective, the approach taken by the Military Tribunal and the German courts is probably the sound way to follow; not the position as judge in a special court as such but the contents and effects of the decisions the judges take should be the basis for evaluation of their guilt.

From an ethical point of view, there are, however, grounds for caution when a regime takes measures because it conceives its judicial system as inefficient or unaccommodating to its need to protect society, especially if such measures are taken in open confrontation with the judges. Judges who accept appointment under such circumstances should be aware that situations may arise where they must choose between being loyal to the system and its rules, on one hand, and the rule of law and fundamental human rights, on the other. In such situations, they must accept that they are held personally accountable for the choices they make and that they cannot shift the blame over to the "law" or to the government. There is all the more reason to hold a judge personally accountable when he has accepted appointment with open eyes to a post that the regime has established specifically because the traditional judges or the normal courts are perceived as insufficient in the maintenance of law and order and internal security under prevailing circumstances.

In many cases, the most prudent line of action will be not to accept such appointments, even though this may cause the regime to circumvent the law and

[18] BGH, Urteil vom 30. 4. 1968—5 StR 670/67.

the courts altogether. If this is the result, the regime will have resorted to means that have no legitimacy in law, and the line of reasoning of the Norwegian Supreme Court in the Mohr case may be employed towards its collaborators. If, on the contrary, the regime is forced to pursue its aims through the court system it has inherited from the time before it deemed it necessary to employ authoritarian means, this might contribute to mitigating the effect of authoritarian measures.

References

Coing H (1947) Zur Frage der strafrechtlichen Haftung der Richter für die Anwendung naturrechtswidriger Gesetze. Süddeutsche Juristen-Zeitung, col. 62

Figge R (1947) Die Verantwortlichkeit des Richters. Süddeutsche Juristen-Zeitung, col. 179–183

Ginsburg T, Moustafa T (2008) Introduction: the functions of courts in authoritarian politics. In: Ginsburg T, Moustafa T (eds) Rule by law: the politics of courts in authoritarian regimes. Cambridge University Press, Cambridge

Kirchheimer O (1961) Political justice: the use of legal procedure for political ends. Princeton University Press, New Jersey

Law reports of trials of war criminals, vol XIV. United Nations War Crimes Commission, London, 1949

Lippman M (1992–1993) They shoot lawyers don't they? Law in the Third Reich and the global threat to the independence of the judiciary. Calif West Int Law J 23:257–318

Loewenstein K (1948) Reconstruction of the administration of justice in the American occupied Germany. Harv Law Rev 61:419–467

Müller I (1989) Furchtbare Juristen – Die unbewältigte Vergangenheit unsere Justiz. Knaur, München

Radbruch G (1946) Gesetzliches Unrecht und übergesetzliches Recht. Süddeutsche Juristen-Zeitung 105–108 [English translation Statutory Lawlessness and Supra-Statutory Law, Translated by Bonnie Litschewski Paulson and Stanley L. Paulson, 26 Oxford Journal of Legal Studies 2006, pp. 1–11]

Schorn H (1959) Der Richter im Dritten Reich Geschichte und Dokumente. Vittorio Klostermann, Frankfurt am Main

Trials of War Criminals before the Nuremberg Military Tribunals, vol III, the Justice Case, Washington, 1951

Chapter 11
Justification of Judicial Oppression

Judges may find themselves in situations where they contribute to or are the direct perpetrators of substantial and obvious infringements of individual rights. Despite this, it may not always be just to prosecute them and hold them criminally responsible for this. As we have seen, judges are under pressure from different values and ideals when it comes to their duty to uphold the law. The decision of whether to stay on the bench, giving support to the regime while trying to do justice as far as possible, or to resign is not an easy decision. Since open defiance often will undermine the effective role of the judiciary as a modifying factor, it is also hard to know to what extent it serves justice to apply techniques to modify suppressive measures. For such reasons, judicial responsibility must be confined to the more obvious infringements of fundamental rights. But even in these cases, there may be circumstances excluding individual criminal responsibility for the judge. Such circumstances may be found under the principle of culpability under the general principles of the ICC Statute, Articles 30–33.

According to the principle of culpability, punishment presupposes that the court is convinced that the defendant is personally reproachable for the crime he has committed.[1] This entails that a person is responsible only if the material elements of a crime are committed with intent and knowledge [Article 30 (1)]. In addition, Article 33 excludes responsibility for crimes committed under superior orders unless the orders are manifestly unlawful. But since crimes against humanity and genocide per se are manifestly unlawful, superior orders will never exclude responsibility of judges as I have defined the material elements here. Culpability is excluded under Article 32 where there is a mistake of fact on the side of the defendant. Mistake of law shall, in general, not be a ground for excluding criminal responsibility. It may exclude liability "if it negates the mental element required by such a crime". But it is only a ground for mitigation of punishment if the defendant

[1] Jescheck (2004), p. 44.

H.P. Graver, *Judges Against Justice*, DOI 10.1007/978-3-662-44293-7_11

should have known the unlawfulness of the act.[2] Article 31 (1)(d) excludes liability where the act "has been caused by duress resulting from a threat of imminent death or of continuing or imminent serious bodily harm against that person or another person, and the person acts necessarily and reasonably to avoid this threat, provided that the person does not intend to cause a greater harm than the one sought to be avoided".

Criminal Intent

The Eilifsen Case

To punish a person for an offence, it is normally not sufficient to establish that an offence has been committed. Normally, it also has to be established that the accused committed the offence with the necessary criminal intent. The Military Tribunal expressed the requirement of criminal intent in the following way:

> As applied in the field of international law that principle requires proof before conviction that the accused knew or should have known that in matters of international concern he was guilty of participation in a nationally organized system of injustice and persecution shocking to the moral sense of mankind, and that he knew or should have known that he would be subject to punishment if caught. Whether it be considered codification or substantive legislation, no person who knowingly committed the acts made punishable by C. C. Law 10 can assert that he did not know that he would be brought to account for his acts. Notice of intent to punish was repeatedly given by the only means available in international affairs, namely, the solemn warning of the governments of the states at war with Germany. Not only were the defendants warned of swift retribution by the express declaration of the Allies at Moscow of 30 October 1943. Long prior to the Second World War the principle of personal responsibility had been recognized.[3]

The requirement of criminal intent is more specific when applied to particular acts of judicial oppression. In such cases, the judge must know not only that he is participating in an organised system of injustice but also that the particular verdict for which he is accused was illegal and would lead to consequences prohibited by the law. The following case from Norway gives an illustration of this. The case was one against two Norwegian judges in the special court set up to try Gunnar Eilifsen.[4] As Chief Superintendent of the Police, Eilifsen supported five of his subordinate police officers who, in August 1943, refused to carry out orders to arrest three women for refusing to assemble to work duty under the Nazi authorities. The refusal was reported to Reichskommissar Terboven, who decided that it was necessary to set an example and demanded that Eilifsen be sentenced to death.

[2] Jescheck (2004), p. 47.
[3] The Justice Case (1951), pp. 977–978.
[4] Reported in NRT 1949, p. 935.

To accommodate this, Quisling signed a law that retroactively made it possible to punish Eilifsen's offence by death and established a special court to try Eilifsen.

The Court was set up with three members: Justice of the Supreme Court Egil Reichborn Kjennerud, Chief of the State Police Karl Martinsen, and Head of the Department of the Order Police in the Ministry of Justice Egil Yngvar Olbjørn. The members of the Court were told by the Minister of Justice and the Chief of Police that the Germans demanded Eilifsen be sentenced to death but that the sentence would be commuted to a prison term by Quisling.

In spite of this, Reichborn Kjennerud and Olbjørn voted for a prison sentence. When the judgment was brought to the Minister for his signature, the Minister and the Chief of Police were furious and demanded that the Court reconsider its sentence. The two judges were told that they would be shot in addition to Eilifsen if they did not return with a death sentence, and they were also reassured that Eilifsen would be pardoned if sentenced to death. The Court reassumed its deliberations, and Olbjørn gave in to the pressure with the result that the Court returned with a 2–1 vote for the death punishment. Eilifsen was not pardoned, and the execution took place later on the same night.

In the subsequent case against Olbjørn, the trial court stated that participation in the special court in itself was an act of criminal collaboration with the enemy. The proceedings were therefore illegal, and Olbjørn was charged with accessory to murder. On the charge of murder, the Court held that since Olbjørn was told that Eilifsen would be pardoned, he could not be found guilty of deliberate murder due to lack of criminal intent. On the other hand, it was seen as negligent of him to place his trust in this promise, so he could be convicted for manslaughter.

Ignorance of Law

The basic barrier against punishing judges is not to establish that an offence has been committed but to establish that the act has been committed with the necessary guilty state of mind. The problematic issue is not with judges who consciously disregard the law to further the oppressive aims of the state he is serving. As stated above, it is not the "monsters" we are concerned with but the good judges and the extent to which they can be held accountable for their participation.

Many of the instances of departures from basic elements of the rule of law are undertaken by honest judges performing their duties as they perceive them under the law and without malicious intent. In the words of high judges from the apartheid regime of South Africa:

> There were certainly a significant number of cases with a high public profile which it can be argued could have been decided differently quite legitimately without any violation of the judicial oath of office. What compounded the disappointment of many was that some of those decisions were decisions of the Appellate Division. But that does not necessarily mean that those who decided them did so perversely, knowing that their conclusion was not the right one, simply in order to please the government of the day, or to give vent

> consciously to their own ideological positions. Any assertion to the contrary is a grave assertion indeed and clear evidence would be required to support it.[5]

In his famous article on statutory non-law and supra-statutory law, Radbruch posed the question: can a person, educated in the legal belief in positivism, be blamed for regarding the laws of the regime as binding law? He does not answer his question but leaves the answer hanging in the air: justice may have been wronged by these judges, but their ignorance may exonerate them. In later works, he is more elaborate to the fact that the positivistic outlook should exonerate judges who committed evil by applying the law in a situation where they knew no alternative.[6]

Helmut Coing offered a slightly different track. Referring to Radbruch's article, he emphasised that the German judges were unprepared for the situation they were faced with under the Nazis and that legal theory did not offer them any tools with which they could defend themselves when the state required them to apply laws that gravely contradicted any notion of justice. He pointed the finger not at any particular legal theory as such but at the lack of institutions and doctrines of legal review and standards by which to judge legislation and other orders of the state. Coing employs the lack of tools and standards to perform a judicial review of the statutes the judges were required to apply as an excuse for their actions. Because they had no tools of resistance, they could not be expected to resist.

The importance of positivism as an explanation for the development of German law in the Nazi period was overrated by Radbruch and his followers.[7] Despite the weaknesses in this position, this was the explanation that was established as the accepted explanation in postwar German legal theory and understanding. There is of course a vast difference between using a factor as an explanation and using it as an excuse. One may explain the acts of a criminal with reference to his desire for the stolen object and lack of impulse control, but few would accept such an explanation as an excuse for his behaviour, and certainly not as a justification.

In his great thesis in defence of the judges who remained "true to their people" during the Nazi period, Hubert Schorn surveys positivism as an excuse and states that "their traditional approach to application and assessment of legislation was not without influence as a cause for the attitude of the judiciary towards National Socialism".[8] He maintains that the attitude to legislation formed a favourable ground for National Socialism, together with the fact that most judges lacked schooling in legal philosophy. They were therefore not equipped to evaluate the Nazi laws against general legal principles and the rule of law. Many judges applied

---

[5] Submission to the South African Truth and Reconciliation Commission by the following members of the Supreme Court of Appeal: Mr. Justice J.W. Smalberger, Mr. Justice C.T. Howie, Mr. Justice R.M. Marais, and Mr. Justice D.G. Scott, 115 S. African Law Journal 1998, pp. 45–46.

[6] See Paulson (1994).

[7] See Chap. 14 below.

[8] Schorn (1959), p. 23.

Nazi laws because they believed that enacted laws were expressions of the law and that they therefore were obliged to follow them.[9]

Over several pages, Schorn describes various theoretical and practical relationships between legal positivism and the legitimacy of the state and the legislator before he draws the conclusion: "One cannot deny many of the judges who applied NS Criminal law the defence of good faith, when they judged what they thought was the law, as they believed it was just to apply the law".[10]

Where South African judges are referring to cases where less oppressive results could have been legitimately reached within the legitimacy of the system itself, Radbruch and Schorn discuss the matter as if the judges had no choice, no scope of discretion within the system. While this does not mean that they thought that judges to whom legitimate alternatives were available were eligible for punishment, they do set up a stronger test case. For if it is possible to show that the subjective conditions for criminal liability are fulfilled for judges who had to step outside of the legitimacy of the system itself in order not to commit serious violations, this must be even more the case for judges who could have avoided becoming violators within the rules of the system itself. This also means that it is easier to defend liability for judges in supreme courts that have a greater scope of shaping the law than for judges in lower courts who are bound by precedents.

Neither of the South African judges, Radbruch and Schorn, mentions the fact that error in law does not normally count as a justification or excuse in criminal matters and that the error of positivism at least merits a discussion as to whether it should count as an error in law or an error in fact. If a judge, for instance, is unaware of the fact that if he denies habeas corpus for a person detained by the police this person will be tortured and put in an extermination camp, he is not acting with criminal intent regarding the torture and murder of this person. If a judge is aware of this but believes it to be the law, unaware of the fact that he has a duty not to apply laws that substantially and obviously violates the person's rights, then we have the issue of whether the requirements for punishing the judge are fulfilled. Ignorance or misunderstanding of the law will, in many jurisdictions, not exclude the establishment of criminal intent unless the misunderstanding is excusable.

The error of positivism and the good faith of a person believing he is following the law were not accepted as an excuse by Norwegian courts when assessing the guilt of judges who accepted appointment to the Quisling courts. In the case against Arnvid Vassbotten, who accepted the position as a judge in the Quisling Supreme Court, the trial court stated:

> The defendant has related to the occupation as a lawyer and directed his whole behaviour based upon crafty, but also subtle interpretations of international law, of which he regarded himself to have special knowledge of.
>
> Both the judgment of the Supreme Court of February 10, 1941 and the whole attitude of the defendant, are dictated by the formal legal view that the Norwegian population had a

[9] Schorn (1959), pp. 30–31.

[10] Schorn (1959), p. 31.

> duty to maintain the operations of the state in cooperation with the German occupiers, and by a theoretical consideration of his duties as a government official towards the Germans under international law.
>
> By a light retouch of the words of the defendant in the pamphlet mentioned afore one might say that it is discouraging to observe how legal thought and sober considerations darken and overshadow his patriotism and national insight.
>
> From the defendant's view on the power and legal status of the occupying forces one must acknowledge that his motives have been honourable, and that he, like many others who have betrayed their country, has not had the direct intention of aiding the enemy.
>
> He has acted out of his individual opinion on what served the country best, and completely forgotten or set aside the faithfulness and obedience to the lawful authorities of the nation, to whom he as an official of the state owed special obedience.[11]

As we see, the Court here accepted that Vassbotten acted not out of condemnable motives but out of a belief in law and a perceived obligation of obedience. Nevertheless, his erroneous belief was not an excuse for criminal liability. There is, on the other hand, a difference between Vassbotten and the German judges. Whereas Vassbotten with his belief was the odd man out in Norwegian society, the German judges who believed in their obligation towards the Nazi regime were the vast majority of their profession.

Initially, in cases against members of other professions than judges, German courts did not accept ignorance of the law as a valid excuse against criminal punishment. Many of the accused in the euthanasia cases invoked the secret Act from Hitler of 1939 as the excuse for their contribution. This order made the action legal, they claimed, at least in the mind of the perpetrators who could not be blamed for believing that their actions were legal. Initially, this defence was rejected by the courts that argued a decision to kill defenceless people out of reasons of social utility was contrary to the core of any conception of justice. For the same reason, the defendants could not be heard with their pretence that they had believed in the legality of the Act.

From the beginning of the 1950s, however, the courts' treatment of mistakes of law changed, and it was recognised that such mistakes could be exculpating for lack of criminal intent on the hand of the defendant. Applying this rule, the courts' view on euthanasia shifted, and some judges started to argue that the present attitude was not self-evident since society's attitude had varied and that euthanasia has been defended by authorities such as Seneca, Thomas More, and Martin Luther. Based on such reasons, courts started to acquit doctors of murder charges, especially in cases of euthanasia of children.[12]

The judges were treated even more understandingly than the doctors since the courts did not even question the reasonableness of their claim that they acted from a belief that they were upholding the law. In the Rehse case, the German Supreme Court stated that a judge could only be punished for voting for a death sentence if he so voted for nefarious reasons.[13] Hans-Joachim Rehse had been a member of the

[11] NRT 1946, p. 1268.

[12] See Freudiger (2002), pp. 336–350.

[13] BGH, Urteil vom 30. 4. 1968-5 StR 670/67.

People's Court, "the most notorious Nazi judicial innovation", in the words of Telford Taylor,[14] and had been co-assessor with the infamous Roland Freisler in many of his capital cases. The Supreme Court stated correctly that each judge serving on the bench has individual responsibility for his own vote and must be judged on his own account. Freisler had been an intimidating person, but Rehse was nonetheless responsible for his own actions.

The Court did not discuss the issue of whether the grounds for the convictions of the People's Court were legal or not; it seems to have taken this as established. Thereby, it appears that the Supreme Court rejected the opinion expressed by Radbruch in his article from 1946 since the main task of the People's Court was to enforce laws that "governed solely by the momentary necessities of intimidation, disregarded the varying gravity of offences and threatened the same punishment, often death, for the slightest as well as the most serious of crimes".[15] In practice, however, this may not have had such a great effect. Whether the acts of a judge were illegal or not, a judge who exercises his function as a judge in a proper way without jeopardising the independence of the court or taking into account irrelevant factors will not have the necessary intent to commit a crime, according to the Supreme Court. And a judge who willingly and knowingly steps outside of these lines can be punished, according to the Supreme Court, for misconduct in office and, according to Radbruch, for committing the crime of murder, detention, or whatever wrong he inflicts on the persons he sentences. Under both approaches, a judge who keeps to his functions as a judge will be immune to criminal sanctions no matter how unjust the laws are that he bases his judgments on. And this seems to have been the approach of the West German courts after the war, since scarcely any judge was punished for rulings given during the Nazi period.

Proving the intent to do wrong by misapplying the law or by employing the law for extralegal purposes is a difficult task for a prosecution. Additionally, such a requirement makes any postulation of a duty of the judge to abstain from applying the most oppressive laws without practical relevance in criminal law. According to this standard, only undeniably evil judges can be punished. Even the fanatics, the ones who pursue the evil aims of an oppressive regime to the very end, are acquitted as long as they believe that they are performing judicial functions within the scope of the law.

In cases against judges and prosecutors of the GDR regime, the German Supreme Court stated that a prosecutor or judge who believed his actions were legal because they were obedient and loyal to the regime might be regarded as being in error of the law and that this error in any case could not be of the kind to excuse the act and make it less culpable under criminal law.[16]

In a 1995 case against a member of the GDR Supreme Court, the defendant was accused of voting for penalties that were grossly disproportional in relation to the

---

[14] The Justice Case (1951), p. 38.

[15] Radbruch (1946).

[16] See Senat, NJW 1995, p. 3324, and BGH, Urteil vom 16.11.1995 5 StR 747/94, p. 857.

crimes. The defendant admitted that he had felt that the punishments were too strict, but he had nevertheless chosen to vote with the majority. The German Supreme Court acknowledged that his experience that the punishments were disproportionate did not in itself amount to knowledge that his colleagues were in fact violating their duty not to commit substantial and obvious violations of individual rights. Such actual knowledge was, however, not necessary to punish the judge for his contribution to the verdict. In the words of the German Supreme Court:

> Faced with the particularly high requirements that must be fulfilled to establish the violation of a duty in an objective sense since this is limited to obviously serious and intended violations of human rights, it is inconceivable that a professional judge will not see the obvious illegality of his decision.[17]

The Supreme Court also pointed to the fact that the procedures followed in some of the cases had been deficient and that one trial was not free from elements of being a mock trial where the object was more to deter through annihilation of the defendant than to seek justice. This also contributed to the establishment of the necessary criminal intent.

In the Justice Case, the US Military Tribunal recognised that a condition for finding a person guilty was that the accused knew or should have known that he was guilty of participation in a nationally organised system of injustice and persecution shocking to the moral sense of mankind and that he knew or should have known that he would be subject to punishment if caught. The Tribunal however treated any ignorance of the illegality of the acts committed by the judiciary as non-exonerating ignorance of the law.[18] The Tribunal did not inquire into the actual knowledge of the accused of the rules of international law or the intent of the Allies to bring them to force. If this knowledge had formed part of the requirement to establish criminal intent, such inquiries would have been necessary on the part of the Tribunal. As it stands, after the judgment of the Tribunal, knowledge of the fact that war crimes and crimes against humanity are punishable under international law, and of the fact that legality under municipal law is no excuse, is not a necessary requirement to establish criminal intent.

Duress

A different defence, related to the question of criminal intent, is the allegation that the judge was under coercion and that he ruled as he did out of fear of severe sanctions. If the judge had passed judgment out of the belief that he was merely fulfilling his normal functions of a judge, he would lack the necessary criminal intent. If he ruled out of fear, however, his sentence was motivated by extralegal reasons. His decision would no longer be a judicial decision but an intentional

[17] BGH, Urteil vom 16.11.1995 5 StR 747/94 p. 857 on p. 862.

[18] The Justice Case (1951), p. 978.

departure from the duty to decide the case solely on the basis of the facts and the law. Should it exempt him from punishment if he could prove that he judged the way he did out of fear of his life?

The defence of coercion was also put forward by Radbruch in his 1946 article. This excuse of coercion was contested by some writers in the postwar discussion on judicial responsibility in Germany. Kurt Oppler pointed out in an article from 1947 that German judges were not in fact coerced or were at least not threatened with loss of life or office. The many instances where judges did not follow the will of the party without losing their office prove this.[19] Apparently, no judge who was put on trial in Germany after the war made the claim of coercion. A principled argument against exonerating judges because of coercion was delivered by Robert Figge.[20] He pointed out that there are several professions where the members of the profession are expected even to sacrifice their life in the line of duty: soldiers, police, firemen, and sailors. He argued that the judge in the same way has a duty to sacrifice his job, and even his life, to protect law and justice. If this is the case, then fear of coercion can be no legal defence for a judge. He has a duty to stand up for the protection of justice and defend it, if necessary, with his life.

This might seem like a harsh demand. The same approach was nevertheless taken in some cases where the judge had been threatened to return a particular verdict. In the Eilifsen case from Norway mentioned above, the members of the special court were pressured into acting as judges and also threatened that they would be shot by the Germans if they did not pass the death sentence on Eilifsen. The Court rejected this defence, however.[21] According to the Court, he had no right as a judge to jeopardise the life of another to save himself from punishment, even from the threat of execution. In any event, the Court stated, it did not see it as likely that the Germans would execute a Norwegian judge for refusing to impose the death penalty.

Hannah Arendt argues that the choice between acting out orders and taking the consequences of refusing is a free choice between alternatives, even when the consequences of refusal are severe punishment. "If someone points a gun at you and says 'Kill your friend or I will kill you,' he is *tempting* you, that is all".[22] Choosing to do evil only entails that the person prefers doing wrong to suffering wrong, which is something different from being forced to do something.

Nevertheless, the law often exonerates a person who is acting at the point of a gun. When this is the case, it is often by a doctrine of duress or necessity that the surrender of one good is necessary to save another. This can also be applied when one is out to save oneself, for example when breaking into a cabin in the mountains during a winter storm to seek shelter from the deadly weather.

---

[19] Oppler (1947).

[20] Figge (1947).

[21] NRT 1949, p. 935.

[22] Arendt (2003), p. 17, quoting Mary McCarthy.

According to the ICC Statute, Article 31 (1)(d), there must be a threat of imminent death or of continuing or imminent serious bodily harm against that person or another person for duress to be an excuse. As we saw in the Eilifsen case, this condition is seldom fulfilled in the case of a judge. The other condition is that the person acts necessarily and reasonably to avoid this threat and does not intend to cause a greater harm than the one sought to be avoided. This defence will always imply a balancing of the stakes, and the gain that is won must outweigh the good that is relinquished. On this account, one might say that one should never be permitted to commit the grave acts of substantial and obvious violations of the rights of another in order to save oneself. Grave personal danger might be counted as a mitigating circumstance towards a lower sentence but not as a reason for acquittal. This, I think, is in accordance with general criminal law in many countries.

Discussion

A conclusion of this survey is that in the context of holding judges accountable for sentences that entail obvious and substantial violations of individual rights, ignorance of the fact that this could be deemed a criminal offence is no valid defence. This is well established in international law and is also well in line with how ignorance of the law is treated by criminal law in many national jurisdictions. It is a paradox in the German postwar cases against Nazis that those of whom one should expect the highest knowledge of the law were treated with most understanding when it comes to the effect of their ignorance on their guilt. Overall, there was a tendency of the courts to treat crimes of defendants from the upper social strata such as lawyers, doctors, and military officers more leniently than crimes of people from the lower strata. The treatment of judges was, however, even in this picture exceptionally lenient.[23]

There are scant grounds to treat judges differently from others and allowing them to invoke ignorance of the law to a greater extent than others when accused of similar violations. The Norwegian Supreme Court turned the arguments around. In the case against Mohr, who accepted the position as president of the Supreme Court after the judges appointed before the occupation had resigned, it was stated that "it had to be apparent to a man with the defendant's legal education and experience as a judge that the occupying power were engaged in the breaking down of the defences set by international law in favour of an occupied state".[24] If anything, one should expect higher standards from judges, not lower.

---

[23] Freudiger (2002), p. 416.

[24] NRT 1946, p. 1139.

That judges are acting in fear of loss of their careers, jobs, or even their personal safety under oppressive regimes cannot be an excuse. In tyrannies, many people are acting in fear. They must still be held responsible for evil and wicked deeds.

References

Arendt H (2003) Responsibility and judgment. Schocken Books, New York

Figge R (1947) Die Verantwortlichkeit des Richters. Süddeutsche Juristen-Zeitung, col. 179–183

Freudiger K (2002) Die juristische Aufarbeitung von NS-Verbrechen. Mohr Siebeck, Tübingen

Jescheck H-H (2004) The general principles of international criminal law set out in Nuremberg, as mirrored in the ICC Statute. J Int Crim Justice 2:38–55

Oppler K (1947) Justiz und Politik. Deutsche Rechts-Zeitschrift 2:323–326

Paulson SL (1994) Lon L. Fuller, Gustav Radbruch and the "Positivist" theses. Law Philos 13:313–359

Radbruch G (1946) Gesetzliches Unrecht und übergesetzliches Recht. Süddeutsche Juristen-Zeitung 105–108 [English translation Statutory Lawlessness and Supra-Statutory Law, Translated by Bonnie Litschewski Paulson and Stanley L. Paulson, 26 Oxford Journal of Legal Studies 2006, pp. 1–11]

Schorn H (1959) Der Richter im Dritten Reich Geschichte und Dokumente. Vittorio Klostermann, Frankfurt am Main

Trials of War Criminals before the Nuremberg Military Tribunals, vol III, the Justice Case, Washington, 1951

Chapter 12
A Special Immunity for Judges?

Obligations and Orders

In his famous article from 1946 on statutory lawlessness, German politician and legal scholar Gustav Radbruch compares the slogans "orders are orders" and "law is law" and concludes that the Nazi regime employed both of them to ensure the loyalty of its subjects. But whereas the obedience of the soldier has never been regarded as absolute, because orders may be illegal, positivism ensures that the law's requirements are limitless. This was the attitude of the prevailing legal thought that, according to Radbruch, rendered the legal profession defenceless in the face of its Nazi masters.

Perhaps one could claim that the excuse of following the law is just the lawyers' variety of the more general excuse of following orders—an excuse that was rejected in the trial in Nuremberg against the major war criminals. According to Article 8 of the Nuremberg Charter, "the fact that the defendant acted pursuant to order of his government shall not free him from responsibility". The Military Tribunal in the trial against the major war criminals interpreted this in the following passage:

> The provisions of this Article are in conformity with the law of all nations. That a soldier was ordered to kill or torture in violation of the international law of war has never been recognized as a defense to such acts of brutality, though, as the Charter here provides, the order may be urged in mitigation of the punishment. The true test, which is found in varying degrees in the criminal laws of most nations, is not the existence of the order, but whether moral choice was in fact possible.[1]

What is implicated in the term "whether moral choice was in fact possible" is open to interpretation. One alternative is that an order in itself is never an excuse, but the fact that the defendant acted according to an order can be one of the facts considered when determining whether he acted with the necessary criminal intent.

---

[1] Trial of the Major War Criminals before the International Military Tribunal, Nuremberg, vol. 16, 466.

H.P. Graver, *Judges Against Justice*, DOI 10.1007/978-3-662-44293-7_12

With regard to the more serious crimes, misunderstanding of the law should not exclude criminal intent regardless of whether the misunderstanding is due to an order or other circumstances.

Are there reasons to accept that a judge, because of his special function and responsibility, should be allowed to invoke the defence of 'just following the law' in situations where others are condemned, despite the fact that they are acting on superior orders? Or should the defence of the judge be construed so as to coincide with the defence of superior orders? Legal scholar and political scientist Otto Kirchheimer points to a basic difference between a soldier and a judge with regard to superior orders. While both the soldier and the judge owe loyalty, the objects of their loyalty are different. The soldier owes loyalty to the command structure, whereas the judge owes loyalty to the mandate of the law.[2] The law is not a chain of command, and the judge, unlike the soldier, is expected to exercise his own discretion in determining the contents of the law. This difference means that, in some respects, less is at stake for the judge than for the soldier—blind obedience is not expected of the judge, and he may object to the interpretation offered by others. On the other hand, the loyalty expected from him is in a sense greater since he has a measure of freedom and choice. These questions take us into the heart of the issue of judicial immunity: should a judge who follows the law be immune to later charges of responsibility for the consequences of his ruling?

Under the Allies' war crime trials against German judicial officials, judicial immunity was recognised as a defence where judges in occupying territories were charged with sentencing persons charged with, for example, espionage or assaults. The pleas of judges in such cases were that such people were tried and convicted according to the rights of occupying powers under international law. This plea was allowed to prevail if it were shown that the victim was accorded a fair trial.[3] In many cases by national courts against war criminals, judges were convicted, however, for denying the accused the right to a fair trial. The United Nations War Crimes Commission gives the following examples:

1. that captured airmen were tried "on false and fraudulent charges" and "upon false and fraudulent evidence",
2. that the accused airmen were not afforded the right to a defence counsel,
3. that the accused airmen were not given the right to have an interpretation in their own language of the trial proceedings,
4. that the accused fliers were not allowed an opportunity to defend themselves.

The Commission also stated that "it is a violation of the law of war, on which there could be a conviction if supported by evidence, to inflict capital punishment on prisoners of war without affording to them opportunity to make a defence".[4]

[2] Kirchheimer (1961), p. 176.

[3] Law Reports of Trials of War Criminals, vol. 15, p. 161.

[4] Law Reports of Trials of War Criminals, vol. 15, p. 163.

If a judge is awarded immunity, it cannot be because of the fact that he is not regarded as a responsible agent as such. One could argue, of course, that when the judge applies the law, it is the law that should be blamed and not the judge. But in this respect, there is no difference between the judge and the person following an order. Criminal or moral responsibility does not presuppose that the agent executing an act also is the author of the act. It suffices for blame that the actor had a possibility to refuse.

Hannah Arendt makes a case that there is no such thing as obedience in political and moral matters. Although every organisation demands obedience to superiors and to the laws of the land, those who obey actually support, and without such support, "no man, however strong, can ever accomplish anything, good or bad".[5] Obedience is, in other words, participation and support.

Immunity and the Role of the Judge

If the judge should be excused for following the law, it can therefore not be for the fact that the judge is fulfilling a duty. The reason must lie in the nature of the judge's role that immunity from consequences of performing a judicial role is important or necessary to society in order for the judges to fulfil the tasks required of them. In his article, Radbruch states:

> The culpability of judges for homicide presupposes the simultaneous determination that they have perverted the law, since the independent judge's decision can be an object of punishment only if he has violated the very principle that his independence was intended to serve, the principle of submission to the statute, that is, to the law.[6]

Radbruch here invokes the independence of the judge as a basis for immunity: a judge who serves the law cannot be punished.

The traditional argument for judicial immunity is that the judge should be free to apply the law without fearing the consequences in order to be able to apply the law in an independent and impartial way. If the judge is under the pressure from other factors than the relevant facts and law in the case, his decision may be influenced by factors outside the scope of the law, and justice will not be done.

This is a different argument than the argument that the judge is just following the law. If the law is perceived as determined and formal, the situation of the judge becomes more like the situation of a soldier following an order. But to the extent the judge has a scope of discretion and must make a professional choice, immunity becomes more important to protect the integrity of this choice. This choice should not be made under the influence of parties or others trying to influence the judge in an extralegal manner, nor should it be made under the influence of fear of consequences the judge may encounter after the decision by action of disappointed

[5] Arendt (2003), p. 46.

[6] Radbruch (1946).

parties or public officials. The point is presented in a clear way by former Chief Justice of South Africa M.M. Corbett in his presentation to the Truth and Reconciliation Commission:

> In order to be true to his judicial oath and to administer justice to all persons alike "without fear, favour or prejudice" a judge must enjoy independence from the legislature, from the executive, from any other body or authority which could be tempted to influence his decisions. Only under those circumstances can justice be done in the courts.[7]

This is an important point. Most would agree that it is illegitimate to approach a judge before the ruling in order to try to influence or intimidate him. Likewise, there is a general consensus as to the inappropriateness of the judge letting himself be led by considerations outside of the scope of the facts and the law of the case. In principle, there should be no difference whether the external factors are matters that are known to him in advance or whether they concern possible consequences or repercussions that he may be confronted with in the future. We do not want judges who allow their rulings to be influenced by a real or perceived need to cover their backs.

Immunity for judges is a compelling legal principle in some jurisdictions. Common law countries are notable examples.[8] It is also an internationally recognised principle. The UN Basic Principles on the Independence of the Judiciary state in section 4 that "there shall not be any inappropriate or unwarranted interference with the judicial process, nor shall judicial decisions by the courts be subject to revision".[9] Immunity for the judge is seen as important to ensure that the judge can determine cases as he sees the law without fear of criticism or repercussions. There is no immunity from liability for criminal activity, and judicial immunity does not apply to disciplinary actions against judges for violations of professional and ethical standards that pertain to their conduct.

Since the judge is not immune from being charged with crimes, this should settle the matter: judicial immunity is not a defence for the judge charged with violating basic rights when applying oppressive laws. On the other hand, the lenience that is shown to such judges, even after contributing to the most unthinkable atrocities, indicates that there is a reluctance to make judges responsible for their contributions. Some of this reluctance may be based on the concept that the judge should be immune from sanctions when he is being obedient to the law and is applying it in a professionally recognised manner.

In common law, judicial immunity is a deeply entrenched doctrine. It has been used to guard judges from common law causes of action, including false imprisonment, malicious prosecution, and libel, as well as from statutory causes of action for the deprivation of civil liberties and constitutional rights.[10] Although judicial immunity is not recognised as a formal defence in criminal or disciplinary cases,

[7] Corbett (1998), p. 20.

[8] See Shaman (1990).

[9] For a presentation of the principles, see Lippman (1992–1993), pp. 311–317.

[10] Shaman (1990), p. 2.

the application of sanctions on judges for their decisions, even if they clearly disregarded the law, is so seldom that it, in practice, amounts to a judicial immunity. In the US, there is a long-standing reluctance to sanction judges for decisions made on the merits of the case. The sanctions that are applied, if at all, are mild and presuppose patterns of errors or obvious or egregious errors made in bad faith.[11] The state of the law is such that it can be questioned if the judge even has a duty to apply the law.

A doctrine of judicial immunity has been used to escape facing criticism for contributing to a breakdown of the rule of law. In South Africa, judicial officers (both judges and magistrates) declined to attend the hearing of the Truth Commission on the institutional hearing on the legal community; their responses took the form of a few written submissions.[12] Chief Justice M.M. Corbett explained their refusal in the following manner:

> This does not mean that a judge is not accountable or above the law. He is accountable to a superior court of appeal; he performs his duties openly and in public and is thus subject to daily scrutiny and criticism; and in the last resort there is impeachment. Outside these parameters, however, a judge may not be called upon to account for his or her judgments or to debate and justify before, for instance, governmental bodies or commissions. To require such accounting before the TRC would, in my view, be contrary to and subversive of the principle of judicial independence.[13]

The fact that the purpose of the hearing was not to establish guilt or hold individuals responsible and thus was not of a judicial or quasi-judicial nature did not have any bearing on the judges' willingness to appear.[14]

Judicial immunity, however, is by no means universally recognised. In Germany, for instance, judicial immunity is no defence against the crime of "bending the law" (*Rechtsbeugung* according to the Criminal Code, section 339).[15] It is also interesting to note that the concept of judicial immunity is not made an explicit part of the UN Basic Principles on the Independence of the Judiciary or the Bangalore Principles of Judicial Conduct.

Should we allow judicial immunity as a defence for judges accused of undermining the rule of law by enforcing and expanding oppressive legislation and repressive regimes? The heart of the matter is that in cases where the law is evil, we *want* the judge to be influenced by factors outside of the law. Law is never completely rational, and questions of law and fact are never completely determined. This means that elements of judgment, and thus morality and ethics, enter into any

---

[11] Brand-Ballard (2010), pp. 61–70.

[12] Report of Truth and Reconciliation Commission of South Africa, Volume 4, 29 October 1998, p. 93.

[13] Corbett (1998).

[14] Dyzenhaus speculates that there may have been other reasons for the reluctance of the judges to appear; see Dyzenhaus (1998), pp. 36–46.

[15] It has been claimed that the German Supreme Court, through a restrictive interpretation and application of section 339 (previously 336), has created what amounts to judicial immunity in practice; see Spendel (1996), pp. 809–812.

legal decision-making. We want judges to act as moral agents in extreme situations and to protect the rule of law when it is under attack. Historical experience shows that the main problem we face is not rogue judges deviating from the law but obedient judges who, for various reasons, contribute to authoritarian regimes, evil laws, and erosion of the rule of law. Since judicial immunity can only be defended from the perspective of rule of law, it should not be constructed in such a way that it contributes to the erosion of the rule of law. "When judges make themselves complicit in state oppression they cannot cite their independence as an 'insurmountable obstacle' to their being made accountable".[16] Rather, judicial immunity should be constructed so that it can foster the defence of the rule of law. This would entail that judicial immunity is not available as a defence to a judge who is accused of violating fundamental aspects of the rule of law.

On the other hand, one could argue that if one does not recognise judicial immunity as an absolute principle, this would put judges in authoritarian regimes in an even more precarious position. It is a fact that many repressive states seem reluctant to interfere directly in the operations of the courts in such an overt way that would entail sanctioning a judge.[17] Even in Nazi Germany, sanctions against opposing judges were mild, as long as the judges kept their opposition to the bench and did not engage in subversive activities. It would, therefore, be an argument against limiting the scope of judicial immunity if this could encourage authoritarian regimes to engage stronger measures to discipline judges than they seem to do.

Particularly in the case of Germany, however, there is reason to doubt whether the restraint of the regime towards the judiciary can be explained with reference to a principle or rule of judicial immunity. The regime certainly had no second thoughts in departing from basic principles and commands of the rule of law. Why should it be different with a rule protecting judges from being held personally responsible for undesirable rulings? The explanation lies probably elsewhere than in the existence of a nationally and internationally recognised rule of judicial immunity.

The Nazi Party opted for a strategy to achieve its position by ostensible legal means and took great pains not to be blamed for discarding the concept of the "Rechtsstaat". This policy of striving for legitimacy by reference to legality, albeit grounded in new concepts such as "the need of the German people" and "the will of the Führer", required that independence of the judiciary be formally upheld. The need for legitimacy was also probably what protected judges who sought to mitigate the harshness of the Nazi legislation, not a norm of judicial immunity. Any reference to such a norm would easily have been brushed away as unwarranted "normativism" and a liberal reminiscence of the old regime.

The relative restraint of the Nazis towards the courts is not exceptional. In many authoritarian regimes, formal independence of the courts is respected, but judges are protected only as long as they are useful. A norm of immunity will not protect

---

[16] Dyzenhaus (1998), p. 146.

[17] See pp. 39–45 above.

them. The only effect of maintaining a norm that protects judges who apply evil law will therefore only be to protect evil judges when the times change. Such a rule is therefore more to the benefit of authoritarian regimes than to the rule of law.

Judicial Independence and Immunity

Judicial immunity is only granted to judges acting in a judicial capacity. As a consequence, a judge acting on the instruction of another, be it one of the parties or an organ of the state, should not be able to invoke judicial immunity as a defence of his actions. A judge acting under instructions from the government is no different from an administrative functionary.

The Military Tribunal in the Justice Case stated that Nazi judges were "not entitled to the benefit of the Anglo-American doctrine of judicial immunity because that doctrine is based on the concept of an independent judiciary administering impartial justice".[18] The pressure and coercion applied to the judges was, in other words, a reason for not granting them the benefit of judicial immunity.

On the other hand, the very same lack of freedom has been cited as an exonerating circumstance for judges of the Nazi period. Hubert Schorn details in his book how the judges were directed through the secret "Richterbriefe" of the Ministry of Justice and, more informally, by doctrinal writings of Nazi legal scholars and repeated criticism in the SS press. "It goes without saying that such repeated proclamations and assertions influenced the judiciary, and that the constant drumfire against their competence made them unsecure and courage-less", writes Schorn.[19] The judges were put under the normal regulation of civil servants and were obliged to swear allegiance to Hitler. Both Hitler himself and the leading echelons of the judicial system served as bad "role-models" to the judiciary.

If we accept a certain scope for the defence of judicial immunity, which many jurisdictions do, we still have to decide on the conditions that must be fulfilled to apply the defence. A precondition for judicial immunity under the doctrine of judicial immunity under common law is that the judge is not in clear absence of jurisdiction and is performing judicial acts. This seems a reasonable starting point. There is no reason for exonerating a judge performing pure acts of administration to a greater extent than the official in a public office.

But what about other conditions? Should judicial immunity be awarded on the basis of the purely formal criterion that the act in question is ostensibly a judicial act? Judicial immunity is normally reserved to the substance of the judge's ruling. The judge is not immune to disciplinary reactions if he departs from basic procedural requirements or acts in a way that is contrary to his duties as a judge. But to

[18] The Justice Case (1951), pp. 1024–1025.

[19] Schorn (1959), p. 79.

what extent should such circumstances also deprive him of the defence of judicial immunity towards attacks on his substantive decisions?

Even if the judge is acting in a court with general legitimacy, a lack of independence—for example, a prior agreement between the judge and one of the parties on how the case will be decided—will deprive the ruling of its judicial nature and thereby expose the judge to liability. What applies to agreements must also apply to a situation in which the judge is acting under clear orders or under coercion, for example from political or judicial authorities, to decide a case in a certain way. As stated in a private letter by Rudolf Oeschey, who was a judge in Nuremberg during World War II, a system where the judge is told how to decide individual cases renders the judge superfluous.[20]

The same view is expressed by Jeffrey Shaman in his presentation of the doctrine of judicial immunity under common law:

> After all, a prior, private agreement by a judge to rule in a particular way is totally incompatible with the judicial role of deciding cases impartially on the basis of evidence and arguments presented in court with all parties present.[21]

The basic reasoning behind such statements is that a decision that is prearranged is not a judicial decision and that the judge is therefore not acting in a judicial capacity when he sanctions it. Taking orders from a party is corruption; taking orders from the government is acting as a part of the executive branch and not the judicial branch of the state.

US courts have decided that advance agreements or conspiracies by a judge to rule in favour of a party are within the scope of judicial immunity, so long as the judge is not acting in the clear absence of jurisdiction.[22] In other jurisdictions, this has been seen differently. In the Justice Case, the Military Tribunal went into detail in examining the way the Nazi Party, the Ministry of Justice, and the SS sought to pressure and influence judges. After summarising the evidence, the Tribunal concluded:

> In view of the conclusive proof of the sinister influences which were in constant interplay between Hitler, his ministers, the Ministry of Justice, the Party, the Gestapo, and the courts, we see no merit in the suggestion that Nazi judges are entitled to the benefit of the Anglo-American doctrine of judicial immunity. The doctrine that judges are not personally liable for their judicial actions is based on the concept of an independent judiciary administering impartial justice. Furthermore, it has never prevented the prosecution of a judge for malfeasance in office. If the evidence cited supra does not demonstrate the utter destruction of judicial independence and impartiality, then we "never writ nor no man ever proved." The function of the Nazi courts was judicial only in a limited sense. They more closely resembled administrative tribunals acting under directives from above in a quasi-judicial manner.[23]

---

[20] The Justice Case (1951), p. 1020.

[21] Shaman (1990), pp. 12–13.

[22] Shaman (1990), p. 12.

[23] The Justice Case (1951), pp. 1024–1025.

The same principle is enshrined in many national jurisdictions. Otto Kirchheimer states in his book on political justice:

> The judge who mortgages his freedom in advance, whether out of fear or out of subservience, does not, as both German and French courts had occasion to insist, want to act as a judge.[24]

An action with fixed results may be called a trial for purposes of propaganda but will nevertheless not merit the label of a trial. It is important to distinguish between trials that are conducted for political purposes or that have elements of a political trial, on one hand, and a "spectacle with prearranged results", on the other.

We find a notable example where the results of nominal court proceedings were found not to be judicial at all in the case of the so-called *Waldheimer-prozesse* of the former GDR. In 1950, the regime arranged for the trial and conviction of 3,432 persons who had been detained and held by the Soviet occupying forces in Germany. The trials were conducted by special prosecutors and judges who had been trained for this purpose and who had been instructed by the Party rulers on how to proceed and decide. The trials were held over a few weeks in secret, apart from ten cases that were held as public show trials. The proceedings resulted in 32 capital sentences, 24 of which were executed, and in long prison sentences for most of the accused. Not one accused was acquitted. In a subsequent ruling from 1954 on the legality of the trials, a West Berlin court stated:

> In effect the proceedings were not those of courts established and staffed according to the Judicial Procedures Act, but rather of commissions established by the Soviet–German administration with the sole task of passing verdict on the said group of people. They must be seen as Special Courts similar to their predecessors of the Nazi time that were prohibited by to the orders of the Allied Occupying Forces, and that also are prohibited according to provision 134 of the Constitution of the GDR which states that "No citizen may be deprived of the right to be judged by statutory judges. Special courts are inadmissible . . ." Their judgments can therefore not be recognized as binding; the verdicts that they have passed—according to the authorities more than three thousand—are as non-existent, that is they are null and void.[25]

But how strong should pressure be when applied on a judge before it can be said that his independence and impartiality breaks down? In situations where the judge is acting under an oppressive regime or when the social pressure on the judge to limit rights is strong, one may ask when the judiciary ceases to be independent. Formally, the German judges retained their independence throughout the Nazi regime and individual judges were seldom told in advance how to decide individual cases. In reality, however, they were under strong pressure from the Nazis and the leading judicial authorities to decide the cases according to Nazi ideology.

This question of course entails a subjective side. If the judge bends to pressure and his judgment is motivated not by the law but by the instruction or pressure he is under, he is no longer acting independently. He is then not fulfilling his obligation

---

[24] Kirchheimer (1961), p. 339.

[25] K.G. Berlin, Beschluss vom 15.03.1954—1 RHE AR 7/54.

to follow the law, and consequently he cannot appeal to the law as an exonerating circumstance for the consequences of his decisions.

But the issue can also be seen from an objective side. Not any expression of wish for an outcome by responsible political authorities or any criticism of judicial rulings can amount to instructions or pressure that causes the independence of the judiciary to break down. Even in Nazi Germany, there were cases were judges refused to follow instructions with the argument that instructions could not create legal duties for independent judges.[26] If fact, evaluations of the situation in Nazi Germany show that the threshold is quite high before one must conclude that the courts are not acting independently.[27]

From this, we must conclude that even under circumstances where the judges are under extreme pressure from a coercive regime, the performance of the courts may be judicial in nature. The significance of preserving the immunity of the judges against individual sanctions is no less under such circumstances. It is of vital importance that this is the one bar that even oppressive regimes are reluctant to cross.

Responsibility is an individual matter. In instances where we cannot say that independence has broken down as such, we must draw a line between institutional independence and independence in the individual case. In its first case against the judges of the former GDR after the reunification of Germany, the German Supreme Court expressed it in this way:

> Even when the courts are not de facto independent, they can resolve conflicts and punish satisfactorily to the extent that they approach the parties in a neutral way with an aspiration to do justice.

Therefore, pressure and independence must be assessed in the individual instance. The conclusion of the Justice Case was that judicial independence in general had broken down, so the defendants could not invoke the doctrine of judicial immunity in their defence. Their reasoning does not, therefore, give guidance on how to draw the line in individual cases.

However, there are other cases from the trials of judges from the Nazi period that may give guidance.

In the few cases that came before the West German Supreme Court, the threshold to regard court proceedings as mere mock trials was set very high. In its ruling from 1956 in the case against Otto Thorbeck and Walter Huppenkothen, the Court did not find that the proceedings of the special courts against Canaris and several of his associates in the concentration camps of Sachsenhausen and Flossenbürg on 6 and 8 April 1945 had not been independent trials.[28]

The trial court had found that the trials were mere scams ordered by Hitler, Himmler, or Kaltenbrunner in order to dress up the execution of the prisoners in a

---

[26] For an example, see Schorn (1959), p. 443.

[27] See above pp. 177–185.

[28] BGH, Urteil vom 19.06.1956—1 StR 50/56 (LG Augsburg).

legal form. The trials were held immediately after Hitler had ordered the extermination (Vernichtung) of the prisoners, after reading extracts from Canaris's diary discovered in an Abwehr safe by the Gestapo a few days earlier. The accused had at that point been held as detainees of the Gestapo for months, but no trial had been initiated due to lack of evidence.[29]

Although there was no haste due to the long period that had already passed since the prisoners were detained, the trials were held as expedient SS summary trials within days of the decision to try the prisoners. The crimes they were accused of dated as far back as a year, 1 even 7 years. Even Thorbeck himself was surprised when he learned this.[30] The prisoners were tried by SS courts, although by rank and status they should have been put before military courts. They were held in the confines of the concentration camps, which were also the place of execution; they bore evidence of having been tortured; and the prisoners received no prewarning and were not given the aid of a defence counsel. One of the prisoners, Hans von Dohnanyi, was taken from his sickbed on a stretcher probably unconscious due to medication. The prisoners were executed immediately after sentencing.

The trial court regarded it as established that both Thorbeck and Huppenkothen were aware that the purpose of the trial was not to establish the guilt and sentence of the defendants but to get rid of inconvenient prisoners under the facade of legal proceedings. Under these circumstances, the point was not whether the accused in the trial actually were guilty of treason; the point was that the trial was a show trial, and for this reason the result was not a legal execution but murder of the accused and both Thorbeck and Huppenkothen were therefore guilty as accomplices to murder.

This left the case as a matter of judicial immunity. If it could be proven that the trials were mere show trials performed at the command of a higher authority, the participants would have to answer for the consequences. The Supreme Court, however, regarded the trials as ordinary trials and based its ruling on the avowal of the defendants that they had perceived themselves free to perform their functions as judge and prosecutor according to the merits of the cases at hand. The deficiencies of the trials were regarded as mostly "formal". In light of the burden of proof that must be met in a criminal case, it could not be established that the trials were not real trials, and it could not in any case be established that the defendants did not perceive them as real trials. Based on this, they were both acquitted, although Huppenkothen was punished for participating in the execution of the sentences without receiving the necessary confirmation of them from the higher authorities.

The same view on judicial immunity was stated even more clearly by the Supreme Court in 1968 in the case against the People's Court justice Hans-Joachim Rehse.[31] Rehse became a judge in 1931 and acted as an assistant judge at the People's Court, starting in 1934. He was charged as an accessory to murder and put

[29] Smid (2002), pp. 453–455.

[30] Schminck-Gustavus (1995), p. 37.

[31] BGH, Urteil vom 30.4.1968—5 StR 670/67.

on trial for sitting on the bench with the notorious Roland Freisler in seven instances where the People's Court condemned the defendants to death.

The Supreme Court stated that members of a court all operated individually, even in Freisler's court. Members of the People's Court were independent, equal, and only bound by the law. Their sole duty was to follow their own legal conviction. No one, not even the president of the court, could deprive them of this autonomy. This meant, according to the Supreme Court, that if a judge were guilty of a criminal offence, it would be as a principal actor and not as an accessory. The Court also drew the conclusion that a judge could only be liable to punishment if he was motivated by malicious reasons in reaching his conclusion.

In a comment to these two cases in 2002 in relation to the 100-year anniversary of Hans von Dohnanyi, a former justice of the Reischsgericht (the German Supreme Court) who was killed as a consequence of the trials against Canaris and his men, President of the German Supreme Court Prof. Dr. Günter Hirsch stated that these rulings of his predecessors of the Court were a shame and, in effect, made it impossible to punish any of the Nazi judges.[32]

The reasoning of the Supreme Court was directly in contradiction to the view of the Military Tribunal, which had stated that judicial independence had ceased to exist in Nazi Germany at the time. How independent the judges in fact were in the later phases of the Nazi regime is a matter for the historians today. Angermund claims that although the judges were under heavy pressure, especially after 1942, they were not totally bound in their duty. At least the freedom to review the facts and to measure out the punishment remained. Many judges may have felt that their judicial freedom was more limited than it in fact was and repercussions for diverging judgments harsher than they in fact were. Harshness in sentencing developed independently of the circulars from the Ministry of Justice, and the Ministry, in fact, also found it necessary to warn the judges against excessive use of harsh punishments.[33]

The approach of the German Supreme Court was not extraordinary compared to the approach of courts in other countries. In a Norwegian case from 1949, where three German judges were accused of murder for their participation in a German special court (*Standgericht*) that sentenced five Norwegian patriots to death, the Norwegian Supreme Court took a similar view to that of the German Supreme Court.[34] The background for the case was the assassination by members of the Norwegian resistance movement of the Norwegian Chief of the State Police, Karl Martinsen, on 8 February 1944. On the same day, as a response to the assassination, the German *Kommissar* for occupied Norway, Joseph Terboven, ordered the setting

[32] 100. Geburtstag von Hans von Dohnanyi Ansprache des Präsidenten des Bundesgerichtshofs Prof. Dr. Günter Hirsch beim Festakt aus Anlaß des 100. Geburtstags von Hans von Dohnanyi am 8 March 2002, http://www.bundesgerichtshof.de/cln_134/DE/BGH/Praesidenten/Hirsch/HirschReden/rede08032002.html?nn=544442, accessed 10.01.2013.

[33] Angermund (1990), p. 245.

[34] The Latza Case, reported in *Law Reports of Trials of War Criminals vol. XIV*, United Nations War Crimes Commission, London 1949 and NRT 1948, p. 1088.

up of a *Standgericht* (summary court) as a countermeasure against the growing sabotage and terror activities of the underground movement. The Standgericht was to try several people who were regarded as the brains behind the resistance movement.

Four of the persons to appear before the Standgericht were arrested in the course of the same afternoon and taken directly to the trial venue before the trial started. They were not involved in, and were not accused of being involved in, the assassination of Martinsen. It seemed evident that the purpose of the trial was to send a message to the Norwegian resistance by executing some of its leading members as a reprisal for the assassination of Martinsen.

The presiding judge of the Standgericht was Hans Paul Helmut Latza (1908–1975). He was SS-Obersturmbannführer and a judge in the SS und Polizeigericht Oslo from 12 May 1940 to 7 May 1945. He took part in the discussions at Terboven's office prior to setting up the trial. At these discussions, he, according to the Norwegian trial court, "must have learned that the whole trial was nothing but a camouflaged act of reprisal with only one possible outcome to those to be tried—the death sentence".

Latza was first found guilty of murder, but the conviction was overturned by the Supreme Court on appeal. In the next round, Latza and the other judges were acquitted by the trial court, a decision that was sustained by the Supreme Court after appeal by the prosecution.

In assessing the guilt of the defendants, Supreme Court Justice Berger stated that the decisive legal issue was "whether the procedure before the Tribunal met with the minimum demands which form the prerequisites for proper court proceedings—in the first instance whether the Tribunal as an independent court took its decision after a fair investigation of the question of guilt, or whether the outcome of the trial was predetermined by directives given to the tribunal".[35] This was used as the legal standard for evaluating the guilt of the defendants.

There were several objections that could be made to the procedure of the Standgericht regarding the rights of the defendants. In the opinion of the Supreme Court, however, the lack of normal requirements of due process did not entail that the decision by the Standgericht to pass a death sentence on the accused lacked the qualities of a judicial decision. Justice Berger thus did not attach decisive weight to the facts that the charges made against the accused before the Standgericht had not been put in writing beforehand, the accused had not been assisted by a counsel for the defence, the evidence presented and accepted had been of an indirect nature only, the proceedings had taken a short time and were of a summary character, and the compulsory confirmation of a death sentence seemed to have been procured and prepared in a very superficial way.

The crucial point was whether there had been a fair trial before independent judges who delivered their judgment according to their free conviction. Based on the facts, there were, in the opinion of Justice Berger, insufficient grounds to

[35] Law Reports of Trials of War Criminals, vol. 14, p. 80, NRT 1948, p. 1089.

conclude that this was not the case and that the judges were acting on explicit or implicit instructions. The other justices of the Supreme Court concurred with the opinion of Justice Berger, and the German judges of the Standgericht were acquitted.

In its notes on the case, the UN War Crimes Commission remarked:

> While the Supreme Court may be thought to have taken a view of the denial of a fair trial which was more favourable to persons accused of such denial than the view taken by some other authorities, its finding does serve to underline the truth of the statement made in the notes to the Justice Trial that the denial of anyone of the rights enumerated on pp. 103-104 of Volume VI would not necessarily amount to the denial of a fair trial, and the courts have had to decide in each instance whether a sufficient number of the rights which they have regarded as forming part of the general right to a fair trial were sufficiently violated to warrant the conclusion either that the offence of denial of a fair trial has been committed, or that the defence plea that a killing or other injury was justified by the holding of a previous trial has been disproved.[36]

This is understating the point. If judicial immunity applies to a judge who believes his job to be an assessment of the case based on the applicable laws and presented evidence, no matter the content of the laws, no matter how summarily the evidence is established and the proceedings are held, there is certainly a very limited scope for holding a judge responsible for his contribution to injustice.

Some of the statements by the UN War Crimes Commission and by the US Military Tribunal seem to indicate that there is such immunity for judges. But there is an internal tension in the ruling of the Military Tribunal. On one hand, its states sweepingly that the German judges worked under such conditions that their undertaking cannot properly be characterised as judicial and that judicial immunity therefore does not apply. On the other hand, most of the defendants who were found guilty by the Tribunal were convicted not for their activities as judges or prosecutors but for their undertakings in the Ministry of Justice and therefore responsible for the development and setting into force the Nazi legal programmes against Jews, Poles, and resistance in the occupied territories. Judges and prosecutors who were convicted for their judicial activities, had either undertaken these in a discriminatory fashion, thus participating actively in the persecution of Jews or they had taken part in the illegal "Night and Fog" programme. Those judges who were not actively implicated in such activities were acquitted, disregarding the facts that they as judges in the special courts or the People's Court had contributed to the general breakdown of the rule of law. The war crime cases in the occupied countries followed the same line and only convicted German judges where there was evidence that there was not even pretence of a fair trial involved when summarily convicting resistance fighters or prisoners of war.

Based on postwar cases, it seems that the defence of judicial immunity is generally accepted and available even to judges who operate under conditions where they are subjected to quite high levels of pressure to decide their cases in a

[36] Law Reports of Trials of War Criminals, vol. 14, pp. 84–85.

certain way. But this again brings back the question discussed above: why should judges under orders have a wider defence than others?

A basic difference between the convictions of the Military Tribunal and acquittals of national courts is that the convictions of the Tribunal were for the breach of very basic internationally recognised rules to protect against discriminatory persecution. Here, there are even stronger arguments for not accepting judicial immunity as a defence than when judges are accused of departing from basic elements of the rule of law in national courts. But instead of focusing on the differences between international and national settings, perhaps it would be better to state outright that, in certain cases, judicial immunity cannot be defended, whether the judge is acting independently or not. Judicial independence should not be an argument used to exonerate judges from a responsibility for their choice to enforce legislation when the effects are obvious and serious violations of fundamental rights. In that way, there is no contradiction between the Military Tribunal and national courts over the judicial nature of the German courts under Nazi rule. The extent of the defence of judicial immunity could then be approached directly instead of indirectly by inquiring into the nature of the judicial decision.

The relevant question ought to be: what should be the substantial scope and limits of judicial immunity in order to protect the position of the judiciary and thus ensure and promote the rule of law? When expressed in this way, the answer should be that there is no immunity for the judge who commits obvious and substantial violations of individual rights, even when this takes place in the exercise of normal judicial functions in accordance with the law. Such violations are criminal under international law, there are no conclusive reasons against punishing those who have committed these violations retroactively under municipal law, and ignorance of these two basic tenets should not count as an exculpating factor. These are the standards that should be applied to any representative of a regime engaged in a widespread or systematic attack directed against basic human rights. To wield power through law is to commit to a form that conditions or disciplines what one can do in the name of the law.[37] There is, therefore, no good reason why the standards of personal responsibility for obvious and substantial violations of individual rights should not also be applied to judges, even if they are acting independently.

Division of Power

A slightly different argument for judicial immunity is that the proper role of the judiciary is to respect and give effect to legislation that has been enacted according to the basic rules of the legal order. Judges should not undertake to engage in a

[37] Dyzenhaus (2010), p. 286.

legislative activity, and consequently they should not be held responsible for actions and consequences that can properly be ascribed to the legislator.

This was the basic tenet of the approach of the South African judiciary under apartheid. In the words of Chief Justice Steyn of the Appellate Division:

> [It would] be an evil day for the administration of justice if our Courts should deviate from the well recognized tradition of giving politics as wide a berth as their work permits. It is one thing, and a very proper one, for a judge to point out defects in a statute or to draw attention to results, in all probability not anticipated or appreciated, which work hardship or injustice, i.e. to matters which Parliament might presumably want to rectify. It is a very different thing, and in my view a very improper one, for a judge to rush into a political storm or into the wake of it, in a strongly contested matter in which Parliament has, by way of firm deliberate policy, knowing what it was about and in the valid exercise of its legislative powers, laid down what is to be done.[38]

The same argument is used by Justice Thomas of the United States Supreme Court in his dissent in Graham v. Florida, where the Court restricted the use of life sentences on minors to other than homicide cases. Justice Thomas, with the following of justices Scalia and Alito, stated here:

> That the Court is willing to impose such an exacting constraint on democratic sentencing choices based on such an untestable philosophical conclusion is remarkable. The question of what acts are "deserving" of what punishments is bound so tightly with questions of morality and social conditions as to make it, almost by definition, a question for legislative resolution. It is true that the Court previously has relied on the notion of proportionality in holding certain classes of offenses categorically exempt from capital punishment. See *supra*, at 4. But never before today has the Court relied on its own view of just deserts to impose a categorical limit on the imposition of a lesser punishment. Its willingness to cross that well-established boundary raises the question whether any democratic choice regarding appropriate punishment is safe from the Court's ever-expanding constitutional veto.[39]

When it comes to making policy choices in a well-functioning democracy, this is a sound, albeit controversial, argument based on a constitutional theory of division of power between the legislative, executive, and judicial branches of government.[40] The positivism argument of Nazi Germany and the parliamentary supremacy argument of South Africa show that this constitutional theory is taken well beyond its setting in a theory of constitutional democracy. And even in a democratic setting, this can hardly be an argument to exonerate judges from a responsibility for their choice to enforce legislation that has, as its effects, obvious and serious violations of fundamental rights. Whereas the democracy argument may have a right place in a theory on how to establish what justice entails in a specific societal setting, and how to rightly balance conflicting rights and interests, it can scarcely have a place when it comes to the types of violation that may form the basis of individual responsibility for state officials. The issue here is not whether the measures that the judges are enforcing are undemocratic or lack legitimacy from the point of view

[38] Dyzenhaus (2010), pp. 116–117.

[39] Dissenting opinion in Graham v. Florida 560 US—08-7412 (2010).

[40] For an example and overview, see Allan (2011).

of political theory but whether they are so contrary to any conception of justice from the point of view of the rule of law that they may be deemed unacceptable under any setting.

References

Allan J (2011) Statutory bill of rights: you read words in, you read words out, you take parliament's clear intention and you shake it all about – Doin' the Sankey Hanky Panky. In: Campbell T, Ewing KD, Tomkins A (eds) The legal protection of human rights sceptical essays. Oxford University Press, Oxford

Angermund R (1990) Deutsche Richtershaft 1919–1945. Fischer, Frankfurt am Main

Arendt H (2003) Responsibility and judgment. Schocken Books, New York

Brand-Ballard J (2010) Limits of legality: the ethics of lawless judging. Oxford University Press, Oxford

Corbett MM (1998) Chief Justice of South Africa, presentation to the truth and reconciliation commission, 27 November 1996. S Afr Law J 115:17–20

Dyzenhaus D (1998) Judging the judges, judging ourselves truth, reconciliation and the apartheid legal order. Hart, Oxford

Dyzenhaus D (2010) Hard cases in wicked legal systems pathologies of legality, 2nd edn. Oxford University Press, Oxford

Kirchheimer O (1961) Political justice: the use of legal procedure for political ends. Princeton University Press, New Jersey

Lippman M (1992–1993) They shoot lawyers don't they? Law in the Third Reich and the global threat to the independence of the judiciary. Calif West Int Law J 23:257–318

Radbruch G (1946) Gesetzliches Unrecht und übergesetzliches Recht. Süddeutsche Juristen-Zeitung 105–108 [English translation Statutory Lawlessness and Supra-Statutory Law, Translated by Bonnie Litschewski Paulson and Stanley L. Paulson, 26 Oxford Journal of Legal Studies 2006, pp. 1–11]

Schminck-Gustavus CU (1995) Der "Prozeß" gegen Dietrich Bonhoeffer und die Freilassung seiner Mörder. J.H.W. Dietz Nachfolger, Bonn

Schorn H (1959) Der Richter im Dritten Reich Geschichte und Dokumente. Vittorio Klostermann, Frankfurt am Main

Shaman JM (1990) Judicial immunity from civil and criminal liability. San Diego Law Rev 27 (12):4

Smid M (2002) Hans von Dohnanyi Christine Bonhoeffer, Eine Ehe in Widerstand gegen Hitler. Gütersloher Verlagshaus, Gütersloher, pp 203–209

Spendel G (1996) Rechtsbeugung und BGH – eine Kritik. NJW 809–812

Trials of War Criminals before the Nuremberg Military Tribunals, vol III, the Justice Case, Washington, 1951

Chapter 13
Holding Judges Responsible

A Fixed Core of Justice

The analysis has shown two contradictory inferences that can be drawn from historical and legal material. On one hand, judges can be held responsible for exercising judicial functions within the law if by that they contribute to obvious and substantial infringements of individual rights. This is demanded by the rule of law even if it means that legislation is applied retroactively in order to achieve it and is also an obligation under international human rights regimes.[1]

On the other hand, judges almost never are brought to account for their misdeeds under oppressive settings. Indulgence towards the judiciary was not only a German phenomenon. In contrast to most other countries, Germany at least had a debate where even the Supreme Court at one point stated that disproportional punishments were against an unwritten basic assumption of German criminal law, opening up the door for the view that it could be illegal for courts to apply formally valid legislation. This was not to be the final word of the Supreme Court in its dealing with Nazi judges. But the debate left the door open for the next stage.

When German courts were asked to consider judicial crimes again after the breakdown of the GDR, they answered differently. This time they did accept that a judge could be performing an illegal act when applying laws in the way envisaged by the legislator and the rulers. They reached this result partly by including ratified international human rights instruments in their reasoning, arguing that when ratified these also form part of the positive law that the judge has to take into account. But they went one step further than this by not limiting the argument to treaty-based international obligations, thus reasoning also from basic elements of justice. International human rights are hence an expression of justice and not its only source.

The finding that judges in the GDR were breaking the law when applying valid statutes in contradiction of basic elements of justice would probably not have been

[1] See Brems (2011), pp. 286–287.

H.P. Graver, *Judges Against Justice*, DOI 10.1007/978-3-662-44293-7_13

possible without the existence of case law on judicial responsibility and the discussions this instigated. The case of the Nazi judges, how they judged and how they were later judged, thus has a significant bearing on the question of the responsibility of judges for contributions to oppression and oppressive regimes. The German experience shows that judges can be held accountable by successor regimes and transition trials for their judicial functions in upholding oppressive laws.

The Nuremberg trials showed that judges can be held responsible under international law, not only for war crimes but also for administering the law against a country's own nationals. The Military Tribunal established that it was a crime for judges to administer laws that were part of the regime's discriminatory policy and extermination of Jews and Poles and to undertake an arbitrary and brutal enforcement of oppressive laws "shocking to the conscience of mankind".

As a result of the findings of the Tribunal, even judges may be held accountable under the Rome Statute of the International Criminal Court. Based on the statute, judges can be guilty of genocide and crimes against humanity also when applying and enforcing municipal law. According to Article 7(2)a, an attack against any civilian population means a course of conduct "pursuant to or in furtherance of a State or organizational policy to commit such attack". Thus, enforcing the laws of the regime cannot be a defence but is, on the contrary, an argument to substantiate that the condition of furtherance of a state policy is fulfilled.[2]

International law is, as we know, not directly applicable in municipal law in all jurisdictions, at least not as a sufficient legal basis for applying criminal sanctions or to supplant rules of domestic law. Whether judges can be held responsible by national courts must therefore be answered within each legal order according to its own legal principles and rules. But the German experiences, together with the fact that judges can be punished by international courts and tribunals, give valuable insights and arguments to be considered when addressing this question in national legal contexts.

It seems at the outset quite reasonable that there exists a core of justice, present in the minds of "all civilized people", and that to this core belong substantial and manifest human rights violations, intolerable disproportionate punishments, and substantial violations of the right to a fair trial. On the other hand, the words of the US Military Tribunal on the draconic punishments meted out by German courts during the war, with the minimum of procedural guarantees, are a note of caution to finding self-evident requirements of justice:

"Every nation recognizes the absolute necessity of more stringent enforcement of the criminal law in times of great emergency" and "in the face of a real and present danger, freedom of speech may be somewhat restricted even in America. Can we then say that in the throes of total war and in the presence of impending disaster those officials who enforced these savage laws in a last desperate effort to stave off defeat were guilty of crimes against humanity?"[3]

---

[2] See The Justice Case (1951), p. 984.

[3] The Justice Case (1951), p. 1026.

What seems beyond question to many people today may not be so straightforward to people in a totally different setting tomorrow. At least, it was not so to the defenders of democracy and the rule of law in 1948. On the other hand, for a practice to become a rule of international law, it need not be a universally recognised practice but only one accepted by civilised nations *in general*.[4]

It appears to be very difficult to find a fixed core of justice that can be seen as intuitively valid as law under all conditions and at all times. Regimes may decide to depart from international obligations in their own internal law, and judges may be put under an obligation to enforce these laws. Morally, they may be under an obligation to refuse, resign, or find ways to bend the law, but to say they are guilty of crimes under their own law is a different question. At the same time, however, they may be committing criminal acts from the perspective of international law.

Why Are Not Judges Punished?

A pressing question is why judges are acquitted even when there are no compelling legal arguments against convicting them. One probable reason has more to do with transitional justice in general. It is rather the exception than the rule that dictators and their supporters are punished after a change of political system.[5] Often, amnesty is part of the deal for surrendering power to democratic forces. There is also often a social need for reconciliation and looking forward. The extent of implication in the workings of the old regime might have been so far-reaching that looking for accomplices may have deep and rupturing effects for social stability.[6] International relations, politics, and a perceived need to balance between peace and justice often lead to the non-enforcement of criminal liability.[7]

But as we have seen, even in cases where perpetrators of oppression and terror are punished, judges often go free. After Nazi Germany, the most obvious explanation to this is that it was the judges of the old regime who continued into the new regime.[8] They punished guards and soldiers, and to a certain extent doctors, officers, and bureaucrats, but let their own off.[9] Another factor is that the cases against the judges came rather late and not until the late 1940s and the early 1950s. By this time, the prosecution of Nazis in Germany and in the rest of Europe was on

[4] See Law Reports of Trials of War Criminals, vol. XV Digest of Laws and Cases, United Nations War Crimes Commission, London 1949, p. 10.

[5] See Werle (2001), p. 3001.

[6] For a discussion on the prosecution of human rights violations under apartheid in South Africa, see Berat (1993), pp. 199–231.

[7] See Einarsen (2012), pp. 51–62.

[8] For an account of the continuity of the community of judges and officials of the legal system, see Müller (1989), pp. 204–221.

[9] See Freudiger (2002), p. 416.

the wane.[10] This, however, does not explain why judges were not prosecuted earlier.

One thing is how the leniency towards the judges in general came about being accepted by society. The need for experienced judges when building democracy based on the rule of law may have prohibited a general purge of all judges with a Nazi background. This was different in the Soviet Occupied Zone, where they started from scratch with a new type of lawyers schooled in Marxist–Leninist ideology.

Another matter is why even the obvious Nazis were not put on trial and convicted. Once it was accepted that it was necessary to maintain a large number of the judges from the Nazi regime, the path was laid out: under these circumstances, it was more important to infuse into the judges the new ideology of the rule of law than to purge the Nazis. They had all, more or less, been involved in the crimes of Hitler. A crusade mounted by the judges who had kept clear of the worst crimes of the system would easily have antagonised many colleagues and created deep rifts in the judiciary. When only a few are truly innocent, the exculpation of even the most profoundly guilty is the most convenient for all.[11] This also created a need to "normalize" the judicial practice of the Nazi time—it would have been difficult to integrate the judges into the new order of the Federal Republic while simultaneously stating they had been responsible for a practice amounting to illegality by the standards of the same Federal Republic.[12] Judging for the future of the Federal Republic may, in this light, have seemed more important. Better to close the ranks and forget.

Similar reasons may explain the leniency with which judges have been treated in other situations. The Norwegian Supreme Court showed a great deal of professional courtesy towards the German judges of the special courts under the occupation. Several of the procedures they directed could easily have been said to not satisfy even the minimum requirements of a fair trial and thus treated as war crimes. Many participated as prosecutors in sending Norwegians to the "Night and Fog" programme, an act that was characterised as a war crime by the US Military Tribunal. In Norway, they were acquitted.[13]

The remarks by the US Military Tribunal on the use of harsh laws and draconic punishments during war are also very empathetic towards the predicaments of their German colleagues.[14] They demonstrate that a judge on trial could maybe expect an understanding from the bench not so readily available to others. But not only judges were extended this kind of sympathy: South African judges got away with boycotting the Reconciliation and Truth Commission.

[10] See Pendas (2009), pp. 357–358.

[11] See Pendas (2009), pp. 360–361.

[12] See Freudiger (2002), p. 402.

[13] See NRT 1948, p. 116.

[14] See pp. 132–133 above.

The Commission addressed the balance between the need to integrate all judges in the undertaking of building the rule of law under the new order against the justice of accountability in the following way:

> The Commission has a good deal of understanding for the 'collegiality' argument, which says that the non-appearance by those judges willing in principle to appear will create greater mutual trust among the 'old order' and the 'new order' judges and so advance the cause of constitutional democracy. However, such benefits, if achieved in this way, are outweighed by the powerful symbolic effect of the judiciary showing themselves publicly and humbly to be accountable. For this is what the hearing was about and what the Constitution demands of a judiciary that is granted the onerous power of constitutional review. It is required that the judiciary display some sense of being able to balance its necessary and justifiable demand for independence with a measure of accountability to the South African nation it serves.[15]

Surprisingly, it does not seem to harm the social acceptance of the judiciary that many judges have a tainted past of betraying the rule of law under oppressive times. People's faith in the courts seems independent of the extent to which it contributes to oppression. Under apartheid in South Africa, the confidence in the legal system among the blacks and the coloured was on a level with the confidence among the whites.[16] Those most sceptical, maybe with a cynical view, where the ones with the closest knowledge of the system, namely the black lawyers who regarded the system as "morally bankrupt".

Based on such experiences, it does not appear that it is necessary to restore faith in the legal system to punish judges who have applied and enforced oppressive laws, even with appalling results. Under some circumstances, it may even seem more important to concentrate on marshalling authentic and sound support among the judiciary for democracy and the rule of law and the new values of the future society. This cannot, however, cover the truth that justice demands equal treatment of judges and others who violate rights for the purpose of political oppression.

The Hurdle of Retroactivity

The approach that the German Supreme Court took in the cases against the GDR judiciary has been criticised as overly formal when the Court stated that the judges did have a scope of interpreting the GDR law under the authority of international human rights and a common core of justice. Although this might be correct from reading textbooks of legal interpretation, it is far from how the law was perceived in the GDR at the time.[17] From this point of view, the German Supreme Court undertook a new reading of the law of the GDR and applied its reading retroactively to the GDR judges.

---

[15] SA Truth and Reconciliation Commission Final Report, pp. 107–108.

[16] See Ellmann (1995), pp. 425–426.

[17] See Marxen and Werle (2007), p. XLIV with citations.

Certainly, from a legal realist point of view, this seems correct. It is, in my opinion, more satisfying to the way society and judges perceive the role of the judiciary to say that a successor regime that punishes past judges for manifest violations of human rights, intolerable disproportionate punishments, and substantial violations of the right to a fair trial is enacting a new legal regime that it is applying the law retroactively, at least if the oppressive regime has lasted for so long that it would be a fiction to say that one is applying the law previous to this regime.

On the other hand, I believe that a transitional justice should allow for such retroactivity.[18] This is in accordance with the view taken by the European Court of Human Rights.[19] In the case brought by Streletz, Kessler, and Krenz against Germany, the Court stated:

> The Court considers that it is legitimate for a State governed by the rule of law to bring criminal proceedings against persons who have committed crimes under a former regime; similarly, the courts of such a State, having taken the place of those which existed previously, cannot be criticised for applying and interpreting the legal provisions in force at the material time in the light of the principles governing a State subject to the rule of law.[20]

The applicants had occupied senior positions in the GDR's state apparatus and the Socialist Unity Party leadership. They had been members of the National Defence Council, the body whose decisions were a necessary precondition for the issuing of orders concerning the GDR's border-policing regime, where 264 people were killed trying to escape to West Germany. The European Court of Human Rights thus accepted the German courts' interpretation of GDR law, by explicitly accepting that a successor regime applies general principles of rule of law when interpreting the laws in force under oppressive circumstances. Technically, the courts are engaging in a reformulation of the law by legal interpretation parallel to what happened in Germany in the transition from the Weimar Republic to the Third Reich. Substantially, however, the courts now are engaged in protecting the rule of law, whereas the courts then were engaged in breaking it down. This makes the whole difference from the point of view of the rule of law.

The effect of the position of the European Court of Human Rights is that it is permissible to reinterpret oppressive legislation in a way to make it conform to international human rights instruments, even when this leads to retroactive punishment. This means that in regimes that maintain an ostensive commitment to fundamental rights, those violating these rights will not have a legitimate expectation that their actions will be regarded as legal at a later time, regardless of whether they are perceived as legal by the regime's authorities or courts at the time.

The European Court of Human Rights even took a step further and stated:

[18] In the same direction, Werle (1995), p. 82.

[19] See Brems (2011), pp. 298–301.

[20] ECtHR case of Streletz, Kessler and Krenz v. Germany, (*Applications nos. 34044/96, 35532/97 and 44801/98*) Judgment 22 March 2001, p. 32.

> The Court considers that a State practice such as the GDR's border-policing policy, which flagrantly infringes human rights and above all the right to life, the supreme value in the international hierarchy of human rights, cannot be covered by the protection of Article 7 § 1 of the Convention. That practice, which emptied of its substance the legislation on which it was supposed to be based, and which was imposed on all organs of the GDR, including its judicial bodies, cannot be described as "law" within the meaning of Article 7 of the Convention.

With this statement, the Court leaves no doubt: legislation that flagrantly infringes human rights, and above all the right to life, is not "law" within the meaning of Article 7 of the European Convention. This approach resembles the Radbruch formula. The difference here is that by interpreting Article 7 of the Convention, the Radbruch formula is transformed to positive law. When legislation authorising human rights violations is disregarded in relation to Article 7, the prohibition against such violations stand and punishing the ones responsible will be according to law.

Whether one chooses the approach of reinterpreting the law in light of human rights or one takes the view that criminalisation may be applied to violations after the fact, the position from the point of view of the European Court of Human Rights is the same: one can never commit gross violations of human rights with the legitimate expectation that one will not be punished.

That retroactive punishment is allowed under international human rights law does not in itself make it permissible under municipal law. As we have seen, the position of the German courts has been that the principle of prohibiting retroactive punishment bars punishing acts that were not criminal at the time they were committed. The courts, on the other hand, circumvented this by the fiction that the state-sanctioned atrocities of the Nazis and of the GDR regime were prohibited at the time.

The issue of retroactive punishments is central to transitional justice and may be described as a rule of law dilemma of transitional jurisprudence: "If ordinarily the rule of law means adherence to the settled law, to what extent are periods of transformation compatible to the rule of law? In such periods, what does the rule of law mean?"[21] The issue is not confined to the question of the responsibility of the judiciary but applies to all instances where oppression was performed under policies enacted with legal means. It is difficult to see why the argument of retroactivity should apply to judges to a greater extent than to others accused of committing crimes against the basic sense of justice. With the US Military Tribunal, one could say that crimes of oppression become even worse when they are performed by the dagger under judicial robes. When oppression is legitimised by the courts, this strengthens the other organs of an oppressive state and weakens the case of any opposition. Judges should therefore not be protected from retroactive punishments to any greater extent than others who commit state violations.

[21] Teitel (1996–1997), p. 2017.

Other courts have also found that the principle against retroactive punishment is not absolute and that it does not completely set a bar against punishing acts committed by the legal authority of state institutions. In Denmark, after the war, there was no specific constitutional provision that prohibited retroactive legislation. There was, nevertheless, a discussion on whether one should enact legislation that retroactively criminalised acts committed during the German occupation.[22] Even if the constitution did not entail this principle, it must still, as part of the principle of *nulla poene sin lege*, be regarded as a fundamental principle of the rule of law. It could, however, not be applied fully in such extraordinary situations as the occupation of the country. The acts that were criminalised were of such character that the guilty could not have been in reasonable doubt about their illegitimacy. Departing from the principle by enacting retroactive legislation could, of course, contribute to a lessening of the respect for the rule of law and must therefore be done with caution. Letting the acts go unpunished could, on the other hand, also contribute to the undermining of this respect and must therefore also be taken into consideration. The result was that the Danish Parliament, in June 1945, enacted a law to be applied to acts committed during the German occupation.

In the Netherlands, the second in command of the German occupying forces invoked the defence of retroactivity. The crimes he was accused of had been made criminal offences by a decree of 1947. His defence was rejected by the High Court with the following words:

> The appellant wrongly asserts that the criminal character of such actions has only now, afterwards, been provided. In doing so he loses sight of the fact that for a long time such transgressions have been known all over the world as 'oorlogsmisdrijven,' 'crimes de guerre,' 'war crimes,' 'kriegsverbrechen,' etc., while even before the Second World War the imposition of punishment for such acts took place in several countries, among them Germany.[23]

The United Nations War Crimes Commission commented:

> The main argument of the Court on this point was that, at least in the field of international criminal law as related to war crimes and crimes against humanity, express provision for the type and severity of punishment was not an essential pre-requisite. Decisive was the fact that, in view of its seriousness, the offence was deserving of punishment under all standards of criminal justice of civilized nations. The above findings are in accord with those made by the International Military Tribunal at Nuremberg in the case against the major Nazi war criminals.[24]

In Norway, the Constitution, Article 97 states that "no law must be given retroactive effect". During the occupation, the Norwegian cabinet continued their activities in exile in London. From there, they enacted provisional laws

[22] See Tamm (1984), pp. 737–744.

[23] Law Reports of Trials of War Criminals vol. XIV, United Nations War Crimes Commission, London (1949), s. 119.

[24] Law Reports of Trials of War Criminals vol. XIV, United Nations War Crimes Commission, London (1949), s. 120–121.

criminalising collaboration and treason. They also extended the possibility of using capital punishment, which, in the laws in force when Norway was attacked, was limited to times of war. Had this not been done, it would not be possible to use capital punishment in proceedings initiated against collaborators and traitors after the war.

The government and the top officials of the Ministry of Justice were of the opinion that under the extraordinary situation of the occupation, laws could be enforced retroactively. This was, for the most part, not accepted by the courts.[25] One notable exception was in cases against members of the German Gestapo who had been involved in torture during interrogations, in some instances with the death of the suspect as a result. Here, the courts enforced a provisional law, enacted in 1945, that permitted the use of capital punishment in cases of war crimes. Although there was no provision in Norwegian criminal law that allowed the use of the death penalty for murder or torture at the time the acts were committed, the Norwegian Supreme Court, by a majority of 11 against two, accepted it in the Klinge case.[26] Justice Skau argued that war crimes were crimes according to international law, and international law allowed for use of capital punishment. He also stated that the protection against retroactive punishment is a requirement of justice meant to protect the citizens against their authorities and should not be used to protect foreign violators who are citizens of a state that is attacking these authorities. The opinion of the majority was given support by the United Nations War Crimes Commission, which stated:

> It may be added that no shadow of an objection could be raised to the sentence on the ground that it constituted an unjust use of the discretion thus permitted by International Law, since it was shown that a death had resulted from the ill-treatment meted out by the accused.[27]

Nevertheless, the decision has been met with criticism by the legal doctrine in Norway. In a case against a war criminal from Bosnia–Herzegovina in 2010, the Norwegian Supreme Court reversed the decision.[28] Here, a Bosnian national was on trial for crimes against humanity during the Bosnian–Serb war. At the time of the war, crimes against humanity had not been made part of Norwegian criminal law. The Court voted in plenary session, and all the judges agreed to a reversal of the Klinge decision, even though there was disagreement over the actual case.

The Court rejected the Klinge formula in a rather formal way: "In our country article 97 gives absolute protection in the area of criminal law, and this protection must be given to everybody".[29] The rejection is unfortunate and was unnecessary as the defendant could be and was punished for the same crimes under other provisions

---

[25] See Andenæs (1979), pp. 120–121.

[26] NRT 1946, p. 1139.

[27] Law Reports of Trials of War Criminals vol. III, United Nations War Crimes Commission, London (1948), s. 13.

[28] NRT 2010, p. 1445.

[29] Justice Møse, paragraph 119.

of the penal code. Consequently, there was not much at stake for the defendant in this case from the point of view of the rule of law. Although protection against retroactive punishment and punishment without a clear legal basis are important elements of the rule of law, the Supreme Court here leaves Norway in a position where it is difficult to punish the responsible for oppression enacted and enforced by legal means should such a situation arise. In such a case, Norwegian courts will therefore have to resort to the fiction employed by the German courts in order to bring the ones responsible to justice—that law is not law when reinterpreted in retrospect by courts under new circumstances more favourable to the rule of law.

Does the Responsibility Go Far Enough?

Some might object that holding judges responsible for enforcing laws that flagrantly infringe human rights and thereby committing substantial and obvious infringements of individual rights does not go far enough in sanctioning contribution and support of oppression. What about laws and decisions that are not so grave that they must be perceived as substantial and obvious? Why should judges be permitted to walk away from violating individual rights at all?

The case law of the German Supreme Court against the judges of the GDR has been criticised for being too lenient and for accepting legal convictions against critics of the GDR regime based on far-fetched analogies and misconstructions of the facts of the cases.[30] It is true that with the legal construction adopted by the Supreme Court, it was compelled to endorse as legal under GDR law many court rulings that were oppressive and contrary to the basic rights of citizens under internationally recognised civil and political rights. In particular, the many cases of punishing with long prison terms minor demonstrations of discontent with the regime's policy to prohibit citizens to travel abroad give illustration of this.

It is, however, not obvious that the answer to this is for a successor regime to deem such judicial acts as criminal acts and to hold the judges responsible. The examples from international and national cases that have been reviewed above show that the practice until now has been to construe the criminal liability of judges narrowly. To go much further than what the German Supreme Court has done would lack backing in international law and practice and would soon raise much more difficult issues regarding the principle of retroactivity. As we shall see in the following chapters, holding judges responsible for a wide range of judicial activities under oppressive regimes or laws will also easily challenge the principles of judicial independence and immunity.

The standard "substantial and obvious infringements of individual rights" might be considered by some as vague and of little guidance to the determination of the extent of the obligation of judges and hence in itself is in contradiction to the rule of

[30] Schröder (1999).

law. The way the standard has been applied gives little credence to this objection. It could, on the other hand, be useful, not least in the guidance of judges who find themselves in a difficult situation to give the standard a little more substance. A useful starting point can be found in the Rome Statute of the International Court of Criminal Justice. Articles 6–8 define the crimes of genocide, crimes against humanity, and war crimes as they are under the jurisdiction of the ICCJ.[31] Prohibitions against slavery, genocide, racial discrimination, and torture are among the norms frequently cited as jus cogens, that is, basic norms of international law that are universally binding, which cannot be contracted away.[32]

Central to the definition of genocide is the intent to destroy, in whole or in part, a national, ethnical, racial, or religious group. Central to the definitions of crimes against humanity and war crimes is a widespread or systematic attack or as part of a plan or policy or as part of a large-scale commission. Use of legislative means will often include intent, policy, and actions on a widespread or systematic scale. When giving effect to such laws, judges will therefore easily be in a situation where these conditions are fulfilled, as shown by the US Military Tribunal against the Nazi lawyers. In its introductory comments to the application of Control Council Law No. 10 as legal basis for punishment, it stated:

> As we construe it, that section provides for punishment of crimes committed against German nationals only where there is proof of conscious participation in systematic government organized or approved procedures amounting to atrocities and offenses of the kind specified in the act and committed against populations or amounting to persecutions on political, racial, or religious grounds.[33]

The inclusion of a condition of "systematic government organized or approved procedures" as by the Military Tribunal or of "widespread or systematic attack or as part of a plan or policy or as part of a large-scale commission" as by the Rome Statute in addition to the condition of "substantial and obvious infringements of individual rights" lends more substance to the norm as a basis for criminal sanctions. Based on historic experience, it seems unlikely that successor regimes will go much further than this in their dealings with offenders of predecessor oppressive regimes. To include a requirement of systematic attacks will therefore probably not reduce the efficiency of transitional justice in dealing with the aftermath of dictatorship. But it will heighten the standard of rule of law in such proceedings and check arguments based on assertions that "substantial and obvious infringements of individual rights" is too vague a standard to apply in criminal proceedings against a judge who had been applying the law of the time.

The nature of the violations covered by the Rome Statute can be comprehended by studying the list of abuses recorded as crimes against humanity in Article 7:

---

[31] See Jescheck (2004) on the relationship between the Nuremberg trials and the ICC statute.

[32] Einarsen (2012), p. 8.

[33] The Justice Case (1951), p. 982.

(a) murder;
(b) extermination;
(c) enslavement;
(d) deportation or forcible transfer of population;
(e) imprisonment or other severe deprivation of physical liberty in violation of fundamental rules of international law;
(f) torture;
(g) rape, sexual slavery, enforced prostitution, forced pregnancy, enforced sterilisation, or any other form of sexual violence of comparable gravity;
(h) persecution against any identifiable group or collectivity on political, racial, national, ethnic, cultural, religious, gender as defined in paragraph 3, or other grounds that are universally recognised as impermissible under international law, in connection with any act referred to in this paragraph or any crime within the jurisdiction of the Court;
(i) enforced disappearance of persons;
(j) the crime of apartheid;
(k) other inhumane acts of a similar character intentionally causing great suffering or serious injury to body or to mental or physical health.

Of particular note to judges under circumstances when they are charged with enforcing authoritarian or oppressive measures are the prohibitions against "imprisonment or other severe deprivation of physical liberty in violation of fundamental rules of international law and persecution against any identifiable group or collectivity on political, racial and other grounds". These prohibitions will easily be violated when enforcing measures of interning people without access to due process of law and measures directed against opposition and criticism of the regime in power. When such measures are enacted in, for example, emergency legislation, they must readily be regarded as systematic and as part of a plan or policy. The same is the case if justice is systematically denied members of a political or ethnic group.

For deprival of the basic minimum of a fair trial or for grossly unjust punishments, it is not obvious that there needs to be any element of discrimination. The ECtHR has recently stated that fundamental principles of justice may limit the punishments that can legally be inflicted by a state upon defendants in criminal cases. In its judgment of 17 January 2012, ECtHR accepted that a grossly disproportionate sentence could amount to ill-treatment contrary to Article 3, even if matters of appropriate sentencing largely fall outside the scope of the European Convention.[34] However, the Court also considers that "gross disproportionality" is a strict test, and it will only be on "rare and unique occasions" that the test will be met. A standard to be applied is if the sentence would "shock the conscience" or violate principles of fundamental justice. The Court did not consider a mandatory sentence of life imprisonment a violation of Article 3 as such, absent any gross

[34] Case of Vinter and others v. the United Kingdom Applications nos. 66069/09 and 130/10 and 3896/10.

disproportionality in light of the crime and any mitigating circumstances. The case is pending a decision by the Grand Chamber after an appeal by the applicants.

This does not mean, of course, that a judge who imposes a disproportionate punishment is committing a criminal offence. But it does give support to the holding of the German Supreme Court in the GDR cases that intolerable disproportionate punishments are contrary to the basic principles of justice and that the legality of such sentences can be disregarded even should they be according to the positive law that the judge is applying.

References

Andenæs J (1979) Det vanskelige oppgjøret. Tanum-Norli, Oslo

Berat L (1993) Prosecuting human rights violators from a predecessor regime: guidelines for a transformed South Africa. Boston College Third World Law J 13:199–231

Brems E (2011) Transitional justice in the case law of the European Court of Human Rights. Int J Transitional Justice 5:282–303

Einarsen T (2012) The concept of universal crimes in international law. FICHL Publication series No. 14, Torkel Opsahl Academic EPublisher

Ellmann S (1995) Law and legitimacy in South Africa. Law Soc Inq 20:407–479

Freudiger K (2002) Die juristische Aufarbeitung von NS-Verbrechen. Mohr Siebeck, Tübingen

Jescheck H-H (2004) The general principles of international criminal law set out in Nuremberg, as mirrored in the ICC Statute. J Int Crim Justice 2:38–55

Law reports of trials of war criminals, vol III. United Nations War Crimes Commission, London, 1948

Law reports of trials of war criminals, vol XIV. United Nations War Crimes Commission, London, 1949

Marxen K, Werle G (eds) (2007) Strafjustiz und DDR-Unrecht Dokumentation, Band 5/1 Teilband Rechtsbeugung. De Gruyter, Berlin

Müller I (1989) Furchtbare Juristen – Die unbewältigte Vergangenheit unsere Justiz. Knaur, München

Pendas DO (2009) Nazi trials in postwar Europe. J Mod Hist 81:347–368

Schröder F-C (1999) Der Bundesgerichtshof und der Grundsatz "nulla poena sin lege". NJW 89–93

Tamm D (1984) Retsopgøret efter besættelsen. Jurist- og Økonomforbundets forlag, København

Teitel R (1996–1997) Transitional jurisprudence: the role of law in political transformation. Yale Law J 106:2009–2080

Trials of War Criminals before the Nuremberg Military Tribunals, vol III, the Justice Case, Washington, 1951

Werle G (1995) We asked for justice and got the rule of law: German Courts and the Totalitarian Past. S Afr J Hum Rights 11:70–83

Werle G (2001) Rückwirkungsverbot und Staatskriminalität. Neue Juristische Wochenschrift 3001–3008

Part III
The Moral Side of Judging

Chapter 14
The Positivism Thesis

The Reasons for Judicial Complicity

Disregarding the question of whether the immoral law is "law" or not and the question of the duty to follow the law, a judge is also a human being, an individual, and a member of society. As such, he has moral responsibilities. In oppressive situations, he is faced with the question, as Hannah Arendt puts it, of asking himself to what extent he is able to live with himself after having committed certain deeds.[1] Many seek to hide behind the law and to regard themselves in the mirror as an upholder of law and justice and live well with this, even if upholding law and justice means participating in the oppression of other human beings.

As we have seen in Part I of this book, judges regularly contribute to the oppression of authoritarian regimes. The fact that they have been trained and have functioned as judges under the rule of law does not prevent this. We have seen in Part II that, although they also do this under circumstances that are not justifiable, they are often excused and seldom brought to justice. From the point of view of criminal law, their actions are understandable and often perhaps more worthy of pity than of blame. The rule of law includes an ideology where judges are the protectors of the rights and the integrity of the individual and where the law applies equally to all, even to the bodies of the state. But the ideology of the rule of law does not seem to stop judges from participating in transforming the law into an instrument of oppression and persecution. Even where the conditions for punishment are not met, we may still ask the question why judges so blatantly betray the high ideals of the rule of law, of which they are supposed to be the prime guardians, and, further, whether the responsibility for this lies first and foremost in the law itself, in the judicial role, or with the individual judge himself.

At first sight, the reasons for judicial complicity may seem obvious. Judges are expected to adhere to the law even when it contradicts their own notion of morality.

[1] Arendt (2003), p. 44.

H.P. Graver, *Judges Against Justice*, DOI 10.1007/978-3-662-44293-7_14

Most writers on law and legal theory seem to be of the opinion that judges have a duty to adhere to the law and are legally and morally prohibited to disapply a legal rule even if it leads to a morally bad result. On the other hand, many seem to agree that this duty does not apply in cases where the result is manifestly bad or extremely unjust and that judges in very bad regimes have no reason to adhere to the law at all.[2] Nevertheless, judges still obey the law and even defend this position, as we have seen from the argument put forward by South African judges to the Truth and Reconciliation Commission.[3] How can this be?

From a sociological point of view, the answer is quite clear. Judges, as do others, have to give way to overwhelming force. Although judges have normative power over the use of the coercive power of the state, they do not control it. In situations of public hysteria of fear of destruction of the state or of internal or external threats to life and social stability, persons trained in law are not exempt.[4] And to the extent that judges try to resist such drives of hysteria, they are liable to become the targets of public criticism that can effectively influence their behaviour. In such situations, the judiciary lacks backing from strong voices of civil society in support of legal freedoms. Elements of individual fear may also come into play. Although experience from many situations shows that dictators do not apply direct force on the judiciary, this does not mean that judges do not give their support out of fear of their personal safety.[5]

A second explanation is that authoritarian rulers often have support from the elites of society, and judges with their background and profession belong to these elites. In situations that are considered extreme, members of the legal profession and judiciary shed their professional logic and act out of class interests.[6] The judges of South Africa offer a clear illustration of this. They were all members of the white minority and upheld its oligarchy over the majority of the population of the country. They also contributed to the transformation of the oligarchy into an authoritarian state with totalitarian elements. Politics, social forces, and class interests go a long way in explaining judicial behaviour and support to ruling elites. But politics and psychology are interwoven, writes Jonathan Glover in his moral history of the twentieth century.[7] This is because both authoritarian rulers and schemes and institutions set up to avoid authoritarianism need the support of officials and of the public for their policies and measures to take effect. The climate of the public opinion can make a difference as to whether a disaster is unfolded or avoided.

Judges have many individual and institutional reasons to adhere to the law.[8] Judges, like others, are disposed to finding ways of furthering their own careers.

---

[2] See Brand-Ballard (2010), pp. 126–130.

[3] See p. 16 above.

[4] See Halliday et al. (2007), pp. 26–27.

[5] See Curran (1998–1999), p. 42.

[6] See Karpik (2007), p. 475.

[7] Glover (2012), p. 401.

[8] See Brand-Ballard (2010), pp. 70–73.

Playing along with the regime provides job security and promotions. Many judges of Nazi Germany played along with the Nazi regime because they saw in this an opportunity to re-establish a social position that they had all but lost during the Weimar Republic. A third explanation is that the courts are, after all, organs of the state. By continuing to serve on the bench, the judges accept the office of applying and enforcing the laws of the state. They are in a way morally or, at least, psychologically committed to uphold the laws under which they hold their position and power. Finally, judges may seem to find themselves in a position where they have no choice, and where the alternatives to participation seem much worse, from the perspective of the rule of law too. Some measure of judicial contribution may be better than naked force employed outside the scope of the law.

Convincing as social and political explanations may be, they still do not answer the question of how judges justify their choice to support the regime and how they reconcile this choice and the actions that they perform as a consequence of it with their inbred ideals of the rule of law and protection of individual rights. And they do not give the whole picture. There are, after all, judges who do not protect their own class interests or seek to further their own careers. The common law judges of South Africa are a powerful example of this. And as we have seen in Chap. 5, there are examples even from Nazi Germany. Judicial complicity varies under conditions that are not so easily explained by recourse to common interest and opportunism. How do we explain the differences in judicial collaboration with the German occupiers in Belgium, Denmark, the Netherlands, and Norway?

Despite the rather obvious sociological and ideological facts, judging by the academic debate within legal theory, there seems to be a pressing need for an explanation of the contribution of judges to repression. One reason for this may be that the facts of persecution and repression are so contrary to the notion of the rule of law in the western legal tradition that it is difficult to accept that the prime officers of the law take part in it. This may be particularly difficult for members of the legal profession and the judiciary because they like to think of themselves as the guardians of the rule of law. So a question that seems to have rather obvious answers from the perspective of social theory has been subject to major controversy within the field of legal theory.

From the point of view of legal theory, there must be something flawed with the legal system where judges can contribute to atrocities. Either what seems to be a legal order is not a legal order at all or there is something wrong with the approach and methods of judges in oppressive societies since they depart from their task as guardians of the rule of law. The answer may be a combination of both if one claims that it lies in the inability of such judges to distinguish between law in the true sense and the oppressive non-law of authoritarian regimes.

For the purpose of understanding judges, the most interesting part of the discussion is the discussion on the role of legal reasoning. The discussion on whether unjust laws constitute law in a real sense is of theoretical interest, but it begs the question when it comes to understanding the judge, who in any case must be able to draw the distinction in practice. And this brings us back to the question of the methods available and applicable. In the discussion on the importance of the legal method for explaining judicial contribution to oppression, different positions have been taken. As we shall see in the following, there are those who claim that judicial participation is due to the method they adhere to, whether it is legal positivism (Radbruch) or the "free law" movement (Behrends). On the other side, there are those who deny the importance of legal methodology (Rüthers, Curran) and hold that different legal methodologies provide the judges with different rhetorical forms (Osiel). And there are those who emphasise the political side of methodology (Dyzenhaus).

In the following, I will review this discussion with emphasis on the discussion on the cases of Nazi Germany and South Africa. After considering and rejecting the most common theory—that legal positivism can account for judicial atrocities—I turn to the question of to what extent the answer lies with the judge himself. I will also discuss the tenability of the position that acting as a judge for an oppressive regime to temper its oppression can be defensible as the lesser evil. Then I will consider the importance to the discussion of the last few decades' rise of international law regimes to protect fundamental and human rights. In conclusion, I will show the politics of legal reasoning. Legal reasoning becomes political under certain conditions, namely when legislation and law can no longer be seen as two parallel forces. When the legislator wages war on law, legal method becomes a political issue both in the sense that the legislator will seek to demand a specific method and a redefinition of the legal undertaking and in the sense that the judge has to make a choice. What consequences different legal approaches have depend on the specific circumstances. One can therefore not in advance say that one method favours the rule of law whereas the other favours tyranny. The choice the judge makes of which method to employ has direct consequences for the extent of his participation in the oppression of the regime.

Radbruch and the Discussion on Nazi Germany

Sebastian Haffner gives a vivid account of the instant transformation of the Kammergericht (Court of Appeals) of Berlin from a proud Prussian court to a subdued instrument of Nazi law. He tells how the deliberations of the judges change subsequent to one judge of Jewish origin being replaced in April 1933 with a young jurist coming from the Amtsgericht (a lower court), an open-faced, blond man with glowing cheeks, who was "something high up in the SS":

> The deliberations themselves were also often strange. The new member of the senate produced unheard-of points of law in a fresh, confident voice. We *Referendars*, who had just passed our exams, exchanged looks while he expounded. At last the president of the senate remarked with perfect politeness, 'Colleague, could it be that you have overlooked paragraph 816 of the Civil Code?' At which the new high court judge looked embarrassed, like a candidate who had just slipped up in a viva, leafed through his copy of the Code and admitted lightly, 'Oh yes. Well, then it's just the other way around.' Those were the triumphs of the older law.

> There were, however, other cases in which the newcomer did not back down but held eloquent speeches, in a somewhat over-loud voice, stating that here the paragraph of the law must yield precedence; he would then instruct his co-judges that the meaning was more important than the letter of the law. He would quote Hitler. Then, with the gesture of a romantic stage hero, he would insist on some untenable decision. It was piteous to observe the faces of the old *Kammergerichtrats* as this went on. They looked at their notes with an expression of indescribable dejection, while their fingers nervously twisted a paper-clip or a piece of blotting paper. They were used to failing candidates for the Assessor examination for spouting the kind of nonsense that was now being presented as the pinnacle of wisdom; but now this nonsense was backed by the full power of the state, by the threat of dismissal for lack of national reliability, loss of livelihood, the concentration camp... They coughed; they said, "Of course we agree with your opinion, but you will understand..." They begged for a little understanding for the civil code and tried to save what could be saved.
>
> That was the *Kammergericht* in Berlin in April 1933. It was the same *Kammergericht* whose judges had stood up to Frederick the Great 150 years earlier and, faced with a cabinet decree, had preferred jail to changing a judgment they considered correct in the King's favour. In Prussia, every schoolchild knows the story of the miller of Potsdam which, whether it is true or not, gives an indication of the Court's reputation. The King wanted a windmill removed because it disturbed the view from his new palace of Sans Souci. He offered to buy the mill. The miler refused, he wanted to keep his mill. The King threatened to dispossess the miller, whereupon the miller said, 'Just so, your Majesty, but there's still the *Kammergericht* in Berlin.' To this day the mill can be seen next to the Palace.
>
> In 1933 the *Kammergericht* toed the line. No Frederick the Great was needed, not even Hitler himself had to intervene. All that was needed was a few *Amtsgerichtsrats* with a deficient knowledge of the law.[9]

Haffner observed how the Prussian justice system caved in before his eyes within a few months after the Nazis came to power. How could this come about, not only in a court of appeals in Berlin but throughout the whole of the judiciary of Germany?

In his famous essay, *Gesetzliches Unrecht und Übergesetzliches Recht* (Statutory Lawlessness and Supra-Statutory Law), Gustav Radbruch presented the argument that positivism was the cause of the German judges' commitment to the policies of the Nazi regime. And not only did their positivism leave the judges defenceless against laws with arbitrary and criminal contents. But also positivism, with its total lack of defence against misuses of legislation, should now finally be overcome in Germany in order to arm it against any future return to a lawless state.

Radbruch's thesis that legal positivism was the main cause found resonance among many contemporary observers. Karl Loewenstein, a refugee from Nazi Germany to the United States in the 1930s and who cannot be accused of being apologetic towards the German jurists, wrote:

> The truly exasperating feature of the Nazi legal system lay in the fact that the most arbitrary and unjust of its acts were couched in the form of a statute, decree, or similar enactment, which, because of its formal character as a legal norm, was applied by the judge as "law" regardless of its inherently arbitrary character. The German judge worships the written law and slavishly follows its letter. He is unaffected by intellectual doubts as to the intrinsic justice of the legal rule he has to apply, provided it is enacted by the authority of the state,

---

[9] Haffner (2003), pp. 189–190.

> and he does not question whether the authority is legitimate or not. He is confirmed in this attitude by his class situation much more than in Anglo-Saxon countries, where the judge at one time or another has been a member of the bar and, as such, has usually participated in trials combating the state.[10]

Positivism quickly established itself in the postwar self-consciousness of the German legal community, not only as an explanation for the actions of the German lawyers but also as an excuse and an exonerating factor. The positivism thesis was also actively maintained by lawyers who, acting as Nazi ideologists, had attacked positivism fiercely during the 1930s. In his answers to Robert Kempner, the American prosecutor in Nuremberg, well-known legal theorist Carl Schmitt during his interrogations blamed the German belief in legality for the readiness of the higher officials of the German state to follow Hitler. He claimed that legal positivism was the unchallenged view on law in Germany at the time. According to the positivist outlook, norms and commands enacted by the competent state authority all qualified as "law" as such, and this was all that was law. "During the French Revolution, the terror of the Jacobins was met with 'what crimes can be committed in the name of liberty!' Of the complicity in the crimes of Hitler of the judiciary and public administration it can now be said, that these crimes were possible in the name of a fully functionalised legality", Schmitt wrote.[11]

Schmitt stated that the empowering law was perceived by most as conforming to the requirements of legality and thereby formed the source that made all subsequent enactments legal. Evidently, he was not so sure about this in 1933 and 1934. In his 1933 comment to the empowering law, Schmitt warned against a widespread "liberal constitutionalism" and called for "guarding against undermining the legal grounds of the new state with the sophistry of the old Party-State. With the state, also the constitutional law and the constitutional law doctrine must be cleansed and renewed".[12]

After the purge of the SA in 1934, where Röhm, the Chief of Staff of the SA since 1931, and the "old guard" of the SA were massacred without trial and without warning by Hitler's orders, an opportunity was taken to murder a large number of people who at one time or another had opposed Hitler. Hitler enacted a law that retroactively claimed that all the killings were legal executions. In a comment, Schmitt accentuated his warning against liberal thinking and wrote about the "liberal legality's blindness to the law". Applauding the massacre as "a protection of the law by the Führer against its gravest misuse", he called for the need for a revision of "our prevailing methods and modes of thought, the dominating opinions and existing case law. We should not see blindly at legal concepts arguments and decisions that all stem from the old and ailing times". Only the Führer himself could truly see the inner justness of the law. "But in a society ordered in such a way with the unity of state, movement and people, this inner justness belongs to all sectors of

[10] Loewenstein (1948), p. 432.
[11] Schmitt (2000), p. 108.
[12] Schmitt (1933), col. 455–458.

life and society that are sworn to loyalty to the Führer".[13] Evidently, Schmitt, in 1933 and 1934, saw the need to vanquish the dominating "liberal legality" in order to make room for the "inner justness" of Nazi law, and he did not believe in legality as an explanation for what legal measures were necessary under the new regime.

When Schmitt after the war invokes positivism as the explanation, he indirectly suggests that all the efforts of himself and the other Nazi legal ideologists to convince the legal community of the failings of positivism were in vain—they still clung to their positivist inclinations. On the other hand, by this very fact, they adopted and applied the Nazi ideology and transformed the liberal legal order into an order of oppression. Quite convenient for Schmitt and his colleagues, who by this have no blame in the transformation that took place?

Positivism is a common explanation for judicial contribution to oppression. Radbruch's positivism thesis was expanded and endorsed by renowned American legal scholar Lon L. Fuller in his debate with British legal theorist and positivist H.L.A. Hart.[14] The judges of South Africa explained their enforcement of apartheid and oppressive security measures with the doctrine of parliamentary sovereignty and positivism. This explanation is also supported by influential observers of the South African legal system. Professor of law John Dugard wrote in a comment in 1987:

> Although lawyers and judges in South Africa (or elsewhere) seldom engage in sophisticated jurisprudential speculation, there is considerable support for the two basic principles of Austinian positivism: first, that law is the command of the sovereign, and, second, that a strict division must be maintained between law as it is and law as it ought to be—that is between law and morality... This jurisprudential outlook possibly accounts for the manner in which judges have applied the 'laws of apartheid'.[15]

Positivism has also been the explanation offered for the support by the Chilean judiciary of the military dictatorship.[16] Similar explanations are used to describe the support of judges of the United States to slavery in the nineteenth century and disproportionate sentencing in current times. J.C. Oleson wrote in an article from 2007:

> Even today, American judges are plagued by the moral-formal dilemma. While neither as egregious nor as obvious as the abuses of the law that flourished under the Nazis, the Supreme Court of the United States still wrestles with laws that, while valid, incense and outrage commentators... Many federal district judges chafe against mandatory minimum sentences, frustrated by blunderbuss laws that require them to impose sentences they believe to be unjust.[17]

At its crudest level, positivism is offered as an explanation for motive. The motive might stem from a normative fact: positive obligations enacted by the ruler

---

[13] Schmitt (1934), col. 945–950.

[14] Fuller (1957), pp. 630–672.

[15] Dugard (1987), pp. 496–497.

[16] Hilbink (2008), p. 118.

[17] Oleson (2007), pp. 676 and 679.

are binding law. Alternatively, it might stem from a psychological inclination to accept as binding that which is ordered by an authority; that is a disposition towards obedience. It is difficult to discern when positivism is offered as a normative and when it is offered as a psychological explanation. At the normative level, the positivist theory on Nazi Germany was wrong. Legal positivism was not the dominating theory or method in Germany before the Nazi rule, and certainly not during it. At the psychological level, Stanley Milgram has shown that obedience to authority is a strong motive, so strong that many are unable to disobey even when they are experiencing even extreme tension when being ordered to harm others.[18] Such tension is reported by Norwegian public defender Leif S. Rode from a case decided by the SS Polizeigericht Nord, where 11 defendants received the death sentence on shaky evidence. "The judge's hand trembled so much when reading the sentence", writes Rode, "that he had to support it with his other hand. He was obviously under great personal distress at this moment".[19]

The positivist explanation accords well with the concept that many judges have of the judicial role. This self-understanding is stated in a typical way by South African Supreme Court judges for the South African Truth and Reconciliation Commission:

> The law reports abound with cases decided against the government by ostensibly government-supporting judges, and cases decided in favour of the government by judges known to be opposed to the government's policies. That is no more than one should expect from any judge who is true to the office: that he or she will decide the case in accordance with his or her understanding of the law of the land, whether or not he or she approves of the result of the application of that law. That is the inevitable consequence of the taking of the judicial oath of office and it could hardly be otherwise[20]

That an explanation agrees with the self-understanding of a social actor is no guarantee of it being correct, though. Using positivism as an explanation for why the legal profession became a willing instrument for the implementation of Nazi policy through the judiciary was already problematic at the outset.[21] Bernd Rüthers and many after him have shown that Nazi lawyers did not employ a formalist method true to the legislation in their dealings with the law. Rather, it was the use of non-positivist sources defined by the ideology of race and the common good and purpose of the German people that guided interpretation and application of statutes and general legal concepts and principles. The traditional obligation of the judge to follow the legislation was substituted by an obligation to follow the will of the Führer, which required a plethora of legal approaches and methods.[22]

---

[18] Milgram (2004), p. 43.

[19] Rode (1983), p. 334.

[20] Submission to the South African Truth and Reconciliation Commission by the following members of the Supreme Court of Appeal: Mr. Justice J.W. Smalberger, Mr. Justice C.T. Howie, Mr. Justice R.M. Marais, and Mr. Justice D.G. Scott, 115 S. African Law Journal 1998, p. 43.

[21] See Paulson (1994).

[22] Rüthers (2012), p. 277.

References

Arendt H (2003) Responsibility and judgment. Schocken Books, New York

Brand-Ballard J (2010) Limits of legality: the ethics of lawless judging. Oxford University Press, Oxford

Curran VG (1998–1999) The legalization of racism in a constitutional state: democracy's suicide in Vichy France. Hastings Law J 50:1–96

Dugard J (1987) The judiciary in a state of national crisis – with special reference to the South African experience. Wash Lee Law Rev 44:477–501

Fuller LL (1957) Positivism and fidelity to law – a reply to Professor Hart. Harv Law Rev 71:630–672

Glover J (2012) Humanity a moral history of the 20th century, 2nd edn. Yale University Press, New Haven

Haffner S (2003) Defying Hitler: a memoir. Phoenix, London

Halliday TC, Karpik L, Feeley MM (2007) The legal complex in struggles for political liberalism. In: Halliday TC, Karpik L, Feeley MM (eds) Fighting for political freedom comparative studies of the legal complex and political liberalism. Hart, Oxford and Portland

Hilbink L (2008) Agents of anti-politics: courts in Pinochet's Chile. In: Ginsburg T, Moustafa T (eds) Rule by law: the politics of courts in authoritarian regimes. Cambridge University Press, Cambridge

Karpik L (2007) Postscript political lawyers. In: Halliday TC, Karpik L, Feeley MM (eds) Fighting for political freedom comparative studies of the legal complex and political liberalism. Hart, Oxford and Portland

Loewenstein K (1948) Reconstruction of the administration of justice in the American occupied Germany. Harv Law Rev 61:419–467

Milgram S (2004) Obedience to authority, New York 1974 published by Perennial Classics with a foreword by Jerome S. Bruner New York

Oleson JC (2007) The antigone dilemma: when the paths of law and morality diverge. Cardozo Law Rev 29:669–702

Paulson SL (1994) Lon L. Fuller, Gustav Radbruch and the "Positivist" theses. Law Philos 13:313–359

Rode LS (1983) De tyske krigsretter, in Den Norske Advokatforening, Advokaten – rettens og samfunnets tjener Den Norske Advokatforening 1908–1983, Oslo, pp 329–362

Rüthers B (2012) Die unbegrenzte Auslegung: Zum Wandel der Privatrechtsordnung im Nationalsozialismus 7. Ausg. Mohr Siebeck, Tübingen

Schmitt C (1933) Das Gesetz zur Behebung der Not von Volk und Reich. Deutsche Juristen-Zeitung col. 455–458

Schmitt C (1934) Der Führer schützt das Recht zur Reichstagsrede Adolf Hitlers vom 13. Juli 1934. Deutsche Juristen-Zeitung, col. 945–950

Schmitt C (2000) Antworten in Nürnberg, Herausgegeben und kommentiert von Helmut Quaritisch. Duncker & Humblot, Berlin

Chapter 15
What Positivism?

Undefined Positivism

How could the reference to positivism survive for so long as an explanation of the readiness of German judges to accommodate the oppression and tyranny of the Nazi regime? First of all, "positivism" was used in an undefined manner without a clear concept of "legal positivism" and with emphasis on different things. Radbruch equals the situation of the judiciary with the situation in the army: in the army, the slogan was "an order is an order"; in the administration of justice, it was "a law is (a) law" (Gesetz ist Gesetz). But what conception of legal positivism lies behind such a conception of law?

The most formalised concept of legal positivism at the time was that of Hans Kelsen. Setting aside the fact that Kelsen's legal theory was by no means the predominant one in Germany before the Nazis, in fact his *Reine Rechtslehre* was only first published in 1934, Kelsen's theory presupposes that the different rules of the legal system can be justified according to a basic norm. But there was no such justification of the rule of the Nazis according to any basic norm in force when the Nazis took power. On the contrary, they based the legitimation of their system on an assertion of a revolution, where the basic norm of the Weimer Republic was not carried over into the new order.

In his criticism of a court ruling from the Special Court of Darmstadt, Ernst Rudolf Huber, professor in Kiel, Leipzig, and Strasburg and one of the leading constitutional lawyers of the Nazis, explained how all of the constitutional principles of parliamentarism, federalism, distribution of power, and individual rights had been smashed by National Socialism, not through legislation but directly in a revolutionary manner, immediately through the seizure of power by the National Socialist Party.[1] The basic principles of the National Socialist state were the importance of the German people, the Führer principle, and the totality of politics.

[1] Both the case and the comments are published in Juristische Wochenschrift 1934, pp. 1744–1747.

H.P. Graver, *Judges Against Justice*, DOI 10.1007/978-3-662-44293-7_15

These formed the founding basis for the constitution of the National Socialist state and were as such supreme principles of law. Single provisions of the Weimar constitution were only valid as far as they explicitly or implicitly were recognised by the National Socialist state and were then to be interpreted in line with the principles of the Nazi constitution and not according to their traditional interpretation.

In the ideology of the time, the Nazi takeover was thus presented as a revolution, with a front against the rationalism and positivism of the liberal state. Positivism is a danger to the state, wrote professor of public law Ulrich Scheuner, author of the thesis Die nationale Revolution: Eine staatsrechtliche Untersuchung, "because no ethically based conception of the state can grow from it. Every state must be grounded on specific customary and political values from which it serves its people, draws its authority and combats its enemies. A relativistic basis must by necessity lead to a weakening of the consciousness of the state and to an undermining of its authority".[2]

Another way of perceiving Kelsen's theory is by taking it as expressing that the basic norm changes with the identity of the legal system. Under a revolution, the old legal system is replaced with a new one that is now considered as the valid legal order. The old basic law is replaced by a new one. This conception of law cannot, however, explain why anyone should obey the new legal order. The basic norm is not a normative part of the law but a postulation like an axiom, used for descriptive and analytical purpose. A judge can therefore not invoke Kelsen's theory as a reason for obedience to the new regime.[3]

On this basis, it can be concluded that the "positivism" of Nazi law could not have been the positivism of Kelsen in the sense of an obligation to adhere to a basic norm that gave Nazi law the quality of law. Despite the fact that the Nazi takeover of power claimed its legality in a provision of the Weimar constitution, its legal self-understanding denied this constitution the status of a basic norm for the regime and shifted the focus of judicial loyalty from positively enacted legislation to metaphysical concepts of "needs of the German people" and "will of the Führer".

It therefore seems that the positivism Radbruch refers to is a concept of law where law equals orders from a sovereign who has power to enforce his commands, regardless of how these orders conform to any basic law or anything else. This understanding is supported by the fact that Radbruch himself, in the beginning of his article, juxtaposes the two maxims "an order is an order" and "a law is a law". Stanley L. Paulson points out that Radbruch employs two different concepts of positivism—the broad obedience to authority concept when he seeks to explain the actions of the German judges and the narrower statutory legal positivism when he seeks to exonerate them.[4] The same concept is employed by Carl Schmitt when he speaks of the belief in legality with reference to Max Weber's thesis of legitimacy

[2] Scheuner (1934), p. 190.

[3] See Mahmud (1994), pp. 110–113.

[4] Paulson (1994).

through legality and legality tied to any norm or command by an empowered organ of state.

This is a very broad concept of legal positivism, conflating positivism with obedience to authority. On the other hand, this concept of law accords well with the change in attitude that the Nazis brought about. The traditional loyalty to legislation was substituted by a new loyalty to the current will and policies of the dictator.[5] This positivism is described in an illuminating way by Herman Jahrreiss to the International Military Tribunal in the trial against the major war criminals:

> Hitler's will was the final authority for their considerations on what to do and what not to do. The Führer's order cut off every discussion. Thus a person who as a functionary of the hierarchy invokes an order by the Führer is not trying to claim exemption from punishment for an illegal action but opposes the assertion that his conduct was illegal; for it is his contention that the order with which he complied was legally unassailable.[6]

The position of Adolf Hitler in the perception among German jurists was described in the following way by one of the defendants at the US Military Tribunal in Nuremberg in a way that endows Hitler with mythical qualities like some dark force taken from the writings of J.R.R. Tolkien:

> However, something entirely different has occurred; with the Führer a man has risen within the German people who awakens the oldest, long forgotten times. Here is a man who in his position represents the ideal of the judge in its perfect sense, and the German people elected him for their judge – first of all, of course, as 'judge' over their fate in general, but also as 'supreme magistrate and judge.'[7]

We see this reverence of Adolf Hitler demonstrated by Carl Schmitt in his article after the SA purge in 1934, where between 150 and 200 people were arrested and liquidated by SS, SD, and army forces. On 3 July, Hitler enacted the Act on Measures to Defend the State, with its sole article: "The measures taken on 30 June and 1 July and 2 July to surmount the treason against the nation and state are lawful as defensive actions". Schmitt wrote that "truly, the act of the Führer was judicial in the real sense. Acts of the Führer are not subject to law but are themselves the highest law".[8] The headline of the article was "The Führer Protects the Law".

This relationship of the Führer to the law is also reflected in the methodological dictum that National Socialist ideology formed the highest source of law. Again, in the words of Schmitt: "All law stems from the right of vitality of the people. Any enactment of the state, any judicial decision contains law only in as far as it flows from this source. The rest is not law, but rather a network of norms of force that are mocked by a competent criminal". This hostility to law was directed not only

[5] See Rüthers (2012), p. 277.

[6] Trial of the Major War Criminals before the International Military Tribunal, Nuremberg 14 November 1945–1 October 1946, vol. 17, p. 489.

[7] The Justice Trial, p. 1012.

[8] Schmitt (1934), col. 947.

towards the received laws from the previous regime but also towards measures enacted by the Nazi regime itself.

This description may accurately describe how Hitler's commands were perceived as laws. It nevertheless disregards both basic facts of how the Nazi legal order operated and basic elements of most versions of legal positivism as this concept is understood by its adherents. It does, however, agree with the Nazis' revolutionary concept of law, which was presented as "simply the regulations given by the supreme authority of the state, regardless of their contents", as opposed to the old concept of laws as "sovereign rules accepted by the national assembly according to specified procedures".[9] This was a new and revolutionary concept of law introduced by the Nazis—not something they carried over from the old regime or from established legal theory. This concept of law could therefore not be the reason why the judges accepted the Nazi rule; it was rather a result of their accepting it. The question to be asked is, therefore, not why the German lawyers followed the law but why they were so obedient to the authority of Hitler and the Nazi Party.

Positivism as Separation of Law and Morality

In his article "Positivism and the Separation of Law and Morals", H.L.A. Hart discusses Radbruch's thesis.[10] According to Hart, the central tenet of positivism is not the command thesis but the separation of law and morals. Postulating law as something that exists does not necessarily mean that law equates to commands but that law is something that can be seen to exist as opposed to law as something that is desirable or something that ought to exist. What lies at the root, says Hart, is not that of a command but "what it is for a social group and its officials to accept such rules".[11]

What Radbruch and Schmitt characterise as legal positivism is therefore, according to Hart, misleading because legal positivism as such does not offer an authoritative explanation of *why* a social group and its officials accept laws as laws. It only states that norms that *are* accepted can be characterised as law. But the whole point of Radbruch and his followers is to offer an explanation to explain and to guard against similar developments in the future. The commands of the Führer were accepted and must as such, according to legal positivism, be deemed as the law of Germany at the time. But they were not accepted because they were law according to the previous concept of law; they were accepted despite the old doctrines of loyalty to legislation.

[9] Scheuner (1934), p. 202.
[10] Hart (1957).
[11] Hart (1957), p. 603.

The reality was therefore rather the opposite of the positivist theses: the will of the Führer was law because it was accepted as such. To invoke legal positivism as an explanation is therefore circular—they were accepted because they were accepted. The theory of Radbruch amounts to a postulate that German jurists acted according to a theory of law that stated that "anything deemed to be a law by any official with a claim to legal power ought to be accepted and obeyed as law without question". This was not the prevailing concept of law among German lawyers before 1933, and if it was, it could hardly be characterised as a typical position of legal positivism.

Studies of the lawyers of the Weimar Republic and of the Nazi period reveal that positivism had already lost its position as a leading school of thought in the Weimar Republic and that National Socialist legal thought was diametrically opposed to positivist thinking.[12] So, in conclusion, it is fair to say that the basic concept of law that Radbruch and Schmitt ascribe to German lawyers is not legal positivism, and this concept does not accurately portray the attitude of the Nazi courts. In fact, as pointed out by Paulson in his arguments against Fuller, the leading positivists under the Weimar Republic were against the Nazis, and the Nazis and the legal theoreticians who supported them were fully aware of this fact. Further, in the debates between the positivists and the others in the years preceding the Nazi takeover, the non-positivists won the day. Finally, the mainly conservative judges of the time were basically not strictly loyal to the positive legislation of the Weimar Republic. These facts together indicate strongly that it is incorrect to explain the attitude of German judges under the Nazi regime with positivism.[13] As Rüthers points out, positivism presupposes a certain stability and confidence in the legitimacy of the state. But this confidence was shattered in Germany, initially by the First World War and then by the monetary crisis of the 1920s.[14]

In fact, the legal theorists who were the strongest proponents of positivism as a legal theory were precisely those who did not come to terms with the Nazi regime, like Radbruch himself.[15] Nazi legal theory was rejected by the positivists; it was the non-positivists that accepted it. Even if we should accept such a broad concept of legal positivism as presented by Radbruch and Schmitt, their explanation fails because they do not coincide with the facts of how the Nazi legal system operated. Nazi law was not perceived as something positive, separate from customs and morals. In fact, Hitler himself, as early as 1933 in a speech to a meeting of German lawyers in Leipzig, proclaimed that in the Third Reich law and morality are identical.[16] As can be seen already from Schmitt's writings from the 1930s, Nazi law was presented as something inherent in the German people and the Nazi order and as something separate from and above positive law. Law was also presented as

---

[12] Ott and Buob (1997), p. 462.

[13] See Paulson (1994).

[14] Rüthers (2012), p. 95.

[15] See Paulson (1994), p. 325.

[16] See Fraenkel (1941), p. 110.

"what benefits the German people". The idea of the authoritarian state was given status as an absolute ethical value.[17] The Nazi legal order could not be disconnected from morals and ethics but presupposed a definite ethical universe that was given precedence over positive law.

It is evident that the Nazi concept of law in no way conformed to the basic element of legal positivism to separate law as something that exists from law, as how it ought to be, or as ideals found in morals, ideology, or something else outside the scope of positive law. Law is therefore something outside of not only the legislation from the old regime but also the legislation issued by the Nazi authorities. Legislation of the time did not entail "law" in this sense but merely hinted at "law" in a more or less obvious way.[18] As we also can see from numerous cases, the non-positive sources of Nazi ideology were an important part of legal interpretation. A clear example can be found in the interpretation and application of the Nuremberg race laws in the case law of the Supreme Court of the 1930s.[19]

Positivism as Formalism

The second part of the positivist thesis is that not only did the judges have to obey the law, but also they had to apply it without a measure of personal discretion. Not the judiciary but the legislator was the cause of the atrocities of the regime. In this way, the lawyers and judges can be absolved from most of the blame for the atrocities committed through and sanctioned by the law. This argument confuses positivism with formalism and mechanical decisions. Hart shows in his article that formalism is not a necessary component of positivism.[20] Both a positivist and a non-positivist can employ a legal rule in a mechanical way.

A person being held responsible for his decision will often resort to the excuse that his decision was dictated by the law. But is this a true characterisation of the situation of the German judges? If they had a choice when interpreting and applying the law, they cannot lay the burden of their rulings on the Nazi legislator.

There is ample evidence of the fact that German judges went far beyond a mere mechanical application of the law as given to them in the books of legislation. On the contrary, the development of the law from a liberal, democratic rule of law and legal order to a totalitarian dictatorship in the earliest years of the Nazi regime was the result not first and foremost of legislative activity but of the activity of the courts.[21]

---

[17] Scheuner (1934), p. 203.

[18] See Maus (1989), pp. 80–103.

[19] See also the summary by Hattenhauer (1989), p. 26.

[20] Hart (1957), pp. 610–613.

[21] Rüthers (2012), p. 505.

In their application of the wicked and oppressive laws of the regime, the Nazi judges were exercising choice. Hart describes judicial choice as something exercised in "hard cases" in the "penumbra" of legal concepts and rules based on extralegal factors.[22] This seems to entail that if one rejects Hart's theory of law and his theory that rules have a binding core and a penumbra where the judge is unbound by the law, one also rejects his assertion that the judges are exercising a personal choice when they follow or oppose the measures of a regime. This is the position of Dyzenhaus when explaining the South African judges under apartheid. Based on his analysis of their judicial reasoning, he maintains there is a consensus among judges that legal reasons fully determine their conclusions.[23] Judges who applied the authoritarian laws from a plain fact approach, giving best possible effect to the oppressive aims of the legislator, obviously thought they were required to do so under the law in the same way as those judges who opposed a common law approach thought that this was what the law demanded of them. To the extent that Dyzenhaus is correct in his observations, it seems crucial to the issue of judicial complicity or protection whether they ascribe to some version of legal positivism or to some other theory of law.

The weak point of this criticism is that legal theory is not prescribed by law. The application of a plain fact approach, a common law approach, or any other interpretative approach or theory for that matter is not dictated by the law. The judge may choose his approach, and his approach may have consequences for the answers that he comes up with to questions of law. He may or may not choose an approach strategically to obtain the result he deems favourable for reasons outside the law. The choice may be made consciously or unconsciously. Nevertheless, his choice, and thus the legal result of it, is not determined by the law. The judge is making a choice, either on a legal solution directly or on an interpretative approach that indirectly influences his solution. This means that the decision to employ an interpretative approach not only is a theoretical decision but also may be a moral and a political decision. If his approach leads him to condone or, worse, to impose injustice, he is under a moral obligation to reconsider his approach. One does not have to ascribe to Hart's theory of core and penumbra to recognise this moral choice of the judge when applying wicked laws. One must, in any case, question whether the positivism of German jurists up to the 1930s included formalism.

Alternatives to Positivism

There were commentators in Germany after the war who offered other explanations than legal positivism. A judge from Koblenz, Landesgerichtsdirektor Dr. Rotberg,

---

[22] Hart (1957), p. 607.

[23] Dyzenhaus (2010), pp. 174–175.

pointed to the participation of the judges in politics.[24] Many judges were engaged in party politics before 1933, and this was perceived as a matter of fact. After the Nazi takeover of power, employing the judges in the interests of the party became a main part of judicial policy. Judges were recruited and scrutinised for their political loyalty and their ability to live up to the slogan that "law is what benefits the people". In this way, the judiciary was turned into "politics' whores", in the words of Dr. Rothberg. In order to avoid similar situations, judges need to be independent not only from orders and instructions but also in their minds. Judges should also be above party politics to ensure their real and apparent impartiality in societal conflicts that they are called upon to decide.

Rothberg was challenged by Ministerialrat Kurt Oppler, who called for more political judges, not less.[25] He shared Rothberg's analysis that the Nazi judiciary was characterised by politicised judges but claimed that the judges all in all had been politicised before the Nazi takeover and that the majority during the Weimar Republic had been committed against democracy and against the Republic. The majority of the judges, who were not active members of any political party, were the ones who rapidly joined the Nazi Party after 1933. To ensure a democratic development of Germany after the war, its judges had to be firmly committed to the policy of democracy and rule of law and thus had not be above the important strives of politics in society. Participation in politics should therefore be regarded as a qualification and not a disqualification for a judge, although a judge of course should refrain from active party politics after taking office.

Since there were many alternative legal theories in Germany at the beginning of the twentieth century, one could speculate that the acceptance of Nazi law was caused by other schools of thought, apart from legal positivism. Okko Behrends finds the sources of Nazi legal theory in the so-called free law movement of the late nineteenth and early twentieth centuries. This school of thought was a reaction to the formalist conceptual jurisprudence and emphasised the judicial decision as the heart of the law. The judicial decision should be curtailed not by abstract concepts and doctrines but by the particulars of the case and the social reality surrounding it. According to Behrends, this school of thought broke the ground for Nazi legal theory with its voluntaristic approach to law, romanticising the judicial decision and the release of the judge from all bindings to the doctrinally developed legal concepts and values.[26]

Behrends gives a convincing account of how the main thoughts of the free law movement could be and actually were adopted by leading Nazi ideologists like Carl Schmitt and Roland Freisler. In addition to hailing the judge as the law's sovereign, the free law movement emphasised the social reality in a romanticised way as the living will of the people that constitutes the life and body of law. In this way, the free law school differed from other movements in legal theory in that it put the

[24] Rotberg (1947).

[25] Oppler (1947).

[26] Behrends (1989), p. 38.

judge and his decision in the centre position and freed him from normative constraints. Similar theories of law were developed at the same time in other jurisdictions than the German, notably by the American and the Scandinavian realists.

Both the positivism thesis and the free law thesis imply that if German lawyers had stuck with their systematic, conceptual constructivism, they could have avoided turning the judicial system into an instrument of Nazi terror. It goes without saying that in order to employ the judiciary and the legal system for their purposes, they needed a theory of law. As we have seen above in Chap. 3, the Nazi leaders put great emphasis on preserving the forms of legality during the takeover of power. Since they, in their own self-understanding and in real terms, strived for a revolutionary change and a clean break with the "liberal rule of law state", it was not possible to operate with a legal theory that emphasised continuity and systematic identity between delivered concepts, values and law, and new laws and decisions. They needed to free the legal application from the normative constraints of the past. They also needed the application of law to be instrumental according to the aims of the system at any time. The judges therefore had to be made apprehensive to the basic ideology and the changes in this ideology as society developed. This was basically achieved by the setting of the basic values of race, blood, and people and by the introduction of the mystical source of the Führer will.

It is therefore easy to show that the needs of the Nazis could not have been fulfilled so easily by theories that emphasise coherence in law over time. In the same way, positivism understood as a separation of the law, that is, from the law that ought to be, would have barred the Nazi courts from letting the ideology of the Nazi Party override or modify legislation enacted before the Nazi takeover. If the courts had adhered to positivist doctrine as the Prussian Administrative Appeals Court did,[27] they would not have given "the needs of the German people" or "the purity of the German race" status as a superior source of law and would thus not have had grounds to disregard or reinterpret provisions of the BGB and other laws in the way that they did.[28]

On the other hand, this is not something particular to the Nazis. It is not their legal theory that separates the law of the Nazis from the law of other places and other times. Legal scholars and practitioners change and adopt legal outlooks for a reason, and outlooks compatible with the needs of the Nazis have served the needs of other societies as well. Societies sometimes seek stability, and sometimes change. They are sometimes marked by harmony and homogeneity and other times by conflict and diversity. The plethora of legal theories is also a function of the size and diversity of law as an academic discipline and not part of the law as such. It therefore requires extralegal argumentation to show that one theory is preferable to all others. Where some value change, others value adaptability; where some value foreseeability, others value substantive justice.

---

[27] See pp. 98–100 above.

[28] See Hempfer (1974), p. 103.

But change, stability, foreseeability, and substantive justice cannot be regarded independently from the value of what it is that is going to change, stabilise, be foreseeable, or determine justice. In the moral and political fields, there is, therefore, no escape from evaluating the specific issues at hand. When the basic political issues of society concern the very issue of continuity or change, choice of legal method becomes political in itself. This can be seen from many historical examples, such as under the New Deal in the US under the 1930s, in the breakthrough of the welfare state in the Nordic countries in the middle of the twentieth century, and in the Europeanisation of law that is taking place currently in most European countries. When, in addition, the legislator wages war on the rule of law, the choice also becomes a moral choice. The correct question to ask of the judges of Nazi Germany is consequently: should they have contributed to persecution on racial grounds, deprivation of basic rights, and ruthless and unjust punishments? And not: should they have departed from this or that legal methodology? Since the question of participation or not was related to the choice of legal method, it shows that under such conditions, the choice of method and legal theory becomes not only a question of legal theory but also a matter of politics and morality.

References

Behrends O (1989) Von der Freirechtsbewegung zum konkreten Ordnungs- und Gestaltdenken. In: Dreier R, Sellert W (eds) Recht und Justiz im "Dritten Reich". Surkamp, Frankfurt am Main, p 38

Dyzenhaus D (2010) Hard cases in wicked legal systems pathologies of legality, 2nd edn. Oxford University Press, Oxford

Fraenkel E (1941) The dual state a contribution to the theory of dictatorship. Oxford University Press, New York

Hart HLA (1957) Positivism and the separation of law and morals. Harv Law Rev 71:593–629

Hattenhauer H (1989) Wandlung des Richterleitbildes. Im 19. und 20. Jahrhundert. In: Dreier R, Sellert W (eds) Recht und Justiz im "Dritten Reich". Surkamp, Frankfurt am Main

Hempfer W (1974) Die nationalsozialistische Staatsauffassung in der Rechtsprechung des Preußischen Oberverwaltungsgerichts. Dunker & Humblot, Berlin

Mahmud T (1994) Jurisprudence of successful treason: Coup d'Etat and common law. Cornell Int Law J 27:49–140

Maus I (1989) "Gesetzesbindung" der Justiz und die Struktur der nationalsozialistischen Rechtsnormen. In: Dreier R, Sellert W (eds) Recht und Justiz im "Dritten Reich". Surkamp, Frankfurt am Main, pp 80–103

Oppler K (1947) Justiz und Politik. Deutsche Rechts-Zeitschrift 2:323–326

Ott W, Buob F (1997) Did legal positivism render German jurists defenceless during the Third Reich? In: DeCoste FC, Schwartz B (eds) The Holocaust's ghost: writings on art, politics, law and education. University of Alberta Press, Edmonton

Paulson SL (1994) Lon L. Fuller, Gustav Radbruch and the "Positivist" theses. Law Philos 13:313–359

Rotberg HE (1947) Entpolitisierung der Rechtspflege. Deutsche Rechts-Zeitschrift 107–110

Rüthers B (2012) Die unbegrenzte Auslegung: Zum Wandel der Privatrechtsordnung im Nationalsozialismus 7. Ausg. Mohr Siebeck, Tübingen

Scheuner U (1934) Die nationale Revolution Eine Staatsrechtliche Untersuchung. Archiv des Öffentlichen Rechts 166–220
Schmitt C (1934) Der Führer schützt das Recht zur Reichstagsrede Adolf Hitlers vom 13. Juli 1934. Deutsche Juristen-Zeitung, col. 945–950

Chapter 16
Alternative Approaches to Legal Interpretation

The Plain Fact Approach to Legal Interpretation

The increased authority of the legislator under authoritarian conditions has been studied in depth by David Dyzenhaus in his study of the South African Appellate Division under apartheid. Dyzenhaus rejects positivism as an explanation for judicial acquiescence of oppressive measures by the rulers in power. Instead, he accredits it to what he calls the "plain fact approach". In the plain fact approach, law is applied as it exists and not according to what morality requires. The judge "looks to a pattern that exists as a matter of historical fact in the legal acts and decisions of the past, mainly those of the legislator".[1] The pattern to be applied is the result of an intentional design by the actual authors of the acts, the holders of power over legislation.

The plain fact approach to statutory interpretation has similarities to what continental lawyers call the subjective approach or the subjective theory of interpretation, that is, that the judge is bound by, and should strive to establish, the meaning held by the legislator when enacting the statute. Because of this approach, South African judges felt compelled to give decisive significance to the racist ideology of the legislator and to interpret its statutes so as to give this best possible effect as can be seen in the extreme when applied so that "the greater the expressed restrictions (on personal liberty), the greater the implied restrictions".[2] In light of this, principles embedded in common law, such as equality and rule of law, had to yield to the clear discriminatory intent of the apartheid legislator.

Part of the plain fact approach is the reading of the statutes as pointers to this pattern. These pointers are taken as counterpointers to what would otherwise follow from general principles of law.[3] A good example of such a reading of the law is the

[1] Dyzenhaus (2010), p. 48.

[2] See Dugard (1987), p. 491.

[3] Dyzenhaus (2010), pp. 61–69.

H.P. Graver, *Judges Against Justice*, DOI 10.1007/978-3-662-44293-7_16

Roussow v. Sachs case, where a person interned under the 90-day rule was denied access to reading matter and writing material during the duration of his detention because this would make the detention less effective and thus defeat the purpose of the legislator. By this reading, a statute that authorises the administration to make controversial decisions implies departures from due process since due process would make the decision-making "barely manageable",[4] a statute that authorises separation of people on the grounds of colour and race implies powers to make separations that are unreasonable since this is "inevitable",[5] and a statute that authorises great restrictions to imply even greater restrictions shows a parliamentary intent for the restrictions to be effective.[6]

In Dyzenhaus' view, the plain fact approach is an attitude of the judge that he brings with him when he comes to the statutory interpretation and serves as the interpretative context.[7] Obstacles encountered by materials or arguments are seen in light of this context. In light of this, principles embedded in common law such as equality and rule of law had to yield to the clear discriminatory intent of the apartheid legislator.

In the South African context, the judges were dealing with the relationship between apartheid legislation and rule of law principles based on common law. The legislation interpreted by the judges was, for the most, legislation passed by a legislator infused by the apartheid ideology. In Nazi Germany, this was different as the vast body of legislation predated the Nazi rule and was clearly passed with a legislative intent more favourable to individual rights and the rule of law than the Nazi rulers. The judges therefore had to depart from a subjective approach to statutory interpretation and interpret the statutes so as to give them an "objective" meaning in light of the present circumstances. German judges consequently employed the *objective approach* to interpretation of statutes.[8] In the objective approach, the distinction between the statute and the legislator is crucial. The statute is interpreted "objectively", that is, independently of the subjective intentions of the legislator. As a method of statutory interpretation, this has parallels to what Dyzenhaus labels the "common law approach" where the interpretative context and not the intent of the historical content is the "master over legal meaning".[9]

The prime elements of the interpretation of the Nazis were the wording of the statute, its aims, and their realisation in the current setting, where the ideology of the Nazi Party formed the interpretative context. The new ideology was not constructed as in opposition to the existing law but as part of its subject matter.[10]

[4] Cassem v. Oos-Kaapse Kommittee van die Groepsgebiedraad 1959 (3) SA 651 (A).

[5] Minister of the Interior v. Lockhat 1961 (2) SA 587 (A).

[6] Roussouw v. Sachs 1964 (2) SA 551 (A).

[7] Dyzenhaus (2010), p. 81.

[8] See Rüthers (2012), pp. 178–185.

[9] Dyzenhaus (2010), p. 85.

[10] Rüthers (2012), p. 174.

In this way, the Nazi lawyers could untie the bonds between legislation inherited from the old regime and its rule of law values and apply them in light of the ideology and requirements of the new times without departing openly from their inbred loyalty to the law. Although this approach was of most importance when applying legislation that predated the Nazi takeover, the approach also ensured that the regime was not limited even by its own legislation. Adherence to the statute in its originally intended meaning or to the strict interpretation of its wording was scorned by the Nazis as "normativism".

On the face of it, this seems to be an approach that differed from the one taken by the courts in South Africa for the respect of legislative authority. The South Africans stuck firmly to the authority of the legislator, whereas the German judges seemed to undermine it. If we go deeper, we see, however, that there are similarities. The Nazi judges showed great adherence to their current legislator and authority in power. By the means of traditional legal techniques, such as the construction of new legal concepts and ideas, the use of basic principles, restrictive interpretation, contextual interpretations, and analogies, they sought to construct a coherent and applicable normative body of principles from the programme and ideology of the Nazi Party.[11] In most cases, departures from the previous legislation and from the rule of law were substantiated not through open evaluations of conflicting values but through arguments based on positive legal sources and through traditional legal techniques such as extensive or restrictive interpretation, analogies, or systemic arguments to fill gaps in the law.[12]

The main task facing the German judiciary was different from the South African context as the whole existing body of law had to be reinterpreted to be applied as a tool for National Socialism. The basic element of how the judge approached statutes and the other legal material of relevance seemed nevertheless to be the same: the basic ideological pattern of the ruling party is taken as the interpretative context and most authoritative source of law. The South African judges who extended apartheid took their interpretative pattern from the apartheid legislation and the ideology pursued by the legislator. Since the basic law that had to be reformed by this legislation was the unwritten law of the common law, this entailed taking a subjective approach to statutory interpretation. The ideological pattern was constructed both from positive law in the form of legislation and from non-positive law in the form of the ideology of the National Party and the white ideology of the differences of races and the perceived need to protect the white Christian civilisation of the South African community. The German judges also took their interpretative pattern from the ideology pursued by the legislator. But since the law that had to be reformed in their case mainly consisted of statutory law in the civil law tradition, this entailed taking an objective approach to statutory interpretation. Also, their ideological pattern was constructed both from positive and non-positive sources.

---

[11] See Rüthers (2012), p. 116 and Adami (1939).

[12] Rüthers (2012), p. 174.

Taking this into account, Dyzenhaus' plain fact approach seems to fit the approach of the Nazi judges quite well if we shift their emphasis from the pattern intended by the legislator of the past to the pattern intended by the rulers of the present. The German judges looked to the ideology of the Nazis as an interpretative context to be applied both to the legislation of the old regime and to the legislation of the Nazi regime. Only Nazi legislation was taken as pointers to the intent of the legislator, however, and these pointers were used as counterpointers to consequences to be drawn or inferred from the older legislation, as well as new legislation.

The result of the two approaches was the same: to achieve a realisation of the positive morality of the rulers in power. We see the same results when we compare Germany and South Africa as we see when we compare Nazi Germany and Vichy France. Also here, we see that German and French lawyers came to similar results regarding the reinterpretation of the law to accommodate the racial category of Jewishness, despite divergent and even contradictory interpretative methods. The problem then is not related to this or that legal approach or method but to the relationship between the judiciary and the governing standards of evaluation held by those in power. Judges adapted their method of interpretation to fit the rulers and the ideology of the day. The steady compass that is used for navigation is not a method of interpretation but a loyalty to the society they are serving as an important branch of the ordering state. As maintained by Rüthers, legal methodology is intended not as an instrument *against* the societal sense of justice but as a method for its *realisation*.[13] The argument was made in more general terms by Hannah Arendt, who pinpoints it nicely:

> The total moral collapse of respectable society during the Hitler regime may teach us that under such circumstances those who cherish values and hold fast to moral norms and standards are not reliable: we know now that moral norms and standards can be changed overnight, and that all that then will be left is the mere habit of holding fast to something.[14]

Why is it that the authority of the legislator is even more persuasive to the courts when the legislator is oppressive and challenges the values of the rule of law? One answer to this could be that under such conditions, the legislator asserts his authority more forcibly than under more normal conditions. We have seen that the ideological and political pressure exerted on the judges after the Nazi takeover was severe. This was not only a negative pressure but also a positive one in the sense that the Nazis promised the return of the old order, the respect for authority, and the resurrection of the position of judges as important members of society.[15] Also, many judges supported the ideology of the Nazi regime, particularly the racial and nationalist parts of it.

Such factors may have been important, but could they be sufficient to induce conscientious judges acting under the ideology of the rule of law to depart from this

---

[13] Rüthers (2012), p. 443.

[14] Arendt (2003), pp. 44–45.

[15] See Angermund (1990), pp. 66–67.

ideology in individual cases, with the victims of the oppression face to face with them in the courtrooms? In any case, they cannot explain the support given by judges who do not sympathise with the political aims of the regime. Lisa Hilbink found in her interviews with justices of the Chilean High Court that only 6 of the 36 acting judges actively supported the military regime, whereas 14 were clearly at odds with it and were well aware of the historical and international standards of democracy. Sixteen judges were "in between" and asserted different levels of disagreement with and distance from the regime.[16] Despite these facts, the Court in its rulings consistently supported and upheld the oppressive measures of the military dictatorship. Not even all German judges under the Nazi dictatorship supported the Nazi party. In fact, in the military courts, which were an important instrument in the Nazi war effort and oppression of opposition, a large number of the judges were at odds with the Nazi ideology. This did not prevent them from accepting that all opposition must be strictly and forcefully put down with harsh methods.[17]

We know that judges often find and employ methods to alleviate the consequences of harsh rules when they feel the need to do so. Why then is their obedience to legislative authority so strong under oppressive conditions that they abandon such techniques? We see that judges under such conditions even employ their creative legal minds to bring the ideology and intent of the legislator even more efficiently into practice than what is required by alternative legitimate interpretations of the law.

The Dissonance Theory of Robert M. Cover

In his study of antislavery and the judicial process in the United States in the nineteenth century, Robert M. Cover launched the idea that the psychological theory of cognitive dissonance could offer an explanation. Antislavery judges faced with legal rules compelling them to find in favour of slavery must have experienced strong conflicts between their ethical beliefs in the evil of slavery and their loyalty to the law and their judicial role. Cover points out that a judge caught in this way between law and morality has the option to apply the law against his morality, to disregard the law and follow his morality, to resign, or to state that the law is not what he honestly believes it to be.[18] None of these options are psychologically attractive, and most people will seek to find some compromise.

The initial conflict for these judges was to choose between liberty and slavery. Framed in this way, the issue was morally easy. But as a consequence of their role as judges, the choice was not this but rather between values such as between liberty

[16] Hilbink (2008), p. 115.

[17] Garbe (2000), pp. 106–107.

[18] Cover (1974), p. 6.

and ordered federalism, between liberty and fidelity to public trust, and between liberty and adherence to the common undertaking of American nationhood.[19] The judges were drawn into a situation where application of their own formal principles and general acceptance of their role as judges led to the inevitable application of immoral laws. Cover's dissonance hypothesis then predicts in this situation that the judges who were the most troubled by results that favoured slavery would be most likely to exhibit some behaviour that reduced this dissonance. This dissonance could be reduced by elevating the formal status of the law, by retreating to a mechanical formalism in the application of the law, and by ascribing responsibility for the result elsewhere than to the personal choice of the judge.[20]

All these three patterns of reasoning can be backed by reference to rule of law values. The authority of the legislation is connected with how law in general is legitimised and also with values such as equality and predictability. A formal approach to the application of law can also be justified by reference to predictability and impartiality and adherence to authority and precedent. The proper role of the judge is to apply the law and nothing else. Ascription of responsibility to the legislator is in accord with the doctrine of division of power and the separation between the role of the legislator and the role of the judge.

A retreat to a plain fact approach or to emphasising of the obligation to obey the legislator and not only the law as such is therefore not in contradiction with basic principles of rule of law. Outright refusal to give obedience to the legislator in general is untenable for a judge and difficult to reconcile with the judicial role. The alternative is then to apply the law but reserve the right to censure the worst excesses. In this position, the judge also remains responsible for the application when he does not exercise judicial review, and this may be a difficult position to uphold for a person who morally disagrees with the basic assumptions and ideology behind a law. It must be easier then to capitulate and undertake the position of "the mouth speaking the law".

Dyzenhaus contests Cover's theory by saying that there is little evidence that judges who portray their adherence to the will of the legislator are trying to evade personal responsibility. They interpret legislation in this way because they view their role under the constitutional order "not primarily as the guardians of liberty, but the servants of the popular will expressed in the statutes of the elected assembly".[21] But this begs the question why these judges hold this view of their judicial responsibility. For one, this explanation presupposes that judges view their role consistently, which they often do not. Dyzenhaus himself mentions the case law of the English Lord Denning, showing that his approach to interpretation of statutes was different in cases that concerned national security and cases that did not.[22] On the same note, former Chief Justice William Rehnquist argues that civil liberty

[19] Cover (1974), p. 198.

[20] Cover (1974), p. 229.

[21] Dyzenhaus (2010), p. 82.

[22] Dyzenhaus (2010), pp. 266–270.

cannot occupy as favoured a position in wartime as in peacetime and that the courts should pay attention to the government's claims of necessity as a basis of curtailing civil liberty.[23]

One does not need to accuse judges of misrepresenting their beliefs and judgments to ascribe to Cover's theory. His theory is on a different level; it is a theory about why judges hold the beliefs that they do. Dyzenhaus' case analysis shows what beliefs they hold regarding their constitutional role and approaches to interpretation and application of statutes and in many ways confirms Cover's hypothesis. We find both when we study the US antislavery judges, the judges of South Africa, and the judges of Nazi Germany that they emphasised the authority of the legislator strongly, that they made reference to ideology and values held by the legislator, and that they employed this ideology to extend the application of the statutes even beyond their wording. In the case of Germany, the prevailing ideology was also used to reinterpret and, if necessary, disapply legislation enacted under the previous regime. The issue is not whether the judges believed that they were obliged to adjudicate in this way but why they held such beliefs.

There is another argument that can be made against Cover's dissonance hypothesis, however. The one established legal tradition where the plain fact approach has been the dominant approach to legal thinking over a sustained period of time has been the Scandinavian legal tradition. From the middle of the twentieth century until its end, the traditions of Denmark, Sweden, and Norway were strongly influenced by the school of thought called "Scandinavian legal realism". At the same time, these were liberal societies with solidly entrenched democracies and systems of representative government. It is difficult to perceive that judges frequently encountered serious conflicts between the law and their moral conscience in these countries during this period of time. In fact, it can be argued, as Dyzenhaus observes, that in a morally decent legal system where the legislator generally enacts morally sound statutes, the plain fact approach will lead to morally better results overall.[24]

Undoubtedly, the mainstream approach to legal method in the Scandinavian legal tradition was, and still is, the plain fact approach as described by Dyzenhaus. Legislation forms the dominant part of the legal sources, and the approach to legislation is based on the concept that the role of the judge is mainly to give effect to the stated intents and aims of the legislator. For this reason, judges not only are allowed but also are obliged to study the preparatory material to the legislation as an important part of their legal method. The most important documents are the reports prepared by the government to Parliament where an Act is proposed, but often there are also expert reports preceding the report by the government. These documents are not only important as sources of information to the background and aims of the proposals for new legislation; they are also used as guidelines for interpretation, so

[23] Rehnquist (1998), Kindle edition loc. 3670.

[24] Dyzenhaus (2010), p. 171.

they often contain supplementary norms to the enacted statutes. Sometimes, these are even given preference over the text of the statute.

The expressed intent of the legislator is an important guide to interpretation in dominant Scandinavian legal thought. This intent may be expressed in a special section of the Act stating its purpose. It is also often expressed and elaborated in the preparatory material. The Scandinavians have even defended this approach as a way of implementing EU legislation. In a case of implementation of the directive "unfair terms in consumer contracts", the Swedish authorities argued that "according to a legal tradition well established in Sweden and common to the Nordic countries, the preparatory work is an important aid to interpreting legislation. The incorporation of the annex to the Directive in the preparatory work thus seemed the most suitable solution".[25] The published preparatory material is used to guide the discretion that the judge must exercise when applying a statute and may also be used as a basis for an expansive or analogical application and also a restrictive application of the legal rule.

Scandinavian realism has, on the other hand, been quite hostile to the application of general legal principles and for a long time did not recognise that statutes could be restricted or reviewed by reference to legal principles. In the textbook used for the education of lawyers at the University of Oslo from 1971 and the rest of the century, the concept of "legal principle" does not exist.[26] The book is based on a realist approach to law. In addition to plain facts such as legislation, preparatory material, case law, and the legal practice of administrative authorities, it recognises the evaluations of the judge as a source of judicial decisions. These are, in a way, beyond the reach of the law insofar as they are not guided by norms entailed in the plain fact sources.

The authority of the legislator over legislation is very similar in Scandinavian legal thinking to the legal thinking we have been reviewing regarding oppressive situations. The social and political settings are, however, very different. This shows that a plain fact approach does not necessarily have to be a result of confrontations between the force of the legislator and the moral beliefs of the judge, that is, a result of cognitive dissonance. Maybe it can also be the result of complacency.

The Scandinavian societies after the Second World War were basically socially and culturally homogeneous societies with high levels of social solidarity. The contradictions between labour and capital of the industrialisation and the economic crisis of the early twentieth century were replaced by social democracy and the common social project of building the welfare state. The level of the populations' trust in the government was high, as too were the expectations that social and economic problems could be solved by government intervention. The countries had some of the world's largest public sectors by GNP and the highest levels of public spending, financed by direct and indirect taxation.

---

[25] See Judgment of the Court of the European Union (Fifth Chamber) of 7 May 2002 in Case C-478/99, European Court reports 2002, p. I-04147.

[26] Eckhoff (2001).

These social conditions formed the background for the legal and judicial approaches to legislation. The legislative policies had broad backing in the population and in the elites, and neither the policies nor government interventions were seen as manifestly threatening to the rights and interests of individual members of society. To the extent that there were problems, these were regarded as problems to be solved by the legislature and not by the courts.

The enactment of the Public Administration Act in Norway can illustrate this point. Part of the background for this Act was concerned with the very broad discretionary powers that the legislator wished for the administration. Some of these concerns came from liberal circles, some from business circles. The Public Administration Act was a national compromise where broad discretion was maintained but where other interests were accommodated by institutional solutions giving the private sector insight into and influence over administrative decisions and by procedural rules to ensure due process.

The Scandinavian experience suggests that a plain fact approach may seem appropriate when the level of conflict in society is low and there is a high degree of shared values between members of society. Under such circumstances, there are few arguments for resisting the formal rule of law value of the authority of the legislator. The emphasis that the welfare state puts on substantive justice even outweighs the formal principles of predictability and consistency and thus impartial application of the law. The situation is characterised by a mutual respect between the legislative and judicial institutions, based on the respect of the will of the legislator and the independence of the judiciary. The judiciary trusts the legislator not to misuse its power, and the legislator trusts the judiciary to apply the law in a loyal fashion, even when it is not spelled out in a clear and predictable way. Under such circumstances, *departures* from a plain fact approach are maybe more want of an explanation than resorting to it. There are few legitimate reasons that could be given in favour of such a departure.

In past decades, these circumstances have changed in Scandinavian countries. A major factor behind this change is globalisation, which has led to more socially and culturally differentiated societies due to immigration. Individuals and minorities are more often in need of protection from the majority than previously. Another factor is the globalised economy and the expansion of a doctrine of individual liberty. Individualism and liberalisation of the market has heightened the level of conflict over public interferences in the private sphere. International legal regimes endow national judges with the task and means to review national legislation, and national law is reviewed by international courts.

Nevertheless, the Scandinavian experience shows the attraction of the plain fact approach where there are no counterforces such as legal principles protecting the individual or controversies over the basic values and policies in society. This would probably also apply when judges share the values and policies of the legislator, even in situations when these are in conflict with other segments of society. Judges are employed in the service of the existing legal order. This is an important part of their institutional role, whether the legal order is just or unjust and whether the state is determined by the rule of law or not. In all different formations of the state, judges are conformists as part of their defined function. To expect judges to break with oppressive legislators is, therefore, to expect them not only to oppose the authority of the current ruler but also to depart from their institutional role as judges of the regime. On the other hand, they are also under a normative expectation to protect the rule of law and the central legal values inhered in this ideology.

This may therefore be an explanation for the use of the plain fact approach by judges who shared the basic ideological assumptions of racism in Germany and South Africa, by judges who agreed with the rulers in force for the need for emergency measures against communism and subversive elements, and by judges who accorded with the policy of eugenics to combat social problems. Judges who approve of the values of oppressive rulers and judges who experience conflicts of conscience may therefore find each other in a common plain fact approach to the oppressive legislation. Together they forge an alliance with considerable persuasive power over their fellow judges.

References

Adami FW (1939) Das Programm der NSDAP und die Rechtsprechung. Deutsches Recht 486–491

Angermund R (1990) Deutsche Richtershaft 1919–1945. Fischer, Frankfurt am Main

Arendt H (2003) Responsibility and judgment. Schocken Books, New York

Cover RM (1974) Justice accused antislavery and the judicial process. Yale University Press, New Haven and New York

Dugard J (1987) The judiciary in a state of national crisis – with special reference to the South African experience. Wash Lee Law Rev 44:477–501

Dyzenhaus D (2010) Hard cases in wicked legal systems pathologies of legality, 2nd edn. Oxford University Press, Oxford

Eckhoff T (2001) Rettskildelære 5. utgave ved Jan E. Helgesen. Universitetsforlaget, Oslo

Garbe D (2000) Im Namen des Volkes?! Die Rechtlichen Grundlagen der Militärjustiz im NS-Staat und ihre "Bewältigung" nach 1945. In: Nolz B, Popp W (eds) Erinnerungsarbeit Grundlage einer Kultur des Friedens. Lit Verlag, Münster

Hilbink L (2008) Agents of anti-politics: courts in Pinochet's Chile. In: Ginsburg T, Moustafa T (eds) Rule by law: the politics of courts in authoritarian regimes. Cambridge University Press, Cambridge

Rehnquist WH (1998) All laws but one civil liberties in wartime. Vintage Books, New York (Kindle edition)

Rüthers B (2012) Die unbegrenzte Auslegung: Zum Wandel der Privatrechtsordnung im Nationalsozialismus 7. Ausg. Mohr Siebeck, Tübingen

Chapter 17
Beyond Legal Theory as Explanation

Do Legal Theories Influence Judicial Action?

Legal positivism is the explanation that is most often suggested to explain why judges contribute to the atrocities of authoritarian regimes. A reason for this is that this explanation accords with two basic facts of judicial behaviour. The first is the tendency judges have, as everyone else, to adhere to authority. Obedience to authority is one of the most important factors that explain why people agree to commit the most horrible offences when ordered to. The second is more particular to judges and has to do with the ideology of not getting involved in politics. Particularly in situations with great political conflicts, taking a stand on the decisions and measures of the leaders of the government is perceived by judges as political action. Therefore, these measures are not reviewed but taken as a basis for the interpretation and application of the law.

As we have seen, these two factors have little to do with positivism as a particular theory of law and less to do with particular legal methods. We are here dealing with explanations at different levels. Authority and avoidance of getting mixed up in politics are explanations at the psychological and ideological levels. Legal theory and methodology are at the normative level and at the level of justification. Do legal theories actually influence and explain judicial practice at all? Marc Osiel states in his study of judges in Argentina and Brazil that "there need not be any moment of ethical epiphany, no point at which one feels compelled—either internally or by circumstances—to identify with the rulers or against them". The judges "may merely evince the disposition to exercise independent judgment in a profession where competent practice requires it".[1] Legal theories, in the opinion of Osiel, rarely impel the judge to resistance. They merely provide him with alternative rhetorical forms that the judge can apply in support or in opposition to a regime.[2]

---

[1] Osiel (1995), p. 482.

[2] Osiel (1995), p. 484.

H.P. Graver, *Judges Against Justice*, DOI 10.1007/978-3-662-44293-7_17

A similar conclusion is drawn by Bernd Rüthers in his thorough study of German private law in the Nazi years. Substantial parts of the judicial practice during the Nazi period are impeccable from the point of view of the legal methodology employed. For this reason, the search for a legal methodology that might protect the legal order from being misused for authoritarian purposes is bound to fail.[3] In his opinion, "a legal theory that is reduced to questions of methodology and social engineering is like a navigator who commands excellent instruments and methods of calculation, but lacks trustworthy points to navigate from such as stars, lighthouses and radio beacons".[4]

Vivian Grosswald Curran observes that German and French lawyers came to similar results regarding the reinterpretation of the law to accommodate the racial category of Jewishness, despite divergent and even contradictory interpretative methods. Where the German judges used the established method of reasoning with general clauses, the French, in contrast, used their established method of avoiding reference to general legal principles. "Natural law and principles of equity, like all other legal principles and perspectives, will be colored and defined so differently at individual moments of history, that it is not they, but, rather, the values of the individual and institutional legal actors that will determine whether law is a force for or against humanity at any given moment in history".[5]

Richard H. Weisberg shows in his study how the legal community through "a 'desiccated Cartesianism', a uniquely French desire to see the elaborate interpretation of the religious laws through every logical conclusion... [created] an indigenous system of rationalised persecution" of the racial laws of the Vichy regime.[6] By formulating and discussing issues of how to interpret the racial statutes at a low level of generalization, and thus avoiding taking a stance on the very principle of racism, legal doctrine contributed to bringing about a pervasiveness and acceptability of the statute.[7] Different approaches in other words lead to the same results: on the basis of relatively minor pieces of legislation, the legal system is transformed by legal interpretation. "To believe in a high correlation between the philosophical or methodological theory a judge applies and the specific outcome of cases is to overlook the indeterminacy embedded in the judicial decision-making process", writes Curran.[8]

Otto Kirchheimer concluded his discussion of the influence of legal theory with the following: "In short, legal theories may dimly reflect community attitudes, and serve as welcome rationalizations, but they are scarcely primary determinants of judicial action".[9]

---

[3] Rüthers (2012), p. 444.

[4] Rüthers (2012), p. 526.

[5] Curran (2005), p. 488.

[6] Weisberg (1996), p. 48.

[7] Weisberg (1996), p. 81.

[8] Curran (1998–1999), pp. 39–40.

[9] Kirchheimer (1961), p. 212, note 78.

There was a consensus regarding policy that Kirchheimer refers to that is evidenced in the practice of the German courts from 1933, both in their willingness to accept National Socialist ideology as underlying principles for legal interpretation and in the effect given to this ideology in cases regarding the status and rights of persons of Jewish origin.[10]

In any case, both formal and substantive approaches to interpretation of statutes may, in fact, be employed in order to temper the oppressive legislator and to correct popular ideas and values.[11] The formal approach was applied against oppressive measures by the Prussian Administrative Appeals Court in the 1930s. By refusing to reinterpret provisions for the protection of individuals that were not explicitly repealed by the Nazis, the Court sought to maintain judicial control with the police. Once these provisions were overridden in clear terms by the Nazi legislator, this defence line fell. As Osiel points out, "the more willing rulers are to enact their most repressive policies into positive law, the less legal positivism can provide a professional rationale for judicial resistance".[12]

South African judges of opposition employed what Dyzenhaus labels the common law approach, where statutes and precedents are interpreted in accordance with the rule and reason of the common law, including principles of equality before the law, due process, and habeas corpus.[13] Based as it is on common law with its doctrine of parliamentary sovereignty, this approach must also give way to the plain terms of legislation. It is unthinkable that judges, by employing pertinent methods of interpretation, can function consistently as a power contrary to the policy of the ruling power and the dominant societal values in the long run and maintain their position as judges of the regime. As pointed out by Rüthers, the law is the establishment, and the practical fact is that the approach to law in any state and of any given legal theory is to serve the establishment.[14]

Psychological Factors

The Radbruch theory is no longer accepted in contemporary theory as an explanation for the atrocities of the Nazi judges. As shown above, positivism is incompatible with the legislation of the Nazi period, judicial practice, and the legal ideology that was developed by the Nazis to influence, curb, and direct the judges. The plain facts approach is an approach to legal interpretation and application that may serve as a methodological instrument for judges when applying the law to accommodate authoritarian rulers. Once this approach is established and employed as mainstream,

[10] See pp. 60–68 above.
[11] See the analysis of Osiel (1995), pp. 489–510.
[12] Osiel (1995), p. 544.
[13] Dyzenhaus (2010), p. 53.
[14] Rüthers (2007), p. 558.

judicial oppression follows almost automatically if this serves the ideology and aims of the present legislation. But what can explain the establishment of this approach as mainstream besides the psychological explanation offered by Cover? Cover's explanation does not, after all, offer any reasons beside the adherence to the authority of the legislator for this choice of action by judges. After all, in the famous experiments on obedience to authority by Stanley Milgram, one-third of the subjects did not bow to the authority of the experimenter.

Milgram distinguished between "binding factors" and "adjustments in the subject's thinking" in explaining the subject obedience.[15] The binding factors lock the subject into the situation and include politeness, a desire to honour the initial promise to contribute to the experiment and the awkwardness of withdrawal. Adjustments in thinking help the subject maintain his relationship with the experimenter, while at the same time reducing the strain brought about by the experimental conflict.

The binding factors operating on the judge are obvious. On the one hand, we have the commitments stemming from the judicial role and the perceived legal and professional duty to uphold the law. As long as he stays on the bench, the judge perceives this duty. The awkwardness of withdrawal from a collective or a group is thoroughly examined in other studies that show that people go to extremes in order not to break out into nonconformity. Group pressure operates through a basic identification among the members of the group and a strong urge not to separate oneself.[16]

Adjustments in a judge's thinking are evident in the emphasis on the binding effect of the law and the stating that the law leaves no choice to the judge. Also, the strong drive to separate legality from morality and human consequences of the application of the law can help the judge to overcome the cognitive conflict that exists between his application of oppressive law and his rule of law ideals.

One would expect that judges who are critical of the ideology and aims of an oppressive legislator would find ways to justify not obeying the authority of the law as construed to serve this legislator. As we can see from the experiences of South Africa, some did and employed what Dyzenhaus terms the common law approach, but many more did not. Obviously, many other factors than mere obedience to authority are at play.

Adherence to authority may be part of an explanation, but it can only be part. After all, not all judges participate in the oppression of authoritarian regimes. Judges have both independence and a choice in determining the law and applying it. Why do they not do more to avoid obvious departures from the rule of law? One explanation could be that they develop a "moral blindness" that prevents them from relating to the consequences of oppressive measures.

Moral blindness is illustrated by the example of SS judge Konrad Morgen, who went to the Eastern Front and the extermination camps and witnessed the

[15] Milgram (2004), p. 17.

[16] Browning (1998), p. 71.

extermination of Jews and at the same time took up prosecution of persons involved in the killings for corruption and transgression of orders. In their study of this judge, Pauer-Studer and Velleman cite his self-understanding as a "fanatic for justice". Pauer-Studer cites Morgen's answer to his interrogators at Nürnberg about his visit to Auschwitz: "After inspecting the extermination machinery in Birkenau, Morgen was interested in the SS personnel who were administering 'this apparatus'. Morgen stated that by looking at the guard room 'he experienced for the first time a real shock'. Instead of 'spartan simplicity' he found in the guardroom an ensemble of couches on which SS personnel were dozing with glassy eyes, having obviously consumed a lot of alcohol during the night. Morgen found it equally revolting that these SS men were served potato pancakes by four or five young Jewish girls who were wearing civilian clothes rather than prison uniforms. What Morgen found most objectionable, indeed unbelievable, was that the SS men and these female prisoners were addressing each other by the familiar 'du' instead of the formal 'Sie'".[17] Pauer-Studer draws the conclusion that "Morgen's endeavours were flawed not so much because of a blind commitment to the orders of the supreme authorities—he sometimes ignored them and sought ways to evade them. The problem is that Morgen's moralised self-conception, drawing on a deeply moralised understanding of law, prevented him from seeing that the political context and perverted normative background of his legal activities undermined their point and meaning".[18]

Moral blindness is not limited to situations with tyrannical regimes. Many liberal states from the 1920s onwards, and as far up as to the 1970s, went quite far based on perceptions on eugenics in repressive means against people who were perceived as mentally degenerate. Those who supported measures such as enforced sterilisation were not motivated by a desire to protect the race from inferior genetic material; many of the supporters were motivated by social policy reasons, to protect against crime and antisocial behaviour and even to prevent new individuals being born into social misery and poverty. The oppressive measures were generally accepted and enforced by the judiciary. In the infamous opinion of Justice Oliver Wendell Holmes: "instead of waiting to execute degenerate offspring for crime, or to let them starve for their imbecility, society can prevent those who are manifestly unfit from continuing their kind... Three generations of imbeciles are enough".[19]

How can we explain such warped senses of morality and justice? Harald Welzer speaks of the three circles of the process that drives people to abandon their moral ideals and inhibitions against committing atrocities.[20] The first is a societal process where the lines of conflict and division between "friend" and "enemy" are established. The employment of lethal means against the enemy in the persecution

[17] Pauer-Studer (2012), p. 386.

[18] Pauer-Studer (2012), p. 389.

[19] Buck v. Bell, Superintendent of State Colony for Epileptics and Feeble Minded, 271 U.S. 200 1927.

[20] Welzer (2007), Kindle edition loc. 160.

of Jews and communists during the eastern campaign of the German army in 1941 changed the prohibition against murder to an obligation to kill. The second circle consists of the social situation of the actor and his interpretation of this situation. The third, the innermost circle, is the actor's own perception of the options that are open to him. These are, to a large extent, influenced by psychological binding factors and factors adjusting the actor's thinking. By this, we see that the participation of judges in oppression is the result of the interplay between changes in the political and social situations of society, the professional and personal interests of the judge relating to this situation, and psychological factors operating on the individual judge.

Such binding factors may influence a judge's thinking to such an extent that he does not see the unreasonableness or injustice in oppressive measures. As we have seen, the South African judges extended the apartheid laws of racist South Africa much in the same way as the Nazi judges extended the discrimination of the Jews. In the case from 1934 on the post office in Transvaal, the crucial issue was whether discrimination between races was a sensible and rational measure, which in itself could not be seen as unreasonable. Justice Stratford of the Appellate Division could not see that dividing the community into white and coloured was itself unreasonable "for such conclusion runs counter to accepted principle and good sense". Justice De Villiers distinguished between discrimination on gratuitous grounds and discrimination for which "reasons may be conceived upon which such discriminations might justify and reasonably be made" and placed discrimination based upon race and colour in the latter category.

Moral blindness is cultivated by distance. The distance may be psychological, institutional, or physical. Psychological distance is created by tribal thinking and by dehumanisation of the victims of our actions. These are well-known factors in explaining how people can commit evil deeds on others. We see them in action in the racial jurisprudence of Nazi Germany and of apartheid. We also see them when people brought to trail are defined as antisocial enemies in a "war" to defend national security. Institutional distance is created by thinking about people in abstract categories, as holders of rights or duties, as offenders and defendants, instead as whole persons. This distance is inherent and necessary to legal thinking. It is worth to think about the dangers it entails in fostering moral blindness in situations where the law turns oppressive. Physical distance weakens sympathy. A special form of physical distance is the one where atrocities take place in unreal and distant settings. As Glover points out, sympathy can be weakened by a sense of unreality.[21] Auschwitz was, as he points out, "another planet", which made it possible to think that "this is not really happening". This effect could contribute to the moral blindness of Konrad Mogens. Matters such as these that create distance in different ways are common psychological patterns that overwhelm, weaken, and narrow human responses.

[21] Glover (2012), pp. 407–408.

Institutional Factors

In a reflection after two occurrences with totalitarian rule in Germany, Bernd Rüthers points out the decision the individual judge takes on whether to submit to the authority of the regime or not is not a free decision. The decision is influenced by the socialisation he has been through in becoming a judge, his family status and dependents, his social and economic means of subsistence, and many other factors.[22] This makes the decision a moral decision that can be explained, understood, and justified or criticised. In order to pass judgment, it is important to understand the situation that the judges are in.

Institutional factors obviously contributed to the readiness of German judges to accept the demands of the Nazi regime. Already at the time of the Nazi takeover of power, there was almost universal agreement on the necessity for total legal reform within the legal profession. For this reason, they offered themselves at the disposal to the reform programme of the Nazis.[23]

Most judges were critical of the Weimar Republic and were estranged by its policies. The reasons for this were social, political, and economic.[24] Members of the legal profession belonged to the conservative classes. To approach a judicial career entailed long years on meagre salaries. For this reason, it was, in practice, reserved for people with private means, exactly those parts of society that were hit the hardest by the hyperinflation of the 1920s. At the same time, unemployment among legal candidates was high. "The rude shock of the 1918 defeat, the political rise of the working class, and especially of the middle classes' impoverishment through rapid inflation in the beginning of the twenties, had alienated the judiciary from the political establishment", writes Kirchheimer.[25]

The judges and the legal doctrine were at odds with the social democratic rulers in power in the Weimar state. Gustav Radbruch, as Minister of Justice, commanded the judges to adhere to a strict legal positivism and to uphold the legislation that was passed by the political majority.[26] The judges, though, maintained the necessity of correcting the "mistakes" of the parliamentary legislator through judicial review and judicial independent interpretation of the laws. On the other hand, no review was exercised over the emergency legislation enacted by the President of the Reich against the Weimar Parliament. "The judiciary went overboard in supporting the government against its enemies on the left, but established a consistent pattern of refusal to tackle political law breakers on the right".[27]

---

[22] Rüthers (2007), p. 563.

[23] Rüthers (2007), p. 502.

[24] Angermund (1990), pp. 66–67.

[25] Kirchheimer (1961), p. 211.

[26] Angermund (1990), pp. 35–40.

[27] Kirchheimer (1961), p. 213.

After the takeover of power, the Nazis appeared to judges to be willing to re-establish social order albeit under an authoritarian signature.[28] In all accounts, the Nazi rulers were seen as capable of restoring the "law state" (*Rechtstaat*). The emergency measures were seen as temporary revolutionary measures, which did not fundamentally influence the role of the judges. Even the purge of the judiciary under the law to the Restoration of the Civil Service did not result in any major change in the composition of the judiciary. The ideological pressure and enforced membership in the union of National Socialist lawyers were probably perceived as unwelcome to most, but even so the judiciary experienced its social status and importance being increased after the Nazi takeover of power.

Similarly, institutional factors may explain the compliance with the demands of authoritarian rulers of judges in Latin America. The legal systems of Argentina, Brazil, and Chile were quite similar and were, compared to other legal systems, strongly hierarchical, oriented towards the exclusive authority of state institutions and towards the implementation of policy rather than the resolution of conflicting values and interests. Despite this, the regimes exercised their powers of repression in different ways with distinct relationships between the military and the judiciary. Such differences can partly be explained by the different histories of the role of the military in political relations in the three countries.[29] Thus, the institutional arrangement of the legal order and the judiciary influences the response of the judiciary to oppressive legislation.

The legislator is not the only forceful authority within a community of judges. In Germany, the law professors and legal doctrine are awarded status as important authorities. The Nazi takeover of power received broad support among the academics, and legal doctrine was soon employed to legitimise the new regime and to develop the law into national socialist law.[30] Other institutions regarded with awe are the highest courts of a jurisdiction. This authority is formally institutionalised in jurisdictions with a doctrine of *stare decisis* and is also widespread in civil law countries that do not recognise the binding force of precedence.

The fact of the persuasive power of the higher courts means that if these can be turned to support oppressive measures of a regime, the other courts will follow. At the least, the regime has an instrument to ensure judicial support in important instances.

Judge Cassell of the United States District Court of Utah voices the situation of a lower court judge forced to decide against his own conscience and opinion of the law by case law from the Supreme Court:

> The court is keenly aware of its obligation to follow precedent from superior courts—specifically the Tenth Circuit and, of course, the Supreme Court. The Supreme Court has considered one case that might be regarded as quite similar to this one. In Hutto v. Davis, the Supreme Court held that two consecutive twenty-year sentences—totaling forty years—

[28] Angermund (1990), pp. 48–61.

[29] Pereira (2005), location 887–896.

[30] See Pauer-Studer (2014).

> for possession of nine ounces of marijuana said to be worth $200 did not violate the Eighth Amendment. If Davis remains good law, it is hard see how the sentence in this case violates the Eighth Amendment. Here, Mr. Angelos was involved in at least two marijuana deals involving $700 and approximately sixteen ounces (one pound) of marijuana. Perhaps currency inflation could equate $700 today with $200 in the 1980s. But as a simple matter of arithmetic, if 40 years in prison for possessing nine ounces marijuana does not violate the Eighth Amendment, it is hard to see how 61 years for distributing sixteen ounces (or more) would do so... In light of these continued references to Davis, the court believes it is it obligated to follow its holding here. Indeed, in Davis the Supreme Court pointedly reminded district court judges that 'unless we wish anarchy to prevail within the federal judicial system, a precedent of this Court must be followed by the lower federal courts....'[31]

We see that in sentencing cases, the Supreme Court of the US has even asserted its authority on the lower courts explicitly. Indeed, one of the core elements of the rule of law is that the law is applied in an equal way to all. The formal qualities of the rule of law support upholding unjust legislation and also support adherence to rulings of higher courts. In addition, the fact that it is higher courts that speak gives the result the added legitimacy of judicial support. The issue can no longer be framed as a question of whether the judiciary should support the legislative or administrative measures of an oppressive regime because the regime already has this support.

Oppressive regimes regularly seek to secure support from the highest courts. In Chap. 3, we examined several cases where new regimes substituted judges in the highest court or secured support by "court packing", appointing additional supportive judges.

Chile is an example of a case where the authority of the Supreme Court was important for the judicial support of the dictatorship. Chile had a tradition of independent courts before the coup in 1973, and the Junta in no way interfered with the independence of the courts. Despite this, the courts never sought to challenge the legitimacy or politics of the military government but cooperated fully with the regime.[32] The history of democratic practice and respect for legality was longer and stronger in Chile than in Argentina and Brazil. Nevertheless, in contrast to their Argentinean and Brazilian counterparts, the Chilean courts did not exhibit any form of opposition against the regime.

In Chile, judicial appointment, evaluation, discipline, and promotion were controlled by its Supreme Court, and this system was left in place by the military leaders. On this basis, Lisa Hilbink offers an institutional explanation, different from the psychological explanation offered by Cover, for the support by the Chilean Judges for the military dictatorship of 1973–1990.[33] Hilbink points to the institutional structure of the Chilean judiciary with a hierarchical career structure where judges would enter at a young age into the badly paid service as a district court judge and work their way up in the hierarchy to more prestigious and better paid

[31] D. Utah, 2004 U.S. v. Angelos 345 F.Supp.2d 1227.

[32] See Hilbink (2008), p. 102.

[33] Hilbink (2008), pp. 120–129.

posts. To do so, a judge had to attain favour with his or her superiors. The higher judges also have the responsibility to oversee subordinate judges for any judicial faults or abuses. The ultimate responsibility for recruitment, advancement, and disciplinary measures over the judiciary lay with the Supreme Court.

This bureaucratic structure produced strong incentives for judges to comply with the opinions and attitudes of the courts above. In this way, a conservative minority in the higher courts could effectively control the whole judiciary. This was emphasised by the internal purge of opposing judges undertaken by the Supreme Court in 1974. The Supreme Court also exercised direct discipline over the judges during the authoritarian regime. For instance, a judge who announced that he would not apply the amnesty law to a case of disappeared communist leaders or turn the case over to the military courts was suspended by the Supreme Court for two-and-a-half months on half pay.

This structure does not explain the attitude taken by the Supreme Court justices themselves. Why did they abandon the rule of law and support the dictators? The explanation Hilbink offers here is that the judges who reach the Supreme Court have spent their careers being discouraged from creative, independent, and innovative decision-making and have learned to emulate and please their superiors. In addition, the institutional ideology of the judiciary as being apolitical promoted their support of the oppressive regime, which portrayed itself as above politics.

Another reason could lie in the controversies that the Supreme Court had engaged in with the previous Allende regime.[34] Allende wanted to overhaul the Court; the Court responded that the proposals were unconstitutional. The response of the government was to refuse to implement the Court's decisions. Against this background, the Court seemed to welcome the coup of Pinochet, who claimed that his aim was to restore the rule of law. In this way, the situation in Chile has likenesses to that in Germany in 1933 where the judges welcomed the Nazi's promise to re-establish social order and respect for the law. Estrangement in the relations between a regime and the courts may prepare the grounds for judicial acceptance of authoritarian rule. In these cases, judges seem to have valued their own personal and institutional status and autonomy higher than the protection of the rule of law and individual rights.

Hilbink's explanation is based on the specific organisation of the Chilean judiciary. The authority of the Supreme Court here rested on its formal position in relation to the recruitment and advancement of the judges. Her explanation, however, underlines that institutional arrangements are more generally of importance in explaining the attitudes and actions of judges and that there are more ways of securing adherence to the authority of higher courts than a doctrine of precedents.

---

[34] See Verner (1984), p. 483.

Entrapment and Erasure of Moral Identity

Jonathan Glover holds that entrapment may be an important factor in accounting for participation in evil.[35] Individually, participation in evil may be both undesirable and against the interests of the participant. Collectively, however, there are few options for resistance. His description of the situation of soldiers during the First World War may easily also fit the situation of judges under an authoritarian regime. Judges may not be consistent or unanimous in their evaluation of the legality and legitimacy of the measures taken by the regime. A refusal to obey is likely to achieve very little unless it spreads rapidly to the judiciary. This is difficult to organise, and without any organisational effort, it is unlikely to take place.

Solidarity among the judiciary can also be a factor. Psychological research shows the importance of peers when it comes to influencing human behaviour. Christopher Browning's examination of the files of the trials against German *Einsatzgruppen*, the task forces of the security police employed against Jews on the Eastern Front, makes this point clear when it comes to the worst atrocities. Loyalty and duty to one's comrades when faced with gruelling tasks is a strong motivating factor; fear of unconforming, likewise. A judge who refuses to apply oppressive laws knows that if he resigns or applies for a transfer, a colleague of his will have to take over the job.

The realistic alternatives to abiding by the regime and applying its measures are few. As time goes on, each person also gets more deeply involved and therefore also complicit in the oppression of the regime. As Stoltzfus maintains, the year for Germans to protest against Nazi Jewish policies successfully was 1933, not 1943.[36] According to contemporary observer Sebastian Haffner, the Berlin Kammergericht collapsed as an institution on March 31, 1933, when the Court without protest allowed the SA to enter the premises and throw out the Jewish judge, lawyers, and clerks.[37] When the German judges accepted the purge of Jewish colleagues in March and April 1933, they gave the regime encouragement to continue with their racial persecution and also, to a large extent, acquiesced to the legitimacy of such measures. This made it much harder for judges to go up against the racial policy of the regime at later stages when cases came before the courts.

Early measures of resistance are important not only because they may be more effective at this point. They also contribute to counteracting the moral entrapment that many undergo, which makes resistance at a later point less likely. Glover relates the story of the resistance of the Dutch people against the measures against the Jews taken by the Germans right after the occupation in 1940. The banning of Jews in the civil service met with protests and student strikes. A rounding up of 400 Jews in Amsterdam was met with a total strike in Amsterdam and the nearby towns. According to Glover, these protests must have created a self-respect that

[35] Glover (2012), Chapter 19.

[36] Stoltzfus (1996), p. 261.

[37] Haffner (2003), p. 151.

helped the many Dutch people who gave Jews shelter during the occupation, thus leading to the saving of 25,000 people who were hidden in Dutch homes during the occupation.[38]

John Dugard makes the same point regarding the situation of judges in South Africa. He points out that if judges in South Africa had resigned or protested in large numbers in 1955, when the Appellate Division of the Supreme Court was packed by the government to ensure support for its legislation, or in 1967, when indefinite detention without trial was introduced, the resignations could have had considerable effect. But by the 1980s, they had "missed the boat".[39]

The Belgian judges under German occupation, in contrast, did protest against the occupying authority right from the beginning. They refused to apply laws enacted by the occupying authority on the grounds that they only had power to apply Belgian national law. On these grounds, they also refused to apply laws passed by the Belgian administration that were enacted according to a delegation from the occupying power. Enactments by the Belgian administration had to have basis in the emergency and war powers given by Belgian constitutional law. They also protested against the purge of Jews from the bench and the bar, which may be a factor in explaining why they were later able to resist introducing racial categories and elements into Belgian law. The Belgian courts mounted a fairly successful resistance to the German occupation throughout the war, in contrast to the courts of the Netherlands and Denmark. There may be many reasons for this, but no doubt it was easier for the courts in Belgium to resist the more oppressive measures that were demanded of them when they had resisted from the very beginning.

The difficult question to decide is at what point the regime has engaged on a path to authoritarianism. When does it depart from the liberal constitution in such a way that it is timely for the courts to protest? In situations where there is an obvious break, such as with foreign occupations or coups d'état, this decision is relatively easy. The issue for the courts in such situations is to decide whether they should continue their work on the basis of their old powers or whether they should accept operating on the basis of powers conferred or implied by the new regime. Even though most courts in practice opted for the latter alternative, experience shows that this is a dangerous path to tread. In these cases, it is very difficult for the courts to mount effective protests later when the oppression of the regime exceeds all limits. Once the courts have accepted operating on the basis of loyalty to the new regime, they can hardly avoid becoming instruments of the oppression of the regime.

The only morally viable alternative in such situations is for the courts to continue on the basis of the old constitution. As long as this is possible, this will temper the measures of the new regime, provided that it is a constitution based upon the rule of law. This may, in the long run, prevent the regime developing the most oppressive policies by forcing it to abide by the constitution, or it may not. It may develop into a confrontation between the regime and the judiciary, which the judiciary will

[38] Glover (2012), p. 385.

[39] Dugard (1984), p. 292.

almost certainly lose in the first run. The courts cannot force the regime to respect their rulings or enforce their decisions. They cannot prevent the regime from creating new tribunals and appointing new judges or forcing the old judges to resign. But they can withhold the legitimacy that recognition by the established courts or cooperation of the corps of judges entails. And in some cases, this will temper the regime as we have seen, even under such oppressive circumstances like the Nazi occupation of Belgium.

A condition for such resistance to be effective is that it comprises more than the Supreme Court. Regimes can force the Supreme Court into submission by packing it, such as in South Africa, or purging it, such as in Argentina, and still obtain the legitimacy of the courts if the remaining judges remain loyal to the regime. A protest against the new regime must include larger parts of the judiciary.

The situation is much more difficult when oppressive measures are enacted by a regime that does not purport to act according to a new formal power basis. Measures may be enacted against specific groups, such as sterilisation measures against the feeble-minded or harsh punishments against notorious criminals or public enemies, or they may be enacted in specific situations of emergency. In such situations, the courts must decide whether authoritarian measures are legitimate measures in defence of the rule of law or whether they are the first steps on the slope towards authoritarianism.

In times of trouble, judges are often faced with the question of whether to allow a departure from fundamental rights to protect society in public emergencies. Emergencies may be due to a threat from without, such as foreign terrorist attacks, or from within, such as grave social unrest. In fact, even the international human rights instruments have provisions that allow for the restriction of certain rights, when it is "necessary in a democratic society" or under "war or other public emergency threatening the life of the nation". Similar provisions are included in many national constitutions.

Such emergency provisions are often the legal basis used by dictators to seize power, for example in Weimar Germany and in many countries of Latin America. Emergency powers can also be misused by a regime to defend oppressive policies, such as was seen in South Africa during apartheid and in the US in its war against terror after 9/11.

The issue in law of to what degree the state should be allowed to limit rights for the protection of public goods and its own existence is a difficult question. A lesson to be learnt from history is that the answer to this question, even by democratically minded courts deeply entrenched in rule of law values, will vary according to how the issues are perceived in society at the time. It should suffice to mention the attitude of British and US courts to the internment of the Nazis and the Japanese during the Second World War or the attitude of the courts of many of the western countries during the 1940s and 1950s to freedom of speech and Communist parties.

In the case of Liversidge against Sir John Anderson, the Home Secretary, the House of Lords had to decide to what extent the courts should review decisions to detain alleged Nazis during the war.[40] Instead of applying basic principles of liberty recognised in common law, to interpret the law restrictively the majority accepted the measures taken by the government with the words of Viscount Maugham:

> If there is a reasonable doubt as to the meaning of the words used, we should prefer a construction which will carry into effect the plain intention of those responsible for the Order in Council rather than one which will defeat that intention.[41]

Similarly, the majority of the United States Supreme Court in the case of Dennis v. the US accepted the Smith Act, making it a crime for any person to knowingly or wilfully advocate the overthrow or destruction of the Government of the United States by force or violence as constitutional.[42] In the case, which was against leaders of the Communist Party, Chief Justice Vinson, speaking for the majority, held:

> If Government is aware that a group aiming at its overthrow is attempting to indoctrinate its members and to commit them to a course whereby they will strike when the leaders feel the circumstances permit, action by the Government is required.

The fact that international and national courts today, under the present circumstances, take a more restrictive view to limits to human rights is no guarantee for they will continue to do so under drastically different conditions. This is all but evident from the repressive means that were employed by the American administration after the terrorist attack on 11 September 2001, which included internment of suspects without access to courts and the use of torture in the examination of prisoners. Initially, the administration received support from the courts, and even now judges are deeply divided over the legality of such means.[43]

After the tide, in the transition to democracy and normal times, the matter is often seen in a different light. Most people today would not hold the majority opinions of the Liversidge Case in the UK or the Dennis Case in the US as good law. But does this mean that we have grounds to criticise the judges of that time for their departure from the rule of law? And more importantly, by what means, if any, could we support the rule of law under similar conditions, to prevent judges from giving way to oppression, which seems necessary to the rulers in charge? This is not only a matter of spelling out the law because what is at stake is the way the law is construed and applied by the highest legal authorities when the stakes are high.

US Chief Justice William Rehnquist has argued that the reluctance of courts to decide a case against the government on an issue of national security during a war is desirable.[44] On the other hand, we know that the authority of Liversidge was important for the South African courts in their acquiescence to the indefinite detention without trial enacted under emergency legislation. And emergency

[40] For a critical discussion of the case and the law and circumstances surrounding it, see Simpson (1988).

[41] Liversidge v. Anderson and Morrison (1941) 3 All E.R. 338 (H.L.).

[42] US Supreme Court 341 U.S. 494.

[43] Abel (2007), p. 397.

[44] Rehnquist (1998), loc. 3670.

powers were the legal basis for the Nazi takeover of power and the first measures enacted by the Nazi regime. Seen from a formal point of view, the German courts did not find grounds to question the legality of the Nazi regime. The development is quite illustrating for the mechanism of entrapment, and it is difficult to pinpoint one specific point where the regime departed from its legal basis in the old constitution unless one insists that this took place at the very beginning.

In this respect, legal professionalism represents a challenge to upholding the rule of law since it so often emphasises the separation of law and morality. Lawyers are trained in technical excellence and to leave their own moral convictions and views outside of their professional work. Persons affected by the law are systematically not regarded as persons but as subjects representing abstract categories fitting into the pigeonholes of the law. Lawyers are encouraged not to sympathise with the person as such but to reason from the legal position that he holds.

Professional neutrality may enable the judge to participate in atrocities and at the same time contribute to their legitimation by the law. Vivian Curran shows how the neutral approaches of French legal academics lead them to become complicit in the persecution of the Jews by the Vichy regime.[45] The regime enacted laws that deprived Jews of their rights as citizens and of their property. Over 40 books of legal commentary were written concerning these laws, and law journals created new categories such as "Jews", "Jewish Matters", and "Jewish Issues". The commentators employed the normal approaches of legal science in a neutral way, discussing the aims, concepts, and systematic structure of the laws, and their place in the overall body of laws. Apart from some isolated examples, there was no moral evaluation or criticism of the anti-Semitic and unconstitutional laws.

This neutral and technical approach to individuals may often function for their protection when they are attacked as subhuman, such as when the law accords rights to everyone regardless of race or creed. On the other hand, it may leave the judge immune to the plight of the individual who is targeted by oppressive legislation. In such cases, the training that discourages the judge from looking behind the legal position may prevent him from extending his sympathy to the person and perceiving the actual inhuman effects of the legislation. This is even more difficult if the oppression of the legislation increases in an incremental way, so that by the time the suffering of the affected is so great, it is inevitable that the judge is already entrapped by his contribution and his previous decisions.

References

Abel RL (2007) Contesting legality in the United States after September 11. In: Halliday TC, Karpik L, Feeley MM (eds) Fighting for political freedom comparative studies of the legal complex and political liberalism. Hart, Oxford and Portland

Angermund R (1990) Deutsche Richtershaft 1919–1945. Fischer, Frankfurt am Main

[45] Curran (1998–1999), pp. 27–29.

Browning CR (1998) Ordinary men reserve police Battalion 101 and the final solution in Poland. Harper Perennial, New York
Curran VG (1998–1999) The legalization of racism in a constitutional state: democracy's suicide in Vichy France. Hastings Law J 50:1–96
Curran VG (2005) Law's past and Europe's future. German Law J 6:483–512
Dugard J (1984) Should judges resign? – a reply to Professor Wacks. S Afr Law J 101:286–294
Dyzenhaus D (2010) Hard cases in wicked legal systems pathologies of legality, 2nd edn. Oxford University Press, Oxford
Glover J (2012) Humanity a moral history of the 20th century, 2nd edn. Yale University Press, New Haven
Haffner S (2003) Defying Hitler: a memoir. Phoenix, London
Hilbink L (2008) Agents of anti-politics: courts in Pinochet's Chile. In: Ginsburg T, Moustafa T (eds) Rule by law: the politics of courts in authoritarian regimes. Cambridge University Press, Cambridge
Kirchheimer O (1961) Political justice: the use of legal procedure for political ends. Princeton University Press, New Jersey
Milgram S (2004) Obedience to authority, New York 1974 published by Perennial Classics with a foreword by Jerome S. Bruner New York
Osiel MJ (1995) Dialogue with dictators: judicial resistance in Argentina and Brazil. Law Soc Inq 20:481–560
Pauer-Studer H (2012) Law and morality under evil conditions: the SS Judge Konrad Morgen. Jurisprudence 3(2):367–390
Pauer-Studer H (2014) Einleitung: Rechtfertigung des Unrechts. Das Rechtsdenken im Nationalsozialismus. In: Pauer-Studer H, Fink J (eds) Rechtfertigungen des Unrechts Da Rechtsdenken im Nationalsozialismus in Originaltexten. Suhrkamp, Berlin
Pereira AW (2005) Political (in)justice authoritarianism and the rule of law in Brazil, Chile and Argentina. University of Pittsburgh Press, Pittsburgh (Kindle edition)
Rehnquist WH (1998) All laws but one civil liberties in wartime. Vintage Books, New York (Kindle edition)
Rüthers B (2007) Hatte die Rechtsperversion in den Deutschen Diktaturen ein Gesicht? Juristenzeitung 11:556–564
Rüthers B (2012) Die unbegrenzte Auslegung: Zum Wandel der Privatrechtsordnung im Nationalsozialismus 7. Ausg. Mohr Siebeck, Tübingen
Simpson AWB (1988) Rhetoric, reality and regulation 18B. Denning Law J 3:123–153
Stoltzfus N (1996) Resistance of the heart intermarriage and the Rosenstrasse protest in Nazi Germany. W.W. Norton & Company, New York
Verner JG (1984) The independence of Supreme Courts in Latin America: a review of the literature. J Latin Am Stud 16:463–506
Weisberg RH (1996) Vichy Law and the Holocaust in France. Harwood Academic Publisher, Amsterdam
Welzer H (2007) Täter Wie aus ganz normalen Menschen Massenmörder werden. Fischer Taschenbuch Verlag, Frankfurt am Main (Kindle edition)

Chapter 18
The Lesser Evil

Administrating the Holocaust

Hans Calmeyer was the head of the office for Jewish matters in the Reichskommissariat of the German-occupied Netherlands. On the one hand, he was part of the operations that resulted in 76 % of the 140,000 Dutch Jews deported to the east and killed. He was responsible for the development, interpretation, and application of the *Judenrecht* in the Netherlands, which above all included the legislation that required that all Jews were registered as such in 1941.[1] On the other hand, he and his office were directly responsible for the saving of hundreds of lives.

Apart from requiring all Jews to give information on their heritage and to register, his office was responsible for deciding on the categorisation of persons in instances where the ancestry was doubtful or contested. According to the Nuremberg legislation, only persons with more than two Jewish grandparents were characterised as "full Jews". In addition, persons with two Jewish grandparents were to be regarded as full Jews if they belonged to the Jewish faith. Others with Jewish ancestry were characterised as "mixed" or Aryan. Only full Jews were subject to deportation.

Calmeyer's office dealt with 5,700 cases of doubtful or contested ancestry from 1941 to 1944. In 3,700 of these, it concluded that the person was not a full Jew according to the law. It is a recorded fact that in this work, Calmeyer and his people employed every possibility of discretion and extralegal tricks to decide cases in favour of the respondent. He instigated a complaints procedure, introduced evidence rules in favour of the respondent, and accepted statements and obviously forged documents stating a person's non-Jewish ancestry. He accepted declarations from Jewish mothers that their child was a result of an extramarital relationship with a non-Jew. He even provided lawyers of the respondents with blank documents so that they could provide more convincing forgeries.

---

[1] The presentation of Calmeyer is based on Rüthers (2008), pp. 84–101.

H.P. Graver, *Judges Against Justice*, DOI 10.1007/978-3-662-44293-7_18

An important part of the success of the saving of hundreds of people from extermination in this way was the cover of legality that the decisions were endowed with. Calmeyer was highly respected as an authority on legal issues relating to the Jews by his superiors and by the SS, even though the SS was critical and frustrated by having to postpone deportation of persons because their case was pending in Calmeyer's office. Once a decision was made, however, respected by the SS as according to the law, the person deemed not a Jew was not deported.

Calmeyer's role has been subject to controversy since the war. By some he is regarded as a Nazi bureaucrat complicit in the high rate of extermination that beheld the Dutch Jews. By others he is regarded as a hero of the resistance against the Nazi policy of extermination and as a saviour of hundreds of lives. It is a fact that he contributed to the implementation of the final solution in the Netherlands. Apart from administrating the registration of the Jews in the Netherlands, he also decided 2,000 cases of ancestry against the respondent, thus sending them to their death in the camps. On the other hand, most historians find it obvious that with a dedicated Nazi official in his place, those who were saved by Calmeyer would also have met with certain death.

Hans Calmeyer was at the receiving end of the anti-Jewish legislation and responsible for its implementation. At its originating end and responsible for its development was Bernhard Loesener. He too contributed to the mitigation of the atrocities against the Jews according to his own accounts.

Loesener was in charge of the section regarding racial and Jewish matters in Division I of the Ministry of Interior from 1933 to 1943. He was a witness for the prosecution at Nuremberg in the "Ministries Case" against his superior Wilhelm Stuckart, State Secretary (Staatssekretaer) in the Reich Ministry of the Interior (Reichsministerium des Innern) from 1935 to 1945. He also wrote an account of his years in the Ministry, published in Germany 1961.[2]

In his position as head of the office of racial and Jewish matters, Loesener was the "Jewish expert" of the Ministry. He was instrumental in the drafting of the Nuremberg laws of 1935 and in the bureaucratic wrangles over the subsequent implementing of regulations and decrees. According to Loesener, there was a permanent fight between the Ministry and the Party over the extension of the scope of the anti-Jewish legislation. The Ministry had, according to him, a clear policy to limit and mitigate the effects of the Nazi persecution of the Jews. In his account, he wrote:

> Fortunately the Ministry of the Interior also had quite a few staff members who fought against the Party with every means at their disposal, and continued to do so until the very end.[3]

---

[2] His account and a transcript of his witness statement for the Military Tribunal are published in Legislating the Holocaust: The Bernhard Loesener Memoirs and Supporting Documents by Schleunes (2001).

[3] Schleunes (2001), location 546.

Loesener's account is contested, and independent sources suggest that the Ministry had a much more acting and accepting part in the persecution of the Jews than he admits. But if we take Loesener on his words, can he then be seen as a hero? The first legislative measure was the "Law for the restoration of the Professional Civil Service" of April 7, 1933. This law purged the civil service of Jews and politically undesirable members. According to the definition attached to the law, anyone with at least one Jewish grandparent was included under its measures. This definition was also employed in subsequent purges by private organisations and employers.

The drafting of the Nuremberg laws in 1935 was the first occasion when the legal definition of "Jew" was brought up on a general basis. Loesener had defined it as his first task, "trying to improve the position of the *one quarter Jews*".[4] Prior to the Nuremberg laws, there were battles over the question between the Party and the Ministry. At the meeting in Nuremberg, the Ministry succeeded in limiting the application of the Jewish measures to "full Jews", i.e. persons with more than two Jewish grandparents. Following the first decree to the Reich Citizenship Law, the bulk of the half-Jews and all persons of mixed blood of small degrees were not to be considered and treated as Jews; the same applied in most cases to Jews married to non-Jews, the so-called privileged Jews. In total, this accounted for more than a hundred thousand people within the Reich. This delineation was under constant attack from the Party and the SS, but it held stand until the collapse of the regime.

According to Loesener, the Nuremberg laws were at the time not seen exclusively as laws of persecution. "Many people who had in no way been adherents of the Nazi system, and even those directly affected, viewed them with a certain relief because they promised to put an end to a state of complete legal disarray", he writes.[5] Following the enactment of the Nuremberg laws, Loesener and the Ministry were in constant conflict with the SS and the Party over the scope of the anti-Jewish measures, both over how the concept of a Jew should be defined and over the application of suppressive measures, such as rehousing, wearing of the Star of David, the right to entrance into bomb shelters, and so on, for half-Jews and Jews married to Aryans.

Loesener also used his position to help people in individual cases. He gave advice on legal opportunities and even provided information and warnings on imminent legal or police measures. The Ministry was also the final decision-making body for petitions requesting review of ancestry cases. According to one of his colleagues, under Loesener's direction, all objections of the petitioner were investigated, even if they appeared to be threadbare. He gave advice on how the petitioner's case could be improved upon and always decided a case in favour of the petitioner when there was room for doubt or for the exercise of administrative discretion. For instance, illegitimate children of Jewish women were classified as of mixed ancestry whenever there was any room for doubt as to the identity of the

[4] Schleunes (2001), location 571.

[5] Schleunes (2001), location 787.

father. As long as an investigation into the ancestry of a person was pending, he was exempt from deportation. This measure alone saved the lives of many people.

Loesener's role and contribution to the Holocaust is subject to controversy.[6] Most of what is known about his efforts is based on his own accounts—to the Nuremberg Military Tribunal and in his published recollections. This can lead to an estimation of his actions as more favourable to himself than in actuality and his importance to the saving of persons of mixed ancestry and in marriages to Aryans as exaggerated.

A more probable explanation for the restraint shown towards the half-Jews and Jews married to Germans was the fear the leading Nazis had of popular reactions toward their policies. Popular protests led to the halting of the euthanasia programme against the mentally ill in 1941, and the open demonstrations by German wives of 1,700 Jewish husbands in Rosenstrasse in February 1943 led to their release. Hitler was concerned with the people, not with the bureaucrats who were compelled to support and enforce his policies.[7] Deporting the half-Jews and the Jewish spouses would have involved challenging many tens of thousands of their German relatives and would have challenged concepts of marriage and family life deeply rooted in the German consciousness and traditions.

Seen from the offices of the Ministry of the Interior, the bureaucratic resistance to the more extreme demands of the Party and the SS would nevertheless be seen as important because it appeared effective since the policy of extermination did stop short of half-Jews. It would be natural for those who defended this policy to take credit for the results.

Exemptions from the Rule of Law

These two stories are examples of the argument of the lesser evil in extreme cases. But they show the nature of the dilemma and the difficulties in employing the argument. Can sending thousands of people to their deaths be justified in order to save a few? This is a classic dilemma in moral theory. The situation of the judge is different from the known examples of the runaway tram or the drowning child. Although some of the relevant factors are the same, there are some crucial differences. The judge is instrumental in creating the situation, and he is faced with it repeatedly.

The argument of the lesser evil can be employed on a slighter scale than extermination and still involve difficult dilemmas. Hubert Schorn cites the quandary facing many judges in Nazi Germany due to the existence of a parallel system where the Gestapo took care of the political aberrant and "unwanted elements" in their cellars and camps outside the scope of the law. In many cases, the Gestapo

[6] See the discussion in Essner (2002).

[7] Stoltzfus (1996), p. 259.

apprehended persons who were released by the courts as they walked out of the courtroom. Shorn states that judges in some cases held people in custody to protect them from this, even if they considered that it was unfounded. Some judges even convicted persons they thought were innocent, to prevent the Gestapo from exercising their form of justice.[8]

To evaluate and criticise such reasoning and the choice between protecting society and protecting individuals, we need to take a footing outside of the law. Importantly, such a footing can also provide a platform from where the conscientious judge may reflect on how he should construe the law and whether he should give effect to the will of the government or choose another course.

One approach often taken by people who find themselves in the situation of a judge where emergencies are appealed to for limiting basic rights is that following the course of the government is the lesser of two evils. It is often perceived as a worse alternative to force the government to take action outside the scope of the law or to refuse to contribute with the result that the government appoints other, and more accommodating, judges. The judge may also believe that upholding the government and some measure of law and order is better than the alternative.

Often, the judge identifies with the government in the perception of a threat to society and accepts the argument that limiting the rights of some is the lesser evil. Denmark and Belgium during the German occupation under World War II show two different courses of action in the collaboration of the courts and the police in the oppressive measures of the occupying authorities. In both cases, the courts acted in line with the governments. The Danish government remained intact after the German occupation in April 1940 and entered into a policy of necessary collaboration. This included the police, the prosecution, and the courts. It was an aim of Danish policy to keep Danish jurisdiction over Danish citizens, and the criminal laws and rules of procedure were modified to accommodate the German demands for an effective protection of German interests. The courts contributed and metered out harsh punishments after procedures that departed from the normal requirements of the rule of law. Despite this, the Germans demanded the handing over of Danish prisoners, and by December 1942 80 Danes were in German custody.

To the legal consciousness of the people, it was intolerable that the Danish police should arrest Danes on behalf of the Germans. Nevertheless, the government maintained that it was preferable that the arrests were made by the national police. Even though there were opposing views in the police, the police and courts remained loyal to the government policy of collaboration. An observer noted in 1945 that the grip the German occupier had over the central government automatically extended to the whole machinery of the government due to the habitual obedience and loyalty within the public sector.[9] On the other hand, it is a fact that whereas in Norway 292 members of the resistance were sentenced to death by German and Norwegian collaboration courts during the occupation, in Denmark the

---

[8] Schorn (1959), p. 32.

[9] Tamm (1984), pp. 41–42.

death penalties totalled to 133.[10] All of these were imposed by German courts after the breakdown of the collaboration policy of the Danish government in August 1943.

In August 1943, the Danish government resigned and the Germans declared martial law. The government encouraged the administration to remain in their posts and continue their duties "for the best of the country" for the duration of the emergency situation. In effect, Denmark was governed by the heads of the ministries for the remaining period of the war. The Germans organised units of Danish police under German command. Many of the policemen were recruited from soldiers who had fought voluntarily for the Germans on the Eastern Front. All members of these police forces were later convicted for collaboration with the Germans. But their existence during the last years of the occupation may have protected the ordinary police from becoming too involved in the interests of the German occupiers. After the war, only 1 chief of police and 30 police officers were convicted for collaboration.[11]

In Belgium too, there were controversies between the national administration and the German occupier over the jurisdiction in cases involving Belgium nationals.[12] The German military tribunals exercised competence in cases involving illegal possession of firearms, but the German police was not equipped to handle all the cases. The Belgian authorities wanted exclusive jurisdiction over cases involving own nationals. The Germans demanded that the laws were reformed to ensure convictions and harsh punishment, and the Secretary General of Justice was willing to accommodate this provided the Germans gave a written guarantee that the cases would be handled by Belgian authorities.

The Belgian exile government issued a decree in 1942 prohibiting the handover of Belgian nationals to the enemy. The police abided by this and refused to cooperate with the military administration when this entailed handing over Belgian nationals. The Germans put pressure on the Belgian authorities to ensure cooperation and even considered arresting leading figures of the Belgian judiciary. They decided against this because this would make the cooperation of persons subordinate to them even more unlikely. The Germans finally gave in and gave exclusive jurisdiction to the Belgian courts. A notable exception to the protests by the Belgian courts was, however, the deportation of Jews. Whereas they protested together with the law society against the purge of Jews within the legal community, they did not protest against the German measures against the Jews as such or against the deportations.

In other cases, the judge may not identify with the government or its policies. Still, his identification with a judicial role may compel him to uphold evil measures. Many antislavery judges of the mid-nineteenth century argued in this way. The

[10] Nøkleby (1996), pp. 195 and 188.

[11] Tamm (1984), p. 580.

[12] See Michielsen (2004), pp. 84–89.

same line of argument is presented by current US judges who oppose the strict sentencing regimes imposed upon them by the legislator and by superior courts.

The Lesser Evil Defence

Judges may moderate the excesses of a regime and do justice in individual cases. They may even stem oppressive trends in the beginning and prevent society from developing into a society of oppression. Such contributions will often entail compromises. A judge is, after all, an administrator and executor of the legal policy of the regime he serves. Should contributing to a lesser harm to avoid the greater harm be a recommended way of thinking when a lawyer is asked to contribute to harm and unjustness?

After the Second World War, when the extent of the involvement of the courts in the Nazi oppression was revealed, many German judges sought the lesser evil argument as a defence. Judges in Germany were aware of the "dual state", and the Gestapo in many cases was ready to intervene against any person, without any legal guarantees, for political ends and place a person who had been acquitted in a concentration camp. In the Justice Trial, this line of defence was presented in the following way:

> Schlegelberger presents an interesting defense, which is also claimed in some measure by most of the defendants. He asserts that the administration of justice was under persistent assault by Himmler and other advocates of the police state. This is true. He contends that if the functions of the administration of justice were usurped by the lawless forces under Hitler and Himmler, the last state of the nation would be worse than the first. He feared that if he were to resign, a worse man would take his place. As the event proved, there is much truth in this also.[13]

The judges of South Africa during apartheid defended themselves along the same lines:

> Those of us who were white who chose to remain in South Africa, and who were considered to be properly qualified in both personal and professional respects to perform the judicial function, had to make up our own minds, when asked to accept judicial appointments, whether society as a whole was better served by our accepting appointments than by our declining them. On the answer to that (and of course highly subjective personal considerations) our acceptance or refusal depended. There was also the risk that, if members of the Bar declined to accept appointments, the government might do what it had sometimes threatened to do, and appoint civil servants (magistrates, law advisers, and the like) as judges. We did not consider that to be in the public interest. We thought more good would come of our accepting appointment than of our declining to do so.[14]

[13] The Justice Case (1951), p. 1086.

[14] Submission to the South African Truth and Reconciliation Commission by the following members of the Supreme Court of Appeal: Mr. Justice J.W. Smalberger, Mr. Justice C.T. Howie, Mr. Justice R.M. Marais, and Mr. Justice D.G. Scott, 115 S. African Law Journal 1998, p. 44.

The defence of the lesser evil was rejected by the US Military Tribunal as a matter of law in the Justice Case. The Tribunal discarded the argument that the lawyers were not the worst perpetrators of the Nazi atrocities:

> That their program of racial extermination under the guise of law failed to attain the proportions which were reached by the pogroms, deportations, and mass murders by the police is cold comfort to the survivors of the "judicial" process and constitutes a poor excuse before this Tribunal. The prostitution of a judicial system for the accomplishment of criminal ends involves an element of evil to the State which is not found in frank atrocities which do not sully judicial robes.[15]

Schlegelberger, who argued that his role in the Ministry had been to moderate the Nazi policies and who, to a certain extent, was heard on this by the Tribunal, was nevertheless convicted and sentenced to life imprisonment.

It was also rejected by the Military Tribunal in the Ministries Case. In the case against Wilhelm Stuckart, State Secretary and Loesener's direct superior at the Ministry of the Interior, the Tribunal stated:

> In justice to the defendant it should be said that we are convinced that for a long time he courageously fought the measures against the Mischlings and attempted to intervene in favor of mixed marriages.[16]

Nevertheless, the Tribunal found him guilty with the following words:

> [T]he skill, learning, and legal knowledge of Stuckart was placed at the disposal of those who originated the plan of extermination. The fact that his conscience may have been troubled and the fact that he saw not only the wrong but the folly of the proposals with respect to Mischlings, cannot excuse or condone what he did.[17]

Should we accept an appeal to the lesser evil from a moral point of view, or should we side with Gustav Radbruch in his appraisal of the US Military Tribunal's judgment over the leaders of the Nazi judiciary? To this, we quote:

> Never believe that you can avoid evil by contributing to evil. This experiment has been tried often enough with failure, and is often just an excuse for cowardly complicity. Even when this is not the case, such as with Schlegelberger [German Minister of Justice, 1941–1942], association with the evil inevitably leads to blindness so that one no longer sees the true nature of the evil that one is participating in.[18]

Hannah Arendt is also quite clear on this issue:

"Politically, the weakness of the argument has always been that those who choose the lesser evil forget very quickly that they chose evil... If we look at the

[15] The Justice Trial, p. 1086.

[16] The Ministries Case, vol. XIV, p. 641.

[17] The Ministries Case, vol. XIV, p. 646.

[18] "Glaube niemand, daß es ihm gelingen werde, durch Teilnahme am Bösen Schlimmeres zu verhüten. Dies Experiment ist oft genug gemacht worden und oft genug mißlungen, ist auch oft genug ein bloßer Vorwand feiger Nachgiebigkeit gewesen. Auch wo er das, wie bei Schlegelberger, nicht war, führt er unvermeidlich in Verstrickungen mit dem Bösen, das man bekämpft, und schließlich zu jener Blindheit, die das Böse, das man zugesteht, in seinem wahren Wesen nicht mehr klar erkennt", Radbruch (1948).

techniques of totalitarian government, it is obvious that the argument of "lesser evil" – far from being raised only from the outside by those who do not belong to the ruling elite – is one of the mechanisms built into the machinery of terror and criminality. Acceptance of lesser evils is consciously used in conditioning the government officials as well as the population at large to the acceptance of evil as such".[19] Arendt here points to the dangers of moral blindness and entrapment that have been discussed above. Accepting the lesser evil may easily weaken and narrow the human responses of the judge.

Authoritarian rulers depend upon support and contribution from the sources of power in society. They need the skill and resources of people employed to perform state functions, hereunder also the judiciary. They depend on popular support, and in many cases courts contribute to this by providing the regime with legitimacy. Withdrawal of the support of important institutions such as the courts may weaken and, in the last instance, dissolve the power of the authoritarian rulers.[20]

Refusal to play the tune of the regime, even when it is oppressive, does not, however, always lead to the best results. History shows that critical judges may push the regime to cover its oppression under extralegal schemes and employ police, military, and death squads far outside of public view and the jurisdiction of the courts. Under the military dictatorship in Brazil, the Brazilian Supreme Court refused to implement the most repressive measures of the regime and invalidated them on natural law grounds. As a result, the regime circumvented the law with extralegal terror, in addition to establishing special military courts to deal with political opponents. According to observers, the military courts, with their positivist and cooperative attitude to the laws of the regime, saved more lives than the Supreme Court did with its resistance.[21] Should the results decide?

When situations are as extreme as in Nazi Germany, "the lesser evil" seems an obviously invalid excuse for collaboration in the evil policies of oppression. On the other side of the scale, we have the accepted reservations to individual rights that are recognised even within modern human rights instruments as "necessary in a democratic society". As Chief Justice Rehnquist says, citing Judge Learned Hand: "A society in which men recognise no check upon their freedom soon becomes a society where freedom is the possession of a savage few".[22]

The proportionality test required by such reservations amounts to the balancing of evils and the allowance of a lesser evil to avoid a greater one. So the "lesser evil" is obviously a valid argument under ordinary circumstances. And many a judge who finds himself in a situation where he must inflict pain by his judgment will comfort himself that the result is to the greater good. When is reference to proportionality and the greater good disallowed? This is the critical question that the "good" judge must ask himself.

---

[19] Arendt (2003), p. 35.

[20] See Sharp (2010), p. 19.

[21] Osiel (1995), p. 542.

[22] Rehnquist (1998), location 3620.

The German jurists failed to stem the Holocaust and terror—although some Jews were saved as a result of being processed by the legal system. The law also contributed to saving Jews on account of their being married to German spouses and holding persons with mixed ancestry outside of the extermination programme. The South African judges did not stop apartheid and the repression of the regime to safeguard its existence. On the contrary, the South African Truth and Reconciliation Commission concluded that "part of the reason for the longevity of apartheid was the superficial adherence to 'rule by law' by the National Party (NP), whose leaders craved the aura of legitimacy that 'the law' bestowed on their harsh injustice".[23] But the persons charged under security or racial laws did welcome judicial assistance and did not reject the help of lawyers on the ground that it legitimated the oppression. The Brazilian military courts did save lives, with an acquittal rate of 70 %.[24] Should they be condemned for the 30 % that were convicted according to repressive laws or praised for their acquittals? The testimony of German military court judge Werner Otto Müller-Hill clearly shows that the attitude of the judge matters. Not all German military court judges employed the death sentence in their rulings.

The answer is all the more difficult due to the fact that the interests and values that have to be considered are incommensurable. Consider the antislavery judges of the US in the 1830s–1850s, who upheld the fugitive slave laws against their own convictions of the meaning of liberty and its application to all regardless of race. They did not choose between liberty and slavery but between liberty and an ordered federation of the US, between liberty and fidelity to public trust, and between liberty and the adherence to public undertakings of nationhood. The issue for these judges was whether the moral values served by antislavery outweighed interests and values served by slavery.[25]

When are we faced with oppressive measures that may be countered and moderated by judicial temperance, and when have we passed into the stage of lawlessness? Nazi Germany initially targeted its oppressive laws and measures against the Jews and against political opposition, particularly the communists and social democrats. But was it generally lawless already in 1933? Some claim that it was never a lawless society, that law led directly to Auschwitz, and that even this was not a lawless place. The Nazi experience in this view was not a break with law but part of the normal continuities of history and law in the western legal tradition.[26] "The real focus", writes David Fraser, "one with which lawyers seem to be extremely uncomfortable, should be on the 'politics of law' i.e. on the substantive normative content of laws and on the preferred outcome of judicial interpretation. The question is not, I believe a question of 'not law' versus law but rather what we should, can and must do when confronted with legal evil".[27]

[23] Report vol. 4 from the South African Truth and Reconciliation Commission, (1998), p. 101.

[24] Osiel (1995), p. 538.

[25] Cover (1974), pp. 197–198.

[26] Fraser (2005), p. 10.

[27] Fraser (2005), p. 42.

By this view, "lawlessness" is an inadequate standard by which to draw the line. Many would contest Fraser's view on law and on Germany and draw a line between the oppression of Germany in the 1930s and the lawlessness of the 1940s. Such lines have to be drawn by circumstances outside of positive law. Lon L. Fuller suggested, in his famous discussion with H.L.A. Hart, drawing a line according to the internal morality of law, which he defined as fidelity to law.[28]

But even this leaves open issues to answer. What is "fidelity to law", and by what standards do we measure whether those in power are committed to it? Are we talking about the degree of commitment that the rulers hold to the laws that they derive their legitimacy from and to the rules that they enact? In that case, what shall we make of Hitler's words in his speech in Königsberg in October 1932?:

> I only want to attain the power. When we once achieve this, we will, God help us, hold on to it. We will never let ourselves be removed.

And what of Göbbels in his diary on August 6 1932?:

> Once we have the power, we will never surrender it. It had, in case, to be that they carried us as corpses from our offices.

The intentions of the Nazi leaders were clear and public right from the very start. Does this mean that judges should have refused to give their loyalty to the regime from the very beginning?

This would entail that what we blame the German judges for their staying in office and applying the law right after the Nazi takeover of power. True, a mass resignation of judges would have been a blow to the regime, but is it credible as a strategy to believe in it as a realistic line of action for judges under similar circumstances? Historical experience shows that judges almost never refuse to give their judicial loyalty to new holders of power, even when they achieve their power by non-constitutional means. Even under foreign occupation, many national judges continue to serve and apply the measures of the occupier in a loyal and normal judicial way.

Is it not more credible to demand of judges that they judge with integrity according to the standards of rule of law and in this way try to impose a measure of fidelity to the law on the holders of power? The question is how they should do this and how to distinguish between harsh but legitimate measures to be applied and measures that must count as illegitimate oppression.

Rather than by fidelity to the law, should we measure by the intention of the rulers to do good or evil? This is the line Radbruch suggests when he states:

> Where justice is not even the aim, when equality, which is the core of justice, is consciously denied by the positive enactments, then the law is not only an unjust law, but is lacking even of the legal quality.[29]

---

[28] Fuller (1957).

[29] Radbruch (1946), p. 107.

This demarcation would, if applied on a statute-to-statute basis, for instance, deny the racial laws of apartheid the quality of law and thus demand of judges of South Africa that they be disapplied. On the other hand, it would not as such demand that the same judges refrained from enforcing suppressive measures against opposition to the apartheid regime since they would not obviously be "lawless" by this criterion. We do not have a measure by which to decide if the government is lawless or not if we apply the test only on individual laws.

Perhaps the criteria for fidelity and commitment to justice can be applied in a more general way to a legal regime and not only to specific laws of its legal order. Kristen Rundle has applied Lon L. Fuller's thoughts on fidelity to law to the Nazi persecution of the Jews in order to draw a line between the legal persecution of the 1930s and the extralegal extermination of the Holocaust.[30] Her arguments for accepting the persecution of the Jews in the initial phase as law is that it was implemented in a legal programme that accepted the Jews as agents. She cites both Jewish and Nazi sources to argue that there was a measure of law and stability in the regulation of the Jews up to the pogrom of November 1938. After the pogrom, the Jews were collectively made responsible for the damage that had been caused on their property and lives. From this point on, Rundle argues, something other than legality was regulating Jewish life.[31]

In the exterminatory phases, the Jews were no longer given the status as legal agents and were subject to the disorder of SS terror. Fidelity to law requires that law's subjects are treated as legal agents under a "commitment to the view that man is, or can become, a responsible agent, capable of understanding and following rules, and answerable for his defaults".[32] In the same line, one may say that a regime that, contrary to its own legal norms, systematically practises oppression and terror by extralegal means no longer shows fidelity to law if the courts do not actively resist such practices and demand that the security measures are brought within the scope of the law and the legal institutions. To the extent that the judges are employed in oppression in specific cases, they are contributing to lawlessness if they tolerate the evil that takes place outside of the courts in other cases. Such criticism was directed towards the German judiciary by the Military Tribunal in Nuremberg and towards the judges of Chile and South Africa by the Truth and Reconciliation committees of these two countries.

It is easy to concur with the view that there are crucial differences between persecution and extermination. There should also be differences between a system of rules administered by a structure of courts and rules enforced purely administratively under a regime of terror. Whether the qualification of "law" should be reserved for the former is basically a question to be answered by legal theory and has been a subject of a comprehensive body of scholarship since the famous Hart–Fuller debate. But it is doubtful whether one's position on the concept of law and

[30] Rundle (2009), pp. 65–125.

[31] Rundle (2009), pp. 91–98.

[32] Rundle (2009), p. 106, quoting Fuller.

legal theory should be decisive of the question of legal or moral responsibility of judges who contribute to oppression and evil through their rulings.

Rundle's distinction is framed by the context of looking at law from the perspective of those subjected to law.[33] If one takes a different perspective, that of those responsible for the application of law, the issues are different. Laws regarding how to treat objects such as anti-pollution law or laws on animals' rights are still "law" seen from the perspective of the judge or the administrator, disregarding the fact that its subject matter is objects and not legal subjects. This legal characteristic does not necessarily change when the subject matter is the treating of human beings, although the moral quality of the law may change. Not all laws regarding the treatment of humans have to have the quality of awarding the subjects legal status as holders of rights or of a legal subjectivity in order to pass a moral test. The granting of individual rights in social and health systems is only a recent phenomenon, although we have had laws regulating the rights and obligations of social workers and doctors affecting the recipients of welfare and the patients for a long time. That social and political developments have gone in the direction of the recognition of rights and the recipients of welfare and the patients as legal subjects is recommendable. But if we exclude the previous regulation from our concept of law, we give "law" a very narrow concept if our context is the analysis and evaluation of judges and other legal officials. And we could certainly not, without further qualification, demand that these disapply "law" that does not recognise its human subjects as legal agents in their own right. This does not say that any change in the contents of the law in this respect is not important, especially when it goes from recognition to nonrecognition, but this cannot be used as a criterion for when judges should refuse to cooperate.

The lawyers at Nuremberg were convicted for participation in extermination, for enactment and enforcement of discriminatory laws, and for denial of justice contrary to the laws of war. They were not convicted, however, for denial of judicial agency of their victims and thus not offering them the status of being legal subjects. Their playing field was the part of the system where the victims were regarded as legal agents but of different status. There was fidelity to the integrity and normativity of the positive law as it was given, apart from in the cases of the "evil judges" like Freisler and Rothaug, who went far beyond even the law of the Nazis in their pursuit of their contempt of members of the "lower races". But generally, the reasons given for discriminatory sentencing of Jews and Poles, even by such judges, were not that they were not agents but that they, as agents, committed especially serious offences, such as when Rothaug in a case against a Pole stated:

> The attack of the defendant is directed against the purity of the German blood. Looking at it from this point of view, the defendant showed such insubordination within the German living space that his action has to be considered as especially significant.[34]

---

[33] This is even more pronounced in her article where she investigates how law is experienced in the daily life of its subjects; see Rundle (2012).

[34] The Justice Trial, p. 1149.

The fact that judges conceive the persons against whom they apply the law as legal agents should be no excuse for them. Characterising the defendant's agency in the above case only made things worse: due to the fact that the defendant was a Pole of lesser worth than the Aryans, his insubordination in attacking the purity of the German blood was in need of a particularly harsh punishment. The fact that the Poles who were left to the SS fared even worse was no excuse for the judges who judged in this manner.

The direct killing of Jews, Poles, and the mentally ill was done according to decrees expressing the will of Hitler. In these fields, the decrees were generally secret and, in some cases, not even in writing. They nevertheless expressed the "law" according to the prevailing concept of law at the time, when the supreme legal source was the will of the Führer.[35] The officially stated role of the judiciary was to find and express the will of the Führer and apply all laws accordingly, even when this will was not explicitly expressed by or on behalf of Hitler. This was even more so when it was known and expressed, albeit in secret and oral communications. These decrees and orders were refused recognition as law by German courts after the war, not because they did not treat the persecuted people as agents but because they were in contradiction of a core of justice present in the minds of "all civilized people".[36] The result, however, was the same as proposed by Fuller and Rundle: the Holocaust took place outside of the scope of the law and was fundamentally illegal.

A judge faced with enforcing such decrees should certainly refuse. This was the position taken by Judge Lothar Kreissig and for which he was forced into retirement from his judicial appointment when he refused to commit his wards to the mental doctors for extermination under the euthanasia regime of the Nazis. Although the reason given for his retirement was that he could not continue in this position if he refused to accept the Führer's orders as the ultimate source of law, it is noteworthy that he was not met with stronger sanctions for his refusal. Maybe this was because at this point, the cooperation of the judiciary was ensured anyway, and it was better for the regime to let the sceptics retire quietly than to let them rock the boat by remaining as protesting judges or better for disquiet among the judges that more severe sanctions could have resulted in. It is notable that also within the civil service, and even among the *Einsatsgruppen*, the task forces of the security police engaged in mass murder, those who objected were excused without being subject to personal repercussions.

[35] See Werle (1992), pp. 2529–2535.

[36] See Freudiger (2002), p. 405.

Is Resignation the Only Viable Alternative?

What should a judge do then in a situation where he is forced to participate in atrocities? Many would answer that if a judge cannot avoid contributing to harm in his function as a judge, he should recuse himself or resign. Resignation is, of course, a way of preventing becoming personally involved in oppression. We know that some judges in Nazi Germany resigned because they were unable to go along with the legal oppression of the regime. As we have seen in Chap. 5, Lothar Kreyssig was given the option to resign when he refused to accept the legality of the euthanasia programme endorsed by Hitler, and Hans von Dohnanyi resigned from the Supreme Court after 3 years of service. Another member of the resistance against Hitler, Rüdiger Schleicher, refused an appointment to the Supreme War Court (Reichskriegsgericht) because the position would entail that he would have to convict people who had done things that he personally held as just and because he regarded the independence of the justices, particularly in this court, as "extremely relative".[37]

These resignations had little impact on the regime. Resignation may, on the other hand, be an instrument to weaken the regime by depriving it of legitimacy and perhaps also of the possibility of having a working legal system at its disposal. The resignation of the Norwegian Supreme Court judges at the beginning of the German occupation may have contributed to the general illegitimacy of the Quisling regime in Norway.

On the other hand, resignation is not without its problems. As an individual action, it only leads to another person having to take office and contributing to the oppression of the regime; it is therefore just "passing the buck".[38] It probably makes the oppression worse. The person taking over will either be more disposed in favour of the regime or be in opposition. This means that if a person in opposition resigns, there is a real chance he will be replaced by a person more accommodating to the regime. The liberal judges under apartheid in South Africa knew that if they resigned their office, other judges more sympathetic to the regime would construe the government powers under the emergency laws to be even more oppressive on personal liberties. To require judges under such circumstances to resign from their office is perhaps to show insufficient appreciation for the situation of the judiciary in a society that is unjust and oppressive but not totally lawless.[39]

This reasoning could even be applied to the Nazi regime, at least in its early stages. Lothar Kreyssig writes in his autobiography:

> In the spring of 1933 I drafted my resignation as a judge where I cited a series of elementary breaches of law that were committed or tolerated by the authorities. After a sleepless night I realized that this was too easy. The inconsistency would sink into oblivion and the field left

[37] Gerrens (2009), p. 126.

[38] See Brand-Ballard (2010), p. 177.

[39] Dugard (1987), p. 500.

> to the compliant. Was my decision the wrong one? The uncertainty kept me awake and attentive to the expected conflicts in my duty as a judge.[40]

Kreyssig stayed in office and did not resign until several years later, when his conscience prohibited him from recognising the legality of the systematic killing of the mentally disabled under his judicial ward.

In his inaugural lecture as professor of law at the University of Natal, Durban, in March 1983, Raymond Wachs called for the resignation of judges who found the law of South Africa morally indefensible.[41] He argued that a judge who finds himself in this situation has three choices: to protest, to lie about the law, or to resign. Experiencing a conflict between the law and underlying moral principles, the judge can protest by refusing to apply the law that he finds immoral. Alternatively, he can misconstrue the law and claim that it has a different and more morally defensible content than what he believes it to have from his legal judgment. He would, under both these alternatives, in the words of Clover, choose to act as an insurgent rather than a judge.[42] In both cases, the results are likely to be negligible. If he is not a judge of last instance, his judgment is likely to be reversed on appeal. If he misconstrues the law, he is likely to provoke a reply from the legislator that makes his construction impossible in future cases. And even though he may mitigate the harsh effects of the oppression in individual cases, the system remains largely unchanged.

However, by continuing to serve, judges lend respect and legitimacy to the oppressive regime. According to Wachs, there is really no alternative open to the judge who wishes to square his conscience but to resign. A resignation by an official whose very occupation proclaims the pursuit of justice may "echo, albeit faintly, through the halls of government" and may also have a possible effect on other judges.

The same view was held by South African judges in their written submission to the Truth and Reconciliation Committee:

> A judge, whether positioned by personal conviction on the left, center, or right of the political spectrum, who feels free to ignore the oath of office when compliance with it conflicts with his or her own credo, is no hero. Such conduct is bereft of integrity and is a self-indulgent abuse of judicial power. There are only two honest courses open to a judge in such a situation: either resign or comply with the oath of office.[43]

In a reply to Wachs, John Dugard countered that the state of the law was not such that apartheid provided a complete system in itself.[44] The oppressive laws existed in

---

[40] Cited from Döring (2011), pp. 113–114.

[41] Wachs (1984).

[42] Clover (2012), p. 198.

[43] Submission to the South African Truth and Reconciliation Commission by the following members of the Supreme Court of Appeal: Mr. Justice J.W. Smalberger, Mr. Justice C.T. Howie, Mr. Justice R.M. Marais, and Mr. Justice D.G. Scott, 115 S. African Law Journal 1998, p. 45.

[44] Dugard (1984).

the background of the common law and the Dutch Roman law with their liberal principles, and there was still room for advancement of human rights in the intercedes of the apartheid legal order. He also objected to the singling out of judges as morally complicit. Defence council and attorneys in a political trial also lend legitimacy to the system as their participation testifies to the fairness of the system, and even a tax lawyer who meticulously avoids having anything to do with "political law" is part of creating the impression that the system is a normal system of law. The argument for resignation can thus be extended to everyone and therefore amounts to a support of not doing anything.

According to Gene Sharp, more than 200 specific methods of nonviolent action against authoritarian regimes have been identified, and they can be divided into three main categories: protest and persuasion, noncooperation, and intervention.[45] Judges can engage in all three. They can review the measures of the regime and refuse to recognise them as legal, as what, for instance, the Prussian Administrative Appeals Court initially did with measures employed by the police. Or they can engage in a dialogue either with the dictators or with the elites of society, as the courts of Argentina and Brazil.[46] They can intervene in the operations of the security forces by insisting on habeas corpus and demanding proof for claims made by the authorities. There are many ways in which the courts can contribute to the support of opposition to the regime and provide grounds for questioning its legitimacy. This may be achieved by resigning, as we saw in the case of the Supreme Court of Norway during the first months of the Quisling regime, and resignation is by far the only way. Noncooperation can also be achieved by staying in office, as the case with the Belgian courts during the occupation. The scope of action is much wider than just noncooperation, and judges who resign limit this scope drastically.

The same argument that judges do have a scope for making a difference was made by the German Supreme Court in its review of the actions of the judges under the GDR regime. Despite the fact that the regime was totalitarian and oppressive and practised harsh punishments on defectors and political opponents, there was judicial scope for the protection of fundamental rights according to the Supreme Court of the Federal Republic. In a case against a member of the GDR Supreme Court, where capital punishment was imposed for relatively minor offences, the Supreme Court of the Federal Republic emphasised that the criminal law of the GDR at the time did open up alternatives to capital punishment and that the GDR judges should have exercised their discretion in a "human-rights friendly way".[47] The Court also stressed that, in particular, in Germany on the background of the misuse of the death penalty during the Nazi regime, the judges of the successor regimes were under an obligation to limit the use of capital punishment to the most severe offences, particularly in cases of a political nature. Despite the fact that the

[45] Sharp (2010), p. 31.

[46] Osiel (1995), pp. 548–549.

[47] BGH, Urteil vom 16.11.1995—5 StR 747/94.

Supreme Court here may be criticised for employing a different standard of evaluation from what was perceived as correct in the GDR in the 1950s, the Court does point to arguments that could have been employed by the judges at that time to mitigate the oppressive policies employed by the regime. Judges often have a choice, and it matters how they exercise it.

One should probably not overestimate the effects of either course of action on an oppressive regime. The protests from the liberal judges of South Africa in the 1970s and 1980s did not seem to have any mentionable effect on the regime. The Supreme Court of Brazil protested without much effect on the military rulers. The few instances of protest and resignation of judges in Nazi Germany did nothing to curb the development of the judiciary into a system of oppression and terror. On the other hand, the timely resignation of the Supreme Court of Norway in December 1940 under the German occupation probably did contribute to the delegitimation of the German rule through the Quisling regime. In the same way, the consistent protests of the Belgian courts seem to have contributed to maintaining Belgian jurisdiction over Belgian subjects during the German occupation, without having to make the concessions over the rule of law that were imposed upon the Danish and Dutch courts. And resignations by some US judges over the sentencing regime with disproportionate punishments may be a contributing factor behind the new approach taken by the US Supreme Court on the use of life imprisonment against perpetrators under the age of 18 in Graham v. Florida, 560.[48]

A Realistic Calculus

We see that the dilemmas contained in the lesser evil situations are complex and difficult to resolve. In situations where the regime is oppressive, the lesser evil argument entails clear risks. What then, if any, are the minimum conditions that must be met for the lesser evil argument to be sound? One condition that should be met to accept the argument of the lesser evil is that the evil that is committed with a great measure of probability will directly be instrumental in excluding the greater evil. In general, it is safe to say that sacrificing individual liberty for security will amount to a certain encroachment of liberty but an uncertain result for security. For the argument to be sound, the results for security must be tangible and probable.

On this account, it is easier to exonerate Calmeyer than Loesener. Calmeyer contributed to the evil deportation of the Dutch Jews by fulfilling the duties of his office at the Reichskommissariat for the Netherlands. At the same time, through his actions, he directly saved hundreds from deportation.

Loesener contributed to the persecution of the Jews by drafting the main legislative framework of the Nazi state against the Jews. At the same time, he argued and worked for limiting the measures so as not to include persons of mixed

[48] Graham v. Florida 560 US—08-7412 (2010).

ancestry and Jews married to Aryans. The outcome of this was, however, unsure and indirect. It could easily be argued that the regime would have shown the same restraint without Loesener's efforts from his position. There were others within the administration and party who shared Loesener's views, and the fear of raising public resentment was probably the most important moderating factor. What was said by the Military Tribunal of his boss Stuckard could equally well be said of Loesener—that he placed his skill, learning, and legal knowledge at the disposal of those who originated the plan of extermination. The fact that his conscience may have been troubled and the fact that he saw not only the wrong but the folly of the proposals with respect to Mischlings cannot excuse or condone what he did.

What the examples show is that the lesser evil argument cannot always be discarded. Resignation is not always the best alternative, even if staying on entails contribution to evil. Sometimes a person who stays and works with the regime can use his position to the benefit of individuals in such a way that it is clearly worth the effort. On the other hand, the calculus is often difficult and obscure. Whereas the evil one contributes to by applying and enforcing oppressive measures is definite and measurable, the benefits may be hypothetical and uncertain. This indicates that the reasoning from the lesser evil should be applied with utmost caution.

Avoiding the Slippery Slope

A second condition to be met is that there is a clear direction in the actions of the judge employing the lesser evil argument. It must not be employed as an excuse for just doing the job but be part of a conscious strategy to counter the oppressive means of the regime. It is inherent in law that it legitimises acts that can be construed as unjust and evil: it protects property against the desperately poor; it commits persons to incarceration for the good of society—in some societies, it even takes lives. The application of force always implies sanctioning of an evil for the purpose of avoiding the greater evil. Sometimes the evil that is enacted is substantial and the doing of justice symbolic, for example when a family of immigrants is expelled from the realm for presenting false papers to the immigration authorities. Law is always about proportions and scales. Even the most formalistic reasoning implies substance, where straying from the content of a legal rule is the greater evil that justifies the imposing of consequences that are ascribed. And here lies the key of rejecting the defence of the lesser evil as such. If law is always about applying the lesser evil, this cannot be the defence of a judge accused of evil, for if it were, he could only be blamed for imposing excessive evil, which is a different accusation all together.

On the other hand, this also leads to the necessary conclusion that a judge cannot be blamed for balancing evils and imposing what he thinks to be the lesser evil in the context of the law that he is applying. This is an inherent part of being a judge, be it in a democratic society with respect of rule of law, in an emergency situation, in a society on its way to dictatorship and tyranny, and even in societies that can be regarded as mostly lawless by some standard or other. We cannot answer the question of whether the judge is to blame for his actions by comparing them to alternatives. We must regard them by their own merits and determine whether they amount to unacceptable evils disregarding the intentions held or justifications given.

The greatest danger with the lesser evil thinking is that it may ensnare the judge into the logic of the regime, making him forget that what he does is evil. The lesser evil can, on the other hand, be employed in a systematic way in the opposite direction by the judge who takes incremental steps in order to counter the regime. This is another difference in the actions of Calmeyer and Loesener from a moral point of view. Where Calmeyer applied his skills in order to save as many lives as he could, Loesener's skills were mainly employed into the transformation of the evil policies into law. That he did not go as far as some of the proponents of the regime wished does not mean that he worked to make the regime better; he only worked to prevent it from becoming worse. At the same time, he gave a main contribution into making it become what it became. Calmeyer worked to increase the number of people who could be saved from extermination. In this way, he made a real contribution towards making it better.

The lesser evil is a dangerous guide. The business of applying the lesser evil is an inherent part of the work of the judge. He should, therefore, be especially receptive to Radbruch's and Arendt's warning: that evil leads to blindness for evil and that acceptance of lesser evils is consciously used in conditioning the government officials. Only when the judge employs the lesser evil as part of a conscious strategy to oppose the regime and to systematically achieve incremental improvements can he be sure that he is not entrapped.

References

Arendt H (2003) Responsibility and judgment. Schocken Books, New York

Brand-Ballard J (2010) Limits of legality: the ethics of lawless judging. Oxford University Press, Oxford

Clover J (2012) Humanity: a moral history of the 20th century, 2nd edn. Yale University Press, New Haven and London

Cover RM (1974) Justice accused antislavery and the judicial process. Yale University Press, New Haven and New York

Döring H-J (ed) (2011) Lothar Kreyssig Aufsätze, Autobiographie und Dokumente. Evangelische Verlagsanstalt, Leipzig

Dugard J (1984) Should judges resign? A reply to Professor Wacks. S Afr Law J 101:286–294

Dugard J (1987) The judiciary in a state of national crisis – with special reference to the South African experience. Wash Lee Law Rev 44:477–501

Essner C (2002) Die "Nürnberger Gesetze" oder Die Verwaltung des Rassenwahns 1933–1945. Paderborn, München

Fraser D (2005) Law after Auschwitz: towards a jurisprudence of the Holocaust. Carolina Academic Press, Durham

Freudiger K (2002) Die juristische Aufarbeitung von NS-Verbrechen. Mohr Siebeck, Tübingen

Fuller LL (1957) Positivism and fidelity to law – a reply to Professor Hart. Harv Law Rev 71:630–672
Gerrens U (2009) Rüdiger Schleicher Leben zwischen Staatsdienst und Verschwörung. Gütersloher Verlagshaus, Gütersloh
Michielsen JNME (2004) The "Nazification" and "Denazification" of the Courts in Belgium, Luxembourg and the Netherlands. University of Maastricht, Maastricht
Nøkleby B (1996) Skutt blir den . . . Tysk bruk av dødsstraff i Norge 1940–1945. Gyldendal Norsk Forlag, Oslo
Osiel MJ (1995) Dialogue with dictators: judicial resistance in Argentina and Brazil. Law Soc Inq 20:481–560
Radbruch G (1946) Gesetzliches Unrecht und übergesetzliches Recht. Süddeutsche Juristen-Zeitung 105–108 [English translation Statutory Lawlessness and Supra-Statutory Law, Translated by Bonnie Litschewski Paulson and Stanley L. Paulson, 26 Oxford Journal of Legal Studies 2006, pp. 1–11]
Radbruch G (1948) Des Reichministeriums Ruhm und Ende, Zum Nürnberger Juristenurteil. Süddeutsche Juristenzeitung col. 64
Rehnquist WH (1998) All laws but one civil liberties in wartime. Vintage Books, New York (Kindle edition)
Report of the Truth and Reconciliation Commission of South Africa, Vol. 4, Chapter 4 Institutional Hearing: The Legal Community, 1998
Rundle K (2009) The impossibility of an exterminatory legality: law and the Holocaust. Univ Toronto Law J 59:65–125
Rundle K (2012) Law and daily life—questions for legal philosophy from November 1938. Jurisprudence 3(2):429–444
Rüthers B (2008) Verräter, Zufallshelden oder Gewissen der Nation? Facetten des Widerstandes in Deutschland. Mohr Siebeck, Tübingen
Schleunes K (ed) (2001) Legislating the Holocaust: the Bernhard Loesener memoirs and supporting documents. Westview, Boulder (Kindle edition)
Schorn H (1959) Der Richter im Dritten Reich Geschichte und Dokumente. Vittorio Klostermann, Frankfurt am Main
Sharp G (2010) From dictatorship to democracy a conceptual framework for liberation, 4th U.S. edn. The Albert Einstein Institution, East Boston
Stoltzfus N (1996) Resistance of the heart intermarriage and the Rosenstrasse protest in Nazi Germany. W.W. Norton & Company, New York
Tamm D (1984) Retsopgøret efter besættelsen. Jurist- og Økonomforbundets forlag, København
Trials of War Criminals before the Nuremberg Military Tribunals, vol III, the Justice Case, Washington, 1951
Wachs R (1984) Judges and injustice. S Afr Law J 101:266–285
Werle G (1992) Der Holocaust als Gegenstand der bundesdeutschen Strafjustiz. Neues Juristische Wochenzeitung 2529–2535

Chapter 19
Judges for Justice

Coming Out from Behind the Law

Time has come to sum up the main findings of the book. In the introduction, I stated that the western legal tradition has common roots and a common history. This includes an ideology of law as something autonomous dedicated to protecting more general values such as justice, equality, and the rule of law that bind judges together across time and space. The book has shown how judges struggle to accommodate this ideology when it is under attack by the legislator and the executive, how they defend it, and how they depart from it. The bind is fragile and threadbare at times, at other times almost nonexistent. The fact that it is still there can, however, be seen in the way judges collaborating with authoritarian regimes still try to legitimise their actions with an appeal to this ideology. Some of them are even troubled by a bad conscience. Moreover, we must not forget that even in the deepest darkness of authoritarianism, there are judges who remain true to the ideology and work to counter the oppressive measures of the regime. Does the existence of this bind actually make life better for people living under such conditions subjected to its legal system? Unfortunately, in most cases, it does not. Nevertheless, the fact that it is there gives hope that we can improve the protection it offers. How this can be encouraged is what we turn to now.

We expect judges to be the protectors of individual rights and the rule of law. In cases where the executive and legislative powers of a state attack these basic values of our society, we want the courts to exercise their powers of review to uphold these rights. We like to think of judges as taking heroic stances against authoritarian rulers like the case in present-day Hungary where the constitutional court has been providing checks and balances between the different state organs. However, as we have seen in many recent examples of authoritarian rule in countries within our western legal tradition, the courts have failed to offer such protection.

In fact, many judges believe that, by applying the law, they are defending the rule of law, even under the most oppressive circumstances. In his great apology of

H.P. Graver, *Judges Against Justice*, DOI 10.1007/978-3-662-44293-7_19

the German judges under the Nazi period, Hubert Schorn writes about "those judges who performed their work by following their conscience and who saw upholding the law in a courageous and upraised way as their highest duty".[1] There is no reason to doubt that this expresses the self-understanding of many judges in authoritarian settings. Nevertheless, the consequences of their performance may be horrendous and far removed from any reasonable understanding of the rule of law.

Pressing questions are if and how we can provide safeguards to put judges in a better position to protect the rule of law and to make this judicial conduct more likely. In the constitution of the Federal Republic of Germany, there is a "perpetuity clause" based on the experience of the transition from the Weimar Republic to Hitler's rule. Is it possible in this way to legislate against authoritarianism? An important development in international law since the examples I have reviewed in this book is the development of rules and institutions for the protection of human rights. What security can these provide against developments as those reviewed in the book? Does the answer lie in the training and conditioning of judges in a particular scientific or reasonable methodological approach to the practice of judging? Moreover, how can we make judges better in resisting the psychological forces that urge them into conformity? These are the questions to address in this final chapter.

Constitutional Provisions Against Acceptance of Authoritarianism?

History shows that the existence of a liberal constitution and a judiciary brought up under liberal values with the respect for the rule of law do not prevent a development of judicial acceptance of authoritarian regimes. Weimar Germany had one of the most liberal constitutions of its time, with an extensive catalogue of individual rights. South Africa had its legal traditions deeply embedded in common law. Chile had a tradition of independent courts with constitutional review of legislative and executive measures and ratified the international covenant on civil and political rights in 1973. The Supreme Court of Brazil was a relatively powerful institution and was regarded as a "bulwark for Brazilian democracy".[2] Why did such clear commitments against authoritarianism not a guard against the development of tyranny and oppression?

One could argue that in the cases of Germany and South Africa, the road taken by the authoritarian rulers were provided for by their respective constitutions. In both cases, there were provisions that opened for authoritarian measures against social emergencies. Had these roads been closed, one could argue that they would not so easily have been opened by the courts. This is the basic thinking behind

[1] Schorn (1959), p. 4.

[2] Verner (1984), p. 488.

section 79 (3) of the present German Basic Law, which contains the so-called guarantee of in perpetuity.

Basic Law section 79 (3) states that "no constitutional amendment can abolish the fundamental rights of the constitution or the federal structure of the republic". This provision protects not only from the excessive use of emergency powers but also against a dominant social force changing the rules of the game. Constitutional amendments that suspend or abolish basic rights and minority protection are often difficult to accomplish in social settings where the political majority risks a situation where it loses political power. In such a case, it will be in need of constitutional protection from the new rulers in power. Where power changes hands as a result of elections and the election outcome is uncertain, the probability is that politicians will opt for a legal regime of protection of fundamental rights.[3] If, however, those in power expect that they can hold onto it, their incentives to maintain constitutional constraints on political power will decrease. This is what happened in Germany after the Nazi takeover. Hitler said in his Königsberg speech in 1932: "I only seek the power. Once we get it we will never, so help us God, give it up. We will not allow ourselves to be removed".[4]

The perpetuity clause should guard against such situations where a majority or a dominating political force lacks incentives or the ideology to uphold the protection of the rule of law. Such a provision might protect from amendments made from within the constitution but cannot protect it from the argument that the constitution as such has been repealed. This was the legal construction that was established within Nazi Germany soon after the takeover of power. The regime enacted emergency legislation in accordance with the Weimar constitution, and the enabling Act of 24 March 1933 gave the government power to enact legislation without the involvement of the Reichstag. This included legislation amending the constitution. Nevertheless, it could still be held that constitutional provisions that had not explicitly been repealed were still in force as German law. The Nazi lawyers rejected this argument, and the legal opinion that became established was that the regime was unbound by any other basic law than the good of the German people, ultimately in the way declared or willed by the Führer.

We find an illustrating discussion on whether the Nazi order was a continuation of the Weimar constitution or not in a case of the Special Court of Darmstadt from 26 March 1934 and in the comments that this case received in the *Juristische Wochenschrift*.[5] The Chief of Police of Hessen had issued orders to prohibit assemblies and propaganda of Jehovah's Witnesses and later on to disband the organisation and prohibit membership of it. The legal basis for the orders was the Empowering Act. The defendants in a case before the Special Court of Darmstadt were all charged with breaking the orders. The Court decided that Jehovah's Witnesses were a religious society in the meaning of article 137 of the Weimar

---

[3] See Ginsburg (2003), location 372.

[4] Königsberg 17 October 1932, cited from Strenge (2002), p. 72.

[5] Both the case and the comments are published in Juristische Wochenschrift 1934, pp. 1744–1747.

constitution and that the orders of the Hessen police chief were in contradiction to this provision. The Court argued that article 137 could not have been repealed by the empowering Act since this in itself was based on article 48 of the constitution, which did not allow derogation from article 137.[6] Even though the empowering Act empowered the government to change the constitution by constitutional laws, such laws had not been enacted regarding article 137.

It also argued that the Weimar constitution, as such, was still in force in as far as it had not been expressly revoked by constitutional legislation. If one regarded the constitution as such as abolished, all present institutions and law would be left hanging in the air. The Court also pointed to the fact that large portions of the constitution were not in contradiction of the foundations of the National Socialist state. Freedom of religion had not been abolished by the National Socialist state, and this would, according to the words of the Führer, not happen. Under these circumstances, article 127 had to be respected by the police—the orders against Jehovah's Witnesses were invalid.

The decision was met with prompt and clear criticism by Ernst Rudolf Huber, professor in Kiel, Leipzig, and Strasburg and a leading constitutional lawyer of the Nazis. He stated that the ruling was based on incorrect legal considerations and that it came to the wrong conclusion. The Court had misunderstood what it is for a constitution to be in force. This does not depend, maintained Huber, on whether elements of a constitution are still in force. For a constitution to be in force, it had to be the "unified, comprehensive and single power basis for the political life of a state". The unified character of a constitution is defined by its main supporting principles, which under the Weimar constitution were formal democracy, parliamentarism, federalism, distribution of power, and individual rights. All of these principles had been smashed by National Socialism, not through legislation but directly in a revolutionary manner, immediately through the seizure of power by the National Socialist Party. Against such reasoning, any constitution is defenceless.

The basic problem that faces the judiciary in transitions from liberal rule of law settings to authoritarian rule is the one of constitutional loyalty. If the courts are carried over from the previous regime, they will have been established under the constitutional order of that regime. This constitutional order thus forms the legal basis for their official powers. A regime that seeks to establish its powers from a different legal source, be it a new "revolutionary" legal basis or the "dictates of necessity", has its legal basis partly outside of the previous constitutional arrangement. The courts in such situations are forced to choose between upholding the former constitution and depriving the new regime or its measures of legality and assessing the measures of the new regime under the legal basis that the regime itself claims to be its constitutional foundation. This break may be open in the way that no effort is made to hide the fact that society has undergone a revolution or hidden in

[6] This was in accordance with a view expressed earlier by the Supreme Court in a decision from 23.1.1934, JW 1934, p. 767.

the way that the transition is proclaimed as a (re)interpretation of the prevailing constitutional arrangement. In addition to the two alternatives of upholding the old and accepting the new legal bases, judges may opt to resign or to maintain that a determination of the constitutional basis of the regime is outside the scope of judicial review.[7]

The arguments for each of these four lines of action are complex and may be based in law, legal theory, and ethics. What is certain is that they cannot be solved by legal reasoning alone since they entail not only the interpretation and application of the law but also the choice between different legal regimes. In practice, the courts submit to the new regime in most instances. This may be disappointing from the point of view of the rule of law and of political morality because it means that the courts abstain from protecting and upholding basic rights in the face of authoritarian rule. But a simple and basic argument for this line of action is that it is untenable for a court of law to exist under a regime if it seeks its legal basis in a constitutional arrangement that is not accepted by this regime.

The argument put forward by the Appellate Division of the Supreme Court of Rhodesia after the Smith government declared its independence from Britain illustrates the point. Southern Rhodesia was annexed by Great Britain in 1923. In 1961, the colony was granted a constitution where under, inter alia, its legislature had the power to make laws for the peace, order, and good government of Southern Rhodesia and where "the executive authority... is vested in Her Majesty and may be exercised on Her Majesty's behalf by the Governor".

On November 11, 1965, the prime minister of Southern Rhodesia and his colleagues issued a "Declaration of Independence" purporting to declare that "Southern Rhodesia was no longer a crown colony but was an independent sovereign state". On November 16, 1965, the United Kingdom Parliament passed the Southern Rhodesia Act, which declared that Southern Rhodesia continued to be part of Her Majesty's dominions and that "the Government and Parliament of the United Kingdom have responsibility and jurisdiction as heretofore for and in respect of it".

Pursuant to an arrest made under emergency legislation passed by the Smith government, the Privy Council of the United Kingdom was asked by the wife of the detainee to rule on the legality of the arrest.[8] In addressing this issue, the Privy Council also ruled on "whether or how far Her Majesty's subjects and in particular Her Majesty's judges in Southern Rhodesia are entitled to recognise or give effect to laws or executive acts or decisions made by the unlawful regime at present in control of Southern Rhodesia".

Lord Reid, speaking for the majority, conceded that "Her Majesty's judges have been put in an extremely difficult position". He continued:

> But the fact that the judges among others have been put in a very difficult position cannot justify disregard of legislation passed or authorised by the United Kingdom Parliament... It

[7] See Mahmud (1994), pp. 100–140 for an analysis of these four choices of action and their application in post-colonial coups d'état in common law countries.

[8] In Madzimbamuto v. Lardner-Burke [1969] 1 AC 645.

> is for Parliament and Parliament alone to determine whether the maintenance of law and order would justify giving effect to laws made by the usurping Government, to such extent as may be necessary for that purpose.

The Smith government refused to recognise the decision of the Privy Council and received support from the courts of Rhodesia, even though the judges had been appointed under the old British constitution and had sworn allegiance to it. Two judges resigned in protest. One of them, Justice Fieldsend, was appointed as the first Chief Justice of Zimbabwe when the white minority rule was overthrown.

By continuing to function as courts, the judges, by necessity, accept the fundamental legal basis of the present regime. Arguments between the courts and the holders of power over the protection of rights and the rule of law must therefore, by necessity, take place within the legal framework accepted by the regime. No perpetuity clause from the *ancient regime* can alter this.

International Standards

Most German lawyers did not offer resistance to the Nazi demands; on the contrary, they offered their services to develop the law in line with National Socialist policy. They might have felt obliged to do so, but in their collaboration, they departed from positivism. If they had stood by legal positivism, they would have rejected treating National Socialist ideology and the mysticism of Hitlerism as superior sources of law. Some of those who chose to resist referred to positivism to assist them. With this, for example, the Prussian Administrative Appeals Court was able to halt the reinterpretation of statutes in the light of the new ideology, and it was able to hold the NS legislator to its legislation. But it had few supranational or supra-legal sources from which to draw arguments to curb the contents of the legislation issued by the regime.

On the other hand, the judges in South Africa resisted by applying a common law approach, an approach that referred to general principles of unwritten law. This legislation could be interpreted restrictively and its effects limited. But the common law judges in South Africa too had to yield to parliamentary supremacy and lacked the means of higher laws to overrule unambiguous and clear provisions in legislation.

In the situation today, national judges have the international regimes for protection of human rights as positive legal sources to employ against oppressive measures of national law. International law represents standards for the evaluation of national measures. The interpretation and application of these standards is, in many instances, guided by the case law of international courts and tribunals. The laws and practices of national authorities are monitored and evaluated by independent international authorities and courts.

Independently of the national legislator and ruler, international norms can be held to be binding as positive law on national judges. This was the approach taken by the Nuremberg tribunals after World War II, and it was followed by the German Supreme Court after the breakdown of the GDR and the reuniting of Germany. When asked to consider judicial crimes after the breakdown of the GDR, the German courts accepted that a judge could be performing an illegal act when applying laws in the way envisaged by the legislator and the rulers. They reached this result partly by including ratified international human rights instruments in their reasoning, arguing that when ratified these also form part of the positive law that the judge has to take into account. That the GDR had ratified the International Covenant on Civil and Political Rights in this way became part of the reason for why they could be held criminally liable for enforcing the national law of the GDR.[9]

Today, the individual responsibility and criminal liability for breaches of international law are widely recognised and well established, both in customary law and in the Rome Statute of the International Criminal Court. It is also well established that breaches referred to by the statute can be tried both by international courts and tribunals and by national courts.

International human rights regimes work on the legal orders of participating states in two ways. On one hand, they constitute an authoritative body of law that has legally binding force. On the other hand, this body of law forms a basis for which international pressure can be applied on a violating state by other states. Both these ways can contribute to preventing states from serious violations of individual rights through their municipal law.

Hopefully, the force of international law and of international monitoring regimes will make the participation of national judges in oppression and evil less likely. This is, however, by no means certain. Research on the effect of international human rights regimes cannot show any conclusive results. Statistical analysis indicates, "International rights promotion can help a bit when domestic conditions are right, but it rarely initiates reform on its own. Moreover, it seems to have little impact on many of those countries that need the most help, including those ruled by dictators or plagued by war".[10] As pointed out by Gene Sharp, international pressure may weaken dictatorships somewhat, but their continuation is mainly dependent on internal factors.[11] International support and pressure can, on the other hand, be of great assistance when there is powerful internal resistance.

Regardless of the quantitative effects of human rights standards, international human rights will represent a contradictory body of law when the legislator enacts oppressive laws. In this respect, they will increase the cross-pressure facing the judge. This is, on the other hand, nothing entirely new. In the cases that we have seen before the establishment of the international human rights regime, judges were also under cross-pressure when an authoritarian regime developed in a society that was formally based on a liberal constitution and the rule of law. The German judges

---

[9] See pp. 148–150.

[10] Hafner-Burton and Ronon (2009), p. 373.

[11] Sharp (2010), p. 7.

did not lack standards of protection of the rule of law, but they failed to employ them. The South African judges had standards in common law, which they failed to bring into effect. The Chilean Junta even went through the proceedings of ratification of the International Covenant on Civil and Political Rights at the same time as they perpetrated their terror against political opponents at home.

Even though the existence of norms with the force of positive law prohibiting oppressive and authoritarian measures is nothing new, there are important differences in the situation as it has developed since the turn of the millennium. Whereas the international norms in the twentieth century for the most part were very general and abstract in nature, there exists today a vast body of case law giving specific guidance to their interpretation and implementation in practice. There are also well-functioning international institutions that contribute to their enforcement. The role of the European Commission in the French measures against the Roma in 2009 is a notable example of this.[12] The engagement with Hungary by the European Commission and the Council of Europe is another example.

Institutions are important in that they represent an addition to the mere normative force of an argument. Judges who can invoke the international regime for the protection of human rights against oppressive measures of their regime have a much firmer basis for their resistance than their colleagues of the past. On the other hand, not even institutions are foolproof. Even such a firm institution as the Chief Justice of the US Supreme Court has been openly defied, by the President of the United States. In 1861, Lincoln suspended the writ of habeas corpus in connection with declaring martial law in Maryland. After the arrest of John Merryman, Chief Justice Roger B. Taney issued a writ of habeas corpus. This was not obeyed, and Taney wrote a letter to Abraham Lincoln demanding that he perform his duty as the President of the United States. Lincoln disregarded this ruling and continued to suspend habeas corpus throughout the country.

Lincoln's refusal to abide by the order met with little public criticism. Rehnquist explains this with Taney's authorship of the principal opinion in the Dred Scott Case, which had inflamed the North and cast a shadow over the Supreme Court for at least a generation. He also points out that courts at that time did not form such an important part of public life as they do today.[13] One lesson to be drawn is that courts are not totally immune to currents of public opinion that may undermine their authority. This goes for international institutions as well, of course.

The one important difference today is that judges now have the instruments to oppose an authoritarian ruler. These instruments are available even to a positivistic-minded judge. Therefore, a judge does not have to appear "political" to go against the regime. He can base his opposition in specific norms of positive law, based on traditional legal sources such as enacted norms and case law.

Alas, lack of means is but one factor contributing to the acquiescence of the judiciary in oppression. Loyalty to the authority of the national legislator,

---

[12] See Korando (2012), p. 125.

[13] Rehnquist (1998), location 751.

institutional factors, solidarity to the profession, and entrapment are others. To employ the means available under international law, the judge also needs to break loose from these forces. This can sometimes be difficult. National courts sometimes assert their authority in challenge to international legal opinion.

The international legal protection of human rights also suffers from the vulnerability of constitutional protection, as US judge Learned Hand referred to when he stated:

> Liberty lies in the hearts of men and women; when it dies there, no constitution no law, no court can save it; no constitution, no law, no court can even do much to help it. While it lies there it needs no constitution, no law, no court to save it.[14]

On the other hand, familiarity with the international human rights regime, respect for its legal authority, as well as awareness of the dangers entailed in the situation of a judge when the legislator wages war on the rule of law, may contribute to the maintenance of the spirit of liberty in the heart of the judge.

The Politics of Legal Methodology

Some argue that judges who stick to the correct legal methodology will not engage in undermining the rule of law when it is under attack by an authoritarian legislator. Legal method has been a topic of inquiry since antiquity. Quintilian (AD 32–96), in his Institutio Oratoria, states the following about legal interpretation:

> Moreover every law either gives, or takes away, or punishes, or commands, or forbids, or permits. It gives rise to dispute either on its own account, or on account of another law; and to inquiries either with regard to its wording, or to its intention. As to its wording, it is either clear, obscure, or equivocal.[15]

This could be written in a book of legal method of our own time. The topics, the arguments, and the controversies over legal methodology are integral parts of the undertaking of judges and legal scholars.

Many legal issues are framed not as issues of substance but as controversies over which legal method should apply. In American constitutional law, differences in position over constitutional theory, which determines the correct approach to take in the interpretation of the constitution, are a main divide among both scholars and judges. The development of new legal orders like the order of European Union law is accompanied by the development of new or particular legal methods and approaches to interpretation.

In some situations and some legal jurisdictions, there exists a high degree of consensus on the correct legal method. In present-day Germany, most scholars and judges ascribe to the objective approach to interpretation of statutes. In

[14] Hand (1959), p. 144.

[15] Quintilian, Institutio Oratoria (The Orator's Education) book 7.1.

Scandinavia, in the last half of the twentieth century, there was a high degree of consensus around the realist approach to legal sources. In other situations and in other jurisdictions, the situation is more pluralistic and marked by scholarly controversy. This was the situation in Germany at the beginning of the twentieth century, and it is the situation in the US and many other jurisdictions today.

In most cases, the issue of legal methodology is seen as a theoretical question to be debated and resolved through scholarly debate. Arguments employed in this debate are both theoretical, of the kind that "this and that approach increases the rationality of the legal decision-making", and practical, of the kind that "this and that approach increases legal certainty or justice in the outcome of legal decisions". This is not the place to go into these debates. It is important to note, however, that the solution of methodological issues is most often perceived as something that belongs to the professional and academic sphere. The legislator seldom gets involved, and if so it is customarily only in particular issues, for example to regulate the relationship between national and international laws.

Notwithstanding the claims of some theories, legal orders can fulfil their functions despite the fact that their judges base themselves on very different approaches to interpretation and legal reasoning. This is true even when there are different competing approaches side by side in the same legal order. Different legal approaches often lead to different legal results. This does not mean, however, that it is perceived that the choice between them should be made on account of the legal outcomes they produce. A choice made on this basis will often be accused of being opportunistic and insincere.

Where academics debate, practitioners employ legal methods as part of their everyday routine. In many cases, the employment of a particular method is not a result of a conscious choice but rather a matter of "doing things as they are done" according to established practice. The reasons for seeing the method as obvious can be a result of legal training, theoretical belief, or just everyday habit and routine. But because legal results often follow from the method employed, the law may be perceived as more binding and less open than it actually is. This is an observation that can be made even if one believes, in principle, in the existence of one correct legal answer. The legal theory of, for example, Ronald Dworkin employs the talents of "Hercules" to arrive at the correct answer. However, since normal judges are not Hercules, they have to make evaluations and estimates. Moreover, these evaluations and estimates may be wrong at the same time as they may be dependent upon choices of methodology.

There is nothing wrong about this situation in law; in fact, it is unavoidable. Since we cannot know the right answer, a conscious debate over what methods to employ is rational and prevents single-mindedness. Even though methodological choices influence and sometimes even determine outcomes, these debates are not inherently political as long as there are no direct relations between methodological choices and political interests. In normal times, predictability will, under some circumstances, favour this interest and, under other circumstances, the other—as is also the case with choices such as subjective, objective, or contextual approach to interpretation of statutes.

Oppression can also be legitimised through a variety of legal approaches and methods. This has led some to assume that there is no connection between legal methodology and contribution to oppression through the law. A more probable assumption is that this situation shows the political side of legal reasoning. Legal reasoning is about different ways of valuating stability and change. Is it also about different appraisals of contextual preconditions, legislative purpose, and legal principles? All these are values inherent in the law, where choices have to be made all the time as part of doing law. Nevertheless, in a situation where the legislator is at war with the rule of law, this choice acquires a particular political dimension the judge cannot avoid. The same is the case in other situations of great social upheaval and change. In such situations, the judge cannot only be a judge but must also make a personal choice. And this choice is an inherently moral choice where the judge is accountable.

Lawyers often frame great political issues as issues of methodology. The revolutionary changes that judges under Nazism brought about in private and civil law were mostly not justified by appeal to the new principles and the Nazi ideology. Rather, more typical was the resort to normal and everyday legal arguments, such as extensive interpretation, analogies, and filling of gaps and lacunae in the law.[16] This was not particular to Nazi law. Even after the war and the breakdown of the Nazi regime, German judges were reluctant to use the new sweeping clauses that invalidated laws of the Nazi regime. Instead of seeing the new laws as contrary to the Nazi laws and invalidating them, the laws of the Nazi time were reinterpreted in light of the new liberal laws and ideology.

In many instances, the struggle over authoritarianism directly and overtly involves legal methodology. This was particularly articulated in Nazi Germany where leading Nazi legal theoreticians argued for a new "German" legal method in opposition to the old "Roman" and "liberal" approaches to law. The main object of this approach to law was to mould the Nazi view of the world into a binding basis for legal reasoning. The new order called for a consciousness and character in the judge in order to distinguish between "law and unlaw" (Recht und Unrecht) based on the laws and on his belonging to the community of the German people.[17] Even the Jewish issue became a methodological issue. Carl Schmitt called for removing all books written by Jews from the ordinary collections from the libraries and for the annotation of "Jewish" in all citations of authors with a Jewish background because, as he said, "a Jewish author has no authority, not even on a scholarly basis".[18]

The demand for a new method attacked the "normativism" of liberal legal thought, i.e. the model of thinking through rules and legislation.[19] The Nazi legal ideologists did not let judges hide behind a positivistic and formal approach to the law, and positivism was not an effective way for judges to escape criticism. The

[16] Rüthers (2012), p. 174.

[17] Rabofsky and Oberkofler (1985), p. 97.

[18] Schmitt (1936), col. 1198.

[19] See Rüthers (2012), pp. 123–136.

criticism of the Prussian Court of Appeals presented above, on pp. 100–101, demonstrates this point. Rules should not be seen in isolation from the total legal order based on German people and the Nazi worldview. This worldview, the will of the Führer, and the party programme of the Nazi Party, became main legal sources. It was, however, difficult to construct a coherent theory of law on this basis, and the scholarly doctrine suffered as a result. The judges therefore did not receive the same guidance from legal doctrine as they were used to according to the German condition.[20] As a result, the law became even more indeterminate and open to deviant practices such as the one of the Prussian Administrative Appeals Court. The initiation of the "judges' letters" by the Ministry of Justice in 1942 was also the result of the need to have a more consistent practice and to prevent judges both from underperforming and over-performing with regard to implementing the Nazi ideology in the law.

In other instances, opposition to oppression is framed as a methodological issue. Both the Belgian and the Norwegian judicial oppositions to German occupying rule were framed as an issue of the application of international law in national courts: the Belgian courts, with their position that they would only apply national law, and the Norwegian courts, with their position that they would apply international law and also on this basis perform judicial review of the measures of the German occupier. The Belgians based their position on the experiences of German occupation during the First World War.

The Norwegian position was not based on any previous legal doctrine or experience and may be seen as a consequence of the negotiations with the Germans over the civil administration of Norway after the occupation. In April 1940, after the invasion, the king and the government retreated from Oslo and continued the defence of unoccupied parts of the country. Being the only organ of state left in the occupied part, the Supreme Court took the lead in the negotiations with the Germans over organising the civilian administration. After the occupation of the whole of Norway, with the king and government in exile in England, the Germans wanted the Norwegian Parliament to assemble and to depose the king and elect a new government. The position of the Supreme Court in these negotiations was that this was not possible according to the Norwegian constitution and that the German demand was illegal according to international law.

In the negotiations, the leader of the Norwegian Nazi Party, Vidkun Quisling, sought to be appointed as head of a Norwegian government. The negotiations stranded, and on 25 September the German Reichskommissar, Terboven, declared that he had appointed commissarial ministers to lead the different ministries on his behalf—among these members of Quisling's party. The Supreme Court took the position that these ministers had no legal basis outside of the rights of the occupier under international law since they had their power by delegation from the Reichskommissar. It also took the position that Norwegian courts in matters that

[20] See Rabofsky and Oberkofler (1985), p. 101.

were brought before them should review whether the measures taken were within the scope of international law or not.[21]

This stance on judicial review should probably be seen against the background of the resistance against Quisling and his project and the illegality under Norwegian law of an establishment of a government in substitution for the king and government in exile. The Supreme Court had been quite clear on this position in the negotiations, and had made it publicly known in a statement of 15 June 1940.[22] The same position was taken by the king after a request forwarded by the presidents of Parliament asking him to resign. The position to review the legality of the measures of the administration established by the Reichskommissar was therefore directed as much against the Quisling administrators as against the Germans. When some months later it came to an open confrontation, this was also the case, as the topic of the conflict was a measure on the constitution of the courts issued by the commissarial minister of justice. The basic constitutional issue on the legality of the Quisling administration was therefore decided as an issue of the application of international law by national Norwegian courts.

David Dyzenhaus shows how the approach to legal method was decisive in whether South African judges supported or tried to limit the oppressive measures of the regime. Dyzenhaus rejects a theory that judges chose an interpretive approach in order to find a method of justification that best accommodated their political or psychological need. According to Dyzenhaus, judges regard their answers to legal questions in hard cases as fully determined by law.[23] This means that judges do not feel free to select the legal arguments that lead them to what they regard as the best approach.

What judges believe about law's determinacy or indeterminacy is an empirical question. It is fully possible within an internal perspective of law to regard some issues as delegated from the legislator to the discretion of the judge. In fact, this is the concept of both the legislator and judges in many issues in Scandinavian law. There is no logical or normative inconsistency in claiming that some issues are to be decided by the judge according to his own discretion. This means that the extent to which a certain judge thinks and believes that he has this type of discretion is a matter of discerning this judge's opinion. It is my opinion that Dyzenhaus' claim that "judges regard their answers in hard cases as fully determined by law" is simply wrong. In my experience, many judges believe that they have discretion in many hard cases of law and that the outcome is indeterminate. Many judges who have dissenting opinions from that of their colleagues do not believe that their colleagues are wrong; they simply believe that they disagree.

Therefore, Dyzenhaus' brilliant analysis of cases from South Africa shows, in an excellent way, the political dimension of legal methodology. He shows both in theory and in practice how different methodological approaches were possible and

---

[21] Schjelderup (1945), pp. 185–189.

[22] Schjelderup (1945), pp. 117–118.

[23] Dyzenhaus (2010), p. 174.

how they led to different results regarding the question of supporting the regime or not. Since the choice of method is not normatively determined, the belief of certain judges that their answers in hard cases are fully determined must be labelled a false consciousness that stands in the way of their making an informed choice on the question of their support of oppression or not. When the legislator is at war with the rule of law, there is no escape from this question for the judge.

Legal reasoning becomes political under certain conditions, in particular when legislation and law can no longer be seen as two parallel forces. When the legislator wages war on law, legal method becomes a political issue, both in the sense that the legislator will seek to demand a specific method and a redefinition of the legal undertaking and in the sense that the judge has to make a choice. Michael Stolleis points out that it is misleading to say the German judges were defenceless in the face of the demands of the Nazi leaders since their situation was not that they had no means to defend themselves against the demands of an oppressive legislator. The fact was that the judges themselves employed new methodological techniques to disregard original legislative intent in order to Nazify the law in such diverse fields as family law, labour law, and the law of contracts.[24] The choice the judge makes of which method to employ has direct consequences in the extent of his participation in the oppression of the regime. Which consequences different legal approaches have depend on the specific circumstances. One cannot, therefore, say in advance that one method favours the rule of law whereas the other favours tyranny.

Robert M. Cover has pointed to the tendency that judges faced with morally difficult choices may feel relieved if they believe themselves to be a mechanical instrument of the will of others. To view the results as determined by the law may lighten the burden for the conscientious judge in the way that he does not have to take responsibility for the atrocities he commits. It might also relieve him in another sense in that he does not have to challenge the concept that it is outside of the role of the judge to engage in politics. An open model of legal decision-making where the judge may interpret the law in favour of liberty will constantly raise the question whether the judge is pursuing liberty as an excision of his own personal will or because it is the law.[25] There is, therefore, the paradoxical danger that the conscientious judge perceives the legal method as given and determining of the legal answers, particularly when faced with morally challenging issues, exactly at the time when it is important that he is conscious about the moral and political choices he is making.

The same effect might explain the attitude taken by many French legal scholars to the anti-Jewish legislation of the Vichy regime. In their writings on this legislation, French scholars treated it with the normal approach of legal science, discussing its purpose, categories, and systematic relationships to the rest of the body of law. By treating them as laws like any others, laws that most fundamentally and flagrantly violated the concept of law as developed in France since the

[24] Stolleis (1998), p. 15.
[25] Cover (1974), p. 234.

Revolution were assimilated into the existing legal corpus. The approach was impassive, objective, and neutral, thereby creating the impression that this legislation was normal and entirely permissible from a legal point of view, despite the fact that it blatantly disregarded the Jews' constitutional rights. In fact, the approach of many scholars to this legislation was more neutral than their usual approach in their writings, where they did not abstain from criticising and judging the moral worth of the laws. This restraint could be seen as the result of trying to remain neutral in issues that they personally perceived as very political.[26]

For this reason, awareness of the politics of legal methodology in authoritarian situations is not enough because there are compelling reasons for the judge to disregard the choice that he actually has. The judge, therefore, also needs to be aware of the moral choice he is making in following and applying the law. He should remind himself of Hannah Arendt's words that there is no such thing as obedience in political and moral matters. Everyone always makes a choice, and authoritarian rulers depend upon their subjects choosing to cooperate.

Many have called for the disobedience of judges in situations where the law is blatantly atrocious. Ronald Dworkin recommends that the judge should depart from the interpretative approach where the legal order is immoral. Hercules' counterpart in the evil legal order, Siegfried, should simply ignore legislation and precedent altogether, if he can get away with it, or otherwise do the best he can to limit injustice through whatever means available to him.[27] The editors of the Harvard Law Review encourage judges to "engage in a powerful, symbolic act of civil disobedience... to play a role in ensuring America's substantive commitment to its formal values in an area likely to be ignored by popular government and unlikely to engender a spontaneous, organic, and effective social movement".[28] According to Erhard Blankenburg, the German trials of the GDR leaders and officials established a duty to civil disobedience on the basis of human rights: "Civil disobedience is not only a right of citizens in defending against infringements of governments; it becomes a commitment for public officials if government is infringing on citizens' basic rights".[29]

When faced with a state where the law ostensibly requires an immoral result, one can distinguish between two situations. Either the legal situation is such that there is a possibility within established and recognised methods of interpretation and application that a less oppressive result can be reached (it can be a "hard case" or a case in the "penumbra" within a specific theory of interpretation) or there may be the possibility of applying different methodological approaches, such as the plain fact approach or the common law approach of the South African judges. But the

---

[26] See Curran (1998–1999), pp. 27–29.

[27] Dworkin (1986), p. 105.

[28] Civil Disobedience—The Role of Judges—The Ninth Circuit Confirms Mandatory Sentence—*United States v. Hungerford*, 465 F.3d I i Q (9th Cir. 2006).

[29] Blankenburg (1995), p. 230.

situation may also be such that there is no possibility under established and recognised methods of interpretations of reaching a non-oppressive result.

How and where to draw the line is a matter of one's theoretical and conceptual approach to law, among other things, a matter of whether one believes in determinacy or indeterminacy in law. Consider the Berlin Coffee Case, where the Jews of Berlin where fined for attempting to receive rations announced to the population.[30] Judge Seidel, who acquitted them, argued from basic rule of law principles. By 1940, it could consistently be held that this line of reasoning could not be applied in law to Jews in Germany. In comments by the Reich Minister of Justice regarding the decision, the ruling was criticised and the judge accused of undermining the authority of state bodies before the Jews because even though he thought his result in accordance with the law, he should have chosen a form that "under any circumstances avoided harming the prestige of the food office and thus putting the Jew expressly in the right toward it".

We do not here have to determine whether the judge acted within the scope of German law at the time or whether he broke with it. In either case, we can argue that his decision was morally right and that convicting the Jews would have been morally wrong. If a judge has a scope of discretion in such a situation, or can reach a morally defensible solution by choice of interpretative approach, he should exercise it in order to avoid the oppressive result. And if the law requires him to reach the immoral result, he should arguably break the law.

But can it be morally defensible for a judge not to follow or apply the law? How should we regard the role conception accepted by most that the judge should apply the law and not his own values and moral convictions? A closer examination reveals that it does not follow from the thesis that the law and morality are separate, that there exists a moral duty to follow the law. The separation thesis only implies that the judge should not portray his own personal opinions as law. Whether there exists a moral duty to apply the law or not requires a separate analysis. This applies also to legal theories that hold that moral requirements are part of the law. Consider, for example, the case of abortion. Adherents to Radbruch's, Fuller's, or Dworkin's theories of law, for instance, may, without engaging in theoretical inconsistencies, hold that abortion is legal according to a correct application of the law in a given legal order and at the same time hold that it is immoral according to their own moral convictions. For such a person, the issue of whether he or she is under a moral obligation to uphold this law will also require a separate moral evaluation. Only if one holds the theoretical position that no rule that is immoral or that has immoral consequences can be a legal rule do the issues of determining the law and the moral obligation to follow the law merge into one. But this is not a very common position within contemporary legal theory.

Jeffrey Brand-Ballard argues there are no compelling reasons for stating that the judge has a moral duty to follow the law in specific cases where the result is

---

[30] See pp. 104–105 above.

immoral.[31] Even though citizens in general have a moral duty to abide by even immoral laws, this does not apply to the judge. Brand Ballard's reason for this is that the law seldom compels citizens to cause moral harm or to abstain from preventing moral harm. This is different for the judge, whose actions are about applying force against people. The moral duty not to cause harm when it is morally wrong cancels out the duty to abide by the law. He also rejects the notion that the oath of the office or the role of the judge entails a duty to adhere to the law when the results are morally wrong. Neither a promise nor a job description can make a moral harm defensible. Moral obligations regarding other people's rights cannot be repealed by contract between two parties.

Brand-Ballard's arguments at this level are convincing. The problem, of course, is by what standards we decide what are moral wrongs and whether it is defensible to leave this to the individual judge. As long as the law has legitimacy, he is bound, after all, by norms that have been set in a justifiable way. How can he then defend setting this aside in favour of his own moral intuitions? We could sidestep this problem if we stipulate that the judge is right in his moral evaluation. There are cases when even the legitimate and just law leads to morally indefensible results. Given that this is the case we are faced with in a certain instance, there are no morally compelling reasons for the judge to follow the law and thereby cause moral harm.

This stipulation does not hold true however for all judges in all circumstances, and it sidesteps the difficult issue of how to decide on moral issues in any objective sense. Given the subjectivity of moral reasoning, judges will not agree on moral wrongs, and in the view of some, others will be making mistakes in their moral evaluations. When a judge deviates from the law in one case, this will be a cause for other judges to deviate in other cases, even if they are wrong in their moral convictions. Overall, this may cause more harm from a moral viewpoint than all judges sticking to the law even in instances where it is morally wrong. When we look at the systemic effects of judges departing from the law to avoid moral harms, there is after all a case for a moral duty to abide by the law. According to Brand-Ballard, the system does not, however, require more than that the judges abide by law in most cases. Rule of law does not break down from the fact that judges sometimes deviate from the law. In fact, this happens all the time in all legal orders.

Therefore, the judge is under a moral obligation to deviate from the law in order to prevent moral harm in some cases, as long as he does not do this excessively. He may be right in some cases and wrong in others. This line of action will nevertheless lead to better results in sum than if all judges always follow the law disregarding the moral harm that is caused, provided that judges exercise their judgments with prudence and only depart from the law in situations where they are convinced that following it will cause moral harm.

There are many challenges to Brand-Ballard's arguments relating to the selection of which cases to deviate from the law, to the determination of excessive or

[31] Brand-Ballard (2010).

optimal rates of departure from the law, and to the manner in which the judge should formulate his judgment when he departs from the law. These problems aside, Brand Ballard is probably right in that some departure from the law does little harm overall to the system and that this gives a convincing moral argument for preventing moral harm by departing from the law. If this is the case in reasonably just systems, it must be even more so in authoritarian systems. Also here, the judge must balance between doing justice in the individual case and the general upholding of the rule of law principle that requires judges in general to uphold the law. But when upholding the laws of the regime does more bad than good, judges should depart from the law as much as they can possibly get away with. Their oath of office creates as little moral obligation to uphold the law as an oath taken to serve as a sergeant for the mafia.

Judges must make moral choices when faced with oppressive legislation. It is important that it is recognised that they have both the freedom to make such choices and a scope to act upon them. Legal oppression does not follow from the law but is the result of judges applying and enforcing the law. A law does not execute itself. Even a judge makes a choice to follow the law or break it. The question is not one of law or legal theory but of human choice and action for which the actor is morally responsible.

In making such choices, there is no neutral legal stance. Both siding with the legislator and siding with the rule of law and ingrained legal principles are moral and political choices. The choice is often masked as a matter of legal reasoning, but it is political and moral nevertheless. Thus, the judge should not be dissuaded from taking a stance against the legislator and the executive from fear of acting politically. Historical experience also shows that other fears are often exaggerated. Authoritarian regimes that employ legal order are reluctant to clamp down on judges and show surprising toleration towards judicial opposition. Judges have a larger scope for determining the law independently of the will of the rulers than they often think. An awareness of this fact is important to prevent atrocities by the law in the future.

Resistance for the Rule of Law

Experience shows that legal safeguards are not enough to guard against oppressive measures from authoritarian rulers. Such safeguards are often disregarded, not only by the executive power but also by the courts that should enforce them. The legislative and executive powers of the state put judges in a difficult situation when they employ legal means to undermine the rule of law. The judges have to choose between adherence to the law and respect for values inherent in their legal ideology of the rule of law. Like most others, judges often chose obedience over following their own values under such circumstances. In addition, judges are subject to the same tendency to moral blindness as others when moral panic takes hold over society. To this comes the difficult question of the lesser evil. Even morally conscious judges can have a hard time deciding whether their contribution in enforcing tyrannical measures after all may prevent the regime from employing even worse means of oppression.

How can we provide safeguards to prevent judges from contributing to evil policies and guidance for judges to counter the evil? Is it possible to equip the judiciary with a moral compass to prevent them from departing from the rule of law and the basic requirements of justice? Many have sought recourse in legal theory and a correct methodological approach to law. If only judges approach the law in a correct way, they will be able to uphold the ideals of the rule of law against an oppressive legislator. Experience shows that this is not feasible. Protection must be sought not at the level of legal theory or law. When the regime turns evil, judges are compelled to follow the authority of the law; that is inherent in their role as judges. To the extent they try to temper the excesses of the law and to balance this with their loyalty as judges to the regime, they are forced into the destructive calculus of the lesser evil. Instead, they must step outside their role as judges and ask themselves, as Hannah Arendt observes in her essay on personal responsibility under dictatorship, what the limits are to the consent that they give to oppression.[32]

Judges are, like other people, subject to negative situational forces. As we have seen, the force of authority, moral blindness induced by following the law, and the destructive calculus of the lesser evil allow judges to depart from values of justice and the rule of law that they are otherwise committed to. In order to protect themselves from the development that most judges tend to undergo, the people on the bench must learn to prevent or combat negative situational forces and to resist influences that they do not want or need.

Philip Zimbardo, who has researched how good people turn evil, suggests making use of the same personal and situational factors that turn people to evil to induce them to do good.[33] He suggests employing the "foot in the door" approach, which often leads people to lower their moral guard towards strengthening their moral resistance. Judges could employ this tactic in curbing authoritarian measures little by little. Writing to the judges of apartheid, professor John Dugard wrote: "There is still some room for the judicial advancement of human rights in the interstices of the apartheid legal order, particularly in the interpretation of statutes, the development of the common law, and the review of administrative action and subordinate legislation".[34] He appealed to the judges to employ this room and argued that this would be to act in accordance with their oath of office rather than a misconstruction of the law. In this way, judges could learn by experience that resistance is possible and that they have a measure of independence as long as the regime employs the legal system to maintain legitimacy through legality. Instead of employing their legal reasoning in order to assist the regime in bringing giving their policies legal effect, they should enhance the difficulties.

---

[32] Arendt (2003), p. 46.

[33] Zimbardo (2007), p. 450.

[34] Dugard (1984), p. 291.

Gene Sharp points out that if the sources of power for an authoritarian regime can be restricted or censured for enough time, the initial results may be uncertainty and confusion, likely followed by the weakening of the power of the dictatorship.[35] The confidence of the Nazi rulers over their grip on power was in all likelihood strengthened by the lack of protests from the courts against the purging of Jewish judges and lawyers in the days of March and April 1933. If more courts in Germany had followed the example of the Prussian Administrative Appeals Court in trying to curtail the prerogative state, the dual state may not have been allowed to develop in the way it did with unlimited powers to the security police and the SS.

This example also shows the importance of different forces of opposition working together. It was not only the Prussian Administrative Appeals Court that resisted the unlimited power of the SS and the secret police in the years 1933–1936. This was also resisted by the Ministry of Interior and the Ministry of Justice, which both argued that the operations of the secret police and the conditions in the concentration camps must be subject to the review of the administrative courts. In this, only the Prussian court supported the line of the ministries and stood up against the Gestapo. When the opposition of the two ministries was defeated and the Gestapo had won the political battle, also the court had to give in. Opposition from the court obviously depended upon the opposition from within the state apparatus, and maybe the outcome of the political struggle of the ministries would have been different if more courts had followed the line of the Prussian Administrative Appeals Court.

We may also speculate about the lack of judicial resistance against the euthanasia of the mentally disabled. When Lothar Kreyssig was called to see the minister of justice, he met with von Dohnanyi and talked to him before the meeting began. He asked if the ministry had not received numbers of protests like his own since there, after all, were more than 1,400 judges in Germany exercising guardianship under similar circumstances. To this Dohnanyi answered, "No, unfortunately, yours is the only one".[36] The officials in the ministry, in other words, received no support from the judiciary in its protests against the euthanasia programme.

It could thus have been in the power of the judiciary to prevent Nazi Germany from sliding all the way down the slope to totalitarianism.[37] This could even more be the case of the transformation of the Nazi racial ideology into law. This was, as we have seen, largely the work of the judiciary in rulings giving effect to the anti-Jewish policies of the Nazi Party. This happened in Germany and in France. In both cases, judges had witnessed the removal of their Jewish colleagues from the bench without issuing protests. In Belgium, where the judges protested against the purge

[35] Sharp (2010), p. 20.

[36] Bericht des Amtsgerichtsrats i. R. Dr. Lothar Kreyssig vom 16.10.1969, p. 5, Institut für Zeitgeschichte München-Berlin, Kreyssig, Dr. Lothar ZS-1956 http://www.ifz-muenchen.de/archiv/zs/zs-1956.pdf (last accessed 11.04.14).

[37] See also Nazis in the Courtroom: Lessons from the Conduct of Lawyers and Judges under the Laws of the Third Reich and Vichy France, 61 Brooklyn Law Review (1995), p. 1126.

of their Jewish colleagues, the courts never engaged in transforming racism into law and actually engaged in using legal techniques to resist incorporating German anti-Jewish norms into Belgian law.[38]

This could be developed into an awareness of moments when it is of strategic importance that the regime is challenged and denied legitimacy and legality to oppressive means. Authoritarian regimes are not equally strong all the time, and some situations are more challenging to them than others are. Refusals to accommodate the demands of the regime may have greater consequences under such conditions than others may. We can find an illustration of this in the refusal of deputy commander SS Lieutenant Colonel Nosske of the Einsatzgruppe D to follow the order to round up and shoot the intermarried Jews in Düsseldorf in September 1944. Nosske passed his examinations as assessor in 1934, entered the administration of Justice at Halle in 1934, and was transferred to the Gestapo in 1935. He served as commander for Einsatzkommando 12 from June 1941 until March 1942 and was participant in executing the Fuhrer order of extermination of the Jews in the eastern territories.[39] When he later served in Germany, he received the order of killing the Jews in Düsseldorf, which he refused due to the fact that many of them were considered Germans according to the race laws. The order was revoked, and no sanctions were applied against him, though he suffered some "inconveniences". This happened after an attempt by Goebbels to deport the intermarried Jews of Berlin had been thwarted by popular protests by the wives of the arrested Jews. After this, the regime did not attempt to depart intermarried Jews and "half-Jews" again.[40] One can speculate whether the consequences of a refusal to follow such an order would have been equally benevolent to the Jews and the officer concerned had the attempt in Berlin not been met with the outcry it did. One may also fear for the destiny of the rest of the intermarried Jews of Germany had the order in Düsseldorf been carried out.

As Zimbardo points out, social models are important in this respect. The "common law" judges of South Africa were important even though they did not succeed in stemming the regime. They provided a model showing that an alternative jurisprudence was and is possible. They also provided a beacon of hope for the oppressed and the people brought to trial for political offences. Lothar Kreyssig's brave orders to institutions forbidding them to end the lives of persons under the custody of his Court may or may not have contributed to the end of the Nazi programme of euthanasia. But it definitely serves as an inspiration to future generations of judges showing both that such actions are possible for a judge even under such circumstances as totalitarian Germany in the end of the 1930s and not least that totalitarian governments may be reluctant to meet such judicial actions with the usual terror of the regime.

---

[38] Fraser (2009), p. 211.

[39] The Einsatzgruppen Case (1946–1949), p. 555.

[40] Stoltzfus (1996), p. 256.

Today, also international courts may serve as such role models to a national judge faced with an authoritarian legislature or executive. A promising element in the development of international law in the recent decades is the establishment of international courts and tribunals and the development of a jurisprudence based on the case law from these institutions. These may give inspiration and support to judges looking for models and authority to apply the law in less oppressive ways.

Based on Zimbardo's "Ten-step program to resist unwanted influences",[41] we may point to some factors that judges faced with the task of applying authoritarian measures ought to consider. As Gene Sharp points out, authoritarian regimes are often a passing phenomenon. They are vulnerable and can crumble in a relatively short time space.[42] All regimes that have been the object of this study came to an end, and this was the case of the regimes in central and eastern Europe under the dominance of the Soviet Union. It is therefore important that judges balance their time perspective and situate their position both in relation to the past and to the future to come. When applying laws of the time, they should ask how the application of these laws accords with the ideals of justice and the rule of law of former times.

They should also consider times to come and how the future when the authoritarian rule is brought to an end will regard the measures that they enforce. In some cases, the percentage of anti-government rulings increase once it becomes likely that regime changes will occur. Judges may, in such cases, want to secure their own situation by distancing themselves from the government. As we saw earlier when examining opposition of judges in the twilight of authoritarianism, this was, for instance, the case in Argentina in 1983 and 1989, when it became likely that the current regimes would fall.[43] The same could be seen also in the experiences of the judiciary of Brazil, South Africa, and the Netherlands during the German occupation. Such strategic defections of judges show that judges are able to look beyond mere loyalty to the regime and adherence with its policy and combine this with their judicial role. The challenge is for the judge to take into account the demise of the authoritarian policies before it is obvious to everyone. For this reason, it is important to keep alive memories of both the role judges have played in contributing to evil in authoritarian settings and the way this has been despised afterwards by truth commissions and the public. It is also important to tell the tales of the opposing judges such as the judges of occupied Belgium and the common law judges of South Africa to show that opposition is possible.

In particular, judges should be alert to sacrificing individual liberties for the promise of security. The sacrifices are always real and lead to the implementation of authoritarian measures. Security is often a distant illusion consisting of a threat that is never realised or a future goal that is realised in ways that are difficult to predict and monitor. In his powerful speech in the Belmarsh Case, Lord Bingham

---

[41] Zimbardo (2007), pp. 451–456.

[42] Sharp (2010), p. 15.

[43] Helmke (2002), p. 296.

underlined that protective measures against possible terrorist acts should not go beyond what is strictly required by the exigencies of the situation and that it is for the state to prove that it is so.[44] It is the role of the courts to ensure that the requirements of proportionality are met. The judge should not ask, "could even harsher means have been employed but for the judicial review?" but instead ask, "has the government proven that the harsh means are necessary, that they will be effective and that no lesser means will be equally effective?"

The difficult task is of course for the judge to distinguish between just measures and unjust measures. The positive law gives no answer to this since the question is precisely the limits of the authority of the positive law. The judge must set his own limits based on his own moral intuitions and conscience. In this he may take assistance from the ideology and the principles of the rule of law, protection of fundamental individual rights, and requirements of a minimum of proportionality between the act to be judged and the consequences to be measured out. He may also take assistance from the case law of criminal proceedings against judges by international tribunals and national cases of restorative justice. As we have seen, jurisprudence is not extensive and the requirements that can be extracted from such regarding judicial standards are very basic. Nevertheless, it points in the right direction: there is a limit to what laws a judge can uphold as a judge without the risk of facing criminal sanctions by successor courts. Once this is realised, judges will see that they are personally responsible for what many would like to ascribe to the responsibility of the law and the lawmakers.

The realisation that the judge personally holds responsibility, morally and even legally, for his judicial practice is important because it is the first step in accepting that the judge is personally accountable for rulings and their consequences. Judges, not laws, put men in prison. Obeying the authority of the law always entails consenting to it. People conform more to antisocial groups when they displace responsibility to the others, to the collective, or to the institution. This also holds for judges. The blame put on positivism is an illustration of this. Blaming positivism and the law is a way of reducing the personal responsibility of the individual judge. The German judges could, in this way, move the blame for the atrocities they committed from the person responsible for the application of the laws and over to the person responsible for the enactment of the law, i.e. Hitler himself and his cronies. In this way, the judges could portray themselves as victims of the Nazi rulers instead of perpetrators of Nazi rule. Positivism could also answer the needs of regretful judges coming to terms with themselves and resolve the dissonance between the judgments they passed and their self-images as judges committed to the rule of law.

In order to offer resistance, it is important for judges to remind themselves that they have a choice when applying the law. When a given piece of legislation

[44] A (FC) and others (FC) (Appellants) v. Secretary of State for the Home Department (Respondent), X (FC) and another (FC) (Appellants) v. Secretary of State for the Home Department (Respondent), [2004] UKHL 56.

manifestly challenges basic notions of justice, equality, or the rule of law, there is always a balancing to be performed. We have seen from the historical examples that judges seem to have little problem in performing this balancing in favour of the regime and to bend the laws to accommodate oppression and persecution. But the law can also be bent in favour of liberty. The outcome of this balancing is always the responsibility of the individual judge. This is precisely what is inherent in the notion of judicial independence. As long as there is a minimum adherence to the independence of the judiciary, the judge cannot displace his personal responsibility.

Every lawyer knows that the framing of a legal question more or less determines its outcome. This is what professors teach law students; the important issue when solving a legal problem is casting it in the right "legal" manner. Experienced lawyers know that there is more than one way to frame a question. The answer was already given, when Justice Oliver Wendell Holmes in Buck v. Bell framed the question of the legality of compulsory sterilisation of the "feeble minded" Carrie Buck as a question of, when "the public welfare may call upon the best citizens for their lives", may it "not call upon those who already sap the strength of the State for these lesser sacrifices?" In the same way, the answer is given when we, today, ask whether the state may destroy the reproduction capacity of unconsenting individuals in order to cleanse the race or to pursue goals of social policy.

Amsterdam and Bruner have pointed out how legislators and courts rely on storytelling and how narratives are essential to the practice of law. Law is a means of maintaining continuity in value judgments across times and changing conditions. Legal conflict arise when an existing, legitimate state of affairs have been complicated or challenged by some human action. It is for the courts and the judges to set matters right again.[45] The authoritarian regimes we have studied show the effects of narrative in obvious ways. In Nazi Germany, the Jews and other subversive elements threatened the souls and survival of the German people; in South Africa, the natural order of racial distinctions was threatened by communists and the ANC; in occupied Denmark, the survival of the government and its policy of collaboration was threatened by political opposition and "wild" resistance to the German occupation. Such narratives led to the framing of legal issues as a fight for the survival of society and its institutions, and oppressive means were necessary and justified by the cause at hand. Even the sceptics were convinced that if they did not take part, less scrupulous defenders would employ harsher means.

However, Amsterdam and Bruner emphasise that "a set of contested events can be organized into alternate narratives and that a choice between them may depend upon perspective, circumstances, interpretive frameworks".[46] The case of Rasul v. Bush on whether United States courts lack jurisdiction to consider challenges to the legality of the detention of foreign nationals captured abroad in connection with

[45] Amsterdam and Bruner (2000), pp. 140–141.

[46] Amsterdam and Bruner (2000), p. 141.

hostilities and incarcerated at the Guantanamo Bay Naval Base, Cuba, is illustrative of this point.[47] Justice Stevens told the narrative of the common law writ of habeas corpus: "Application of the habeas statute to persons detained at the base is consistent with the historical reach of the writ of habeas corpus. At common law, courts exercised habeas jurisdiction over the claims of aliens detained within sovereign territory of the realm, as well as the claims of persons detained in the so-called 'exempt jurisdictions,' where ordinary writs did not run, and all other dominions under the sovereign's control. As Lord Mansfield wrote in 1759, even if a territory was 'no part of the realm,' there was 'no doubt' as to the court's power to issue writs of habeas corpus if the territory was 'under the subjection of the Crown'". Under this narrative, the question of stare decisis was a question of whether an earlier case from World War II erected a "bar to the exercise of federal court jurisdiction over the petitioners' habeas corpus claims".

For Justice Scalia, there was a different narrative. He saw the holding of the majority of the court as "not only a novel holding; it contradicts a half-century-old precedent". Drawing on the order necessary in times of war, Scalia expressed: "Departure from our rule of stare decisis in statutory cases is always extraordinary; it ought to be unthinkable when the departure has a potentially harmful effect upon the Nation's conduct of a war. The Commander in Chief and his subordinates had every reason to expect that the internment of combatants at Guantanamo Bay would not have the consequence of bringing the cumbersome machinery of our domestic courts into military affairs. Congress is in session. If it wished to change federal judges' habeas jurisdiction from what this Court had previously held that to be, it could have done so. And it could have done so by intelligent revision of the statute, instead of by today's clumsy, countertextual reinterpretation that confers upon wartime prisoners greater habeas rights than domestic detainees".

The two different narratives, the one on the constant expansion of the writ of habeas corpus and the other on the need to rely on precedent and certainty when conducing a war, lead to two very different conclusions. The judge must be conscious of the power of framing and narrative when faced with legislation encroaching upon individual rights and liberties. This does not mean that civil liberty must occupy as favoured a position in wartime as in peacetime and that the courts should not pay attention to the government's claims of necessity as a basis of curtailing civil liberty. But it does entail that civil liberty should be part of the narrative in order for the judge to make a conscientious evaluation of the extent to which it is strictly necessary to curtail it.

It is easy for a judge to construct alternate narratives under the benign conditions of the US Supreme Court in peacetime. It is another matter under the harsh conditions of dictatorship such as in Nazi Germany, in the military dictatorships of Latin America, or under the apartheid regime in South Africa. Such regimes instil people with terror and fear. Particularly because of this, it is important to illuminate the extent to which opposition from the bench was possible and was left

[47] Rasul v. Bush, 542 U.S. 466 (2004).

untouched by the regime. Opposing judges were subject to criticism and verbal abuse both privately and publicly and were sometimes removed to less prestigious or sensitive posts. Nevertheless, even in Nazi Germany, there is not one known incident of a judge being punished or subject to the claws of the secret police on account of non-conforming judgments. Kreyssig was pensioned off and left in peace at his ecological farm; Dr. Seidel with the Berlin Coffee Case was thrown out of the party and transferred to the civil bench. The common law judges of South Africa were left in place with their dissenting opinions. The German occupiers rattled their sabres against oppositional Belgian judges but overall showed restraint in their employment of harsh measures against individual judges. There are not many martyr judges to tell tales of, not only because judges seldom oppose but also because many authoritarian regimes do not make martyrs of opposing judges.

References

Amsterdam AG, Bruner J (2000) Minding the law how courts rely on storytelling, and how their stories change the way we understand the law – and ourselves. Harvard University Press, Cambridge

Arendt H (2003) Responsibility and judgment. Schocken Books, New York

Blankenburg E (1995) The purge of lawyers after the breakdown of the East German Communist Regime. Law Soc Inq 20:223–243

Brand-Ballard J (2010) Limits of legality: the ethics of lawless judging. Oxford University Press, Oxford

Cover RM (1974) Justice accused antislavery and the judicial process. Yale University Press, New Haven and New York

Curran VG (1998–1999) The legalization of racism in a constitutional state: democracy's suicide in Vichy France. Hastings Law J 50:1–96

Dugard J (1984) Should judges resign? A reply to Professor Wacks. S Afr Law J 101:286–294

Dworkin R (1986) Law's empire. Fontana Press, London

Dyzenhaus D (2010) Hard cases in wicked legal systems pathologies of legality, 2nd edn. Oxford University Press, Oxford

Fraser D (2009) The fragility of law constitutional patriotism and the Jews of Belgium, 1940–1945. Routledge-Cavendish, Oxon

Ginsburg T (2003) Judicial review in new democracies: constitutional courts in Asian cases. Cambridge University Press, Cambridge (Kindle edition)

Hafner-Burton EM, Ronon J (2009) Seeing double: human rights impact through qualitative and quantitative eyes. World Polit 61:360–401

Hand L (1959) The spirit of liberty, papers and addresses of learned hand edited by Irving Dilliard. Vintage Books, New York

Helmke G (2002) The logic of strategic defection: court-executive relations in Argentina under dictatorship and democracy. Am Polit Sci Rev 96:291–303

Korando AM (2012) Roma go home: the plight of European Roma. Law Inequality 30:125–147

Mahmud T (1994) Jurisprudence of successful treason: Coup d'Etat and common law. Cornell Int Law J 27:49–140

Nazis in the Courtroom: Lessons from the Conduct of Lawyers and Judges under the Laws of the Third Reich and Vichy France. Brooklyn Law Rev 61:1121–1164, 1995

Rabofsky E, Oberkofler G (1985) Verborgene Wurzeln der NS_Justiz Strafrechtliche Rüstung für zwei Weltkriege. Europaverlag, Wien

Rehnquist WH (1998) All laws but one civil liberties in wartime. Vintage Books, New York (Kindle edition)
Rüthers B (2012) Die unbegrenzte Auslegung: Zum Wandel der Privatrechtsordnung im Nationalsozialismus 7. Ausg. Mohr Siebeck, Tübingen
Schjelderup F (1945) Fra Norges Kamp for Retten 1940 i Høyesterett. Grøndahl & Søn, Oslo
Schmitt C (1936) Die Deutsche Rechtswissenschaft im Kampf gegen den jüdischen Geist. Deutsche Juristenzeitung, col. 1193–1199
Schorn H (1959) Der Richter im Dritten Reich Geschichte und Dokumente. Vittorio Klostermann, Frankfurt am Main
Sharp G (2010) From dictatorship to democracy a conceptual framework for liberation, 4th U.S. edn. The Albert Einstein Institution, East Boston
Stolleis M (1998) The law under the Swastika studies on legal history in Nazi Germany. The University of Chicago Press, Chicago, p 15
Stoltzfus N (1996) Resistance of the heart intermarriage and the Rosenstrasse protest in Nazi Germany. W.W. Norton & Company, New York
Strenge I (2002) Machtübernahme 1933: Alles auf dem legalen Weg? Ducker und Humblot, Berlin
Trials of War Criminals before the Nuremberg Military Tribunals, vol IV, the Einsatzgruppen Case, Nürnberg, October 1946–April 1949
Verner JG (1984) The independence of Supreme Courts in Latin America: a review of the literature. J Latin Am Stud 16:463–506
Zimbardo P (2007) The Lucifer effect understanding how good people turn evil. Random House, New York

9783662442920